IDENTITY DEVELOPMENT OF COLLEGE STUDENTS

IDENTITY DEVELOPMENT OF COLLEGE STUDENTS

Advancing Frameworks for Multiple Dimensions of Identity

Susan R. Jones
Elisa S. Abes

Foreword by Marcia B. Baxter Magolda

JOSSEY-BASS
A Wiley Imprint
www.josseybass.com

Cover photo: © Goldmund Lukic/iStockphoto
Cover design: Michael Cook

Published by Jossey-Bass
A Wiley Imprint
One Montgomery Street, Suite 1200, San Francisco, CA 94104-4594—www.josseybass.com

Jossey-Bass books and products are available through most bookstores. To contact Jossey-Bass
directly call our Customer Care Department within the U.S. at 800-956-7739, outside the U.S.
at 317-572-3986, or fax 317-572-4002.

Wiley publishes in a variety of print and electronic formats and by print-on-demand. Some
material included with standard print versions of this book may not be included in e-books or
in print-on-demand. If this book refers to media such as a CD or DVD that is not included in
the version you purchased, you may download this material at http://booksupport.wiley.com.
For more information about Wiley products, visit www.wiley.com.

Library of Congress Cataloging-in-Publication Data has been applied for.
ISBN 978-0-470-94719-7 (hardcover)
ISBN 978-1-118-48135-6 (ebk.)
ISBN 978-1-118-48228-5 (ebk.)
ISBN 978-1-118-48230-8 (ebk.)

Printed in the United States of America
FIRST EDITION
HB Printing   SKY10028690_080221

CONTENTS

**SECTION THREE   CRITICAL THEORETICAL FRAMEWORKS AND
                  MULTIPLE IDENTITIES   123**

**SECTION FOUR   EDUCATIONAL APPLICATIONS AND FUTURE
                 DIRECTIONS   213**

LIST OF TABLES AND FIGURES

Tables

Figures

THE AUTHORS

Elisa S. Abes is an associate professor in the Student Affairs in Higher Education program at Miami University in Oxford, Ohio. Prior to joining the faculty at Miami University, she was an assistant professor at the University of South Florida and a litigation attorney at Frost & Jacobs. Abes's research focuses on lesbian identity, multiple social identities, the use of theory in student affairs research and practice, and critical and queer approaches to student development theory. She has served on the editorial board for the *Journal of College Student Development*. She is the recipient of professional awards, including the ACPA Annuit Coeptis award for an emerging professional and the Nevitt Sanford Research Award from the Commission on Professional Preparation. She has also been selected as an Association for College Student Personnel (ACPA) Emerging Scholar. She earned her BA in English from The Ohio State University, her JD from Harvard Law School, and her PhD from Ohio State.

Susan R. Jones is an associate professor in the Higher Education and Student Affairs program at The Ohio State University. Prior to rejoining the faculty at Ohio State, she was an associate professor in the College Student Personnel program at the University of Maryland, College Park. She began her faculty career at Ohio State, where she served as an assistant professor and director of the Student Personnel Assistantship program after a number of years as a student affairs administrator, including as the dean of students at Trinity College of Vermont. Jones's research focuses on social identities, college student identity development, intersectionality, and service-learning. She is also a coauthor of the book *Negotiating the Complexities of Qualitative Research in Higher Education* and an associate editor for the *Journal of College Student Development*. She has received a number of awards, including NASPA's Robert H. Shaffer Award for Academic Excellence as a Graduate Faculty Member, ACPA's Senior Scholar award, the Outstanding Scholar Award from the University of Maryland College of Education Alumni, and Ohio State's Distinguished Teaching Award. She earned her BA in sociology from St. Lawrence University, her master's degree from the University of Vermont, and her PhD from the University of Maryland, College Park.

Chapter Contributors

David Kasch is a doctoral candidate in the Higher Education and Organizational Change program at the University of California, Los Angeles. He serves as a lead editor for *InterActions: UCLA Journal of Education and Information Studies*, and teaches courses on college student development, organizational theory, and qualitative research at the University of Redlands. His research focuses on the influence of social media on college student identity development, the commodification of identity and self-concept in higher education, and college student expressions of microaggressions through social media. David earned a BA in music and recording arts from Loyola Marymount University and master's degrees in college student personnel from Miami University and in higher education from the University of California, Los Angeles.

Stephen John Quaye is an assistant professor in the Student Affairs in Higher Education program at Miami University. He is the recipient of the 2009 NASPA Melvene D. Hardee Dissertation of the Year Award for *Pedagogy and Racialized Ways of Knowing: Students and Faculty Engage Racial Realities in Postsecondary Classrooms*. In addition, he is a 2009 ACPA Emerging Scholar. His research concentrates on difficult dialogues, the influence of race on college campuses, and student learning and development. Stephen earned his BA in psychology from James Madison University, his master's degree in college student personnel from Miami University, and his PhD in higher education from the Pennsylvania State University.

We lovingly dedicate this book to our families,
who are the anchors in our identity stories:

Ann and Brad Jones
Gretchen Metzelaars
Tobi and Frank Abes
Amber Feldman
Shoshana and Benjamin Abes-Feldman

ACKNOWLEDGMENTS

No book is written in complete isolation and without the generosity and help of others. We are both very fortunate to have so many individuals in our lives to whom we can turn for assistance and support on many different levels: from the initial support of our idea; to critical reads of every chapter; to artistic wizardry in graphic design; to collaborations on content, which included making us look smarter than we are; to grounding us in the world of practice; and to extreme patience as our evenings and weekends were taken over by a focus on this book. Our development and writing of this book have benefited enormously from the expertise, support, and encouragement of many.

We are grateful to John Schuh, who took a chance and encouraged us to develop a proposal to Jossey-Bass for this book and then continued to shepherd us through the process. Marylu McEwen offered her usual thorough feedback on an early version of the proposal and continued to encourage us throughout the writing process. We are fortunate to be surrounded by many students who were eager to read our drafts and then offered terrific feedback that kept us grounded in the practicalities of writing for an audience of graduate students. In particular, the suggestions and insights of Mei-Yen Ireland (The Ohio State University) and Kira Newman (Miami University) were incredibly helpful. Claire Robbins (Virginia Tech) read early drafts of several chapters and offered, as always, insightful and thorough feedback. Elisa used a draft of the manuscript in one of her student development classes, so we had an added benefit of incorporating her students' feedback and comments into the final version of the book. We know the book is much stronger as a result of their comments, confusions, and questions. Israel Martin (Ohio State) worked with us to create all the new graphics for the book. We handed him drawings on pieces of paper that we had scribbled in airports, hotel lobbies, and Elisa's dining room, and he made them look exquisite—and like scholarly models. We received immensely helpful and useful feedback from three external reviewers. It was clear to us that they read the manuscript carefully and, as a result, offered us thoughtful feedback that strengthened our final version.

We also greatly benefited from our collaborations with David Kasch (University of California, Los Angeles) and Stephen John Quaye (Miami University) in coauthoring two of the chapters. Their expertise in the areas we were tackling, as well as their good humor, enhanced the substantive content of the book as well as our writing process. We are also grateful for the willingness of Derrick Tillman-Kelly, Ian Prieto, Kira Newman, Alex Hirs, and Mei-Yen Ireland to join us in what is probably the most innovative portion of the book—the creation of borderland models of multiple dimensions of identity. They not only agreed to our invitation but also enthusiastically and seriously took on their assignment to each draw their own model using multiple theoretical frameworks.

Finally, taking on a project of this nature exacts a toll on the everyday "routines" of life, if there are such things. During the time we worked on this book, we experienced moving, births, and deaths in our families. Although writing this book was deeply rewarding, it took our time away from the most significant areas of our lives. Gretchen Metzelaars and Amber Feldman were kind and patient (and somehow put up with us!) when we were at our most focused, and cheered us on—thank you. And Shoshana and Benjamin Abes-Feldman reminded us of what is truly most important in life. Maybe one of them will bring our book to show-and-tell at school!

FOREWORD

Marcia B. Baxter Magolda

Ruthellen Josselson (1996) wrote, "Identity is what we make of ourselves within a society that is making something of us" (p. 28). Her observation captures the complex interplay of personal and societal contexts in human development. Susan R. Jones and Elisa S. Abes explore this complex interplay in *Identity Development of College Students: Advancing Frameworks for Multiple Dimensions of Identity,* bringing to readers' attention just how much context matters in our theorizing about identity development. Their explorations move beyond foregrounding either personal perception or societal power structures to a theoretical borderlands approach that holds both simultaneously. By bringing disparate perspectives into conversation, Susan and Elisa offer a lens that captures the multiple possibilities of identity in the complex and increasingly contentious social context in which we live.

Susan and Elisa not only articulate but also demonstrate the centrality of context in the evolution of identity and theoretical perspectives on identity development. They introduce their own contexts—their intellectual and personal evolution—to show how these contexts frame their research and their beliefs. Robert Kegan (1982) noted that people make meaning "*between* an event and a reaction to it—the place where the event is privately composed, made sense of, the place where it actually *becomes* an event for the person" (p. 2). Susan and Elisa share the events they encountered as well as the meaning they made of them to craft their identities. This rare window into their meaning making illuminates how their particular experiences with both marginalization and privilege shape their personal and professional identities.

Following their lead, I offer a glimpse into the meaning making I bring to writing this foreword. I am a strong proponent of the constructivist-developmental tradition, particularly Kegan's portrait of it, which brings Eriksonian and Piagetian theorizing together to portray self-evolution. I lean toward holistic portrayals of development and become frustrated when contemporary scholars fail to recognize that many earlier scholars (particularly William Perry Jr. and Mary Belenky and colleagues) emphasized the intersections of intellect, identity, and social relations. My twenty-five-year longitudinal study of young adult development, which foregrounds the person as meaning maker, persuades me that a constructivist approach surfaces meaningful possibilities for understanding adult development. As a result of this perspective, I have struggled to understand some scholars' portrayal of intersectionality, critical race theory, and queer theory as incongruent with constructivism. Although I am aware that a constructivist approach does not intentionally foreground power structures, I view it as open to these possibilities and inclusive of the complex interplay between personal and societal contexts. Conversations with many student development scholars, including Susan and Elisa, reveal that many of us struggle with how to position these various perspectives in our attempt to understand the complexity of development. Because we naturally position our own meaning making and ideologies in the foreground, it is challenging to stand outside of them to assume another vantage point. In this book, Susan and Elisa not only show how this tendency mediates our theorizing but also model a way of meaning making that might help us move beyond our own ideologies.

They do so by illuminating how personal and social contexts shape our meaning making, and by modeling how, if we are aware of these contexts, we can stand outside of them to entertain new possibilities. They traverse the theoretical landscape with precision, staying true to the original conceptualizations of theoretical perspectives in their respective contexts while attempting to bridge them to other concepts as they bring perspectives seen as disparate into dialogue with one another. They offer in-depth yet succinct portraits of constructivism, intersectionality, critical race theory, and queer theory as they explore how to create theoretical borderlands. These portraits enriched my thinking about the intersections of personal meaning making and the centrality of power in identity constructions. Susan and Elisa acknowledge points of departure among these theoretical perspectives as well as multiple perceptions of the value of creating theoretical borderlands.

Within this larger theoretical landscape, Susan and Elisa carefully situate their research on college students' identity development. I was intrigued to learn the story behind their multiple collaborations to construct the Model of Multiple Dimensions of Identity (MMDI) and its reconceptualization, the Reconceptualized Model of Multiple Dimensions of Identity (RMMDI). The way they wove the research participants' stories together with their own stories enriched my understanding of the context from which these models arose as well as their nuances. The book then takes an unusual twist as the authors carefully call their models into question, exploring each new theoretical perspective. By asking questions of themselves and readers, the authors push the boundaries of our understanding and dig deeper into the nuances of the interplay of personal perception and societal power structures. Rather than advancing their ideas as complete, they offer them as incomplete and engage readers in critiquing them from multiple perspectives. By creating visions of intersectional, critical race theory, and queered models of multiple identities, Susan and Elisa model theory construction in progress. By inviting graduate students to construct portraits using a borderland approach to the MMDI, they model entertaining multiple contexts and perspectives in an attempt to understand the complexity of identity development.

The student development literature has evolved as though our intellectual, moral, identity, and relational development are somehow separate entities. Intersectional, critical race, and queer perspectives are often framed in opposition to the psychological perspectives that have dominated theorizing about student development. Although they focus clearly on identity in this volume, Susan and Elisa bring together both psychological and sociological perspectives, honoring the specific contributions of each and using the strengths of particular perspectives to compensate for the shortcomings of others. In contemporary society we often observe polarization rather than blending of perspectives. Susan and Elisa move beyond binaries in their work, inviting readers to entertain new, more complex ways of making meaning that honor divergent perspectives and acknowledge development as holistic and dynamic. As a result, the book reflects the complexity of development and the difficult work of theorizing about it. Yet it is accessible because the authors articulate concepts clearly and offer meaningful questions and activities to support the reader in the theorizing process. *Identity Development of College*

Students is a unique contribution to the student development literature because it models complex theorizing, makes the process transparent, and invites readers to hold their own ideologies alongside others in the effort to understand the multiple dimensions of identity. Kegan (1982) defined being a person as "an ever progressive motion engaged in giving itself a new form" (pp. 7–8). *Identity Development of College Students: Advancing Frameworks for Multiple Dimensions of Identity* draws readers into this ever progressive motion, and invites us to give ourselves a new form.

PREFACE

In 1978 student development scholars Lee Knefelkamp, Carole Widick, and Clyde Parker wrote in their New Directions for Student Services text *Applying New Developmental Findings*, "In the past two decades important changes have occurred in the field" (p. vii), and then went on to make the case for the centrality of the study of "college students as students" (p. viii) to the field of higher education and student affairs. Their text, in many ways a precursor to the greatly expanded and highly regarded *Student Development in College,* first published in 1998 and now in its second edition (see Evans, Forney, Guido, Patton, & Renn, 2010), was the first to classify student development theories into theory clusters (for example, psychosocial, cognitive, maturity, typology, and person-environment). For many years, the primary researcher and proponent of psychosocial theory focused on college students (building on the work of Erik Erikson) was Arthur Chickering. His work was published in the seminal text *Education and Identity* (1969) and then revised in a second edition with Linda Reisser in 1993. One would be hard pressed to locate anyone who has completed a higher education and student affairs graduate preparation program who is not at least minimally acquainted with Chickering's Seven Vectors of Development.

Although many would argue that the seven vectors have withstood the test of time, newer conceptualizations of identity development now exist that are useful to understanding the construction of identity among today's diverse college students, who bring to campuses increasingly complex and multifaceted ways of constructing identities and presenting themselves. And just as Knefelkamp and colleagues suggested in 1978, "Important changes have occurred in the field" (p. vii) in the past two decades. Among these changes is the focus on both socially constructed identities and holistic development. Viewing identities as socially constructed locates identity development within larger historical, social, political, and cultural contexts and suggests that identity does not exist outside contingent social realities—and therefore that it is constantly changing amid shifting contexts rather than fixed and stable. Interest in identities as socially constructed led to research, theories, and models on specific identities, such as racial identity, cultural identity, gender identity, ethnic identity, and sexual identity, to name several among myriad possibilities. The focus on holistic development reflects an interest in getting at both a more comprehensive and complete portrayal of the whole student as well as the complexities of identity when considering multiple dimensions of identity (for example, race, ethnicity, culture, gender, sexual orientation, social class, religion and spirituality, and ability) and different domains of development (for example, cognitive, interpersonal, and intrapersonal).

Since the publication of the second edition of *Education and Identity* (Chickering & Reisser, 1993), no text has been presented that explicitly addresses these newer conceptualizations of the holistic nature of college student identity development by integrating a focus on socially constructed identities. Our aim in this book is to concentrate explicitly on college student identity development, tracing the evolution of identity theory from the work of Erikson and Chickering to newer conceptualizations of identity. This focus is the subject of one chapter in the second edition of *Student Development in College* (Evans et al., 2010). Other texts often present identity theories in tandem with many other theories, and not in relation to one another. Further, social identities are typically treated discretely rather than holistically, with a focus on specific populations and the stage-related process that leads to the internalization of race, for example, into one's sense of self. Finally, those who focus on holistic development (for example, self-authorship), highlighting a process of development that leads from following external formulas to generating an internal foundation, do not explicitly address social identities (Jones, 2009; Torres, Jones, & Renn, 2009). That external-to-internal approach does not often acknowledge the influence of larger structures of inequality. In this book, *Identity*

Development of College Students: Advancing Frameworks for Multiple Dimensions of Identity, we focus on what we consider to be an integrative approach to identity, one that treats identity as socially constructed and located in larger structures of privilege and oppression. Our approach presumes the presence of multiple social identities; that is, each individual possesses social identities, such as race, social class, gender, and sexuality, whether or not these identities are personally meaningful. However, we do not address the particularities of each social identity as a developmental process. Rather, we treat social identities as integrally related and a reflection of larger social structures. To get at such a treatment of social identities we focus on several theoretical frameworks, including intersectionality, critical race theory, and queer theory, each of which represents departures from the more typical psychological and constructivist approaches to the study and understanding of identity.

Drawing on both the foundational scholarship and the latest research on identity, *Identity Development of College Students* provides an expanded exploration and discussion of this core area of student development theory, research, and practice. As Vasti Torres, Susan R. Jones, and Kristen Renn (2009) asserted in the fiftieth anniversary issue of the *Journal of College Student Development,* "Student development scholars and student affairs professionals should be open to new theoretical approaches and to exploring new combinations of well-known theories" (p. 593). No one text responds to this call, despite the need for such a text among faculty who teach student development courses and practitioners who apply theory to practice in their direct work with college students. Indeed, our aim was to produce a book that we would want to adopt in our student development theory courses. We hope that this text fills this void.

More specifically, the primary purpose of this book is to describe contemporary perspectives on the identity development of college students in the United States, with an emphasis on multiple social identities. Locating this focus in the historical foundational work of Erikson and Chickering, we trace the evolution of the study of identity in relation to contemporary research and theoretical frameworks. We situate these contemporary perspectives within our holistic description of identity that portrays identity as the intersection of context, personal characteristics, and social identities. As part of doing so, we explore the nature of context, including inequitable power structures, and how context influences and is influenced by multiple social identities. To accomplish this goal, we use our research on multiple identities as a springboard, including the ways in which we have used critical theoretical frameworks (intersectionality, critical race theory, and queer theory) to analyze these relationships. By tracing the evolution of our research, we hope we have created a comprehensive text that enables the discussion of both foundational and newer approaches to understanding identity development and the construction of identity. An outcome of our approach is that the reader is also provided with an example of the evolution of theory development and the intersection of who we are as researchers, our own identities, and theories we are creating. To that end, one could read this book both for the specific content and also as a mirror to our evolving understandings about identity and the identity construction process.

To accomplish our purposes, *Identity Development of College Students* is organized into four sections. Each section is introduced by an overview of the chapters in that section, and in the second, third, and fourth sections there are *interludes,* or pauses from the more academic discussion of content, in which we write about and reflect on how our own stories intersect with the content in the section. The inspiration for including these interludes came from the writing of Robert Rhoads and Patti Lather. In Rhoads's book *Community Service and Higher Learning* (1997), he begins each chapter with a narrative from his childhood. He wrote of his approach,

> We all have a sense of self that we bring to all we do. As we know from our own lived experience, the self is much more than simply a reflection of our present-day circumstances and current feelings. We each have deeply textured social histories, all of which contribute to who we are as a person. (p. 13)

In a book *about* identity, it seemed particularly important to make our own social histories and identities more explicit rather than distancing ourselves from our topic of interest. After all, our interest in the subject of identity came from our own identity explorations, challenges, and negotiations. In her book *Getting Lost,* Lather (2007) incorporates interludes after each chapter as a way to complicate and elaborate on the ideas contained within. Our interludes provide a glimpse into how our thinking has evolved over time and the identity issues with which we have wrestled, both in our research and in our own lives.

We recognize that there are trade-offs in our approach. By focusing on the larger construct of identity and differing theoretical perspectives for investigating and understanding identity, we do not address the identity dynamics for specific groups, and the differences within these groups. That is, you will not find in this book detailed discussions of, for example, racial identity theory, ethnic identity theory, or sexual identity theory. Other texts and book chapters address these specific theories and models, and we suggest that these theories serve as an important foundation for understanding identities and make an important contribution in the evolution of identity scholarship. Still, because of our focus on the theoretical frameworks of intersectionality, critical race theory, and queer theory, identity dimensions of race, social class, sexuality, and gender are foregrounded. Although these frameworks may be applied, with caution and judgment, to other identity dimensions, such as ability and faith, our examples come less from those dimensions than they do from dimensions more specifically congruent with intersectionality, critical race theory, and queer theory. You will also find in this book a discussion of the larger construct of social identities and the evolution of thinking about multiple identities. We do not mean to suggest a return to theories that essentialize specific groups or to imply that identity is the same for all individuals. Instead, we hope to provide a discussion of overarching concepts that may then be applied to particular groups in a way that captures the complexity of identity and the nuances of the identity construction process, rather than distilling the process down to a single story (Adichie, 2009).

Another potential trade-off in our approach comes from the use of our own research as the jumping-off point for our examination of identity in this book. By drawing on our own work, we are returning to data and literature that some may perceive as old. However, we decided on this direction for two important reasons. The first is that the literature we cite is indeed the scholarship that was available to us at the time of our original research, which serves as the foundation for this book. This is not to say that this book is full of only very old material. In fact, it includes, we believe, both a sophisticated treatment of the foundational scholarship on which the study of identity is built as well as the newest thinking about identity. Second, and related to this last point, we find that some scholars and practitioners today are quick to dismiss what seems to them to be antiquated and irrelevant scholarship—sometimes including foundational scholarship. This dismissal is often done without reading the scholarship that is being passed over or without a good understanding of that body of literature. So to that end, our incorporation of what we perceive to be foundational scholarship, including primary sources, in this study of identity represents our belief that we need to understand these theories and constructs, both because much of the subsequent work on identity is anchored in this early scholarship and because much of what these foundational theories convey is still relevant and applicable today. We now turn to a brief description of each chapter in the book.

Section One includes two chapters that broadly address situating identity. In Chapter One we situate ourselves in this work, and lay the groundwork for the interludes that follow. We include our own stories, which narrate how it is that we became drawn to an abiding scholarly interest in the study of identity. We think this is important because who we are influences what we study and how we go about the research process; it also illuminates both our areas of focus and strength as well as what we might miss or remain silent about because of our identities and lived experiences. In Chapter Two we situate the study of identity in different disciplines as well as in higher education and student development scholarship, paying particular attention to the psychosocial tradition in identity theory. Chapter Two offers an evolutionary picture of the study of identity and concludes with the more recent emphasis on identities as socially constructed, which provides the underpinnings for the chapters that follow.

The three chapters in Section Two focus on the development and reconceptualization of the Model of Multiple Dimensions of Identity (MMDI), which serves as the conceptual framework for the book. Chapter Three introduces the three strands of scholarship that anchored the original study from which the MMDI was created: foundational student development theories, particularly those with a focus on identity; identity theories focused on underrepresented groups; and those theories conceptualizing identities as socially constructed, with particular attention to early work on multiple identities. We also discuss two additional works that informed the model, the Multidimensional Identity Model and the constructs of personal and social identities. Chapter Three also provides an introduction to the study itself, including profiles of its participants. In Chapter Four the MMDI is introduced, with particular attention given to the central elements of the model: the core, multiple social identities, the relationship of social identities to the core and identity salience, and contextual influences. In Chapter Five we present the Reconceptualized Model of Multiple Dimensions of Identity (RMMDI), along with details about the study on which this reconceptualization is based. Because the RMMDI integrates a meaning-making element into the model, the scholarship of Kegan and Marcia Baxter Magolda is discussed in relation to the study design and findings. These chapters encourage readers to consider their own self-perceived identities in relation to the various elements of the MMDI and RMMDI, both as a way to apply their own experiences to the models and to ascertain these models' strengths and limitations.

In Section Three we discuss three critical theoretical frameworks that represent a departure from the more typical constructivist approaches to studying identity. Chapter Six addresses intersectionality, Chapter Seven critical race theory, and Chapter Eight queer theory. In each of these chapters we provide detail about the historical origins, core tenets, and characteristics of each framework, referring to primary sources. We also present examples of how these frameworks have been applied in higher education and student affairs research. Finally, we discuss each of these frameworks in relation to the MMDI. We focus here on the MMDI because we consider the RMMDI as the first extension of the MMDI. In applying each framework to the central elements of the MMDI we ask, "How would the MMDI and the RMMDI look different if [theoretical framework] were used? How might each framework shift an understanding of the elements of the MMDI and the RMMDI?" We then present a redrawn model that we created by applying the framework. We redrew the models with some trepidation (discussed more fully in the introduction to Section Three) because we do not believe that there is one right way to capture these complex ideas. However, our focus on these theoretical frameworks and their relevance to understanding identity presented us with several important ideas in relation to rethinking the models. Our redrawn models are designed to capture these ideas rather than to declare a definitive Critical Race Theory Model of Multiple Dimensions of Identity, for example.

In Section Four we tie together the concepts illuminated in the book through two chapters that address the application of these ideas theoretically, empirically, and practically, and then look to the future in terms of new directions for theory building and understanding identity. In Chapter Nine we provide published examples of the application of the MMDI and RMMDI to frameworks for scholarly research, for theoretical investigations, and in practice settings. We also explore the possibilities for applying the three critical theoretical frameworks in practice, and address how doing so might shift the nature of student affairs practice to one that more explicitly considers the role of power dynamics in educational practice. Here we provide several examples of educational contexts that promote critical examination of self and other. Our aim is not to supply specific blueprints for practice, but instead to introduce the paradigmatic shift required to integrate critical theoretical frameworks into practice and the potential outcomes when successful. In Chapter Ten we bring together the theoretical perspectives of constructivism, intersectionality, critical race theory, and queer theory to create theoretical borderlands, an analytic place that draws from multiple perspectives, suggesting that no one perspective is enough for a sophisticated understanding of the complexities of identity. In doing so, the strengths and limitations of each approach are highlighted, particularly in relation to the MMDI, as are the benefits of using theoretical perspectives in combination. Also in Chapter Ten we set the stage for future directions in the area of identity scholarship by providing five examples of a borderland analysis. We invited graduate students who had some prior knowledge of the three critical theoretical perspectives to each draw their own model in a way that illustrates how they would put these concepts and elements together to represent their own lived experiences. We use these borderland models to discuss future directions for research on college students and identity.

In an effort to ensure the usefulness of this text, we conclude each chapter with a list of potential discussion questions and activities that may be used in a classroom setting, either for individual self-reflection or among small groups. We "tested" many of these questions and activities with students in Elisa's student development theory class as we were writing the book, and with graduate students who had some background in the material covered in these chapters. Their feedback was invaluable as we sought to create a treatment of identity that was both sophisticated and accessible.

We end this preface to the book with a favorite quote of ours. This particular quote exemplifies for us what we hope is a significant contribution of this book—that is, a lessening of the strain of this battle to understand self and other by acknowledging that identities are complex, contested, multifaceted, and ever shifting as a result of larger structures of power and privilege. To present these multiple factors at the forefront of analysis and consideration brings us closer to a more authentic conceptualization of identity.

> To be nobody-but-yourself—in a world which is doing its best, night and day, to make you everybody else—means to fight the hardest battle which any human being can fight; and never stop fighting.
>
> **e. e. cummings, 1958 (quoted in Firmage, 1965, p. 335)**

March 2013   Susan R. Jones, Columbus, Ohio
                                                     Elisa S. Abes, Oxford, Ohio

The Jossey-Bass Higher Education Series

IDENTITY DEVELOPMENT OF COLLEGE STUDENTS

SITUATING IDENTITY

The study of identity has long been a hallmark of higher education and student affairs research and practice. The central identity question of "Who am I?" is no less compelling today than it was when the foundational work by psychologist Erik Erikson (1959/1994; 1968) was published. Erikson's conceptualization of identity laid the groundwork for many theorists who followed in his footsteps. However, much has changed in the world since Erikson's day. In this first section of the book, we build the foundation for our approach to this book. That is, we focus both on the evolution of theory (and thus on the role of those who create and develop theories) and on the specific content theories address. To that end, the chapters in this first section situate the study of identity in the evolution of student development theories, and also situate us in this work, as we believe that who we are—the particulars of our identities—have influenced why we are drawn to the study of identity, the approaches we have taken to our work, and the continued evolution of our thinking about identity and college students. As noted in the Preface, among the theoretical underpinnings of this book is that theories are socially constructed; that is, they reflect the historical, political, societal, and cultural contexts in which they emerged. Marylu McEwen (2003) articulated well this framework:

Theories are . . . extensions of social constructions, informed by the
data from which they are developed. Important dimensions of the
social construction of theory include who the theorist is, on whom the
theory is based, for whom the theory is designed, and in what sociohistorical context the theory has been developed. (p. 170)

These are important considerations to keep in mind as you read and
evaluate theories, both those covered in this book and elsewhere.

Further, theories are created by individuals who also are products of
these specific historical, cultural, political, and societal contexts. For
example, Erikson's very close friend, the psychiatrist and prolific writer
Robert Coles (2000), described the relationship between the particulars
of Erikson's upbringing and the moment in history in which he lived and
the focus of his work:

No wonder, then, a psychoanalyst whose ancestry was Danish, but who
lived in Germany, then learned a profession in Austria, only to come to
the United States with a Canadian-born wife, and see his three children,
two sons and a daughter, become Americans, would develop a strong
interest in the way psychology intersects with sociology, culture and
nationalism, history. No wonder, too, a man who had in his background
Judaism and Protestantism, and who was a child during the First World
War, a parent during the Second World War, and saw the continent that
was home to his ancestors, immediate as well as distant, turn into a
region of fear and hate, even murder, despite the so-called
"advancement," the richness of tradition, to be found there—it is truly
no surprise that such a person would give great thought to the effect
events in the world at large have on many of us, no matter the private
or personal aspects of our particular lifetime. (p. 17)

So although theory has evolved since Erikson's pioneering work on
identity, and although some may be quick to dismiss his conceptualizations
of identity as outdated and no longer relevant in contemporary times, to
know something of his background helps explain how his work evolved as
it did. This is the focus of Chapter One in this book, which will leave the
reader with some sense of "No wonder, then, that Susan and Elisa were
drawn to the study of identity."

In Chapter One, Situating Ourselves in the Study of Identity, we continue to draw from Coles's work and adopt his message from *The Call of
Stories* (1989) as an approach to sharing something of ourselves. We enter

into this story of the development of college student identities through our own identity negotiations and journeys. Our narratives, which continue throughout the book as noted in the Preface, provide the reader with some ideas about why we pursue the topics we do and the assumptions we carry with us into our work. Much of what we know about college student identity is anchored in narrative approaches. Despite great variety in epistemological and methodological approaches, disciplinary roots, and sample compositions, the study of identity results in stories that respond to the longstanding and undeniable questions that percolate during the college years: "Who am I?, What will I be?" (Widick, Parker, & Knefelkamp, 1978b, p. 5). These are the questions that serve as the bedrock of the study of identity. And they are the questions that compelled us to engage in scholarly inquiry focused on college student identity development. This focus has been an abiding one for us during our scholarly and professional careers, but we suspect, as Knefelkamp articulated, that "all theory is autobiographical" (quoted in Jones & Abes, 2011, p. 151), and that our interest in identity development and the theories that describe this process was prompted, in part, by an effort to understand ourselves. Finally, because theories represent the worldviews and experiences of those who construct them (McEwen, 2003), we believe it is important for the reader to understand who we are and how our identities intersect with our scholarly pursuits. This perspective also illuminates the theory creation and evolution process. That is, as we have engaged with this work on the study of identity, our understandings have shifted and expanded in directions unimaginable to us when we first embarked on this investigation. The sequence of chapters in this book, beginning with the chapters in this opening section, mirrors the evolution of our thinking and inquiring about identity.

In Chapter Two, Situating the Study of Identity in the Evolution of Student Development Theories, we locate the study of identity in its historical and disciplinary origins as well as under the umbrella of student development theories. Other texts describe in detail these particular theoretical conceptualizations and the specific theories within them, most notably the second edition of *Student Development in College* (Evans, Forney, Guido, Patton, & Renn, 2010), and several chapters in the fifth edition of *Student Services: A Handbook for the Profession* (Schuh, Jones, & Harper, 2011). Our goal in this chapter is not to repeat what is in these texts by fully introducing the specifics of the full range of different theories, but instead to provide enough of an overview of these different conceptualizations that the reader is attuned to the distinctions and nuances among identity theories grounded in psychology, sociology, and social psychology, for example. This overview creates the foundation for what are referred to as "psychosocial" theories of development; the chapter then locates the study of identity in the psychosocial tradition, with attention given to the work of Erikson, James Marcia, and Arthur Chickering. The chapter concludes with a section on social identities and socially constructed identities. Attention to socially constructed identities makes explicit the influence of structures of inequality and privilege and oppression on the identity development process.

Taken together, these two chapters form the springboard for the chapters that follow. We will continue to offer our stories throughout the book in the form of the interludes described in the Preface, as we think the structure of the book should mirror our own evolution as identity scholars and teachers. It is not possible in this book to provide an in-depth orientation to the origins of identity theories, but our hope is that the chapters that follow will motivate readers to explore some of these primary sources and to become more expert in these theories than our overview permits. For example, the use of the term *social identities* is gaining traction in higher education and student affairs research, but often it is presented as a stand-alone phrase without mention of its historical and disciplinary origins. The disposition to more fully investigate the origins of theory is at the heart of theory development—the intellectual curiosity to delve more deeply into theories and then, from that knowledge base, into the questions it evokes, to improve on what exists. In an interview published in 1984, Chickering was asked to comment on the "developmental theory scene today" (Thomas & Chickering, 1984, p. 398). He responded:

> I guess my final word is that we should hold the many theories now available to us with "tenuous tenacity" and maintain a tough-minded and inquiring mind regarding theories. At the same time we need to undertake active experimentation to develop new practices that are systematically oriented toward encouraging human development in the light of the best theory we have at the present time. (p. 399)

We find his response still relevant today, and it serves as a great starting point for approaching the chapters that follow.

CHAPTER ONE

SITUATING OURSELVES IN THE STUDY OF IDENTITY

R obert Coles, author, psychiatrist, and professor, has eloquently written on the relationship between stories and theories. In his book *The Call of Stories*, he urged for "more stories, less theory" (Coles, 1989, p. 27). Coles recounted that during his many years as a psychiatrist he was armed with the best education, superior medical techniques, and widely regarded expertise; however, he was most effective when he was able to nudge his patients to tell him the stories of their lives. He wrote:

> I explained that we all had accumulated stories in our lives, that each of us had a history of such stories, that no one's stories are quite like anyone else's, and that we could, after a fashion, become our own appreciative and comprehending critics by learning to pull together the various incidents in our lives in such a way that they do, in fact, become an old-fashioned story. (p. 11)

Coles (1989) went on to refer to "a respect for narrative as everyone's rock-bottom capacity, but also as the universal gift, to be shared with others" (p. 30).

It is in this spirit that we begin this book focused on the complexities of identity development among college students. The study of identity may be considered an investigation into the stories of one's life; as an individual constructs a sense of self, tempered by the external world, a story unfolds and gets written. As Lieblich, Tuval-Mashiach, and Zilber (1998) suggested, identity stories are "told, revised, and retold throughout life. We know or discover ourselves, and reveal ourselves to others, by stories we tell" (p. 7).

We hope to make explicit the stories that have framed our respective worldviews, our beliefs, and our commitment to an understanding of identity. Thus, we begin by offering our stories to you. And, like Coles (1989) summarizing what he had learned from his mentor in medical school, William Carlos Williams, we believe: "Their story, yours, mine—it's what we all carry with us on this trip we take, and we owe it to each other to respect our stories and learn from them" (p. 30).

Susan's Story

The roots of my interest in identity research took hold long ago. I am a product of the 1960s, and among my most vivid and significant memories is my eighth-grade field trip to Washington, DC, during the Vietnam Moratorium Day—there was a huge antiwar protest, during which we walked alongside those wearing black armbands as a symbol of protest and singing, "Where have all the young men gone . . ." I remember clearly where I was when all four assassinations of my childhood occurred (John F. Kennedy, Malcolm X, Robert F. Kennedy, and Martin Luther King Jr.). I listened carefully to the lyrics of the likes of Peter, Paul, and Mary and Simon and Garfunkel. And at a young age I was reading books like *Soul on Ice, To Kill a Mockingbird,* and *Black Like Me.* I was tuned into injustices, inequality, and the importance of social action as I watched the civil rights movement unfold, large-scale protests against the Vietnam War, and the war on poverty. As a student affairs practitioner, teacher, and scholar for many years now, thinking about, teaching, and researching identity have enabled me to extend these roots and plant new seeds.

My fascination with identity and Erik Erikson began as an eighth grader (apparently eighth grade was a pivotal year for my intellectual growth!) when I wrote my "big" final paper on Erikson's stages of identity as I understood them. I was particularly intrigued by his notion of psychosocial moratorium (a different moratorium than the antiwar protest) because it sounded like something I would want to experience. This introduction to a theory of identity, reflected against what I considered to be my own identity quirks, led me to more formal study of identity and student development, most likely in an attempt to understand my own. When I was in graduate school it was fashionable to have a problem with William Perry Jr. and the other "White guys who studied White students." This led me down paths of both self-reflection on my own social identities that were silenced in what I was reading and critique because of what I perceived as a lack of relevance to my own life. What follows is something of my story and several of the "moments in it" (Coles, 1989, p. 11) as I describe what led me to the study of identity.

For reasons of which I was mostly unaware at the time, I understood at a young age that a privileged background gave me a number of choices and options that others did not have and permitted me a childhood I was able to enjoy. And yet, I also, from a young age, felt like an "other" in the world, and this, I believe, is what propelled me toward such experiences as studying abroad in Kenya for four months in college, working in a dry cleaning factory as the only White person "in the back room," and volunteering in Appalachia (Kentucky) after graduating from college. In all of these experiences I was keenly aware of being different. In one instance, I was ostracized as an "other" and not trusted (Appalachia); in another, I was included and treated as a member of the "family" (Kenya); and in yet another, I was regarded deferentially only because I was White (dry cleaning factory). I thought about what made me similar to the people I was with and what made us different. I wondered about what drew us together and what pushed us apart. I was also aware that in some experiences I was a visitor in another culture, able to return to my comfortable world when I wanted to—an option not always available to those with whom I interacted and worked. These early stirrings of difference inform who I am today.

My earliest feelings of difference I now know are related to my sexual orientation. I carried around this secret about myself for a very long time because I knew my parents would not want to acknowledge this dimension of who I am. When I disclosed my "secret" to my mother, of course she knew. Mothers know these things. But I also think my mother was quite certain that none of her friends had gay children, and if they did, they certainly would not talk about it. So we did not talk about this dimension of my life either. For many years, I lived what felt like a double life. I could present the face of the "dutiful daughter" in some settings and that of the increasingly comfortable lesbian in others. I worked hard to maintain my parents' approval of me while wrestling with how that could include presenting a more authentic self. I made sure that I achieved in all dimensions of my life so that it could never be said that my failings were due to my sexual orientation. I was a good student, an accomplished athlete, and a loyal family member.

It is probably not an accident that I spent ten years working at a Catholic college, which in many ways replicated the identity constraints of my family—"We all know who you are, but just don't talk about it or be too obvious." I experienced the dynamic of feeling at once invisible and silenced because of who I was and highly visible as an "other." I learned how to move through very different environments and, like a chameleon, blend into the setting. This is both the privilege and the potential liability (because it results in inauthentic ways of living) of sexual orientation. However, I think I am the person I am today because of my sexual orientation, or more precisely, because of the process of coming to terms with my sexual orientation. It is why I read the books I did as a kid, chose certain educational experiences, and developed early stirrings of empathy and a social conscience, and even why I research and teach what I do.

In the early 1990s I began a doctoral program as a full-time student after many years of practice as a student affairs administrator. My years as a dean of students were rich and full, providing me with ample experience on which to draw in my doctoral courses. When I wrote my application for the doctoral program, I looked to these experiences to come up with the requested statement of my research interests: leadership development, service-learning, and women college students. However, I also brought with me the question that nagged me during my master's program ten years prior: How could I locate myself in the theories I was studying?

During my first semester as a doctoral student in the college student personnel program at the University of Maryland, I enrolled in a women's studies class titled "Race, Class, and Gender" taught by professor and sociologist Bonnie Thornton Dill, a leading scholar in the areas of African American women and families and Black feminist scholarship (and, as the reader will see in subsequent chapters, a very significant influence on my intellectual and scholarly development). In this class I was introduced to theoretical frameworks and a literature base that helped address some of what I found missing in the student development scholarship (in part because this literature had not been written yet—Carol Gilligan had just published *In a Different Voice* as I was finishing my master's program). The class also placed an explicit focus on populations previously absent from the dominant literature I had studied in my master's program. My final paper in this class focused on African American women college students and represented an early effort to integrate two theoretical frameworks (student development theory and Black feminist scholarship) to extend an understanding of an underrepresented student population.

The next year, I completed a course in phenomenology that introduced me to the philosophical underpinnings of a phenomenological worldview as well as the methods of phenomenological research. In this class I was introduced to and investigated the phenomenological concepts of lifeworld, essence, empathy, and difference. I was intrigued by Jacques Derrida's and Martin Heidegger's concept of *difference* and the relationship between identity and difference. Intertwined with my own experiences of feeling different during my adolescent years was a curiosity about the juxtaposition of identity and difference in relation to student development. Heidegger took on the seemingly incompatible association between difference and identity, suggesting that the trappings of Western thought created a tradition of oppositional frameworks and produced the discourse of identity as sameness and difference as distinct. Instead, Heidegger emphasized the essential relationship between the two and a conception of identity as emerging from the central human experience of difference. I concluded then that exploring identity through the construct of difference requires that multiple dimensions of identity be considered and that individual voices be heard.

At this time, the concept of voice was popular in the identity discourse. Many scholars noted their motivation to "give voice" to some set of previously silenced populations and experiences. It was Dr. Thornton Dill who pointed out to me that "giving voice" is actually antithetical to the presumed empowerment that is to result, as the power differential inherent in one giving voice and the other receiving it suggests. However, the concepts of silence and voice were linked in my mind to the study and experience of identity. Indeed, Belenky, Clinchy, Goldberger, and Tarule (1986), in their landmark study *Women's Ways of Knowing*, concluded that "the development of voice, mind, and self are intricately intertwined" (p. 18). What led scholars to the metaphor of voice was recognition that certain voices were missing from the scholarship on student development and an interest in providing a context for these voices to be heard. Success in this effort was impossible to achieve without wading into the larger structures of power and privilege that created the silencing in the first place. As Reinharz (1994) noted, "Voice, in particular, has become a kind of megametaphor representing presence, power, participation, protest, and identity" (p. 183). These ideas led me to an investigation of identity and difference as part of my phenomenology class.

My dissertation about multiple dimensions of identity was really about me—well, it wasn't about me, but the focus of the study was driven by my own life experiences and questions. I wanted to see myself in the theories I studied. The title of my dissertation reflected a focus on multiple dimensions of identity, but it also included "voices of identity and differ-ence." I suggested then that the experience of difference highlights certain dimensions of identity. That is, power and privilege mediate those dimen-sions of identity that we experience most centrally (or saliently, to use the argot of the field) and those we take for granted; at least this was my experience. The inquiry I began with my dissertation has evolved over the years, but consistent throughout has been my abiding interest in under-standing the complexities of identity construction, especially when social identities and structures of power and privilege are considered. I also real-ized that I could not effectively study these dynamics in others without also carefully considering their role in my own identity construction.

I was very aware of my sexual orientation as a nondominant identity, and of the complications wrought by the intersections of gender and social class. Becoming conscious of my own racial identity, however, was a very different process and began with my experiences during a study abroad program in Kenya during my senior year of college. This process of under-standing has been challenging and ongoing—mostly because, I have come to realize, there are no real prompts for White people to think about their own racial identity. My Kenya experience could have remained all about *them*, and not at all about *me*.

My race and the social class of my background enable me to pass in the dominant culture. My gender—but more significantly, my sexual orientation—push me to the realm of "otherness" and marginality. I found I was able to more fully engage with my racial identity once I began to grapple with my sexual orientation. Despite lots of experiences as a child that highlighted prejudice and racism, and then as a young adult in which I was racially an outsider for a short period of time, I was able to safely keep my own racial identity as White out of any analysis of what I was observing about the "other." This, I learned, is the way the structures of racial inequality and racism work.

I began to see this in the dry cleaning factory when I was asked to move into a management role after one week as a "bagger" and was working alongside individuals who had spent years at the factory. There was one difference, I was White (and educated, although no one really knew that from me), and they were Black. I saw it when I realized that my first Black faculty member was in my doctoral program (and that I had had only two women faculty in my entire undergraduate education)—and when I realized how long it took me to realize this. I saw it in the racial segregation in schools and neighborhoods, and in the racial climates on college campuses. But I really began to see it when I looked at my own racial privileges as a White person and the advantages I accrued in my everyday life simply because I was White. And I saw it when I examined the "details" of my everyday life—what *my* neighborhood looked like, who attended *my* church, who *my* friends were. I was also consistently challenged (and continue to be) in teaching classes about racial identity and tuning in to my own feelings, anxieties, and reactions to classroom dynamics (such as when a White student critiqued Beverly Daniel Tatum's use of the word *racism* as "just so harsh," and a student of color was sitting right next to this person).

Finally, I saw it when I lived for five years in the wealthiest county in the United States, which also had the greatest proportion of African Americans; in a community that was probably 95 percent African or African American; in which my neighbors drove Mercedes, BMWs, and Lexuses and I drove a Honda Civic; in which there were no visible signs of other gay folks and no recognition of the twenty years I had been with my partner; in which there were churchgoing Christians and a HUGE African Methodist Episcopal church; and in which a neighbor showed visible surprise when he inquired if we lived in the house we were standing in front of (when we replied yes, he uttered, "I didn't know White people lived here . . . and where are your husbands?"). So for the first time in my life, I was in a space where my race, social class, and sexual orientation, but particularly race, were very apparent to me; and for the first time in my life, I was a racial minority in my neighborhood. I have lived in towns and cities that boast that they are "diverse" (which typically means the presence of "diverse others" but relatively segregated neighborhoods). I experienced firsthand what it is like to be one of a few in a "diverse" environment (diverse for me)—and not as a result of a study abroad program or part-time job, but because of where I lived, the place I called home. And everyone knew my name!

This highlights for me the centrality of context in the (re)construction of identity and the constant negotiation that occurs between context and self, particularly when structures of power and privilege are considered. I think, then, of identity (including my own) as always in the process of becoming, and as a dynamic interaction between social identities and context. The dynamic nature of these interactions suggests both their multidirectionality, such that context influences identity dimensions and identity dimensions influence context, and that my experience of one social identity—for example, race—also influences the construction of another, such as sexual orientation. Here in this paragraph you see my language become encumbered by my theoretical knowledge and the intersection of story and theory. My own life experiences and process of coming to understand myself led me to the exploration of multiple dimensions of identity and social identities, an enduring interest beginning with my eighth-grade paper on Erik Erikson.

Elisa's Story

Baruch atah adonai . . . Starting as a twelve-year-old girl, and then throughout much of my teenage years, I led Shabbat (Sabbath) services at my synagogue.[1] I read the Torah and led the prayers. I practiced so much that I had much of it memorized. My mother was the principal of my religious school, and I enjoyed spending time in her office or in the synagogue library. I distinctly remember the smell of the Hebrew National corned beef and matzah ball soup at the Jewish deli that we went to every Sunday for lunch after religious school. I looked forward to going to Hebrew school twice a week after "regular" school. I never once was sad that we didn't celebrate Christmas. I loved lighting the menorah for Chanukah and taking turns with my brother lighting candles each night. I always hoped I'd be the one to light on the eighth night when the menorah looked most spectacular. I cherished the Jewish holidays and sharing holiday meals with my family. I never wanted to venture beyond the synagogue or my family's house on Rosh Hashanah or Yom Kippur, because being with people who didn't celebrate these holidays would somehow take away the special feel of the day. As I grew older and moved alone to different cities for school and jobs, I always found comfort in the familiarity and beauty of the music in the synagogue. The melodies were the same, no matter the city, always drawing me back into the security of home. It has been important to me to keep aspects of Kosher. I don't mix dairy and meat, or eat pork or shellfish (I've led a happy life without a cheeseburger, pepperoni, or shrimp). Why? It's tradition. And it's nice to hold on to tradition in a world where life doesn't always play out as planned.

Eloheinu melech haolam . . . I always imagined the day when I would take my own children, always pictured with dark curly hair, to religious school. And I had carefully written down my mom's chicken soup and kugel recipes so I could make them for my own family after Rosh Hashanah

---

[1]Parts of this story were published in Abes, E. S. (2011). Exploring the relationship between sexual orientation and religious identities for Jewish lesbian college students. *Journal of Lesbian Studies, 15,* 205–225.

services or Passover. But Judaism wasn't just about education, holidays, family, and food. It was also about a personal relationship I felt with God. I had and continue to have personal conversations with God, like a close confidant, to always protect my family, especially during my parents' many health scares. I never understood why more prayers didn't include "thank you," as I always believed it was important not only to ask God for protection but also always to express gratitude every time that protection was offered.

Shehecheyanu vkeyamanu . . . So when I was first attracted to another woman and identified as a lesbian—at age thirty—I never questioned my attraction, nor did I ever think there was anything wrong with being gay. Why should there be? Why question whom a person loves? But I did worry about whether or not I would be able to have a family—dark curly-haired children to take to religious school, make matzah ball soup for, light the menorah with. Would I have children who would learn about Judaism from my parents? Questioning whether I would have children was one of the few things that saddened me when thinking about my newfound identity, and this was the subject of my conversations with God. How different would my life look from what I had hoped? Indeed, it's nice to hold on to tradition in a world where life doesn't always play out as planned.

Five years later I met my partner, Amber Feldman, a wonderful Southern Jewish woman who speaks Yiddish, the cultural language of Jewish people, and she, too, wanted children. Three years later, with Amber at my side in tears, I gave birth to our daughter. We followed a Jewish tradition of naming her after a relative who passed away. We named her after my grandmother, my "Amaw," the same one who cooked many of my Rosh Hashanah meals. As a teenager, my grandmother received a small Torah as recognition for being the only woman in her religious school class in the early 1900s, a time when it was uncommon for women to receive a formal Jewish education. That Torah is now one of my most cherished possessions, and I'll give it to our daughter one day. Perhaps at her Bat Mitzvah, when she is called on to read from the Torah as a Jewish adult.

Our daughter's religious naming ceremony took place in the synagogue with her grandparents present. I was moved by the realization that this was her first time in a synagogue; the first time hearing the melodies that have been so comforting to me; the first time being enveloped in the Rabbi's warmth. I will never take for granted how welcoming our Rabbi is of all relationships; his belief that love transcends hate; and his commitment to the Jewish values of loving kindness and justice. Indeed, I shared that same feeling when our Rabbi lovingly presided two and a half years later at our son's *brit milah*, his ritual circumcision, again at the synagogue and again surrounded by family.

V'higayanu lazman hazeh . . . Blessed are you Lord Our God King of the Universe who has kept us alive, sustained us, and enabled us to reach this day. Thank you.

I write this story, which genuinely gets to the essence of me (if there is such a thing), with ease and a sense of fulfillment, keenly aware of how fortunate I am that two identities so important to me have smoothly coalesced. I am aware that this is not the case for many other Jewish lesbians, or for many people who desire positive interactions among other social identities important to their sense of self. I come to the study of identity aware of many of the privileges I have that have facilitated my ability to integrate my identities and curious to understand the nature of this process for others. I also come to the study of identity aware that although my current understanding of identity has its roots in my childhood, that understanding took a long time to more clearly reveal itself to me. I lost sight of aspects of my identity along the way with changing contexts, and my identity is still evolving, as I believe identity continuously does.

Despite my fortune in integrating my two most salient identities, I am aware that these identities make me an "other," different from the norm and lacking certain privileges. Although I have always greatly enjoyed being different as a Jewish person, I am sensitive to some of the negative ways I have felt different, ironically sometimes among other Jewish people. For instance, I was keenly aware as a young child that our family did not have the same financial means as some of the other people in my Hebrew school and Jewish youth groups. Although I had everything I wanted in my loving family, I remember as a child perceiving an unjust hierarchy grounded in social class that made itself apparent during Rosh Hashanah and Yom Kippur services, among the holiest days of the Jewish year. Unofficial seating arrangements for these services seemed to be driven by social class. Those who came from the economically prominent families in the congregation sat in the front of the synagogue, closest to the Rabbi and Cantor, and seemed to find numerous reasons to walk up and down the aisle during services, almost as if the religious service were a fashion show.

My family always sat in the back of the synagogue in the overflow seating. I remember my father, an incredibly kind, very hardworking salesman who unabashedly demonstrates his love for his family, once saying during services that he wasn't comfortable sitting closer to the front of the synagogue because his financial contributions were smaller than those of some of the other synagogue members. I remember how bothered I was by that statement, believing that love and kindness, not money, were measures of a good person—a person worthy of being not only showcased in the synagogue but also, more important, comfortable to pray within a community. Indeed, it was my father's values grounded in loving kindness that were truly consistent with Jewish values, as opposed to behaviors that drew lines between people based on economics. The latter, I realized, perpetuated ill-conceived stereotypes of Jewish people and was a basis of anti-Semitism.

My father's comment was the root of much of my sensitivity toward others who are marginalized and my interest in studying identity from critical theoretical perspectives that explore how systems of inequality shape identity development and identity development theory. Indeed, I find my social class, more so than my sexual orientation or religion, to be the most vexing identity with which to grapple. Despite my awareness of social class differences, I grew up believing we were well-off. My parents always bought me books, and we lived in a well-kept house in a safe neighborhood with a great backyard in which my brother and I wore holes in the grass playing endless baseball. I had no idea how closely my parents watched their budget to provide us with this simple but comfortable life. In college, where I befriended some people of greater financial means, I grew increasingly aware of the differences between my family and those with more disposable income. I considered my friends' luxury spending to be wasteful, and I became more proud of my parents' sacrifices and sensibilities and sensitive to those who struggled more than I did. Still, I was slow to truly understand social class differences and acknowledge the many privileges I had.

Prior to starting my doctoral program in higher education and student affairs, and uneducated about the drain student loans would have on my life for too many years to come, I graduated from a prestigious law school and worked as a litigation attorney in a large, prominent law firm. In the process of doing so, and as a result of some of the choices I made based on my relatively unexamined identity, I became socialized into a cultural status previously unknown to me and into professional expectations that reinforced rather than challenged norms. Although my understanding of my decision to leave the legal profession was not fully formulated at the time, I left knowing that I was not being true to my values and sense of self.

I then enrolled in graduate school, unsure what I was getting myself into and a tad resistant, but hopeful I would find work in higher education more congruent with my values than my previous experience. As a graduate student, I was fortunate to quickly have the opportunity to learn about student development theory in the context of service-learning experiences. The new understanding of identity that I shaped through this opportunity took me back to the seeds planted in my childhood, reminding me how I value the "other" and making my privileges apparent to me, especially those associated with social class and my identity as a White person. Now, as I teach graduate students, especially in the context of intergroup dialogue courses in which we explicitly focus on privilege, power, and oppression in an effort to understand our differences, I learn more about the complexities of identity and my own oversights related to the implications of marginalization from the stories the students graciously share.

Despite some innate sense of inequity, I've always appreciated being different from a norm. Thanks to my growing up Jewish and more recently identifying as a lesbian, the idea of being in a majority is one that feels somewhat awkward to me. Yet I know that I am indeed privileged, including in my race; in regard to ability; and in many ways economically, especially through my numerous educational opportunities, despite the stress associated with maintaining my desired middle-class lifestyle. It disturbs me how unaware I was of these privileges until my thirties (clearly a pivotal decade in my development), instead proud to be color- and other-difference-blind. I am poignantly aware that I talk little of these privileges in this story about myself. I have been educated to understand them; I have been challenged by those with less privilege to open my eyes to how much I still need to learn, and I have pushed myself to continuously do so. I have reached a point where I understand how my identity as a White person is central to how I make my way through the world; and I have committed much of my recent professional life to using my privileges to educate others about systems of inequality and ultimately create change. Still, like many others with privilege, I don't always think of the privileged aspects of my identity as central to who I am, as I do with the interplay between my religion and sexual orientation, with social class mixed in.

In short, my childhood awareness of difference, my current experiences as I begin to teach religious traditions in a family that looks different from what is typically considered "normal," and my professional experiences whereby my understanding about identity is continuously challenged have shaped how I conceptualize identity. Based on my own experience with difference and my sensitivity toward others who experience marginalization, I come to the study of identity believing that identity ought to be studied from a critical theoretical perspective that explores systems of inequality; that identity is a reflection of the intersections of multiple identities; that identity is a complex combination of privilege and marginalization; and that context and identity are inseparable, with both always in flux.

◆ ◆ ◆

We recognize that the identity stories we share here, which have led both of us to explore critically how systems of inequality shape student identity development theory, are only two of many possible stories about our identities. Our identity stories change depending on the time and space in which we tell them. Likewise, we recognize that college students bring multiple identity stories with them to campus every day, also depending on the time and space in which they tell them. Some of these stories are visible, and some are not, both to others and to them.

Nigerian author Chimamanda Adichie eloquently spoke to the nature of multiple stories in a talk titled "The Danger of a Single Story" that she presented as part of the TED Talks series. Referring to the manner in which her African identity has been represented as monolithic, she observed the danger of believing there is just one story that describes a group of people. She explained:

> The single story creates stereotypes, and the problem with stereotypes is not that they are untrue, but that they are incomplete. They make one story become the only story . . . When we reject the single story, when we realize that there is never a single story about any place, we regain a kind of paradise. (Adichie, 2009)

Likewise, there is not only one story that describes an individual person. Changes in context, the passage of time, unfolding memories, new experiences, fresh perspectives, and evolving worldviews all contribute to a person's multiple stories.

It is also in this spirit of multiple stories that we write this book. We offer several different theoretical perspectives, or assumptions about the nature of reality (Guba & Lincoln, 2005), to reveal the multiple ways identity stories might be told, heard, and acted on, depending on one's own assumptions. More specifically, by introducing theoretical perspectives that are critical in nature, we hope to uncover the inequitable ways in which people's stories get told by others, especially those with more power and privilege than they have. As Adichie (2009) stated: "Power is the ability not just to tell the story of another person, but to make it the definitive story of that person." By exposing such power in the realm of college student identity, our hope is that students will more readily be able to create and tell their own identity stories.

The remaining chapters in this book reflect our evolving thinking about the nature of theories pertaining to college student identity development. Our hope is that readers will situate their own stories within these theories while reading. We begin with a review of the evolution of identity development theory, recognizing that just as identity stories change, so, too, must the theories that help make sense of them.

Discussion Questions and Activities

1. Write your own "situating yourself" essay. Specifically, consider what experiences and aspects of your identity shape your interest in and perspectives on theories of identity development.
2. Watch Adichie's TED Talk titled "The Danger of a Single Story" (http://blog.ted.com/2009/10/07/the_danger_of_a/). Have there been times when you have felt that other people have created a single story about you? What has been your reaction to that experience? In what ways do you find yourself creating or relying on single stories about other people? What causes you to do so? What do you see as the danger of a single story for understanding identity? For understanding theory?
3. How do you construct stories about others? About friends? Family? Peers and colleagues? College students? Whom do you include, and whose stories do you tend to miss? What explains which stories you include and which you miss?
4. How might you challenge yourself in regard to the stories you construct about others?
5. From a research perspective, how might studies be designed to counter a "single story"? Are there particular methodological approaches that lend themselves to incorporating multiple stories?

CHAPTER TWO

SITUATING THE STUDY OF IDENTITY IN THE EVOLUTION OF STUDENT DEVELOPMENT THEORIES

The study of identity has long been integral to college student development theory and practice, centering on the seemingly simple question of "Who am I?" As noted student development scholars Lee Knefelkamp, Carole Widick, and Clyde Parker, editors of one of the first texts to bring student development theories together in an organized way, wrote in 1978, "From its inception the college student personnel field adopted a developmental orientation emphasizing the importance of responding to the whole person, attending to individual differences, and working with the student at his or her developmental level" (p. viii). In higher education and student affairs, college student identity development has been linked over the years to achieving "maximum effectiveness" (American Council on Education, 1937/1994, p. 69); achievement (Sanford, 1962); core self-image (Widick, Parker, & Knefelkamp, 1978b); individuation or becoming an individual (Chickering & Reisser, 1993); student learning (King & Baxter Magolda, 1996); and intercultural learning and diversity (Dey, Ott, Antonaros, Barnhardt, & Holsapple, 2010; King & Baxter Magolda, 2005). Put simply, an understanding of identity is necessary if one is to understand college students and their experiences in higher education contexts. However, multiple frameworks and theoretical perspectives on the question of identity exist in the literature, and depending on the framework, disciplinary orientation, or historical context, the definition of identity and the depiction of the identity development process vary considerably and evolve over time.

In this chapter we situate the study of identity under the larger umbrella of student development theories, and then briefly address different disciplinary perspectives on the construct of identity. We then turn our focus to the evolution of psychosocial theories in particular, because this is where the study of identity emerged in the field of higher education and student affairs. We explore in more depth those theories most influential to an understanding of identity in higher education and student affairs, such as the work of Erik Erikson, James Marcia, and Arthur Chickering and Linda Reisser. In doing so we will illuminate both the meaning of the term *psychosocial* and how it has evolved from a concept firmly rooted in psychology (albeit with recognition of the importance of the social world) to one influenced by sociological perspectives and socially constructed perspectives on identity. The final section of this chapter addresses social identities, necessarily introducing the constructs of power, privilege, and identity salience into the discussion of identity, and thereby leading right into the framework for understanding multiple social identities—the foundation for what follows in this book. As we proceed, we will define the major terms and constructs that are central to an understanding of psychosocial theories of development and identity. At the end of this chapter we also include a table (see Table 2.5) that reflects the evolution of identity theories by what we are calling "theoretical era" and identifies several of the bodies of work most influential in each era.

Overview of Student Development Theory

Student development theory emerged in the early 1960s in response to dramatic changes in higher education, such as student unrest during the Vietnam War and the focus on human rights brought on by the civil rights and women's movements (Evans, Forney, Guido, Patton, & Renn, 2010); a growing cadre of student personnel professionals focused on the cocurricular dimensions of campus life; and an interest in understanding the whole student. Drawing on the work of such psychologists as Erikson and Jean Piaget and such sociologists and social psychologists as Emile Durkheim and Kurt Lewin, researchers began to focus their study specifically on college student development, the college experience, and the campus environment. *Student development theory* extends Nevitt Sanford's definition (1967) of development as "the organization of increasing complexity" (p. 47) to the realm of college students. In an effort to capture the complexity inherent in the process of student development, Patricia King (1994) suggested:

> It may be helpful to think of a student's growth and development as a kaleidoscope or mosaic of changing skills, attitudes, beliefs, and understandings, acknowledging that each student represents a slightly different set of shapes, colors, and textures that constitute his or her own personal kaleidoscope, each with its own specific set of developmental attributes. (p. 413)

In the area of student development, the theoretical foundation of the field has typically been organized into what has been called "families" of theories and "theory clusters" (Knefelkamp et al., 1978, p. xi). Initially, the primary families or clusters included theories that focus on psychosocial development (for example, Erikson's theory of psychosocial development); cognitive-structural development (for example, William Perry Jr.'s theory of intellectual and ethical development); maturity models (for example, Douglas Heath's model of maturing); typology theories (for example, Roy Heath's model of personality typologies); and person–environment interaction models (for example, John Holland's theory of personality type and environments). These theories were all considered *developmental theories* at the time they were introduced because they both presume and describe the trajectory of increasing complexity (Sanford, 1967), and because "they are concerned with systematic change over time while in college" (Knefelkamp et al., pp. viii–ix). More recent conceptualizations (for example, Evans et al., 2010; Jones & Abes, 2011; McEwen, 2003) have added to these clusters several theories that focus on social identities, which some argue fall into the psychosocial cluster; developmental synthesis models that integrate clusters, such as the theory of self-authorship (for example, Baxter Magolda, 2001, 2009); theories of organizations, campus environments, and student involvement (for example, Astin, 1984; Bolman & Deal, 2008; Strange & Banning, 2001); and student success theories (Kuh, Kinzie, Schuh, & Whitt, 2005; Tinto, 1993). Marylu McEwen (2003) created a figure that portrays the relationships among college student development theories (see Figure 2.1).

Sanford (1966) also made explicit the role of the campus environment in the development of college students, offering an impetus for student development, and a principle that is foundational to the field, in his call for both challenge and support: "The institution which would lead an

FIGURE 2.1 MODEL OF RELATIONSHIPS AMONG THEORIES
ABOUT THE DEVELOPMENT OF COLLEGE STUDENTS

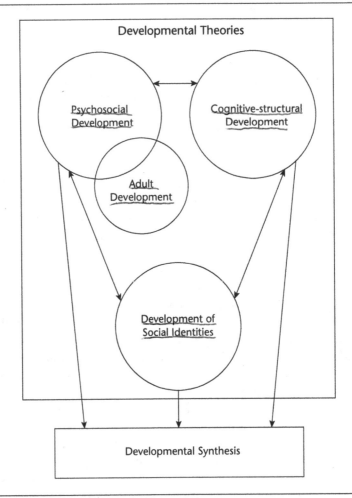

Source: McEwen, 2003, p. 156. Used with permission.

individual toward greater development must, then, present [that person] with strong challenges, appraise accurately his ability to cope with challenges, and offer him support when they become overwhelming" (p. 46). In Sanford's discussion of challenge and support, we see student development as located within the individual, but also as an area that the institution should promote. Knefelkamp and others (1978) made this connection explicit by suggesting central areas of knowledge in which those in higher education and student affairs must be well versed:

> If educators are to encourage development, they must know what development is—what changes can, do, and should take place in students and what particular factors serve to challenge and support them. From our perspective, the creation of a developmental community requires a theoretical knowledge base which describes:
> 1. Who the college student is in developmental terms. We need to know what changes occur and what those changes look like.
> 2. How development occurs. We need to have a grasp of the psychological and social processes which cause development.
> 3. How the college environment can influence student development. We need to know what factors in the particular environment of a college/university can either encourage or inhibit growth.
> 4. Toward what ends development in college should be directed. (p. x)

Although written over thirty years ago now, these questions still provide scaffolding that is relevant to the scholarship and practice of student development.

Early developmental theories were also epistemologically grounded in positivist traditions. *Epistemology* reflects a worldview based on assumptions about the nature of reality, and influences both how we know what we know and what we know about particular phenomena (Glesne, 2006; Guba & Lincoln, 2005). *Positivism* represents an epistemological worldview that emphasizes quantifiable, measurable truths about particular phenomena (such as identity) that can be predicted, discovered, and generalized to the population (Evans et al., 2010; Jones & Abes, 2011). This means development was often presented as a linear and sequential trajectory, and in a series of stages, phases, statuses, or vectors (Jones & Abes, 2011). Several of the theories falling within more recent conceptualizations depart from a positivist worldview and make use of different epistemological frameworks, such as constructivism (which foregrounds participants' meaning making about a phenomenon of interest); critical theory (which illuminates power relations in the interest of social change); and poststructuralism (which deconstructs and decenters taken-for-granted assumptions, such as normalcy and identity) (Jones & Abes, 2011). The epistemological framework used directly influences the role of the researcher, what that researcher knows about particular areas of interest, and how it is the researcher came to know. These epistemological departures from positivism will be more fully discussed and illustrated in later chapters of this book.

Influence of Disciplinary Perspectives on Identity

The response to this alarmingly simple question of "Who am I?" varies depending on disciplinary perspectives (for example, psychology, sociology, cultural studies); epistemological worldview (for example, psychoanalytic, positivist, constructivist, postmodern); and historical context (for example, early conceptualizations compared to those of more contemporary eras). As Sheldon Stryker and Peter Burke (2000) suggested, "The common usage of the term *identity* belies the considerable variability in both its conceptual meanings and its theoretical role" (p. 284). Although identity is most often situated within psychosocial theories of development in higher education research, the study and conceptualization of identity are also anchored in such rich disciplinary traditions as sociology, psychology, social psychology, and human ecology (Torres, Jones, & Renn, 2009). And these disciplinary traditions are also influenced by the prevailing epistemological frameworks and historical contexts. Space does not permit a full discussion on the specifics of each disciplinary tradition or epistemological framework, but instead we provide some general distinctions that influence how identity is approached and, thus, what is known and understood about identity. And despite these distinctions, as Vasti Torres, Susan R. Jones, and Kristen Renn (2009) pointed out,

> Each field locates the study of identity within its own disciplinary lens, but they share commitments to understanding the individual, his or her social context, the influence of social groups, and various dimensions of identity (e.g., race, ethnicity, gender, sexual orientation). (p. 578)

Stuart Hall, a sociologist and cultural theorist, developed an organizing framework for understanding how identity is presented by different disciplines that reflects varying epistemological approaches. Hall (1992), borrowing from an earlier conceptualization of three periods reflecting Western notions of self by experimental social psychologist Kenneth Gergen (1991), identified three competing yet overlapping conceptualizations: the Enlightenment subject, the sociological subject, and the postmodern subject. Identity within the Enlightenment subject is conceptualized as innate and "is the linear development and unfolding of the individual's essential core or self" (Yon, 2000, p. 13). For the sociological subject, identity is produced by cultures and in interaction with the social world, whereas for the postmodern subject identity is always in process, unstable, and fragmented. Identity within the postmodern framework is constructed as performative, fluid, and multiple (Torres et al., 2009; Yon). Summarizing the resultant tensions among these competing conceptualizations, Daniel Yon wrote:

> Much of the growing field of literature on the question of identity is structured by tension between conceptualizations of identity as a category or a process. As a category, identity announces who we are and calls upon notions of nation, class, gender, and ethnicity for definition. But a second way of talking about identities recognizes that identity is a process of making identifications, a process that is continuous and incomplete. This distinction between identity and identification is important because while the former implies an essential and fixed individual, the latter recognizes that identity is a constructed and open-ended process. (pp. 12–13)

As you read on in this chapter and those that follow, you will be able to recognize these tensions and characteristics in both the content of various identity theories and models and the ways in which they have evolved.

Disciplinary approaches also significantly influence perspectives on identity. In most cases, early scholars have provided foundational theories on which others, including those identity scholars in higher education and student affairs, have built. For example, Table 2.1 provides a theoretical genealogy to reflect the evolution of theories in particular disciplines.

However, even this seemingly neat and tidy chart does not accurately capture disciplinary influences, primarily because of the overlaps between psychological and sociological perspectives, which form the foundation for psychosocial understandings of identity. Although many social psychologists are anchored in psychology, some bring decidedly sociological interpretations to their work, primarily drawing on the work of George Herbert Mead and ideas associated with symbolic interactionism. At the risk of oversimplifying, but in an effort to bring some usefulness and clarity to this discussion of the role of disciplinary orientations, we include a helpful outline provided by Rachelle Winkle-Wagner (2009) in her book *The Unchosen Me: Race, Gender, and Identity Among Black Women in College*, which highlights the major differences between psychological and sociological perspectives on identity.

TABLE 2.1 DISCIPLINARY THEORETICAL GENEALOGY

Discipline	Foundational Theorists	Theorists Who Have Extended or Drawn On Foundational Work
Psychology	Erik Erikson James Marcia Jean Piaget Kurt Lewin Robert Kegan	Arthur Chickering and Linda Reisser Ruthellen Josselson William Cross Jr. Janet Helms Jean Phinney Vivian Cass Deborah Taub and Marylu McEwen Marcia Baxter Magolda Patricia King Raechele Pope Rita Hardiman and Bailey Jackson III Nevitt Sanford Corrine Kodama, Marylu McEwen, Christopher Liang, and Sunny Lee
Sociology	George Herbert Mead Sheldon Stryker Emile Durkheim Jürgen Habermas	Kenneth Feldman and Theodore Newcomb Allan Johnson Rachelle Winkle-Wagner Robert Rhoads
Social Psychology	Kenneth Gergen George Herbert Mead	Henri Tajfel James Côté and Charles Levine Kathleen Ethier and Kay Deaux
Cultural Studies	Stuart Hall	Daniel Yon

Assumptions of a psychological perspective on identity (p. 14):

1. It begins by assuming the theoretical priority of the individual and not society.
2. Work on identity, called social identity theory, emphasizes cognitions or mental processes.
3. The self is rooted in cognitions that arise out of a person's experiences.
4. There is an assumption of a single self, a singular identity.
5. Psychological theory discusses traits, characteristics, and personality.
6. Studies often examine perceptions of membership within groups.

Assumptions of a sociological perspective on identity (pp. 16–17):

1. The self develops out of interaction.
2. Society develops first, and a person's identity stems from socialized roles.

3. The self is located in social structures.
4. The self works to organize social life.
5. There are multiple selves.
6. Reflexivity is a central aspect of the self; one is able to reflect on oneself.
7. Sociological work in identity is called identity theory.
8. The sociological perspective underwrites identity theory's emphasis on roles, commitment to roles, and identity salience.

Social psychologists studying identity emphasize three levels of analysis: *personality* (the intrapsychic domain typically studied by developmental psychologists); *interaction* (the behavioral micro domain that addresses day-to-day interactions of individuals in their contexts typically studied by symbolic interactionists); and *social structure* (the political and economic macro systems domain typically studied by sociologists) (Côté & Levine, 2002). As this section on disciplinary influences demonstrates, student development theories, and identity theories in particular, borrow primarily from psychological and sociological perspectives. Typically, the psychosocial foundation of student development is grounded in more psychological orientations (reflected not only in the primary focus on the individual but also in the prevalence of stage-based, linear models of development). As the focus on different dimensions of identity (for example, social identities) has evolved, scholars have drawn on other disciplinary perspectives, such as social psychology, to anchor new understandings. We now turn to examine in greater detail the psychosocial tradition out of which the study of identity in higher education and student affairs emerged, which, as already mentioned, reflects the characteristics of both psychological and sociological perspectives on identity. Combining psychological and sociological approaches to the understanding of identity enables concentration on both the individual and internal developmental processes as well as recognition of the role of the environment, social roles, and sociohistorical contexts in identity development.

Locating Identity in Psychosocial Development

In the field of higher education and student affairs, the study of identity is typically grouped into the psychosocial family of theories. Psychosocial theories of development address the "content" of development (Knefelkamp et al., 1978)—that is, the issues, decisions, and tasks facing college students at particular stages of development (Evans et al., 2010). The origins of psychosocial theories of development are found in Erikson's groundbreaking work. According to Widick, Parker, and Knefelkamp (1978b),

> Erikson's is undoubtedly a psychosocial view; he places the developing person in a social context, emphasizing the fact that movement throughout life occurs in interaction with parents, family, social institutions and a particular culture, all of which are bounded by a particular historical period. (p. 1)

Erikson's characterization of psychosocial identity is one that recognizes the role of the external social world; however, it elevates the role of the individual and internal processes that direct growth and development and highlights the importance of continuity between self and other.

Erikson and Psychosocial Identity

Erikson was a psychologist trained in the psychoanalytic tradition of Sigmund Freud. This is significant because it explains how it is that Erikson and those who followed his lead conceptualized the identity development process. Erikson advanced that the development of identity followed what he referred to as the *epigenetic principle,* suggesting that "anything that grows has a ground plan . . . and out of this ground plan the parts arise, each part having its time of special ascendancy until all parts have arisen to form a functioning whole" (Erikson, 1959/1994, p. 52). Psychosocial theories depict development as a series of *developmental tasks* that characterize specific, and in most cases, age-related, developmental stages. Following the epigenetic principle, development involves the interactions of the physical-biological stage and the external environment and social roles, as well as the individual's internal processing of these interactions. As Widick and colleagues (1978b) summarized, "Since each maturational phase occurs within a particular social and socializing context, the life cycle can be seen as a sequence of 'biological-social' phases, or more properly *psycho-*social" (p. 3). Also characteristic of, and central to, psychosocial theories is the concept of crisis. In each of the phases or stages characterizing psychosocial development, specific developmental tasks must be resolved for growth to occur, with resolution involving a "crisis" or decision-making point. Widick and colleagues defined crisis as "not a time of panic or disruption: It is a decision point—that moment when one reaches an intersection and must turn one way or the other" (pp. 3–4).

Hence we come to the concept of "identity crisis," which has served as the foundation for much of the early writings on college student identity in the psychosocial tradition.

Although Erikson is usually pointed to as the "progenitor of the psychosocial models" (Chickering & Reisser, 1993, p. 21) and "the premier theorist of identity" (Josselson, 1996, p. 6), he cautioned against the overuse and misuse of the concept of identity (Jones et al., 2012). In fact, if he were to read this book on college student identity, he might note the ways in which we have strayed from traditional psychosocial principles that emphasize linear pathways, developmental tasks, and biologically driven development! Nonetheless, Erikson was the first to detail an identity development process, and many followed in the direction of the footprints he left.

Erikson's theory is presented in eight stages, each one characterized by what Erikson referred to as a "psychosocial virtue," "polar orientations or attitudes," and "crises" (Widick, Parker, & Knefelkamp, 1978b, p. 3) for the individual to resolve. Some scholars have attributed precise age ranges for each stage, but Erikson described these developmental stages more generally—although age-specific ranges are implied. Table 2.2 illustrates Erikson's stages of psychosocial development.

It is Erikson's fifth stage, identity versus role confusion, that is the "watershed stage" (Evans et al., 2010, p. 50) for the early understandings of college student identity development. Understanding identity, or answering the question "Who am I?" is the central developmental task of late adolescence. It is important to note that this stage is viewed as the transition from childhood to adulthood, which explains why scholars

TABLE 2.2 ERIKSON'S STAGES OF PSYCHOSOCIAL DEVELOPMENT

Stage (Age)	Psychosocial Virtue	Stage Name (Polar Orientations and Crises)
Infancy	Hope	Trust versus mistrust
Early Childhood	Will	Autonomy versus shame and doubt
Play Age	Purpose	Initiative versus guilt
School Age	Competence	Industry versus inferiority
Adolescence	Fidelity	Identity versus role confusion
Young Adult	Love	Intimacy versus isolation
Adulthood	Care	Generativity versus stagnation
Mature Age	Wisdom	Integrity versus despair

Source: Adapted from Erikson, 1959/1994.

place the traditional-age college student (eighteen to twenty-two) in this stage. Further elaboration on this fifth stage of Erikson's theory in relation to college students was done by Chickering (1969) and Keniston (1971), who "refined Erikson's identity stage, extending it to the traditional college years" (Widick et al., 1978b, p. 4). Erikson (1963) defined identity as "the ability to experience one's self as something that has continuity and sameness, and to act accordingly" (p. 42). Discussing Erikson's definition of identity, Ruthellen Josselson (1987) offered this summary:

> Identity is the stable, consistent, and reliable sense of who one is and what one stands for in the world. It integrates one's meaning to oneself and one's meaning to others; it provides a match between what one regards as central to oneself and how one is viewed by significant others in one's life. (p. 10)

For Erikson, the content or specific issues faced by those in the identity stage of psychosocial development revolved around relationships, vocational decisions, and ideological beliefs and values. It is important to keep in mind that Erikson had men in mind as he described identity. About the identity tasks faced by women, he wrote, "I think that much of a young women's identity is already defined in her kind of attractiveness and in the selective nature of her search for the man (or men) by whom she wished to be sought" (Erikson, 1968, p. 283). To be fair to Erikson and place him in his sociohistorical context, he was a socially progressive thinker in his time, departing from his Freudian training in significant ways and becoming involved in important social causes, such as the civil rights movement. In fact, Josselson (1996) explained that she believes "Erikson was describing social reality as he saw it at the time rather than inscribing how women *must* be in society" (p. 275).

Erikson's theory has been described as "highly descriptive," yet "his constructs do not lend themselves readily to empirical study and validation" (Widick et al., 1978b, pp. 10–11). The first person to apply Erikson's theory to empirical research was developmental psychologist James Marcia. He developed an instrument called the Identity Status Interview, and then, using a sample of men, investigated the process of identity formation in adolescents, and specifically among college students. Rather than emphasizing identity resolution or confusion in the identity stage as Erikson did, Marcia (1966) found that identity is more likely to be characterized by the presence or absence of crisis or exploration and commitment in such areas as politics, religion, relationships, and career

TABLE 2.3 MARCIA'S IDENTITY STATUSES

		Has a Crisis-Exploration Been Experienced?	
		Yes	*No*
Has a Commitment	*Yes*	Identity achievement	Foreclosure
Been Made?	*No*	Moratorium	Identity diffusion

decision making. What resulted from Marcia's research was not a series of developmental stages, but instead a more fluid model of identity statuses (see Table 2.3). The intersections of the axes of crisis and exploration and commitment in these specific areas already noted (politics, religion, relationships, and career decision making), and the presence or absence of each, yield four identity statuses.

Space does not permit a full description of each of the statuses, but it is important to note that these statuses are not intended to suggest a developmental sequence or a permanent identity marker (for example, once foreclosed, always foreclosed) (Evans et al., 2010). Given the limitations of Marcia's sample, Josselson (1987, 1996) investigated Marcia's four identity statuses with a sample of women and developed new names for the statuses and descriptive detail for each. Responding to Marcia's groundbreaking work and Josselson's extension, Côté and Levine (2002) suggested that "the identity status paradigm has produced the most coherent body of empirical research on identity formation to emerge in the field of identity research, in either psychology or sociology" (p. 18).

Chickering and Identity Development

Arthur Chickering arguably contributed the foundational knowledge base on college student identity through his theory of the Seven Vectors of Development. Drawing on the work of Erikson, and concurring with Erikson on the centrality of identity resolution, Chickering proceeded to lay out a theory of college student development. As Chickering and Reisser (1993) noted,

> Since the stabilization of identity was the primary task for adolescents and young adults, it [Erikson's work] was a logical anchor point for Chickering's attempt to synthesize data about college student development into a general framework that could be used to guide educational practice. (p. 22)

This emphasis on educational practice is important because it reflects Chickering's primary area of interest. Chickering himself was quite clear on this point, stating that the book *Education and Identity* "was not written to advance theory per se but rather to improve practice" (Thomas & Chickering, 1984, p. 394). As Widick and colleagues (1978a) pointed out, Chickering was not a developmental psychologist:

> Chickering's model of student development, while psychologically sound, is not the work of a "pure" developmental psychologist; it is the work of an integrator and synthesist. He has logically combined existing theory and evidence extrapolating a pattern of developmental changes in such a way as to make the role of the college environment more apparent in those changes. (p. 20)

Chickering's Background and Methodology Chickering received his bachelor's degree in modern comparative literature from Wesleyan University; his master's degree in teaching English from Harvard University; and his PhD in school psychology from Teacher's College, Columbia University. On completion of his doctorate, he went to work at Goddard College as a psychology instructor and coordinator of evaluation. It was during his time at Goddard (from 1959 to 1965) that he conducted the research that led to his groundbreaking text *Education and Identity* (1969). While at Goddard, a small college in rural Vermont rooted in the philosophy of progressive education advanced by John Dewey—a college consistently regarded as, and proud of being, "out of the ordinary" (www.goddard.edu /history)—Chickering began collecting data from Goddard students to examine the impact of the intentionally designed experimental curriculum on students' development. A significant amount of data was collected via achievement tests, personality inventories, in-depth interviews, and students' diaries of their experiences (Thomas & Chickering, 1984). As director of the Project on Student Development in Small Colleges from 1964 to 1969, Chickering expanded data collection to include students from thirteen other small colleges. The data collected from Goddard students contributed to the development of the seven vectors, whereas the data collected later at other small colleges contributed to the second part of *Education and Identity*, which addresses key influences on student development (Evans et al., 2010). In 1993 Chickering and colleague Reisser published the second edition of *Education and Identity*, which was a revision of the original work based on their review of more recent research from other scholars, rather than on newly collected data they gathered. Their

TABLE 2.4 CHICKERING AND REISSER'S SEVEN VECTORS OF DEVELOPMENT

Vector One	Developing competence (intellectual, physical and manual, and interpersonal)
Vector Two	Managing emotions
Vector Three	Moving through autonomy toward interdependence
Vector Four	Developing mature interpersonal relationships
Vector Five	Establishing identity
Vector Six	Developing purpose
Vector Seven	Developing integrity

Source: Adapted from Chickering and Reisser, 1993.

revision did include the results of students' completion of a developmental worksheet in Reisser's classes and presentations that incorporated students' assessments of and reflections on their experiences (Chickering & Reisser, 1993). The revision included some reordering of the vectors and more inclusive narrative descriptions of each vector.

Seven Vectors of Development Chickering and Reisser's Seven Vectors of Development (1993) are shown in Table 2.4. There is not sufficient space for a complete description of each vector; and, as noted previously, other texts exist that contain this material. Instead we identify several important themes and concepts that will aid in achieving an overall understanding of Chickering and Reisser's vector model of student development.

First, what is a vector? Drawing from mathematics, a vector is a quantity that possesses both magnitude and direction, and this is precisely how Chickering (1969) used the term, although he noted that "the direction may be expressed more appropriately by a spiral or by steps than by a straight line" (p. 8). In his view, development is represented by vectors, or areas of concern, which "describe major highways for journeying toward individuation—the discovery and refinement of one's unique way of being—and also toward communion with other individuals and groups, including the larger national and global society" (Chickering & Reisser, 1993, p. 35). Here Chickering adapted two major constructs in developmental theory, *differentiation* and *integration* (Sanford, 1967), defining development as increasing differentiation and integration. Chickering proposed that development along each of the seven vectors involves cycles of differentiation (for example, seeing the parts of a whole) and integration (for example, putting the parts back together again into a whole), such that "these more differentiated perceptions and behaviors are subsequently integrated and organized so a coherent picture of [an individual] is established" (Chickering & Reisser, p. 21). Development occurs through the resolution of developmental tasks that characterize each vector. Widick and colleagues (1978a) succinctly described Chickering's application of the concept of vectors:

> The vectors specify in psychological terms the nature and range of those tasks. It follows that the vectors also define what the central concerns of the student will be, the tasks which will confront and tend to be sources of worry and preoccupation. Finally, each vector delineates changes in self-awareness, attitudes, and/or skills which are manifestations of successful completion of that task or vector. (p. 21)

Second, Chickering's theory is not only about identity development generally but also more specifically about developing a sense of self. Chickering (1969) explained this by stating, "At one level of generalization, all the developmental vectors could be classified under the general heading 'identity formation'" (p. 78) in that all the vectors lead the individual toward a sense of self. The fifth vector, establishing identity, is more specific to the developmental tasks related to comfort with one's appearance; comfort with self along a full range of dimensions (for example, gender, sexual orientation, and social and cultural context); clarity of self-concept and self-acceptance; and integration of internal and external perceptions of self (Chickering & Reisser, 1993).

Third, Chickering and Reisser (1993) conceptualized development along each of the vectors as not necessarily linear, age related, or rigidly sequential (Evans et al., 2010). Instead, Chickering and Reisser recognized that students will be in different places developmentally that will influence their movement along the vectors; they will experience the college environment differently; and the developmental task or vector that gives one student difficulty will be easily managed by another. Further, students may recycle tasks as internal processing and external demands cause them to reexamine issues related to certain vectors. That said, Chickering and Reisser do suggest that the vectors build on each other, and some work resolving tasks in earlier vectors is required for moving on to later ones, so in this sense the vectors are "developmentally sequential in a general way" (Thomas & Chickering, 1984, p. 397). For example, Chickering and Reisser reported that resolving the fifth vector, establishing identity, requires resolution of the preceding vectors (those pertaining to competence, emotional maturity, autonomy, and mature interpersonal relationships).

Finally, those scholars who have actually conducted research on the transferability of the vectors to diverse populations caution against universal application (for example, Fassinger, 1998; Kodama, McEwen, Liang, & Lee, 2001, 2002; McEwen, Roper, Bryant, & Langa, 1990; Pope, 2000; Straub & Rodgers, 1986; Taub & McEwen, 1991, 1992). Some scholars (for example, McEwen et al., 1990) have found some support for the general content of each vector (for example, developing purpose), but suggest that the ways in which individuals resolve the tasks may differ greatly based on racial or cultural background. They also suggest that additional tasks may be required (for example, developing a spiritual identity). Others (for example, Straub & Rodgers, 1986; Taub & McEwen, 1991) reported that the order of the vectors may differ by certain groups, such as women, or that an individual may delay development in one vector to work on another (see Fassinger, 1998; Pope, 2000). These findings that diverge from Chickering and Reisser's theory have provided some of the impetus for more concentrated attention on social identities in identity theory development and research. We turn to this area of scholarship now.

Social Identities

The use of the term *social identities* is relatively new in the student development literature; however, it builds on longer lines of scholarship from other disciplines, particularly social psychology, sociology, and cultural studies. In higher education and student affairs, interest in social identities emerged from a recognition that many of the foundational theories in student development were based on samples of predominantly White men, White women, or both, leaving out certain individuals and groups from the study of human development. This recognition, coupled with such major social forces as the civil rights movement, women's movement, and gay rights movement and the growing diversity of student populations in U.S. higher education, led to research that explicitly addressed, in both focus and sample, those populations whose experiences had not been represented in the literature. A number of identity theories and models that focused on specific racial, ethnic, and cultural groups, for example, emerged. Our goal in this book is not to provide descriptions of particular social identities, but to introduce social identities as an organizing framework for understanding identity in more complex ways. Social identity theories are discussed again in Chapter Three in relation to the scholarship on multiple identities; here we briefly introduce the origins of social identity theory and several major themes integral to an understanding of social identities.

The first use of the term *social identity* is attributed to social psychologist Henri Tajfel, who, along with his student John Turner, described social identity in relation to intergroup dynamics and perceptions of group membership. In 1982 Tajfel edited a book titled *Social Identity and Intergroup Relations*. Tajfel's conceptualization of social identity emerged out of psychological disciplinary traditions and is defined as "that part of the individuals' self-concept [personal identity] which derives from their knowledge of their membership in a social group (or groups) together with the value and emotional significance attached to that membership" (p. 2). Tajfel went on to suggest that the term *social identity* can never fully address the complexities of the development of identity, but that clearly perceptions of self are influenced somewhat by membership in social groups—and that membership in each group varies in salience for the individual by time and context. Of importance to the discussion here of the precursors to the conceptualization of social identities in student development and identity research is what Kay Deaux, another social psychologist, described as the relationship between personal identity and social identity. Deaux (1993) wrote:

> A number of investigators have proposed distinctions between personal and social identity, although the basis for this distinction is not consensual. Some, such as Brewer (1991) and Turner (1987), posit a temporal trade-off between a sense of personal identity, when one feels different from others, and social identity, when one focuses on shared group characteristics. In this analysis, there is no distinctive content of personal and social identity. Rather, what is personal or social depends on the particular fit of individual to context. Others . . . make a substantive distinction, wherein social identity refers to group membership such as being English or being a professor, and personal identity encompasses more individual relationships, such as daughter or friend, or lover of Bach. (p. 5)

Deaux's own view (1993) was that any distinction made between personal identity and social identity is "somewhat arbitrary and misleading" (p. 5). Instead, she suggested, "Rather than being cleanly separable, social and personal identity are fundamentally interrelated. Personal identity is defined, at least in part, by group memberships, and social categories are infused with personal meaning" (Deaux, 1993, p. 5). Deaux's conceptualization points to the inextricable link between personal and social identities, between the individual, the social world, and the meaning the individual makes of his or her experiences. In the field of student development, the emergence of "social identity" theories grew out of interest in membership in groups that are underrepresented and oppressed.

For example, drawing on and combining their earlier work on Black identity development (Jackson, 1976) and White identity development (Hardiman, 1982), Rita Hardiman and Bailey Jackson III (1997) created a stage-based model of social identity development. They explained that "social identity theory describes attributes that are common to the identity development process for members of all target and agent groups" (p. 23). Although they presented a developmental, stage-based model, they suggested that individuals may be working in several stages simultaneously. Their social identity development model includes five stages: (1) naive or no social consciousness, (2) acceptance, (3) resistance, (4) redefinition, and (5) internalization. Individuals following this progression would move from having no awareness of their particular social group, to accepting internalized roles and norms, to resisting these internalizations, to redefining themselves independent of systems of oppression, to finally internalizing this new consciousness into their redefinition (Hardiman & Jackson, 1997). The developmental sequencing, although the model was not intended to be strictly linear, is mirrored in a number of the theories that emerged during these times that focused on racial, cultural, and ethnic identity, and that grew primarily out of psychological and positivist traditions. These theorists described race and gender, for example, as socially constructed, but their models were firmly rooted in a positivist worldview and developmental frameworks.

Socially Constructed Identities

Despite the differences and nuances in definitions of social identities, several persistent themes exist. The first is recognition of identities as socially constructed. In commenting on the relationship between the literature and research addressing social identities and social constructivism, Evans and others (2010) wrote, "How individuals and groups make meaning of the world they occupy is vital to understanding social identity, making constructivism a worldview and method appropriate to explore these ideas" (p. 235). What Evans and others are referring to here is a way of conducting research that departs from the positivist tradition from which many of the earlier identity theories emerged. They are also identifying an epistemological framework that emphasizes the construction of knowledge rather than its discovery, and acknowledging that these constructions are rooted in historical and sociocultural contexts (Schwandt, 2001). The concept of socially constructed identities is related to constructivism, though they are not the same ideas. The idea of identities as *socially constructed* refers to the concept that "one's sense of self and beliefs about one's own social group as well as others are constructed through interactions with the broader social context in which dominant values dictate norms and expectations" (Torres, Jones, & Renn, 2009, p. 577).

Kenneth Gergen (1991) was among the first to discuss the "dilemmas of identity" (p. x) in contemporary life and to write about the social construction of a person. He advocated that identities are constructed primarily through relationships with others and with the world in which one lives, and that identities are inherently fragmented and disconnected. Gergen wrote, "These relationships pull us in myriad directions, inviting us to play such a variety of roles that the very concept of an 'authentic self' with knowable characteristics recedes from view" (pp. 6–7). Sociologists and scholars in women's studies were more explicit about these relationships, focusing on such socially constructed categories as race, class, and gender. Margaret Andersen and Patricia Hill Collins (2007a) elaborated, arguing that categories' "significance stems not from some 'natural' state, but from what they have become as the result of social and historical processes" (p. 62). Weber (2010) further explained:

> Race, class, gender, and sexuality are *social constructs* whose meaning develops out of group struggles over socially valued resources. Although they may have biological or material referents, race, class, gender, and sexuality are not fixed properties of individuals nor of materially defined groups. Their meaning can and does change over time and in different social contexts. (p. 91)

This conceptualization of identities as social categories that are socially constructed draws attention to the constructs of privilege and oppression because these categories take on their meanings in relation to systems of inequality that rely on privilege and oppression.

Privilege and Oppression

The second theme central to understanding social identities is the explicit role of privilege and oppression. Privilege and oppression are mutually reinforcing; that is, one requires the other to exist. And as sociologist Allan Johnson (2006) suggested, because of this dynamic relationship between privilege and oppression, "All of us are part of the problem" (p. vii). Using the example of race, Johnson explained:

> There is no way to separate the "problem" of being, say, black from the "problem" of *not* being white. And there is no way to separate the problem of not being white from *being* white. This means privilege is always a problem for people who don't have it and for people who do, because privilege is *always* in relation to others. Privilege is always at someone else's expense and always exacts a cost. (p. 8)

In the late 1980s Peggy McIntosh brought the discussion of White privilege to the foreground through the publication of her accessible list of privileges regularly enjoyed by White people (Evans et al., 2010; Johnson, 2006; McIntosh, 2010). She distinguished between "unearned entitlements" (McIntosh, p. 103) and "conferred dominance" (p. 103). Unearned entitlements, according to McIntosh, are those privileges that should reflect the norm for all individuals (for example, feeling safe at school); yet when those privileges are limited to only certain groups of people, then they constitute what McIntosh calls an "unearned advantage" (p. 103). Conferred dominance describes that situation in which one group is systematically overempowered. McIntosh (2010) wrote, "Whiteness protected me from many kinds of hostility, distress, and violence, which I was being subtly trained to visit in turn upon people of color" (p. 102). Conferred dominance and unearned privilege explain, as McIntosh suggested, why, for example, many White students in the United States think that racism does not have an impact on them and that White is not a racial identity.

The preceding example from McIntosh (2010) is reflected in what Johnson (2006) referred to as a paradox of privilege:

> One of the paradoxes of privilege is that although it is received *by* individuals, the granting of privilege has nothing to do with who those individuals are as people. Instead, individuals receive privilege only because they are perceived by others as belonging to privileged groups and social categories. (p. 34)

This means that how others perceive us is what is most important, and it explains how individuals can lose privilege if others do not think they belong to a certain category (for example, a straight male presumed to be gay by others), and how individuals can possess privilege without feeling privileged (for example, a White male from a poor family). These paradoxes create complicated identity dynamics.

Oppression, as Johnson (2006) noted, is the "flip side of privilege" because "like privilege, oppression results from the social relationships between privileged and oppressed categories, which makes it possible for individuals to vary in their personal experience of being oppressed" (p. 38). Marilyn Frye (2007) offered a compelling image to describe oppression using the metaphor of a birdcage, suggesting that if we only look at one wire of the birdcage, we get a myopic view, and it appears that the bird could fly around any time it wanted. But if we were to step back and look at the whole cage and all the wires, a macro view would emerge, and we could see right away how the bird is confined by a system of wires. In applying this metaphor to the oppression of women, Frye summarized,

> It is now possible to grasp one of the reasons why oppression can be hard to see and recognize: one can study the elements of an oppressive structure with great care and some good will without seeing the structure as a whole, and hence without seeing or being able to understand that one is looking at a cage . . . But when you look macroscopically you can see it—a network of forces and barriers which are systematically related and which conspire to the immobilization, reduction, and molding of women and the lives we live. (p. 45)

Social identities are influenced by social constructions that emerge from structures of privilege and oppression. The complex ways in which privileged and oppressed identities intersect have an impact on individual perceptions of self and the identity construction process. Further, privilege and oppression also influence the salience of particular social identities, the final theme we address.

Identity Salience

Salience refers to the prominence or importance attached to a particular experience, idea, feeling, or, in this case, social identity. Like the term *identity*, the word *salience* brings with it differing disciplinary interpretations. For example, Stryker's sociological interpretation emphasizes commitment, identity salience, and role choice (Stryker & Burke, 2000; Winkle-Wagner, 2009). Stryker and Burke (2000) wrote, "Identity salience is defined as the probability that an identity will be invoked across a variety of situations, or alternatively across persons in a given situation" (p. 286). They went on to suggest that "the higher the salience of an identity relative to other identities incorporated into the self, the greater the probability of behavioral choices in accord with the expectations attached to that identity" (p. 286). Stryker and Burke gave the example of salience of religious identity, suggesting that salience of this particular identity predicts time spent involved in religious activities and commitment to social roles based on religion. However, Winkle-Wagner (2009) critiqued Stryker's definition of salience, pointing out that the opportunity of "choice" is not always afforded to all, as was the case in her study of Black women in college. Winkle-Wagner's point reinforces the necessity of attending to the role of structures of privilege and oppression in identity construction, and in the perceived salience of particular identities.

Social psychologists Kathleen Ethier and Deaux (1994) highlighted the relationship between context and identity salience. They wrote,

> Social identity theory and self-categorization theory posit that when identity is made salient, as for example by a change in context, a person will become increasingly identified with his or her group. The concept of salience can be elusive, however, particularly when dealing with long-term changes in context. (p. 244)

They went on to suggest three bases on which one might predict the influence of salience on social identity: (1) those who are highly identified with their group, independent of context (for example, those students who grew up with a strong cultural identity, such as Latina, would experience this identity as salient, even on a predominantly White campus); (2) those for whom there is a contrast between self-perceived social identity and context (for example, individuals whose status is in the minority in their group, such as a gay man in a fraternity or a woman in a STEM major, are likely to perceive those identities as more salient than those from majority groups); and (3) those for whom there is a contrast between past background and current context (for example, the greater the contrast, the greater the increase in salience, such as when moving from a racially homogeneous neighborhood and high school to a racially diverse university) (Ethier & Deaux, 1994).

Psychological perspectives on identity salience emerged from recognition that the discipline of psychology historically has examined the social identities of race, gender, and sexuality, for example, as discrete units of analysis. Growing calls for integration and complexity through the study of multiple and intersecting identities led to the examination of identity salience. The work of psychologist Grace Chen (2005, 2009) explored identity salience and the individual variations in salience of multiple social identities among Asian Americans. Chen (2009) defined salience as "the most prominent—and often most relevant—characteristic, which in this case refers to social identity" (p. 175). Psychological discussions of salience also highlight the influence of shifting contexts and the need to incorporate the great diversity of individual experiences and perceptions of identity. Psychologists Oksana Yakushko, Meghan Davidson, and Elizabeth Nutt Williams (2009) proposed a model of identity salience grounded in theories of social identity, based on ecological models, and designed to assist psychologists engaged in clinical practice. Their model includes two overlapping larger circles that represent the ecological systems of the client and counselor. Each ecological system includes smaller circles that represent the social identities and sense of self of the client and counselor, with salience denoted by the positioning of the smaller circles and the thickness of the lines drawn. These circles are nested within the largest circle, representing the ecological system of the therapeutic context.

The introduction of an explicit focus on social identities into the scholarship and study of identity provides for the discussion of constructs of privilege and oppression, both of which exert an influence on identity. The framework of social identities has advanced an understanding of identity in which such dimensions as race, culture, gender, and sexual identity are considered in relation to both individual, self-perceived identities and the larger structures of race, class, gender, and sexual identity, which influence individual constructions of self.

Summary

The purpose of this chapter has been to provide an overview of the foundation for investigating and understanding multiple social identities, the anchor for the subsequent chapters. We located the study of identity within student development theories in particular, and in varying disciplinary perspectives. We examined the evolution of and context for psychosocial theories, and discussed the foundational contributors to this student development framework. Finally, we addressed the evolution of social identities, which brings to the forefront of analysis such dimensions as race, class, gender, and sexual identity, as well as the influence of structures of privilege and oppression on identity development. This body of scholarship forms the foundation for Chapter Three, which addresses more specifically multiple social identities and the intersection of identities. Overall, we hope that this chapter has demonstrated that the ways in which identity is defined, influenced in part by disciplinary perspectives, and studied, influenced by the chosen epistemological framework, determine how identity is understood. As Côté and Levine (2002) concluded, "The lesson at hand is that we all need to be mindful when telling each other what we think 'identity' is and how it should be understood. We must listen to what the other has to say" (p. 12).

Discussion Questions and Activities

1. Consider the ways in which your identities are socially constructed. Identify two to three specific examples. (For example, think about how others perceive you in relation to how you see yourself.)
2. Thinking about your own identities, identify those identities in which you are part of a dominant or privileged group, and those in which you are part of a subordinate group.
3. Exercise[*] (for a group or class session): Pick an identity in which you have privilege (ability, social class, faith, education—for example, the privilege of sitting in a graduate school class). Each individual in the room should write down, and then state aloud, the identity he or she selected.

    Get into a group with others who wrote down the same privileged identity as you did. In your group, on newsprint or a large sheet of paper, make a list of privileges associated with this identity. Hang this list somewhere in the room.

    Identify volunteers to read aloud the privileges on each page. Then, with all these lists hung around the room, walk around the room and look at the lists—if you get to an identity in which you do not have privilege, you can add additional privileges to the list—you may, from your vantage point as one without privilege

(Continued)

in regard to this identity, see certain privileges that others may not (for example, what a Jewish person might see about Christian privilege; or a person of color might see about White privilege).

Finally, come back as a large group for discussion about observations, addressing the following questions:

- What was it like to see those without privilege add to your list?
- How did it feel if you did not have any privileges to add to the lists?
- How did it feel to add privileges to a list?
- What was it like to do this exercise?
- How does it feel to think about and be aware of privileges?
- What allows us not to be aware of some of our privileges?
- Why are others aware of our privileges and we are not?
- How do privileges influence how we experience our everyday lives? In other words, what do you do that reflects the identity you chose? (For example, "As a White liberal, I listen to NPR, read the *New York Times*, shop at farmers' markets, and eat organic food with my reusable cloth bag; talk about structural inequality; carry a Klean Kanteen . . ."
- Do you have any other observations in relation to social identities?

4. Which of your identities are more salient? How do you understand that? Which are not as salient? Why? How has the salience of your identities changed in recent years or months?

*This exercise was adapted from one used by the Program on Intergroup Relations at the University of Michigan (T. Petryk and R. Fisher, personal communication, November 2009).

TABLE 2.5 EVOLUTION OF IDENTITY THEORIES*

Theoretical Era	Primary Theorists and Scholars
Foundational Theories	Erikson (1959/1994, 1968) Sanford (1962) Marcia (1966) Chickering (1969) Chickering & Reisser (1993)
Socially Constructed Identities	Omi & Winant (1986) Gergen (1991) Frankenberg (1993) Weber (1998) Jones & McEwen (2000) Abes, Jones, & McEwen (2007)
Population-Specific Research	Cross (1971, 1995)—Black racial identity Cass (1979)—homosexual identity formation Josselson (1987)—women's identity development Root (1992)—mixed-race identity Wijeyesinghe (1992, 2012)—multiracial identity Helms (1993)—Black and White racial identity Phinney (1993)—ethnic identity development D'Augelli (1994)—lesbian, gay, and bisexual identity Fassinger (1998)—lesbian, gay, and bisexual identity Renn (2003)—mixed-race identity Liu, Soleck, Hopps, Dunston, & Pickett (2004)—social class
Multiple Identities	Reynolds & Pope (1991) Deaux (1993) Jones (1997)
Intersectionality	Collins (1991) Crenshaw (1991) Weber (2001, 2010) Andersen & Collins (2007b) Dill & Zambrana (2009a) Jones (2009) Abes (2012) Jones, Kim, & Skendall (2012)
Critical Theoretical Frameworks	Fuss (1989)—queer theory (QT) Butler (1990)—QT Lather (1991)—postmodern feminism Tierney & Rhoads (1993)—critical social science Britzman (1997)—QT Ladson-Billings (1998)—critical race theory (CRT) Solórzano, Ceja, & Yosso (2000)—CRT Talburt (2000)—poststructural Delgado & Stefancic (2001)—CRT Delgado Bernal (2002)—CRT, LatCrit Villalpando (2003)—LatCrit Lather (2007)—poststructural feminism Yosso, Smith, Ceja, & Solórzano (2009)—CRT

*We direct readers to a comprehensive chart we developed for the fifth edition of *Student Services: A Handbook for the Profession* titled "Theories About College Students, Environments, and Organizations" (Jones, Abes, & Cilente, 2011, pp. 138–148). That chart is organized by theory family, whereas this one is presented to demonstrate the evolution of theories according to their particular approach and primary focus. This chart is intended to be not exhaustive, but rather illustrative of these different theoretical eras; it provides a few examples of leading scholars contributing to work during these epistemological and theoretical times.

MULTIPLE IDENTITIES AND MODELS

Interludes

Susan

My dissertation focused on "multiple identities" because I was interested in how individuals came to understand their own identities when such dimensions as race, social class, sexual orientation, and culture were considered. I came to this topic entirely through my course work in my doctoral program, beginning with a course titled "Race, Class, and Gender" taught by sociologist Bonnie Thornton Dill. I became fascinated by the ways in which I could bring together the scholarship I was reading from sociology and women's studies with the student development theory and research I was exploring in my classes with Marylu McEwen, my doctoral adviser. However, this was relatively uncharted territory in the college student personnel field, as evidenced by my experience taking my comprehensive exams. Marylu had prepared a question that was to address my cognate area and dissertation focus, coming up with one that asked me to write about "multiple factors" of identity development. Comprehensive exams, by nature, are not conducive to finding easy answers and calmness. I quickly found myself perseverating on the word factors. *What did she mean by multiple factors? Well, I came up with something good enough to enable me to pass my exams, and then, as I wrote the first draft of Chapter One of my dissertation proposal, I transported that language from my exams right into the statement of purpose. "The purpose of this study is to understand multiple factors of identity . . . " And we came full circle when Marylu provided me with the comment that my chapter draft was beautifully written but she wasn't sure what I meant by "multiple factors"! We had a good laugh over this, but it forced me to be much more explicit about what I was after in my dissertation study, and to find what word or phrase best defined my phenomenon of interest. This led me to a focus on multiple dimensions of identity as a way to explore multiple social identities.*

I never dreamed that the Model of Multiple Dimensions of Identity (MMDI) would gain the traction that it has from student development theorists, researchers, and practitioners alike; and I can still remember the day when one of my master's students came to meet with me and proudly showed me how she had "plotted" herself on the model. It never occurred to me that the MMDI would be used in this way. I developed it because I thought it was required in a grounded theory study. And although the MMDI did emerge from the narratives of my participants and provided an "accurate" visual representation of their self-perceived identities, I always worried about including a model because no model could ever convey the richness of their stories or the complexities of identity. In fact, during my dissertation defense, one of my committee members, Dr. Thornton Dill, questioned whether or not the MMDI was actually a "model," presumably because models represent complex phenomena and are developed through rigorous observation and study. I don't think she was questioning the integrity of my study, but more so the wisdom of calling something a model when it is based on interviews with ten college women at one institution. As a result, in my dissertation itself, the presentation of the MMDI was moved out of the results section and into the discussion chapter. It was labeled as an "illustration" of multiple dimensions of identity and discussed as a visual representation of the emerging theory developed from the grounded theory study. It was not until the article published in the Journal of College Student Development *(Jones & McEwen, 2000) that the language of "model" was reattached to the MMDI. A discerning reader will note that the title of this article labels the MMDI as a "conceptual model," this because I continued to hear the caution issued to me by Dr. Thornton Dill and didn't ever want to claim greater impact or contribution than was warranted by my work.*

As I alluded to in the previous paragraph, it caught me by surprise when a number of individuals contacted me for permission to use the MMDI and to apply it to practice contexts. One individual stopped me after a conference presentation to thank me for the model and became visibly emotional and choked up as she explained to me that the model captured her identity struggles as a queer woman from a religious background who was working in an inhospitable environment. I was very humbled and gratified by these reactions, mostly because I saw others taking the work I started and improving on it through application to their own life experiences or research on different populations. One individual who clearly extended the original work on multiple dimensions of identity was Elisa, who came to The Ohio State University to pursue her doctorate in higher education and student affairs after several years as a successfully attorney, and who thought she would explore student leadership for her dissertation research!

Elisa

When I first met with Susan to do an informational interview with Ohio State's Higher Education and Student Affairs doctoral program, dressed in full attorney attire and very naive about what I was getting myself into (wasn't student affairs only about leadership?), Susan told me that she studied "identity." I had little idea what she was talking about, as identity seemed to this corporate litigator to be a self-explanatory topic. My dramatic shift in thinking came about as a result of a service-learning course I took with Susan the following year, in which I examined for the first time at age thirty the meaning of social identities and was introduced to the notions of privilege and oppression, much later in my life than I'm proud to admit. I then learned about the Model of Multiple Dimensions of Identity in Susan's student development theory class, and I was intellectually and personally drawn to this work in ways I had not previously known. Soon afterward, I studied Marcia Baxter Magolda's scholarship on self-authorship. Again, I felt an exciting connection to this material (I am sure in part because it explained so much about my own evolving identity narratives, both social roles—from attorney to graduate student—and social identities—from heterosexual to lesbian) and was intrigued by possible connections among the MMDI, privilege and oppression, and self-authorship. The three seemed to be undeniably connected.

The Reconceptualized Model of Multiple Dimensions of Identity (RMMDI), which brings together these three concepts, naturally flowed from my dissertation research with ten wonderful lesbian college students. I vividly recall Susan's and my intellectual excitement when seeing the connections between my work and hers, and was grateful for the thoughtful time spent with Susan and Marylu constructing the RMMDI together. I did not expect the reconceptualized model to garner the support that it has. Had I, perhaps I would have taken more to heart Kris Renn's candid advice after reviewing it that perhaps we ought to have consulted a graphic designer! Despite its relatively unartful presentation, I am so pleased to know that the model has extended Susan's meaningful work with the MMDI and the ways in which it contributes to students' deepening understanding of themselves. And I now appreciate my own students' insightful analyses of the model, which have continued to push my own thinking about its assumptions about identity in ways I don't believe I could have at the time we constructed it.

◆ ◆ ◆

Chapters Three, Four, and Five all focus on the evolution of the MMDI and the RMMDI. As we both mentioned in our interludes, the attention given to the MMDI and the RMMDI is both humbling and gratifying. In the chapters in this section, we place the MMDI and the RMMDI into the evolution of student development theories, and identity theories in particular, and provide detailed discussions of the development of each model. The MMDI is described by others as the "first student development theory in the literature to offer a conceptual framework for understanding relationships among students' personal and socially constructed identities . . . one of the first holistic models of development" (Evans, Forney, Guido, Patton, & Renn, 2010, p. 247), and as the "standard-bearer in the field" (Renn, 2010b, p. 7) for identity research. In these chapters addressing the two models, we try to provide justification for these laudatory comments.

Chapter Three examines the scholarship and study that led to the creation of the MMDI. In particular, this chapter addresses three strands of scholarship that anchored the study: foundational student development theories, and particularly those with a focus on identity; identity theories concentrating on underrepresented groups in an effort to represent those missing in the foundational theories; and those theories conceptualizing identities as socially constructed, with particular attention to the early work on multiple identities. We also introduce the Multidimensional Identity Model (Reynolds & Pope, 1991) and the work of Deaux (1993), which distinguished between personal and social identities, because these both also influenced the development of the MMDI. It is important for the reader to keep in mind that this section focuses on the literature that was available at the time Susan was conducting her research and constructing the MMDI, so it may appear "old" and outdated. However, this literature is included here to stay true to the evolution of the MMDI and to illustrate how all research is a product of the particular moment in time in which it is designed and conducted. Occasionally we draw on newer research and scholarship to provide a more contemporary framework for this research, and also because several of the scholars whose earlier work was central have continued to publish in these areas. More contemporary research and scholarship will be introduced in subsequent chapters to reflect the work on identity and reconceptualizations of the MMDI that have emerged. Chapter Three also introduces the study on which the MMDI is based. We provide more detail about each participant than journal articles typically permit because we want the reader to learn more about the individuals on whom the model was based. Chapter Three concludes with an overview of the findings from the study, with particular attention to the themes that relate directly to the MMDI, which paves the way for Chapter Four, in which the MMDI is more fully discussed.

Chapter Four delves deeper into the MMDI itself. We provide further detail about the data collection that led to the creation of the MMDI, and then spend the majority of this chapter discussing the model's central elements, with illustrative quotes from participants. These elements include the core, multiple social identities, the relationship of social identities to the core and identity salience, and contextual influences. After the presentation of each element, we provide discussion questions so that readers may reflect on the individual elements and also, using a template of the MMDI, map their own MMDI and develop a visual illustration of multiple and intersecting identities. Engaging readers in this way also paves the way for a discussion of the strengths and limitations of the MMDI, which constitutes the final section of this chapter, as individuals may find elements of the MMDI that resonate with their own lived experiences as well as points of divergence. We also want to point out that in this chapter we stay away from lengthy quotations from the original participants in the study because the data were collected quite some time ago. We want readers to make their own judgments about the current relevance of the elements of the model and the usefulness of the model itself, rather than relying on what had been true.

Chapter Five presents the RMMDI, which was developed based on Elisa's dissertation research on lesbian college students' perceptions of the relationships among their multiple identities. Because the RMMDI incorporates a cognitive dimension into the MMDI through the inclusion of a meaning-making filter, the chapter begins with an overview of meaning making as conceptualized by Robert Kegan and then more fully operationalized by Baxter Magolda. We then go on to introduce Elisa's longitudinal study—and the RMMDI that emerged from the results of this study—using two participants, KT and Carmen, as illustrative of the connections between meaning making and perceived relationships among social identities, as well as how meaning-making capacity evolves given shifting contexts. Carmen's narrative in particular is also offered as an example of the fluidity of the RMMDI—that is, how the power-laden structures of privilege and oppression influence meaning making and in varying ways.

CHAPTER THREE

MULTIPLE SOCIAL IDENTITIES AND INTERSECTING IDENTITIES

Given the background provided in the previous chapter on foundational theories of identity development, this chapter proceeds to address more completely the theories and models that influenced the design of the Model of Multiple Dimensions of Identity (MMDI) and the research that led to its creation. Although some may recognize the model itself and the published article that first introduced it (Jones & McEwen, 2000), our guess is that far fewer are familiar with the original research on which the model is based (Jones, 1997). Reminiscent of the nature of our stories provided in the opening chapter of the book, the title of Susan's dissertation is *Voices of Identity and Difference: A Qualitative Exploration of the Multiple Dimensions of Identity Development in Women College Students* (Jones, 1995). Both prompting and foreshadowing the research to come, the opening paragraph of the dissertation read:

> A growing recognition that some individuals or groups have been left out of the study of human development has resulted in new scholarship which pushes at the veneer of silence and utilizes the metaphor of voice to describe the experiences of those not previously heard in ways consistent with their numbers. (Jones, 1995, p. 1)

In this chapter we present the three strands of scholarship that served as the framework for the study that resulted in the creation of the MMDI. We also introduce the study itself so that readers may learn in more depth

FIGURE 3.1 MODEL OF MULTIPLE DIMENSIONS OF IDENTITY

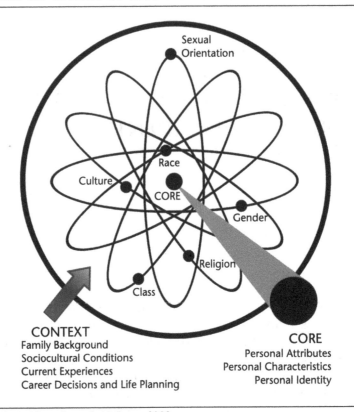

Source: Adapted from Jones & McEwen, 2000.

than typically provided something about the participants themselves and the central findings of the study. Our hope is that providing this level of detail and description will enable readers to see more clearly how the MMDI came to be designed in its original form. Although the MMDI itself is fully presented in Chapter Four, we provide the model (see Figure 3.1) and a brief description of it here so that the reader has some context for the discussion of the scholarship leading to the creation of the MMDI that follows.

The MMDI illustrates identity as consisting of a core or personal identity at the center, made up of personal characteristics and attributes, such as "smart," "responsible," and "caring." The core is surrounded by a number of intersecting rings that represent multiple social identities, such as race, gender, culture, sexual orientation, religion, and social class. The salience of each of these social identities is represented by the dot on each ring and the proximity of that dot to the core. In other words, the closer the dot is to the core, the more salient that particular social identity is to the individual. The core and intersecting social identities are situated within a larger context that includes family background, sociocultural conditions, and current life experiences. The model is drawn to represent a more fluid and dynamic portrayal of identity, and each rendition is a developmental snapshot for a particular individual. That is, among shifting contexts and other circumstances, the elements of the model will also take on new shapes. Having given this brief introduction to the MMDI, we now turn to a discussion of the scholarship from which the study that led to the creation of the model emerged.

Scholarship Leading to the Model of Multiple Dimensions of Identity

The study from which the MMDI emerged was anchored in three strands of scholarship: foundational student development theories, particularly those with a focus on identity; the emerging scholarship at the time that had an explicit emphasis on specific underrepresented social identities (for example, racial identity, gender identity, and sexual identity); and finally conceptual frameworks emphasizing the socially constructed nature of identity, bringing to the foreground the sociocultural contexts in which identities are constructed. The scope of this chapter is not to provide a full discussion of each strand, and some introduction to these theories appeared in Chapter Two. However, each strand will be briefly discussed here, with particular reference to those theorists whose work anchored the study design and provided the framework for the MMDI.

Foundational Student Development Theories

As noted in Chapter Two, nearly all discussions of identity in the student development literature point back to the seminal work of psychologist Erik Erikson, who framed the psychosocial perspective on identity development. Erikson's conception of identity is one that emphasizes "continuity and sameness" (Erikson, 1963, p. 42); considers identity development a largely unconscious process; and holds identity to be influenced by the outside world, such that identity "bridges one's inner life and social roles" (Erikson, 1964, p. 148). Côté and Levine (2002) noted, "By focusing on psychosocial development, Erikson (e.g., 1968) recognized the psychological, as well as the social and personal, dimensions of identity, thereby planting the seeds for a comprehensive, multidimensional theory of identity formation" (p. 14).

Despite the link to the larger social context, Erikson considered the emergence of identity to occur according to the "epigenetic principle," or a "ground plan" (Erikson, 1959/1994, p. 52), which "suggests that the inherent pattern of human growth and its parallel social climate create a universal sequence of psychosocial phases" (Widick, Parker, & Knefelkamp, 1978b, p. 3). In total, Erikson laid out a sequence of developmental tasks to be resolved, yet it is his fifth stage that has been adapted to highlight the importance of identity resolution during what were traditionally the college years for many young adults. Answering the question of "Who am I?" is a central developmental task at this time and is often marked by the experience of "identity crisis" or decision making. It was this question of "Who am I?" that was at the core of Susan's investigation of multiple dimensions of identity.

Because this original investigation focused specifically on college women, Ruthellen Josselson's work was also influential to the study's unfolding. Building directly on the work of Erikson and James Marcia (1966), who was among the first to operationalize Erikson's theory by emphasizing the constructs of crisis and commitment, Josselson (1987) investigated the question of what the identity development process might look like if women were considered. Commenting on the potential differences, she wrote in the introductory chapter to her book *Finding Herself*:

> Although the study of identity formation in men has been a relatively straightforward inquiry, the study of identity formation in women has been fraught with ambiguity and frustration. Men are wont to define themselves by occupation or by their distinctiveness from others, which makes their identity easy to name. Women, by contrast, orient themselves in more complicated ways, balancing many involvements and aspirations, with connections to others paramount; their identities are thus compounded and more difficult to articulate. (p. 8)

Josselson preserved the presentation of identity formation as four statuses or types (foreclosed, diffused, moratorium, and achieved) framed by the axes of crisis and commitment, but added her own descriptions based on her in-depth interview study of sixty women college students. Her objective was not to compare these women to the men in Marcia's study, but instead to provide a thorough profile of women's identity development. Susan's research was not designed to replicate Josselson's work or to locate students within some stage, type, or phase of development. Instead, it was inspired by Josselson's approach to the study of identity in women and the various pathways to identity development. The following statement from Josselson (1987) captures an impetus for Susan's study: "What we need are meaningful ways to compare women with each other. Yet, we are not sure which are the centrally important dimensions, especially in a culture so uncertain about these matters" (p. 5). Thus, the study that resulted in the creation of the MMDI focused precisely on what women college students considered the "centrally important dimensions" of their identity.

Scholarship on Underrepresented Groups

Discontent with these foundational theories of student development, which focused primarily on privileged identities, either through limited samples or claims of generalizability, resulted in scholarly attention to underrepresented populations. A growing move away from an essentialist view of identity (that is, identity can be reduced to core properties and categories) and fixed toward a conception of identity as socially constructed and dynamic resulted in illumination of the identity process for those not typically considered in foundational theories. One of the earlier proponents of identity as socially constructed was social psychologist Kenneth Gergen (1991), who suggested, "What is needed is not another monologue, but a dialogue with those experiencing directly the dilemma of identity" (p. x). As discussed in Chapter Two in regard to the evolution of identity theories, a socially constructed view of identity promotes a move away from seeing identity as essentially an unconscious process leading toward individuation, although one rooted in social context, toward elevating that social context as integral in the construction of identity. That is, one's sense of self and identity is constructed through interactions with others and a larger social context, which includes systems of privilege and oppression, social norms, and societal expectations (Torres, Jones, & Renn, 2009).

What followed from this view of identity as socially constructed were identity theories that focused exclusively on marginalized and oppressed identities, such as racial identity (for example, Cross, 1995; Helms, 1993, 1994); ethnic identity (for example, Phinney, 1993); and sexual identity (for example, Cass, 1979). Although these theories recognized the importance of the social construction of identity and emphasized underrepresented identities and populations, they were still, for the most part, presented discretely and in a stage-like, linear fashion. It was evident in some cases that foundational theories were used as frameworks to extend research to new populations, such as in Jean Phinney's use of Marcia's statuses in her conceptualization of ethnic identity (Marcia, 1966; Phinney, 1993) and Mary Belenky and others' extension of William Perry Jr.'s theory of intellectual development by using a sample of women (Belenky, Clinchy, Goldberger, & Tarule, 1986; Perry, 1968). This approach to the study and understanding of identity resulted in what Weber (1998) characterized as individuals being "typically assigned a single location along a dimension, which is defined by a set of presumably mutually exclusive and exhaustive categories" (p. 18).

As noted in Chapter Two, attention to socially constructed identities, although they were examined discretely, highlighted the importance of also considering structures of privilege and oppression in the construction of identity. Indeed, according to the very definition of social constructions, the examination of the intersections between individual identities and the social context was crucial and brought forward an explicit focus on social identities and how they related to one another. By way of example, Bonnie Thornton Dill (1983) called for more inclusive scholarship about women, recognizing

> the importance of looking at both the structures which shape women's lives and their self-preservations. This would provide us not only with a means of gaining insight into the ways in which race, class, and gender oppression are viewed, but also with a means of generating conceptual categories that will aid us in extending our knowledge of their situation. At the same time, this new knowledge will broaden and even reform our conceptualizations of women's situations. (p. 208)

This body of scholarship, emerging primarily from women's studies scholars, brought into the discourse and study of identity a growing recognition of the importance of examining the intersections of social identities, which had typically been examined discretely, with attention focused only on single identities. A discerning reader, placing this discussion in the context of Chapter Two, will note that the chronology of theoretical understandings of identity is not necessarily sequential. That is, many women's studies scholars, often coming from sociological perspectives, were writing about intersectionality long before those coming from psychological perspectives.

Socially Constructed Identities and Intersections

As discussed in Chapter Two, an explicit focus on socially constructed identities and their intersections is anchored in a sociological perspective that connects individuals with the social structures in which they live. Margaret Andersen and Patricia Hill Collins (2010b) emphasized the importance of this lens, stating, "Race, class, and gender matter because they remain the foundations for systems of power and inequality that, despite our nation's diversity, continue to be among the most significant social facts of people's lives" (p. 1). They went on to suggest that "fundamentally, race, class, and gender are *intersecting* categories of experience that affect all aspects of human life; thus, they *simultaneously* structure the experiences of all people in this society" (pp. 5–6). Although interested in foregrounding the experiences of those previously excluded, Andersen and Collins were also clear that "relying too heavily on the experiences of poor people, women, and people of color can erase our ability to see race, class, and gender as an integral part of everyone's experiences" (p. 4). This last point makes central the study of systems of power that produce privilege for some and oppression for others, and across multiple social identities, such that an individual may possess both privileged and oppressed identities.

In Susan's study an explicit emphasis on privilege and oppression also led to the inclusion of the notion of difference (Jones, 1997), which interrogated more traditional notions of identity as being about sameness and continuity and the idea of salience, or relative salience given context. Thus, Susan's original research built on Eriksonian definitions of identity as sameness, but also added the experience of difference, which introduced the influences of power, privilege, silence, and voice. The metaphor of voice in student development research was a popular one at the time Susan was designing this study; indeed, the title of Belenky, Clinchy, Goldberger, and Tarule's landmark study (1986) is *Women's Ways of Knowing: The Development of Self, Voice, and Mind*, buttressed by a primary finding that "the development of a sense of voice, mind, and self were intricately intertwined" (p. 18). However, little emphasis was placed on the juxtaposition of identity and difference, or on the individual experience of difference in the context of identity development.

Interestingly, the intellectual tradition that did address this relationship came from philosophy and the works of such philosophers as Martin Heidegger and Jacques Derrida. Derrida challenged traditional Western thought by suggesting that *difference* is not easily dismantled into what he called "oppositional predicates"—that one thing is not readily defined by its opposite. Derrida instead advocated for an understanding that emphasizes "this *and* that" (Kearney, 1984, p. 110). The ideas put forward by Derrida and others illuminated the experience of "otherness," or that part of an individual's experience of self that has been concealed from view. As noted in my (Susan's) autobiographical rendering in Chapter One, I was fascinated with the construct and experience of *difference*, most likely because of my own growing up with feelings of difference. In thinking about the design of the study, I began to connect Derrida's construction of difference with Heidegger's call to authenticity. Heidegger's phenomenological conceptualization of authenticity is grounded in one's lived experience and one's ability both to know oneself and to act resolutely and consistently over time (Sherman, 2009). I wondered, what might authenticity look like if one felt different all the time? And how do individuals come to understand those who are different from them? In the context of identity, difference is perceived in relation to that which we are encouraged to become and when we are aware that we do not fit into predetermined categories, including race, social class, gender, sexual orientation, and ability. I wondered whether if we as individuals began to understand the ways in which we are all different, to recognize "otherness" in both ourselves and others, then bridges to understanding would be built. Although this framework of difference and authenticity was not at the fore of the research design, these questions were central in my mind as I embarked on the study.

In addition to the frameworks highlighting the socially constructed nature of identity, two additional theoretical perspectives are important to the research leading to the development of the MMDI: the model developed by Amy Reynolds and Raechele Pope and the distinction between personal identity and social identities advanced by social psychologist Kay Deaux.[1]

---

[1]Deaux's work was used in the manuscript focused on the MMDI (Jones & McEwen, 2000), not in the design of the original study. Nor was the work of Henri Tajfel (1982), discussed in Chapter Two, used in the original study's design. It is interesting to note, in addition to making it clear that these bodies of scholarship were introduced to the work after publication of the original dissertation, that Susan's results affirm many of the concepts discussed by these scholars—that is, the distinction between personal identity and social identities and the importance of both identity salience and context.

FIGURE 3.2 MULTIDIMENSIONAL IDENTITY MODEL

Identify with one aspect of self (society assigned-passive acceptance)	Identify with one aspect of self (conscious identification)
Identify with multiple aspects of self in a segmented fashion	Identify with combined aspects of self (identity intersection)

Source: Reynolds & Pope, 1991, p. 179. Reprinted with permission of John Wiley & Sons, Inc.

Multidimensional Identity Model

At the time when the Multidimensional Identity Model (MIM) was developed, very little research existed that approximated the investigation of multiple identities. The MIM of Reynolds and Pope (1991), however, conceptualized the experience of multiple oppressions and the different strategies an individual may adopt when belonging to more than one oppressed group (see Figure 3.2). Drawing on the work of clinical psychologist Maria Root (1990), who created a model of biracial identity development, Reynolds and Pope proposed four different ways to resolve the realities of membership in more than one oppressed group.

Each option varies on two dimensions or axes of identity development: (1) whether the individual identifies with one or multiple dimensions of self; and (2) whether the individual passively accepts externally defined identities or makes conscious choices about identities. The four options or quadrants of the model are as follows (Jones & McEwen, 2000, p. 406):

1. Identifying with only one aspect of self (e.g., gender or sexual orientation or race) in a passive manner. That is, the aspect of self is assigned by others such as society, college student peers, or family.

2. Identifying with only one aspect of self that is determined by the individual. That is, the individual may identify as lesbian or Asian American/Pacific Islander or a woman without including other identities, particularly those that are oppressions.
3. Identifying with multiple aspects of self, but choosing to do so in a "segmented fashion" (Reynolds & Pope, 1991, p. 179), frequently only one at a time and determined more passively by the context rather than by the individual's own wishes. For example, in one setting the individual identifies as Black, yet in another setting as gay.
4. The individual chooses to identify with the multiple aspects of self, especially multiple oppressions, and has both consciously chosen them and integrated them into one's sense of self.

An important contribution of this model is the acknowledgment that all options or quadrants are possible, acceptable, coexisting, and fluid based on an individual's life situation at a particular time. In addition, the model highlights the important role of context, particularly in negotiating identity resolution. Although oppression and privilege are inextricably connected, this model focuses explicitly on those individuals with multiple oppressed identities rather than simply multiple identities that may be either privileged or oppressed.

Personal and Social Identities

Deaux (1993), a social psychologist, was among the first, particularly in the discipline of psychology, to advance an understanding of identity as multidimensional. As Lisa Bowleg (2008) summarized, "Despite an abundance of theories on social identity within psychology, the prevailing view of social identities is one of unidimensionality and independence, rather than intersection" (p. 313), pointing to Deaux's work as a notable exception. Deaux acknowledged "the parentage" of both Eriksonian and sociological conceptions of identity "by assuming that both categorical membership and personal meaning must be considered in the analysis of identity" (Deaux, p. 5). In particular, Deaux paved the way for inclusion of multiple identities because she recognized the importance of both *personal identity* and *social identities* and their "fundamentally interrelated" (p. 5) nature. According to Deaux:

> *Social identities* are those roles *or* membership categories that a person claims as representative. Here I make no distinction between a group

such as Asian-American and a role such as mother. *Personal identity* refers to those traits and behaviors that the person finds self-descriptive, characteristics that are typically linked to one or more of the identity categories. (p. 6)

Deaux's view of social identity as including social roles is somewhat at odds with the views of scholars who emphasize identity as socially constructed because it enables individuals to avoid scrutiny of such social identities as race, social class, and gender, each of which is shaped by privilege and oppression. Drawing on sociological constructs, such as role theory, Deaux also pointed to the importance of considering the role of context to an understanding of identity. Using results from a study of Hispanic students attending Ivy League universities, Ethier and Deaux (1990) suggested that these students were engaged in an active process of identity work given shifting contexts.

Building on the earlier conceptualizations offered by Deaux, scholars in psychology are now addressing identity in relation to personal identity and social identities (for example, Brewer, 2001; Chen, 2009; Greene, 2000). Chen (2009) suggested that "the aim of social identity models is to theorize individuals' psychological processes related to social group memberships. This includes the individuals' internal understanding of how various demographic variables are integrated into their self-concept" (p. 174). Although the study from which the MMDI emerged was conducted in the mid-1990s, this focus was precisely its purpose.

The theories and frameworks just discussed served as the anchor to the study of multiple dimensions of identity. These frameworks and strands from the literature were integrated in an effort to approach a more holistic view of identity—one that built on pioneering theories of psychosocial development, added specific social identities and considered a perspective on identity as socially constructed, and attended more explicitly to the structures of power and privilege that pattern identity development in both particular and contextual ways. We now turn to the details of the study from which the MMDI was created.

The Original Study: *Voices of Identity and Difference* (Jones, 1995)

I (Susan) set out to investigate self-perceived identities among a diverse group of women college students when such social identities as gender, race, and sexual orientation were considered. I was also interested in the notion of *difference* in the study because this captured the idea that identity construction was tied to structures of power and privilege. Although I was cautious about "difference" as a "seductive oversimplification" (Shields, 2008, p. 303), the juxtaposition of difference as distinct or other (not deficit, as it was often treated in the literature) with identity as sameness and continuity was one that warranted investigation. The stated purpose of the study was therefore "to understand the multiple dimensions of identity development among women college students" (Jones, 1997, p. 377). The guiding research questions were stated as follows (Jones, 1995, pp. 65–66):

1. In what ways do women college students define themselves?
2. How do the dimensions of race, ethnicity, gender, sexual orientation, or other dimensions of difference, inform their understandings of their own identity?
3. Are there particular dimensions of identity that they experience as more salient than others?
4. What meaning does difference have for these women? How do they experience difference?

I investigated these questions using a grounded theory methodology (Glaser & Strauss, 1967; Strauss & Corbin, 1990) because of the study's emphasis on identity development processes and my interest in generating theory to describe these processes. Very few grounded theory studies were present in the higher education and student development literature at the time, but the fit between the phenomenon under investigation and this methodological approach seemed good. In particular, grounded theory ensured a close proximity between theory and the experiences of those being studied; appreciation of context; and reliance on inductive analysis, with the end goal being the generation of theory grounded in participants' lived experience.

Data were collected in this study through in-depth interviews on three occasions with each participant. The purpose of these interviews was to engage participants in conversation about their understandings about their own identity development. The interviews were sufficiently open ended to permit participants to describe in their own words the internal and interpersonal processes by which they defined their identities. Initial questions to participants were broad enough to create room for individual responses and freedom; direct enough to suggest areas of interest;

and personally absorbing enough to engage participants in comfortable dialogue and disclosure (see Chapter Four for a discussion of an activity in which participants engaged to accomplish dialogue and disclosure). I attempted to convey to participants that this was their opportunity to tell their story in their own way (see Jones, 1997, and Abes & Jones, 2004, for more details on methodology and methods).

Sampling Considerations

The participants in this study were purposefully sampled for maximum variation and the potential for "information rich cases" (M. Patton, 2002, p. 46). In grounded theory research, an "excellent participant . . . is one who has been through, or observed, the experience under investigation," and who is considered an "expert in the experience or the phenomena under investigation; they must be willing to participate . . . and they must be reflective, willing, and able to speak articulately about the experience" (Morse, 2007, p. 231).

Guided by these principles and characteristics of grounded theory research, I was interested in a sample of college women who represented multiple social identities, and who had presumably given some thought to these identities. I was quick to identify my sample as a "diverse" one, therefore not replicating the earlier research on college student identity based primarily on singular identity categories. However, Bonnie Thornton Dill, one of my dissertation committee members, cautioned me about this "diverse sample" and what I would be able to say about my phenomenon of interest as a result (Jones, 2002). Her wise counsel was both a comment on sampling procedures and what variation will actually yield in an analysis as well as an important reminder of my role as a White researcher wanting to say something about how women of color construct their identities without essentializing those identities and experiences. Her cautionary advice resulted in my constantly monitoring my own assumptions and interpretations, which I accomplished primarily through the use of a reflexive researcher journal and consistent conversations with peers representing perspectives and social identities different from my own.

Participants in the Study

The limitations in length of journal articles often mean that participants in qualitative studies are never fully introduced beyond their demographic characteristics. This is understandable given the constraints of page limits, but also ironic because one of the reasons for engaging in qualitative inquiry is to provide an in-depth exploration of a particular phenomenon using the voices and experiences of participants. This would suggest that the particularities of participants cannot be disentangled from the words that end up being used to warrant certain claims. The more each participant is introduced and understood by the researcher and readers, the richer the description and deeper the analysis. Rich data, according to Charmaz (2006), "reveal participants' views, feelings, intentions, and actions as well as the contexts and structures of their lives" (p. 14). Here, then, we provide detail about each of the ten participants beyond the demographic descriptors that have appeared elsewhere (Jones, 1997; Jones & McEwen, 2000) in an effort to provide the reader with greater knowledge about not only who these young women were but also what they brought to the study and, hence, our understanding of multiple dimensions of identity. Further, as a researcher, I developed a deep sense of obligation and responsibility to the participants to recount their respective stories in a way that made sense to them. What follows is a profile of each participant, so that their individual life stories remain intact—a mosaic of what is distinct about each of them—and so that what they share in common is illuminated.[2]

JJ JJ was a chemical engineering student who came to the United States from Uganda, where she was born and raised. She married an African American man in the year prior to the study, and had recently purchased a home in a suburban Maryland community. She described herself as a very strong student, bright, and assertive. She missed her homeland of Uganda and made frequent references to "back home." She had a very close relationship with her mother, who taught her many valuable lessons, including the importance of developing a strong internal sense of self. As a bright and talented woman, she was well acquainted with traditional African cultural expectations for women. Moving to the United States introduced her to what she referred to as the "color thing" such that she felt she was "a minority everywhere."

[2]Names are pseudonyms that participants selected at the time of the study, and profiles come from Jones (1995, pp. 69–75), although the tense is shifted here to reflect that data were collected in the past (in other words, so as not to suggest that how participants described themselves then is still current and accurate).

Kumari Kumari was born in Sri Lanka and moved to the United States at a young age so her father could pursue his PhD at a large, prestigious eastern university. Most of her growing up occurred in suburban Maryland. Although she identified strongly with her Sri Lankan cultural background, she described herself as bicultural, as she was most familiar with "American culture." She was aware that she did not fit the mold for Sri Lankan women, but she found strength in being different and unique. She actively sought out friendships with those different from her, and she saw herself as an independent, assertive woman with a strong sense of herself. At the time of the study she was engaged to an African American man, but had not yet told her parents about her plans, knowing that they would be deeply disappointed in her marrying outside of her culture.

Erica Erica described herself as a Black woman and was wrestling with the double burdens of being a member of two marginalized groups. Most of her closest friends were White males, primarily because she identified with the pressures to be strong, which they experienced, and with the privileges they had that she would have liked to have. Erica had had a significant weight problem for most of her life. She described herself as very sensitive and a good friend who occasionally put on masks to hide her pain or to protect herself from the outside world that wanted to see her in a particular way. She was very involved in campus activities and saw herself as a leader.

Jessica Jessica was a graduating senior who was both excited and nervous about her future. She described herself as White and identified strongly with her religious heritage, which was Judaism. She had recently ended a long-term relationship with an African American man. She grew up in suburban Maryland in a very diverse neighborhood and high school. Because of the diversity of her friends, she felt that race was not an issue for her. Jessica articulated an active search for self while trying to move away from some dependent relationships, like those with her parents and old boyfriend. Jessica was raped while in college and believed that this became her impetus for developing a stronger sense of herself, particularly as a woman.

Jenni Jenni was a graduating senior and planned to go on to graduate school to become a teacher. Although well aware of her talents and the career possibilities in the business world, Jenni wrestled with how to combine career success with her plans for a family. She was in a committed relationship with a man from Colombia. She loved what she referred to as the "Hispanic/Latino culture" and had taken the initiative to learn the language and customs of her boyfriend's culture. Feeling no distinct cultural identification for herself, and that being White was "not something I face daily," she enjoyed her "vicarious" connection with the Latin culture. Jenni had struggled with an eating disorder that she said caused her to be more reflective of who she was.

Stephanie Stephanie grew up in affluent and homogeneous neighborhoods outside of Philadelphia and Boston. She was very conscious of the privileges afforded her as a result of her class background. She identified strongly with being Jewish and also called herself a "dyke." She did not like to identify herself as White because she associated White with supremacy groups, and because she was aware that in some countries Jews are not considered White. She identified strongly as an activist and as a feminist. Her course work in women's studies had done a lot to develop what she referred to as her "feminist consciousness." She described her own identity development as occurring by a series of "intellectual epiphanies," yet recognized that she didn't "personally connect" with many dimensions of who she was.

Amy Amy was a graduating senior with a major in government and politics. A summer volunteering in Mexico cemented her commitment to working with underprivileged populations. She had been instrumental in implementing a community service project on campus for Hispanic children in a surrounding community. She didn't "internally connect" with identity terms describing race, gender, or culture because she saw those as "outside identities" that are less complex than individuals really are. She came from a strong, supportive Irish Catholic family outside Boston. Her Irish uncles told the stories of her heritage in Ireland with a colorfulness, zaniness, and vitality that she admired. Amy's sense of herself as a woman had recently evolved and taken on new importance to her. Her father had recently been diagnosed with and treated for cancer, causing her to reflect more on the significance of family in her life.

Ann Ann was actively engaged in a search for her identities as a woman, a Jew, and a daughter. She grew up in an affluent suburban neighborhood outside New York City in a family in which little discussion took place about her background and heritage. She vividly remembered a grade school assignment to draw her family tree and how difficult it was to complete. The tree was seemingly rootless, with few branches and names she could not pronounce. In addition, the assignment seemed to evoke sadness in her mother. The absence of what she perceived to be a distinct cultural heritage made it more difficult for her to define herself. However, this absence had become the motivation for her search for information about which her parents had remained silent.

Nandita Nandita described herself as an intelligent, compassionate, and highly motivated young woman with a clear career goal of practicing medicine. She was born in India and moved to the United States as a very young child. She described herself as "living in two worlds." Most of the time she was able to move comfortably back and forth between these two worlds. Conflicts emerged when she rubbed up against cultural norms for her as an Indian woman. She was developing a serious relationship with a man outside her culture that had evoked dissatisfaction and disappointment from her mother. Her family and her culture were central to her, and she described them as one and the same.

Kenna Kenna was an African American woman from the South, and proud of it! She was raised primarily by her grandparents in a deeply religious household in which church and Jesus explained all there was to consider in the world. Moving to Maryland and beginning college opened Kenna's eyes and prompted a process of self-discovery that included exploration into all the dimensions of who she was. When asked how she defined her identity, Kenna melodically rattled off, "I am a strong, independent, self-reliant, emotionally healthy, religious, African American, Native American, silly, evil, girl woman child," giving rise to the picture of an identity in motion!

These are the individuals and a glimpse into their life stories and self-perceived identities from which the MMDI emerged. In the next subsection we present the central findings from the study.

Findings: Contextual Influences on the Construction of Identity

The focus on multiple dimensions of identity and the juxtaposition of identity and difference brought the role of contextual influences into the foreground. As noted earlier, context was considered important as far back as Erikson's pioneering work (1959/1994), hence the term *psychosocial*. However, the explicit focus on social identities (for example, gender, race, social class, and sexual orientation) rooted in structures of inequality shifted the nature of context from one more general (for example, social climate or socializing contexts and social roles) to one more particular to those individuals from marginalized groups (for example, racism, sexism, or homophobia). This shift in focus resulted in an emphasis on identity salience in the construction and presentation of identity (Rotheram & Phinney, 1987) and signified the recognition of multiple identities (Jones, 1997).

The ten key categories or central themes that emerged from this grounded theory study represent a dynamic interplay of personal identity or core identity, social identities, identity salience, and contextual influences (a list of the ten key categories is provided in Chapter Four). What follows is a description of several of the key categories, as well as the core category, that best illustrate the complexity of the identity construction process. Although all of the key categories were critical to the construction of the emerging theory that resulted from data analysis, the key categories that we are pulling out here for discussion are those that emerged as most central to the continued work on the MMDI. These are the key categories that map directly onto the MMDI and represent issues of multiple identities, identity salience, the core, and contextual influences. These relevant key categories and the core category will be discussed in the remainder of this chapter, and then in Chapter Four we will introduce the MMDI with further elaboration on the relationships among these key categories and the MMDI.

Relative Salience of Identity Dimensions

This key category maps onto the issue of identity salience represented in the MMDI and what creates conditions of salience. The experience of difference influenced each participant's sense of self and prompted identity salience. That is, when difference was keenly felt, identity was shaped. The precise experience of difference varied across such dimensions as race, religion, sexual orientation, and culture, and across certain defining experiences, and included both visible (for example, race) and invisible (for example, eating disorder) differences. For each participant, however, the experience of difference provoked discernment about a dimension of her identity that she might otherwise have taken for granted. For these participants, the feelings of difference emerged from social identities, such as race, gender, sexual orientation, and religion. It also emerged from critical experiences, such as being raped, being overweight, or spending time in a culture outside their own and with individuals very different from them.

These women were aware of the relationships between their experiences with feeling different and prevailing norms and stereotypes. Yet many of them were able to convert these experiences into a source of strength and resilience, bringing their sense of self into sharper focus. For example, Kumari articulated:

> I think I like feeling different. I think I am a unique person and I don't conform to a lot of things, a lot of stereotypes . . . I think of it [difference] more as an asset and I think I can learn from my being different. (Jones, 1995, p. 111)

These women had no interest in conforming to the stereotypes influencing their lives, instead thinking that they were creating their own unique sense of self without giving in to the pressures of externally defined expectations. However, they remained keenly aware of the existence of these expectations. For example, JJ expressed that as a Black woman from an African country, she felt like she was "in the minority everywhere." And although race was not salient to her in her homeland of Uganda, in coming to the United States to pursue her education she encountered for the first time the "color thing" and was perceived by others as only a "Black female with an accent" (Jones, 1995, pp. 111–112).

A number of participants referred to their appearance in relation to their self-perceived identities and how others experienced them. For example, Ann noted, "I don't look Jewish," (Jones, 1995, p. 112) and Nandita related, "I am very fair [skinned] compared to most Indian people, so a lot of Indian people don't even think I am Indian if they don't know me" (Jones, 1995, p. 112). In another example of the influence of appearance on the construction of identity, Erica conveyed her feelings of difference when weight and race intersected:

> The weight thing does definitely add to that whole feeling different, just in terms of I am not even what is considered to be a normal overweight size. And again, all the stereotypes that are associated with large Black women like I am also a nurturer and that whole mammie kind of thing. (Jones, 1995, p. 112)

As these illustrative quotations suggest, salience of a particular dimension of an individual's identity suggests an awareness of that dimension or social identity. Salience emerges out of the interaction between the individual's sense of self and the larger sociocultural contexts external to the individual. However, this interaction is dynamic and influenced by structures of privilege and oppression that produce both taken-for-granted dimensions of identity and identity salience.

Multiple Layers of Identity

This key category relates to the issue of the core in the model and the relationship between the core and multiple social identities. As apparent from the preceding discussion of identity salience, the process of negotiating external influences on identity construction was persistent, and as a result these women distinguished between what they referred to as their inside and outside worlds. For them, a clear difference existed between what they considered to be the "facts" of their "outside identity" and the facts of their "inside identity," the latter representing aspects of their identity that were more personal, complex, and core to who they were. Many of them were quick to point out that their outside identities were easily defined by others (for example, race, gender) and included labels and prevailing stereotypes, whereas their inside identities were more complex and hidden from view, and represented qualities of character and personality (for example, "smart," "responsible," "happy," "caring"). For instance, Amy noted that her "outside identity is much more superficial or less complex," (Jones, 1995, p. 128) and thus, as was the case with other participants, these outside identities carried less meaning, unless the salience of a particular identity came closer to the core. When this occurred, participants were integrating this dimension as part of their inside identity. Kenna spoke eloquently about the importance of self-definition:

> I think people of color and women have historically, their voices have been suppressed. And I think that until you find a language, you can't define your problem. And it is inherently personal and intimate when you create that language for yourself to define your own problem. You can't take someone else's word and then define what's yours. I think we have a problem with defining the problem until we get a language and that language has to be yours, you have to own it in order to begin to deal with it. So I have a problem with people defining other people. (Jones, 1995, p. 131)

The "problem" with which Kenna is wrestling is that of naming herself and coming to terms with who she is, on her own terms. The idea of inside (core) and outside (social) identities represented for these women their chosen language to define themselves, and the distinction helped them preserve those dimensions of their identity that only they would name and that they considered core to who they were at the time.

Braiding of Gender

This key category, although focused on the salience of gender for all the participants in the study, also illuminates the emphasis on multiple identities conveyed by the participants. That is, each participant understood gender as an important identity dimension, but quickly connected gender to other social identities (for example, Indian woman, Black woman, Jewish woman, lesbian woman); to personal or core characteristics (for example, "ambitious," "intelligent," "motivated," "responsible"); and to contextual influences on their identities (for example, sexism, racism, double standards, marginalization, cultural norms and values). This category, in relation to the MMDI, illustrates the dynamic nature of multiple and intersecting identities. It also demonstrates the complexities in identity construction. For example, among these participants, gender was an important identity dimension but not central in and of itself. Gender became more central because of its relationship to other salient identity dimensions.

For example, Kumari, Nandita, and JJ immediately linked gender to their cultural heritage—Sri Lankan, Indian, and Ugandan, respectively. They were keenly aware of cultural expectations and norms for women from each of their cultures and the resulting negotiations. As Nandita explained:

> I keep going back to my family and culture, you know the way I was raised. But I know how Indian women are looked upon and what their roles are and I look at myself and I don't see that. I see two different things because you know I am not quiet and passive . . . why should I change who I am because it has been working for me. (Jones, 1995, pp. 137–138)

Similarly, JJ noted when pointing out the conflict between gender and culture:

> I think they have been in conflict a lot. My being female and being African, because I am not the traditionally African female . . . In the U.S. I probably would be called assertive, but kind of polite. But back home I think they would just call me down right aggressive! (Jones, 1995, p. 138)

Other social identities, such as race and religion, also intersected for participants in ways that were meaningful for them. Even though Erica felt outside pressure to either be Black or be a woman, she resisted this, stating, "I am going to be both at the same time and I cannot separate one from the other. They are a very integral part of me." For Ann, Jessica, and Stephanie, being a woman was linked with being a Jewish woman, although all three were quick to point out that they were still actively defining what that meant to them. What they were confident about was the enduring nature of these identities. Jessica articulated that being a Jewish woman was one of the "least likely things to change about me" (Jones, 1995, p. 135). Stephanie complicated these intersections by describing feminism as the "organizing principle" (Jones, 1995, p. 135) for her identities as a woman, as a Jew, as White, and as a lesbian. She explained that her racial consciousness came in part from recognizing that "not all countries see Jewish people as White people" (Jones, 1995, p. 119), and her identity as a lesbian was shaped in her struggle to come out to her Jewish parents.

Cultural, racial, and religious constructions of gender created experiences for some of the participants in which they encountered sexist attitudes or gender discrimination. The pressure to prove themselves as women was experienced by most of the participants and was amplified when gender was connected to race, religion, and culture, for example. These dynamics involving personal identities, social identities, and contexts combine to illuminate the complexity of identity construction and highlight the importance of contextual influences.

Contextual Influences on the Construction of Identities

The contextual influences on the construction of identities emerged as the *core category*, which in grounded theory research refers to an integrative category and theme. That is, whereas the themes just described highlight individual participants' voices and points of view, the core category is intended to pull these individual voices and viewpoints together into a core story that reflects the experiences and perspectives of each participant. In this study, that core story has to do with the importance of context to the construction of identity because of its influence on all dynamics of identity construction. More specifically, the core category of contextual influences included the social identities of race, culture, gender, and religion, which fused with other contexts, such as family background, current experiences, inclusive beliefs, and career plans and future goals. The core category was shaped by participants' experience of identity as layered and by the relative salience of identity dimensions. Certain dimensions became more salient in particular contexts that prompted an awareness and scrutiny participants had not otherwise experienced. Larger contexts, such as the sociocultural conditions of racism and sexism, reflected structures of power and privilege. Participants' experiences of both privilege and difference mediated their connection with and perceived relative salience of various dimensions of identity. In the original study, the dimensions of identity that were least salient to the individual were those to which the participant was least connected, were taken for granted, and represented unreflected aspects of privilege. Difference was experienced as those dimensions of identity not privileged became more salient.

The particulars of these experiences with difference varied by individual in this study, and included sexual assault, obesity, having an eating disorder, coming out, and holding conflicting values based on culture and religion. All the participants engaged in complex identity negotiations as they managed certain situations and challenges to their identities. They developed strategies to navigate these tensions, such as living a bicultural life, masking difference, keeping secrets, and turning inward. They also talked persuasively about their ability to transform difference into strength and an asset. Each participant expressed an ongoing awareness of her identity and the process of self-discovery in which she was engaged, which involved internal processes as well as external constraints and opportunities.

Summary

In this chapter we discussed the literature that informed the framework for Susan's study leading to the creation of the MMDI. This framework incorporated concepts from foundational student development theories, scholarship on the identity development process

(Continued)

among underrepresented groups, and an explicit focus on socially constructed identities that draws attention to both privileged and oppressed identities as multiple and intersecting. We highlighted two additional works, the Multidimensional Identity Model and Deaux's conceptualization of personal and social identities. We then provided an overview of the study and an in-depth introduction to the study's participants in an effort to present them as more than demographic profiles and to provide the reader with some of the richness of their individual stories. Finally, we highlighted the central themes from the results of the study: relative salience of identity dimensions, multiple layers of identity, braiding of gender, and contextual influences on the construction of identities. In Chapter Four we focus on the MMDI itself, bringing the themes introduced in this chapter into full view.

Discussion Questions and Activities

1. Identify the contributions to an understanding of identity you see in each strand of the literature reviewed. Which strand is most applicable to your own identity development process? What is missing from each?
2. If you were to develop your own iteration of a framework for understanding identity, from which literature strand or strands would you draw?
3. Which findings from Susan's study resonate for you? How do your own experiences depart from these findings?
4. What experiences with difference or otherness have you had? What did you learn from these experiences?
5. How might the results of the study have been different if it had been conducted with all men rather than all women?
6. How would you design a study that investigates multiple dimensions of identity?
7. If Susan's study were replicated today, with access to newer scholarship and research on identity, how would the design look different? Identify three to four research questions that are relevant and important to you.

CHAPTER FOUR

MODEL OF MULTIPLE DIMENSIONS OF IDENTITY

As discussed in Chapter Three, the Model of Multiple Dimensions of Identity (MMDI) is anchored in several areas of scholarship, including foundational theories of student development; research on identity development among underrepresented groups; and sociological and social psychological perspectives that distinguish between personal and social identities, foregrounding the socially constructed nature of identity and the importance of social context. The MMDI grew out of a grounded theory study (Jones, 1995, 1997) exploring perceptions of identity when social identities, such as race, gender, sexuality, and culture, are considered. In particular, as discussed in Chapter Three, the central findings of the study highlighted the relative salience of identity dimensions in relation to difference, multiple layers of identity, braiding of gender, and contextual influences on the construction of identities. The purpose of this chapter is to extend the background information on the MMDI presented in Chapter Three, and to more fully present and discuss the MMDI, including a version of the model that specifically addresses the experience of difference, an element of the original research that often goes unaddressed. In the model's development, the study's central findings were translated into key elements of the model, which are discussed in this chapter. These include the core, multiple social identities, relationship of social identities to the core and identity salience, and contextual influences. We provide details about the study itself and describe the central elements of the model. In discussing the model, we will make more explicit the themes from the findings as well as the model's strengths and

TABLE 4.1 KEY CATEGORIES AND ELEMENTS OF THE MMDI

Key Categories	Element in the MMDI
• Multiple layers of identity • Importance of cultural identification and cultural values • Relational, inclusive values and guiding personal beliefs	The core

• Braiding of gender
• Multiple ways race matters
• Relative salience of identity dimensions
• Searching for identity
	Multiple social identities
	Relationship of social
	   identities to the core
	   and identity salience

• Current experiences and situational factors • Influence of family • Career decisions and future planning	Contextual influences

**Core Category: Contextual Influences on the
Construction of Identity**

limitations, which will pave the way for the reconceptualized model presented in Chapter Five.

In considering the MMDI, it is important to keep in mind that models are by nature representations of complex phenomena and therefore cannot fully capture all of the themes they are intended to portray. As images, models are designed to carefully represent complicated ideas, theories, or elements in a way that is recognizable to the viewer. The MMDI includes several clearly identifiable elements while also integrating the content of the key categories and themes that emerged from the original study. The relationships between the key categories and specific elements of the MMDI are found in Table 4.1. We emphasize this point because it is easy to focus only on the model as a visual illustration of multiple identities and to forget the key categories from the findings of the study that provide the foundation for the MMDI. In recognizing these key categories and themes, an understanding of the construction of identity and a sense of self becomes more complex, contextualized, and nuanced than any illustration may fully present.

Overview of the Model of Multiple Dimensions of Identity

The MMDI provides a conceptual illustration of major themes that emerged from the grounded theory study (Jones, 1995, 1997) of multiple dimensions of identity among a diverse group of women college students (see Figure 4.1). The MMDI contains several central components that

FIGURE 4.1 MODEL OF MULTIPLE DIMENSIONS OF IDENTITY

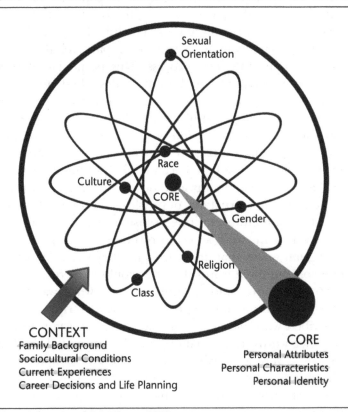

Source: Adapted from Jones & McEwen, 2000.

combine to create a fluid and dynamic image of identity when multiple identities are considered, taking into account the core, multiple social identities, the relationship of social identities to the core and identity salience, and contextual influences. The dynamic nature of the MMDI captures the fluidity of identity. That is, the model represents a snapshot in time and can be continuously redrawn to reflect shifting contexts, the relative salience of particular social identities, and the proximity of social identities to the core.

As discussed in Chapter Three and expanded on in this chapter, the MMDI presumes a distinction between personal identity and social identities. Although social identities may vary in their connection to the core or personal identity and in their relationship to one another, personal identity and social identities were originally conceived as distinct from one another in terms of their content. This conceptualization emerged from the participants in the original study and mirrored what was in the literature at the time. The initial impetus for this distinction in the study came from an exercise each participant was asked to complete as part of the interview process. This particular exercise was designed to focus participants on how they described and defined themselves and on what dimensions of identity were most important to them. The exercise was more fruitful than typical interview questions, as engaging participants in conversation about themselves and their self-perceived identities through interview questions proved challenging for them. We include the exercise here because it helps illuminate where the boundary between personal identity and social identities, as portrayed in the MMDI, came from; how structures of privilege and oppression influence the construction of identity and one's sense of self; and how the MMDI evolved.

Participants were asked to respond to the question "Who am I?" by listing ten words that described who they were. They were then asked to cross off the three words that they could most readily discard, then three more, then three more, until only one word was left on the list. The one word presumably represented the descriptor that most accurately described who they were and was most important to their sense of self. In other words, the remaining word represented the identity descriptor that they were least willing to give up. Two sample lists are provided to illustrate this process and the results of the activity. (We are not using the exact lists provided by participants so as to preserve their anonymity, but these approximate lists that were created by participants.)

Who Am I?

1. ~~Responsible~~
2. ~~Student~~
3. ~~Smart~~
4. Woman
5. ~~Daughter~~
6. ~~Jewish~~
7. ~~Young~~
8. ~~Athlete~~
9. ~~Sister~~
10. ~~Poor~~

Who Am I?

1. Black
2. ~~Woman~~
3. ~~Overweight~~
4. ~~Sister~~
5. ~~Catholic~~
6. ~~Caring~~
7. ~~Funny~~
8. ~~Hardworking~~
9. ~~African Cherokee~~
10. ~~Activist~~

In each of the lists you can identify those dimensions of identity that the individual deemed important, and you can see that each list contains both personal and social identities. The remaining response on each list, "woman" and "Black," respectively, also provides a signal as to the most salient identity to the participant at the time she was asked to complete this exercise. Yet nearly every participant commented that she was uncomfortable leaving only one word to describe all of who she was, preferring instead to think of herself as comprising multiple identities that varied in importance to her at different times or in different circumstances. In addition, the one word remaining on each individual's list was not always the characteristic she perceived as part of the core. This was because, for these women, the core represented those characteristics least likely to be defined by others for them (the core is discussed in greater detail in the next subsection of this chapter). Although this exercise may appear reductionist in that no one person understood herself in a singular way, it did enable participants to respond to the difficult question of "Who am I?" with multiple answers and begin to tease out what was most important to their sense of self.

As the MMDI is introduced and explained in this chapter, use the questions about the model at the end of each of the following sections to reflect on your own perceptions of identity when multiple identities and contextual influences are considered. The discussion of the MMDI is organized by each of the central components of the model as it was initially created based on the results of the grounded theory study of college women. As already stated, these components are the core, multiple social identities, the relationship of social identities to the core and identity salience, and contextual influences. A template for the MMDI is provided at the end of this chapter so you may plot yourself on the MMDI and create a visual illustration that represents your own configuration of multiple identities (see Figure 4.3). Keep in mind that the MMDI is not meant to remain static. The illustration you plot now will undoubtedly shift given changing contexts, new experiences, and growing awareness of self and others. As Erica, one of the study participants, commented, "I guess the one thing that I have really noticed is that identity changes. Identity is far from being constant" (Jones, 1995, p. 160).

The Core

The MMDI depicts multiple layers of identity through the presence of the core, multiple social identities, and larger contextual influences. The key category of multiple layers of identity captures the sense among the participants that identity is complicated and constantly shifting, resulting in their need to negotiate between their internal sense of self (core) and external influences (context). The core in the MMDI appears at the center of the model, reflecting what participants considered their core sense of self. As noted in the previous chapter, the core constitutes an individual's personal, "inner," and "inside" identity or "inner self," and as a result was perceived by the participants as less susceptible to outside influences. The core characterizes personal attributes and qualities, such as "intelligent," "compassionate," "independent," and "good friend" (Jones & McEwen, 2000), and was less visible to an outsider's eye. This quality of the core as impenetrable and protected from outside influence elevated the core in importance to these participants. Although social identities sometimes made participants vulnerable, the core could not be labeled by others or taken away from them. It represented the location in their constructions of self where they had the most agency and experienced the most stability. The key category of *relational, inclusive values and guiding personal beliefs* is represented in the core. Several of the participants articulated core tenets they carried with them as maxims for their personal identity that served as an identity hook. For Kenna, the tenet "If you don't stand for something then you'll fall for anything" (Jones, 1995, p. 155) served as a beacon for how she treated others and decisions she made, and generally nourished her sense of self in the world. Many of the participants were guided by beliefs in justice, fairness, and "activist work."

The core in the MMDI was originally drawn to represent a "core sense of self" situated at the center of one's identity, and therefore participants perceived it as relatively stable. Participants interpreted the core as made up of internally generated characteristics that were important to them and less susceptible to external influence. However, the MMDI also suggests that the more salient social identities are to an individual, the closer to the core they become, which implies motion and change. That is, the core represents an individual's personal identity, and surrounding the core are multiple social identities. Despite a particular social identity's moving closer to the core through the influence of context or self-reflection and awareness, it does not become part of the core. Discussion about the core continues to evolve, exploring further what constitutes the core and the relationship of the core to social identities. The Reconceptualized Model of Multiple Dimensions of Identity (RMMDI) (introduced in detail in Chapter Five) and newer research (discussed in Chapters Six, Seven, and Eight) examine this relationship between the core and social identities in terms of the interactions and overlaps (for example, when a social identity, such as religion, is at the core) and the tensions between privileged and oppressed identities that influence this connection between the core and social identities (for example, the cultural and gender identity negotiations for an Asian American woman) (Chen, 2009; Jones, Kim, & Skendall, 2012; Patton & Simmons, 2008).

Questions

- What is at your core? Using the MMDI template at the end of this chapter, write down a few words that describe your core.
- Does the way in which the core is described here fit with how you see your identity? If not, what is different?
- Is the core a meaningful construct for you? Explain how it is or is not relevant to how you understand yourself.
- How would you characterize and describe what is at your core (personal characteristics, values, personality, social identities)?
- How is it that those characteristics and identities at your core became central to you?

Multiple Social Identities

Multiple social identities are represented in the MMDI as intersecting circles around the core. The critical element is the emphasis on social identities as distinguished from personal identity contained in the core. Further, although foundational research on social identities, as discussed in Chapters Two and Three, highlights the socially constructed nature of identity, Deaux's conception (1993) of social identities emphasizes both social roles and membership in social groups and the interrelationships between personal and social identities. However, Deaux and other social psychologists did not consider the differences among categories of social group membership, instead treating them as "theoretically equivalent" (p. 8). An explicit focus on social identities as socially constructed requires attending to social systems and structures of inequality and privilege (for example, race, gender, culture, sexual orientation, religion, and social class). This moves the discussion away from social roles (such as friend or daughter), which, interestingly, most participants considered more as personal identities than as social identities, and anchors it more on identities situated in social structures. This also brings to light the intersecting nature of personal and social identities in that the role of daughter, for example, may be influenced by cultural norms and expectations. What the MMDI illustrates is that every individual possesses multiple social identities (whether salient or not), and that these identities do not exist independently (although they may be experienced more discretely or in isolation). Instead, these identity dimensions intersect with one another, illustrating that they can only be understood in relation to other dimensions.

Because many theories of college student development and identity treat these identity constructions as internal psychological processes, even if influenced by the surrounding environment, social identities either are not considered at all or lurk in the background of analysis. The foregrounding of social identities in the MMDI exposes systems of power and privilege that pattern development in both particular and systematic ways (Jones, 2009). As a result, the process of coming to know oneself and thinking about the question "Who am I?" is complicated by the socially constructed identities of race, gender, culture, and sexual orientation, and their intersections. For example, the intersection of gender and culture for Nandita meant "living in two worlds" (Jones, 1995, p. 141) to negotiate the conflicts between her upbringing as an "American woman" and the traditional Indian cultural norms held by her parents. Such a dynamic results in complex negotiations, both internally in defining oneself and externally in managing the perceptions others may have, which in turn influence identity negotiation and construction. Reflecting a process that is more fluid and dynamic than a traditional trajectory leading toward an authentic and consistent self, the MMDI illustrates that when social identities are made explicit, certain social identities are more salient than others and are more closely related to the core sense of self. Social identities also shift given contextual influences and the contingent terrain of race, class, gender, and other social identities.

Questions

- Identify five to six social identities that you possess, and label the intersecting circles on your MMDI accordingly.
- What do you notice about the social identities you selected?
- Do you experience any of your multiple social identities as intersecting (if so, which ones and how?); in conflict (if so, which ones and how); or both?
- How is it that you became aware of these social identities? Or how is it that you were able to overlook certain identities?
- What social identities are missing from your MMDI?
- What is the influence of privilege and oppression on the identities you selected? And on those missing?

- What do you notice about the social identities of others? In what ways do you pay attention to the social identities of others more than you do your own?

Relationship of Social Identities to the Core and Identity Salience

The MMDI also captures the relationship of social identities to the core through an illustration of identity salience. Relative salience, or what stands out to an individual, is depicted by the dots on each of the social identity circles and through the proximity of each dot to the core. That is, the closer the dot is to the core, the greater the salience of that social identity to the individual. For example, if race is particularly salient to an individual, the location of race is represented by a dot closer to the core. Similarly, if gender is not at all salient, the dot on that identity circle would be placed farther away from the core. When put in motion, with multiple social identities interacting and the salience of each of those identities identified, the MMDI provides a holistic and dynamic portrayal of how individuals perceive their identities.

The MMDI also offers an explanation for why some identities are more salient than others. As discussed in Chapter Three, one of the research questions in Susan's study (Jones, 1997) addressed difference and what meaning difference held for these women. What the focus on difference illuminated was the importance of privilege and oppression to the construction of self. Salience of particular identity dimensions was integrally connected to structures of inequality and systems of power and privilege. In particular, systems of privilege and inequality were least understood by those who were most privileged by these systems. The more privileged an identity (for example, race), the less salient it was. For example, gender was salient for all of these women; race was most salient for the participants of color, culture for the participants from distinct cultural traditions and with strong connections to their cultural heritage, and sexual orientation for the person who identified as a lesbian in the original sample (Jones, 1997). In more recent research on multiple identities (Jones, 2009; Jones et al., 2012), salience was found to be related to the experience of difference and feelings of "otherness" that prompt identity scrutiny. However, systems of privilege and oppression influenced this experience and created a different set of identity dynamics depending on whether or not the "difference" was visible (for example, race or ethnicity) or invisible (for example, social class or sexual orientation). In this more recent work, results suggested that when a particular social identity was highly visible (for example, race or ethnicity), awareness of difference was experienced at a very young age and persisted into adulthood (Jones, 2009). When the particular social identity was invisible (for example, sexual orientation or faith), a different set of identity negotiations occurred that focused on coming to terms with that particular identity dimension and making decisions about what to disclose to others, a privilege not afforded to those with more visible social identities. The influence of the experience of difference on identity construction exposes the role of privilege and oppression in the process of coming to know oneself. Without an experience of difference, privileged identities remained taken for granted and unscrutinized.

The prism of privilege and difference (see Figure 4.2), although not included in the MMDI, illustrates how both privilege and difference mediated the connection participants had with certain social identities and their relative salience, and shaped the links to these identity dimensions. Pictorially depicted as a prism, difference and privilege mediate the individual's connection to various social identities as the prism influences what is shown to the world and also what is reflected from the world. Technically, a prism both disperses light into a spectrum and also reflects light, an idea that is extended to this version of the MMDI to represent the influences of difference and privilege on the multiple dimensions of identity as well as how individuals respond to difference and privilege in their lives. The prism reflects what participants in the original study (Jones, 1995, 1997) constructed as the distinction between their "outside identities" and their inner characteristics (Jones, 1997). The prism may also represent a lens through which multiple dimensions of identity are understood. Examining identity through a prism of difference and privilege illuminates the influence of contextual factors that both shape and press, or push and pull on, multiple dimensions of identity, and contributes to an understanding of identity development as a dynamic, evolving process continually shaped by these many contexts.

Interestingly, Maxine Baca Zinn, Pierrette Hondagneu-Sotelo, and Michael Messner (2007), in discussing the intersection of gender with other social identities, also used the term *prism of difference* to "analyze a continuous spectrum of people, in order to show how gender is organized and experienced differently when refracted through the prism of sexual, racial/ethnic, social class, physical abilities, age, and national citizenship differences" (p. 148). The construction of a sense of self and identity is understood differently when privilege and difference are considered. Further, the incorporation of multiple identities as well as privilege and difference into the MMDI, and thus into an understanding of iden-

FIGURE 4.2 MMDI AND THE PRISM OF PRIVILEGE AND DIFFERENCE

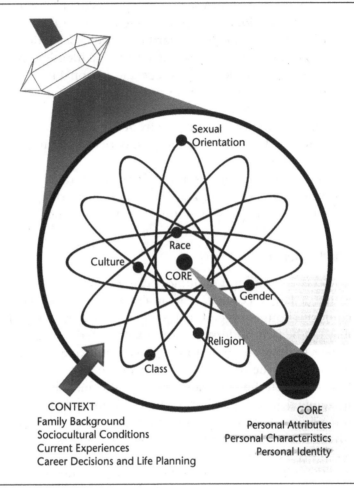

CONTEXT
Family Background
Sociocultural Conditions
Current Experiences
Career Decisions and Life Planning

CORE
Personal Attributes
Personal Characteristics
Personal Identity

Source: Jones, 1995, p. 216.

tity, requires attention to contextual influences, discussed in the next subsection.

Questions

- Using the MMDI template, place dots representing each of the social identities you previously identified. The proximity of each dot to the core signifies its salience to you (for example, if religion is very salient to you, then the dot on the religion circle should be placed very close to the core).

- In what ways do privilege and oppression influence the salience of those social identities you selected? Does salience emerge because of a lack of privilege in regard to a given social identity, or because of personal importance associated with that identity (or some interaction between oppression or privilege and personal importance)? Where do these influences of privilege and oppression come from—outside yourself, or more from the inside? What are they?
- What distinguishes your core from the social identities you identified? How would you describe the boundaries separating the core from your social identities?
- In what ways has a prism of difference operated in your life?
- What influence, if any, did an experience or experiences with difference or "otherness" have on the construction of your MMDI?

Contextual Influences

The core identity and multiple social identities of the MMDI are situated within a larger context. The intent of nesting social identities within context is both to suggest that self-perceived personal and social identities may not be fully understood without considering larger external forces as well as to draw attention to particular contextual influences that made a difference to the participants in the original study on which the MMDI is based. In fact, the core category from the analysis of the data (which, as mentioned in the previous chapter, in grounded theory research is an integrative category that represents the essence of the phenomenon under investigation) was identified as *contextual influences on the construction of identity* (Jones, 1997). Context interacts with other dimensions of identity and thus influences identity salience, the particular intersections of certain identities, and experiences of identities as both privileged and oppressed. Finally, these larger constructs of privilege and oppression could be both externally imposed and internally defined and illuminate the ways in which salient identities are fused with specific contexts.

Emerging from the narratives across all the participants was the central theme that participants' identities were deeply embedded in and created out of contexts. The specific contexts that influenced the identity construction of the participants in the original study included sociocultural conditions (for example, racism, sexism, heterosexism, privilege, and oppression); family background; and their current life experiences, which most notably for them focused on career decisions and life planning. These contextual influences were dynamic and individual; that is, the ways in which context influenced identity varied greatly by participant, and some contexts prompted scrutiny of previously taken-for-granted social identities whereas others did not. For example, when JJ moved from her home country of Uganda to the United States for school, her context shifted significantly. In the United States her race became salient in a way that it was not in Uganda. Similarly, Nandita found herself shifting how she acted depending on the context she was in. When she was at home with her parents, she modeled the cultural values of her Indian heritage, but when she was at the university, she was comfortable breaking out of those values, which she saw as sometimes restrictive in relation to her social life and friendships, and her behavior as an American and Indian woman. In the first example of JJ, we see how a change in context can shift the salience of a particular social identity, such as race. In Uganda, race was not a dimension of her identity that JJ thought about at all, but in the United States she became very aware of the "color thing" and had to consider her race for the first time. In the example of Nandita, the salience of her cultural identity remained strong, although in different ways depending on her contexts; but the particular ways in which her cultural identity intersected with her gender significantly influenced her sense of self. Her parents held very definite expectations for her based on the values of their Indian culture; yet these values were often in conflict with her experiences on campus and with the vision of the woman she wanted to become. Finally, many of these women experienced the press to make career and life decisions as they were approaching graduation from the university, and this, too, exerted a contextual influence on their identities. They were also aware that their identities would continue to be shaped by new contexts, such as work, life planning, and families.

Also important are the ways in which several participants discussed the need to manage context. Participants provided examples of context's remaining invisible or unknown, a dynamic that played a role in the addition of the meaning-making filter in the reconceptualized model, which will be discussed in Chapter Five. In both instances of context as either unknown or invisible, the structures of privilege and oppression are at work and relate back to the discussion of the prism of privilege and difference. The existence of larger contexts of privilege and oppression, such as racism, sexism, and classism, in which identities are constructed resulted in participants' feeling burdened by, for example, expectations to serve as a role model for all Black women, the effort to fit into the fictional ideal of female beauty by becoming bulimic, or the pressure to keep secret an engagement to a man from a different culture because of the disappointment it would cause her parents. These experiences of difference emerging from larger contexts resulted in complex identity negotiations and creative strategies to manage difference. Among these strategies were masking difference, living a hybrid or bicultural identity, and distinguishing between a more public self and a private one. These strategies were also seen in recent research (for example, Jones, 2009; Jones et al., 2012) demonstrating that participants, depending on the context, made decisions about how to present themselves, in some cases downplaying certain aspects of self. These choices relate to perceptions of professionalism, safety concerns, and family backgrounds and expectations.

Another factor to consider in relation to context is present when the influence of context is imperceptible to individuals, a phenomenon that also connects to structures of privilege and oppression. This may be related to an individual's cognitive capacity for recognizing dimensions of context, such as racism or sexism (see Chapter Five); the particular ways in which privileged and oppressed social identities and context intersect (see Chapter Six for a discussion of this dynamic as a characteristic of intersectionality); or the fact that a particular context may simply be unrecognizable to individuals. In both the original research and in later studies on multiple social identities, we found social class to fit into this third category. Largely invisible, social class lurked beneath the surface of participants' narratives, but on closer scrutiny we began to see the very specific ways in which social class was experienced as both a social identity and a contextual influence. In addition, social class intersected with other social identities, such as race, culture, and sexual orientation, in complicated ways (Jones, 2009). The phenomenon of silence around specific social identities and how they intersect is a challenging issue to address in identity research. However, silence signals the ways in which privilege and oppression circulate in the construction of self. Noted poet and essayist Audre Lorde (1980) captured the personal significance of putting voice to silence, writing, "My work is to inhabit the silences with which I have lived and fill them with myself until they have the sounds of the brightest day and the loudest thunder" (p. 46).

Questions

- How do you personally make sense of the core, social identities, identity salience, and context, as well as the relationships among these elements?

- From a personal and professional perspective, what is the purpose of making sense of the MMDI's conceptualization of identity?
- To what extent does the way you make sense of the elements of the MMDI depend on the particulars of your social identities?
- What contextual influences have made the biggest difference in your construction of identity? Being specific, write down some of these influences on your MMDI template. For example, what are the particular experiences, life situations, family dynamics, cultural values, or career decisions that have carried significance for you?
- In what ways have these contexts influenced your identity construction?
- How has your identity influenced the contexts in which you participate?
- How might your MMDI template look different if your current context changed?

Strengths and Limitations of the Model of Multiple Dimensions of Identity

Despite the claim that qualitative studies are not designed with generalizability in mind, the MMDI, which emerged from the results of a grounded theory study of women college students, has garnered quite a bit of traction among identity scholars in student development and higher education and practitioners in student affairs (see Chapter Nine for examples) because of the transferability of the results of the study and elements of the model. The most basic explanation for this, as far as we can tell, is that the MMDI provides a more holistic portrayal of identity, and therefore more closely mirrors the lived experience of identity, than models that focus only on singular dimensions. There are a few other strengths of the MMDI, as well as some limitations, that we address in this concluding section of the chapter. In identifying the limitations of the MMDI, we pave the way for subsequent chapters, which represent empirical and theoretical attempts to address these limitations and extend the model's utility.

Strengths of the MMDI

A significant strength of the MMDI lies in that it is both simplistic and complex. The model is simplistic because it portrays the complexities of identity in a straightforward and clear way; one can look at the MMDI and see the central components of the model clearly represented. The model is complex because it illustrates the nuances of identity by incorporating multiple and intersecting identities and the influence of contextual factors. The MMDI provides for both internal and external definitions of identity, a self-defined core sense of self, and the more macro role of context, thereby opening up discussion and allowing for deepened understanding of the complexities of identity development. The model depicts a more complex and holistic picture of identity than do many models of identity because of the attention to the intersections of social identities and their differing salience, the relationships among social identities and one's internal or core sense of self, and larger contextual influences. A word of caution is warranted, however, as a quick perusal of the MMDI may present a deceptively simple view. As ideally has been made clear through the discussion in these chapters, the MMDI includes multiple concepts and ideas that contribute to its complexity and that should not be missed if one desires to grapple fully with the model and its implications for understanding identity when multiple social identities are considered.

Related to the clarity in presentation and perceived simplicity of the model is another strength, the accessibility of the MMDI. Despite the fact that the MMDI emerged from the narratives and lived experiences of college women, most can plot themselves on this model and thus see aspects of themselves in the MMDI as well as the theory on which the model is based. The MMDI is able to accommodate a wide range of individual differences and contextual influences because it relies on individual responses for its creation. That is, individuals can engage with the MMDI by identifying what constitutes a core identity; specific social identities as more or less salient, as well as these identities' relationship to the core; and particular contextual influences on the construction of identity. What this means is that every MMDI will look different based on the self-perceived identities of the person portraying him- or herself, and thus the MMDI embraces the diversity of individual differences without attaching any judgment to specific identity dimensions.

Another strength of the MMDI is that it provides for a dynamic process whereby identities shift and get shaped and reshaped based on changing contexts and the influence of these contexts both on identity salience and on what is in one's core. In other words, the MMDI is not a static model, but rather a more fluid one that does not contain a developmental end point or presume a linear path to a definitive sense of identity. As such, the MMDI represents a departure from identity models that suggest movement from an identity that is externally defined to one that is internally grounded, or a process that involves a change in awareness of a specific identity from no consciousness or awareness to an awareness that is fully internalized and integrated. These developmental pathways may be present, but representing such trajectories is not the intent of the MMDI. Instead, the MMDI suggests that self-definition is an ever-changing process because of the influence of contexts, which are always nested in structures of privilege and oppression.

Finally, a strength of the MMDI is the recognition, depicted in one model, that individuals may inhabit both privileged and oppressed identities, often represented through the experience of identity salience, and that these privileged and oppressed identities interact. Because of its emphasis on both privileged and oppressed identities, the MMDI also facilitates an examination of identities one might not otherwise consider as a part of oneself. For example, when we consider how privilege and oppression (or "difference," in the prism model) mediate the individual's connection to certain identity dimensions, we can then understand why social class, for example, may not be salient at all for some. The larger societal contexts of privilege and oppression are elevated in importance in the MMDI, but not without equal attention to the more micro experiences of identity negotiations in everyday life.

Limitations of the MMDI

No model is without limitations, and the MMDI is no exception. Further, as the subsequent chapters should demonstrate, we continue to think about and work on the model as we learn more, complete further empirical research, and consider additional theoretical frameworks through which to analyze the identity development process. The limitation that first comes to mind is that the study upon which the MMDI was created (Jones, 1997) and the study that led to the creation of the RMMDI (Abes & Jones, 2004) focus solely on college women, and a relatively small number of them. The sample size in each is consistent with criteria for rigorous qualitative inquiry; however, there will always be those skeptics who doubt that a robust model could be based on a sample of ten. We are also aware that these two original studies (for example, Abes & Jones, 2004; Jones & McEwen, 2000) were conducted a number of years ago now. Subsequent work of ours has both affirmed the components of the MMDI and enabled us to extend it. Further, as already mentioned, the MMDI illustrates an identity snapshot, as each model created represents a point in time. The MMDI does not, therefore, portray identity *development*, but rather is an illustration of how individuals perceive their identity at that moment—and thus is likely to change and shift.

Another limitation is that it is very difficult to graphically represent the complexities of identity and intersecting identities. For example, the core is challenging to articulate in the context of a model. In addition, it is not easy to capture movement in a model, so the MMDI may appear to be overly simplistic and too static (as discussed earlier in the chapter). The core in the MMDI may appear to be too fixed, and the distinction between personal and social identities may seem too rigid. The results of the original study led to a definition of the core as consisting of personal attributes and as protected from external labels associated with social identities; however, the boundaries may be more permeable than this definition suggests. The MMDI also does not fully represent the specifics of the context in relation to systems of power that most influence identity construction. So although the MMDI is intended to represent the influences of a macro context on identity construction, when structures of inequality are made explicit there is an even broader context to be considered.

Questions about the components of the MMDI may also lead to other potential limitations. For example, when individuals identify social identities on their MMDI, this indicates that they have some salience to the individual, even if this salience is only limited. Other social identities (such as social class) may be missing altogether. Further, the MMDI emphasizes certain social identities over others (for example, it focuses more on race than on social identities that emphasize social roles, such as mother, family member, or daughter). One could argue that certain dimensions of self are missing from the MMDI. In addition, the MMDI suggests that salience of a particular social identity is determined by its importance to the individual. Later research has suggested that salience is also created as a result of external forces and specific contexts. Finally, the MMDI represents identity salience by proximity of the social identity to the core. This portrays the existence of multiple intersecting identities and the opportunity for multiple identities to be salient. What is left out of the model is a demonstration of relationships among social identities—a truly intersectional view. Similarly, another dynamic not provided for in the MMDI, in which context is situated as influencing identity, is the possibility that identity may also shape and influence context.

Summary

In this chapter we used the theories that guided the original research and background information about the study presented in Chapter Three to present more fully the Model of Multiple Dimensions of Identity. We focused on the central components of the model—the core, multiple social identities, the relationship of social identities to the core and identity salience, and contextual influences—and presented questions to encourage readers to examine these components in relation to their own lived experience of identity construction. We also introduced the prism of privilege and difference, which more explicitly addresses the influence of power and oppression in the development of a sense of self. By concluding the chapter with a section on the strengths and limitations of the MMDI, we not only highlighted those aspects of the model that have resonated with other identity scholars and practitioners but also paved the way for our discussion of subsequent work on the MMDI (most notably the Reconceptualized Model of Multiple Dimensions of Identity, which will be fully introduced and discussed in the next chapter). We are pleased that the MMDI has served as an impetus for additional work and conceptualizations of identity, as our collective thinking is only enhanced by the ideas of others who share our investment in and commitment to understanding the complexities of identity among college students. The chapters that follow represent how our thinking and empirical research have evolved from the foundational work that led to the MMDI.

Discussion Questions and Activities

1. What do *you* consider to be the strengths and limitations of the MMDI?
2. What was challenging for you as you completed your MMDI template? What new insights do you have about your own identity?
3. What does the process of negotiating identity look like for you? How does your own depiction of your multiple dimensions of identity dovetail with how you think others perceive you? How does your depiction differ from how you think others perceive you?
4. How might the MMDI be applied to your practice? Design three specific uses or applications (for example, a program designed with a specific population in mind, or an advising or counseling session). What needs to be taken into consideration when applying the MMDI to practice?

FIGURE 4.3 MMDI TEMPLATE

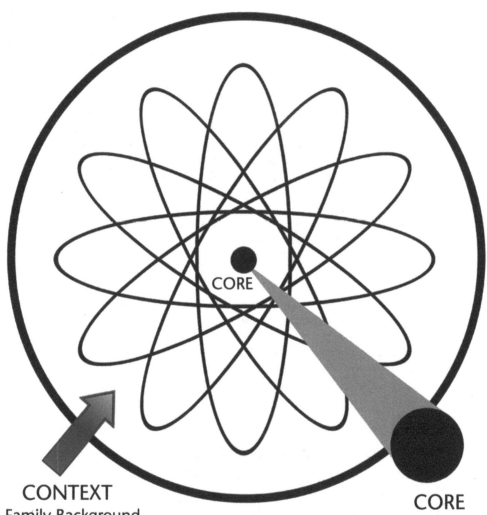

RECONCEPTUALIZED MODEL OF MULTIPLE DIMENSIONS OF IDENTITY

As described in the previous two chapters, the Model of Multiple Dimensions of Identity (MMDI) broke new ground in student development theory through its portrayal of multiple social identities situated within a changing context. Still, the model is limited in that it focuses on only one domain of development, namely identity development. A more holistic portrayal of the relationships among multiple social identities focuses not only on identity development but also on cognitive and interpersonal development. Recognizing this limitation, Elisa Abes, Susan R. Jones, and Marylu McEwen (2007) reenvisioned the MMDI, inserting a meaning-making filter between context and identity. By simultaneously considering both multiple social identities and multiple domains of development, the Reconceptualized Model of Multiple Dimensions of Identity (RMMDI) offers a more comprehensive portrayal of college student identity than does the original model. In this chapter we describe the research that led to the RMMDI as well as the notion of meaning making, and then turn to the elements of the RMMDI. In the final section we discuss some of the strengths and limitations of the model within the context of systems of inequality, calling for a flexible application of the meaning-making filter in relation to the other elements of the model. That last section sets the stage for the discussion of critical theoretical approaches to representing the MMDI, which we explore in detail throughout this book.

Meaning-Making Capacity

The RMMDI grew out of Abes and Jones's research (2004) on lesbian college students' perceptions of the relationships among their multiple social identities. We therefore explain that study in some detail here. Given the central role of meaning-making capacity in that research and the introduction of the meaning-making filter into the MMDI to create the reconceptualized model, we begin with a review of meaning-making capacity as described by Robert Kegan and Marcia Baxter Magolda. We focus significant attention on meaning-making capacity because this construct creates a filtering process between contexts and the salience and meaning of social identities.

Drawing on several of the ideas developed by noted psychologist Jean Piaget (1952), Kegan (1994) developed a theory of self-evolution that describes a series of increasingly complex meaning-making structures. He defined meaning-making structures as sets of assumptions that determine how an individual perceives and organizes his or her life experiences. These structures constitute the organizing principles of how one makes sense of and interprets the world. He explained that a person actively interprets life through meaning-making structures, and that "there is no feeling, no experience, no thought, no perception independent of a meaning-making context" (Kegan, 1982, p. 11). For example, the way a student interacts with central figures in his or her college experience, such as professors, academic advisers, and student organization mentors, might depend on whether that student's interpersonal meaning-making structure allows him or her to define relationships or only to be defined by relationships. Kegan (1982, 1994) explained that we use a particular meaning-making structure until doing so no longer makes sense for us as a result of differences between that meaning-making structure and our current reality. For instance, a student whose meaning-making structure contributes to being defined by a relationship with an academic adviser might start relying less on that meaning-making structure when beginning to receive guidance from the adviser that is not consistent with a growing internal sense of what might be a rewarding academic major. Letting go of a particular structure can be an emotionally trying experience, as the meaning-making structures one has been using offer a familiar way of making sense of the world.

In Kegan's theory of self-evolution (1982, 1994), a developmental theory that spans from birth through adulthood, Kegan refers to meaning-making structures as "orders of consciousness." He describes five orders of consciousness, each of which represents increasingly complex ways of understanding oneself and one's relationships with others. It was within this theory of self-evolution that Kegan coined the term *self-authorship*, a meaning-making structure that occurs when a person reaches the fourth order of consciousness.

Baxter Magolda has made significant contributions to student development theory through her application of and expansion on Kegan's theory of self-evolution, especially the concept of self-authorship, in the context of college students (for example, Baxter Magolda, 2001, 2009). Baxter Magolda has traced the development of 30 participants (originally 101) in her twenty-five-year longitudinal study, which started as an exploration of epistemological development and evolved into a study of multiple, integrated domains of development. She began her research with these participants when they were first-year students in college, and has continued to study their development through annual interviews (these same participants are now in their forties). Working from the results of her extensive research, Baxter Magolda (2001, 2009) has elaborated on the process of development toward increasingly complex orders of consciousness most often found among traditional-age college students.

Among the significant contributions of her work is the detail with which she portrays development from external to internal meaning making as a process that encompasses three interconnected domains of development. That is, she makes explicit how meaning making consists of cognitive, interpersonal, and intrapersonal development. The cognitive domain refers to how people construct knowledge, specifically whether they perceive one reality or multiple realities and whether reality is externally or internally defined. The interpersonal domain refers to how people define their relationships with others, specifically whether they define themselves *in* relation to others or *through* their relationships with others. Do their relationships define them (external meaning making), or do they define their relationships (internal meaning making)? The intrapersonal domain refers to how individuals understand their sense of self, including their personal and social identities. Is one's sense of self externally or internally defined? Baxter Magolda's research (2001, 2009) has demonstrated the interconnectedness of these three domains: development in one domain often contributes to development in another.

Baxter Magolda has found that Kegan's third order of consciousness (1994), or external meaning making, is the most prevalent meaning-making structure among traditional-age college students. At the third order of consciousness, knowledge is defined externally, and individuals define their identity through their relationships with others as well as through other external influences, such as social norms and campus climate. Without the ability to see multiple realities, maintain an identity apart from a relationship, or develop an internal belief system, a person who makes meaning at the third order of consciousness is unable to resolve conflicts among competing sources of knowledge or expectations. Individuals define themselves through others' knowledge, expectations, and worldviews rather than having the ability to define their own perspectives. All of these external influences make up the context in which a person lives. Context can be as broad as the surrounding sociopolitical environment, or it can be more local, such as the family and friends with whom one interacts. At the third order of consciousness, individuals *are* their context. No filtering mechanism exists between the two.

Students making a transition between external and internal meaning making are at a "crossroads" in their development (Baxter Magolda, 2004). During this transitional period dominated by tensions and unresolved conflicts between their developing internal voice and external influences, students gradually question the external influences that have shaped their perceptions of knowledge, relationships, and identity, as these influences are increasingly incongruent with their developing internal ideas and values. At a crossroads, though, it is difficult to be confident in these growing internal beliefs, or even certain as to their precise nature, making acting on emerging internal ideas a struggle or an impossibility. A person starts to develop an internal voice, but that voice is drowned out by the much louder noise of the many external influences in which the person is situated, and which that person has been accustomed to internalizing as his or her own. For example, a college student who is starting to develop her own beliefs about the meaning of her African American identity might struggle to truly know how she defines this aspect of herself when she has for many years understood her race through the manner in which family, friends, the media, stereotypes, and schooling defined it for her. She might simultaneously hold some of her own tentative beliefs but also still cling to contradictory beliefs she has internalized for years prior. At the same time, acting on her newly developing beliefs is often a challenge if they differ from the beliefs of those important to her, those she sees as having more authority than she, and those that are more pervasive.

Fewer college students make meaning at the fourth order of consciousness, or using an internal meaning-making structure. Internal meaning making is characterized by self-authorship (Baxter Magolda,

2004), which requires complexity in cognitive, interpersonal, and intra-personal domains of development. Specifically, Baxter Magolda (1999) explained that self-authorship is "an ability to construct knowledge in a contextual world, an ability to construct an internal identity separate from external influences, and an ability to engage in relationships without losing one's internal identity" (p. 12). Self-authoring individuals have developed their own system for making sense of the many external influences that affect them and can draw on that internal system when faced with conflicting expectations or expectations that are not in line with their beliefs. Using this mature meaning-making structure, individuals can use their own voice to engage authentically with the many external voices surrounding them.

Using the same example of the African American woman described earlier, if she is using a self-authoring meaning-making structure, she would have an awareness of and some influence over how her race is shaped by others' perceptions, portrayals, and expectations, and she would be able to make her own sense of those external influences and define the meaning of her race according to her own value system and desires. The way in which she perceives her race is not fixed, but she understands and has some influence over the changes. With her study participants now in their forties, Baxter Magolda has been able to explore in greater depth the process of self-authoring one's life. She has found that development toward self-authorship is not a linear trajectory that is the same for all people, but that instead people take different paths "based on their personal characteristics, experiences, the challenges they encountered, and the support available to them" (Baxter Magolda, 2009, p. 330). Figure 5.1 depicts the relationships among the domains of development and the movement from external to internal meaning making. The figure is drawn to show that the three domains of development are integrated at all points along the developmental continuum. The wavy arrow is intended to illustrate that the external-to-internal continuum is not an inflexible, linear path.

Meaning-Making Capacity and Multiple Social Identities

With Kegan's and Baxter Magolda's theories describing external-to-internal meaning making as an informing framework, we explored relationships among lesbian college students' multiple social identities (Abes & Jones, 2004). We grounded this study in a constructivist perspective because we

FIGURE 5.1 DEVELOPMENT TOWARD SELF-AUTHORSHIP

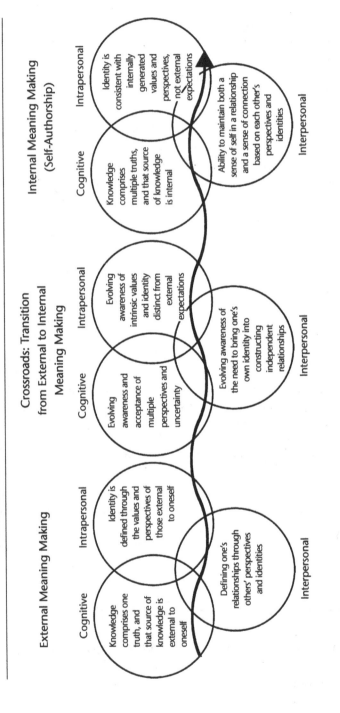

External Meaning Making

Crossroads: Transition
from External to Internal
Meaning Making

Internal Meaning Making
(Self-Authorship)

Cognitive

Knowledge comprises one truth, and that source of knowledge is external to oneself

Intrapersonal

Identity is defined through the values and perspectives of those external to oneself

Interpersonal

Defining one's relationships through others' perspectives and identities

Cognitive

Evolving awareness and acceptance of multiple perspectives and uncertainty

Intrapersonal

Evolving awareness of intrinsic values and identity distinct from external expectations

Interpersonal

Evolving awareness of the need to bring one's own identity into constructing independent relationships

Cognitive

Knowledge comprises multiple truths, and that source of knowledge is internal

Intrapersonal

Identity is consistent with internally generated values and perspectives, not external expectations

Interpersonal

Ability to maintain both a sense of self in a relationship and a sense of connection based on each other's perspectives and identities found this to be conducive to understanding students' meaning-making capacity. Constructivism is an interpretivist theory rooted in the notions that multiple realities exist and that realities are coconstructed between the researcher and participants through dialogue (Denzin & Lincoln, 2000; Lather, 2007). We used narrative inquiry methodology to understand how the participants made meaning of their identities. The purpose of narrative inquiry is to understand the wholeness of human experience through data collected in the form of stories (Clandinin & Connelly, 2000; Lieblich, Tuval-Mashiach, & Zilber, 1998). We selected narrative inquiry because it is consistent with our belief that identity and stories are intertwined (Chase, 1995).

Using purposeful sampling to obtain information-rich cases (M. Patton, 1990), we selected ten women for our sample. All ten women, ages eighteen to twenty-three, were attending the same large, public research university in the Midwest. Five were students of color (one Black; one Latina; one Puerto Rican and White; one Trinidadian and White; and one African American and White); five were White. There were two Jewish women, one agnostic, one pagan, one agnostic pagan, one Protestant Christian, and one Catholic, and three did not identify with a religion. In terms of gender expression, eight identified as female, two as androgynous. Six women identified as middle class, one temporarily poor, one working class, and two upper-middle class. We collected data through three open-ended interviews with each participant. During the second interview, we gave each participant a copy of the MMDI and asked her to plot her identity on the model. That is, we asked each participant to identify what aspects of identity were core, to note the salience of multiple social identities in relation to the core, and to indicate what aspects of context were most relevant to how she perceived the salience of her social identities. We did not instruct the participants as to which identities to include on their model. We used these depictions as the basis for additional interview questions. We then took a constant comparative approach to data analysis (Lieblich et al., 1998) to understand the themes within and across the women's stories.

Our results demonstrated that the participants' meaning-making capacity served as a filter through which they interpreted external influences, or context, prior to those influences' shaping self-perceptions of sexual orientation identity and its relationship to other social identities. How context influenced these perceptions depended on the complexity of participants' meaning-making capacity. Participants with complex meaning-making capacity, or those who were closer to using an internal meaning-making structure, were able, more so than those with capacity that was less developed, to filter external influences, such as family background, peer culture, social norms, and stereotypes, and to determine how these factors influenced their identity. Complex meaning making contributed to the ease with which sexual orientation integrated or peacefully coexisted with other social identities, and increased the extent to which participants' perceptions of their social identities were consistent with the sense of self they hoped to achieve. In short, we learned that a relationship exists between students' development toward self-authorship and how they understand the meaning of and relationships among their multiple social identities.

Reconceptualized MMDI: Partnering the MMDI and Meaning Making

The RMMDI portrays this connection between meaning-making capacity and relationships among students' multiple social identities. That is, we partnered the MMDI with Kegan's and Baxter Magolda's theories of development toward self-authorship. In doing so, we created a model that incorporates both multiple domains of development and multiple social identities. The RMMDI is illustrated in Figure 5.2.

We worked with Marylu McEwen to develop that model given her role in creating the original MMDI as well as her in-depth knowledge of how the model is situated within the larger body of student development theory. In the RMMDI, the core and multiple social identities are represented similarly to how they are depicted in the original model. Contextual influences, such as peers, family, social norms, and campus climate, are drawn as arrows moving toward identity. Meaning-making capacity is drawn as a filter, similar to a screen, between context and identity. How context moves through the filter depends on the permeability of the filter, and the permeability depends on the complexity of the person's meaning-making capacity. To illustrate complex meaning-making capacity, the filter is drawn with narrow screen openings; less complex meaning-making capacity is represented by wider grid openings. The wider the screen openings, the more permeable the filter. Contextual, external influences more easily move through a highly permeable filter (representing less complex meaning making), thereby having a stronger influence on a person's perceptions of identity than they would if the filter were less permeable (representing more complex meaning making). To reiterate the nature

FIGURE 5.2 RECONCEPTUALIZED MODEL OF MULTIPLE DIMENSIONS OF IDENTITY

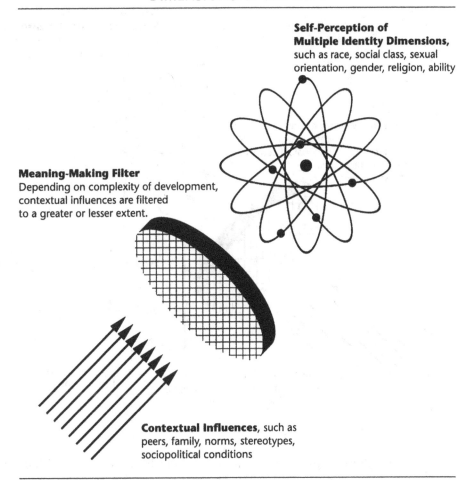

Self-Perception of Multiple Identity Dimensions, such as race, social class, sexual orientation, gender, religion, ability

Meaning-Making Filter
Depending on complexity of development, contextual influences are filtered to a greater or lesser extent.

Contextual Influences, such as peers, family, norms, stereotypes, sociopolitical conditions

Source: Adapted from Abes et al., 2007, p. 7.

and purpose of the filter, Figure 5.3 illustrates that the meaning-making filter represents a person's development toward self-authorship. The permeability of the filter depends on whether a person makes meaning externally, internally, or at a crossroads between the two.

Regardless of differences in meaning making, and the corresponding differences in the permeability of the filter, identity is always shaped within contexts. The filter does not block context, but differences in the

FIGURE 5.3 RMMDI AND ITS RELATIONSHIP TO SELF-AUTHORSHIP

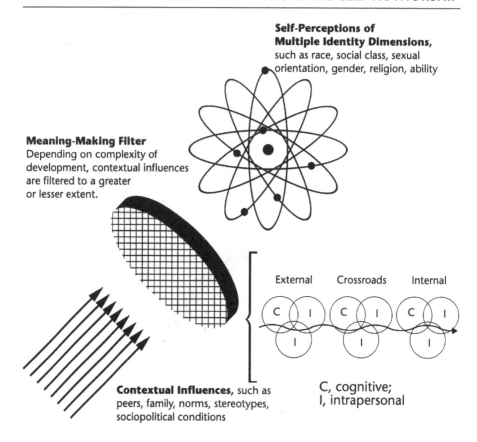

Self-Perceptions of Multiple Identity Dimensions, such as race, social class, sexual orientation, gender, religion, ability

Meaning-Making Filter Depending on complexity of development, contextual influences are filtered to a greater or lesser extent.

External   Crossroads   Internal

Contextual Influences, such as peers, family, norms, stereotypes, sociopolitical conditions

C, cognitive; I, intrapersonal

permeability of the filter result in distinctly different ways in which context influences the nature of identity. For a person with primarily external meaning-making capacity, context directly shapes identity perceptions. For instance, if the campus climate sends messages that celebrate only heterosexual relationships, through traditional notions of homecoming kings and queens, a Greek system grounded in heterosexual dating rituals, or an alumni association that recognizes only heterosexual marriages among alums, women students may not even perceive the possibility of identifying as a lesbian. The external context steeped in heterosexuality moves through the filter unchanged and results in the women perceiving their identity the same way that context defines their identity. Unfiltered, context *is* their identity. Individuals with internal meaning-making capacity, by contrast, are able to make their own sense of how context shapes identity. That same campus climate moves through the filter, but as it does so, individuals are able to reshape for themselves its meaning and control to some extent what aspects of context will influence identity—and in what ways. Individuals with an internal meaning-making structure might be able to understand that there are multiple possibilities for relationships, and that what the campus climate celebrates is only one possibility. They might also have a strong enough sense of self in relation to others to be able to remain true to their own identity despite a context that does not recognize who they are.

To provide a more in-depth example of how the RMMDI portrays the influence of a person's meaning-making capacity on the nature of relationships among social identities, we share the story of two participants from our study (Abes & Jones, 2004). For four years following the completion of the research that was described in our study, Elisa conducted follow-up interviews with eight of the ten participants. She conducted two interviews, one to two years apart, to understand through longitudinal data the link between meaning-making capacity and perceptions of relationships among multiple social identities. Although the RMMDI was developed from only the first phase of this longitudinal study, in the next section we use data from all three study phases to provide an example that demonstrates how increasingly complex meaning-making capacity filters the ways in which context influences perceptions of relationships among multiple social identities.

KT's Story: Meaning-Making Capacity and Relationships Among Sexual Orientation, Religion, Social Class, and Gender

KT received her undergraduate degree in physical education during the first study phase.[1] After receiving her master's degree, she worked as a physical education instructor during the remainder of the study. A White woman raised as Catholic, KT realized she was a lesbian near the end of high school. Her mother strongly disapproved, telling KT that as a lesbian she could not practice Catholicism, be professionally successful, or be feminine. As KT came out to her college friends about her sexual orientation, most everything she knew about what it meant to be a lesbian was

[1]Much of KT's story is drawn from Abes & Kasch, 2007.

based on negative stereotypes she heard from her mother. Soon after, it became important to KT to be her own person as a lesbian, but before she could consider that possibility, she had to learn whether or not the stereotypes were true.

The first study phase was marked by KT's experiencing dissonance between her mother's perspectives and the new perspectives she was exploring. This dissonance is typical of an early crossroads between external and internal meaning making and often spurs cognitive, interpersonal, and intrapersonal development. Although KT was encouraged by glimmers of perspectives different from those of her mother, she was not ready to develop her own ideas on what it meant to be a lesbian and how that related to her religion, gender, and social class. Over the next eighteen months between the first two study phases, KT continued moving through the crossroads. Still investigating multiple perspectives on what it meant to be a lesbian, KT was tentatively developing her own perspectives and starting to understand that her social identities were not mutually exclusive. In the third phase, a little over one year later, KT spoke with much more confidence about her own perspectives on her identity and felt comfortable defining her identity separate from the way her mother had taught her. We describe in the following subsections KT's development in how she made meaning of some of these social identities.

Sexual Orientation and Religion

KT had a deep faith in God, and reconciling her religion and sexual orientation was among her most significant challenges. During the first study phase, KT reflected on a time when she believed her mother's perspective that identifying as a lesbian precluded her from being religious. KT sought out other perspectives to help her learn that her mother's interpretation of the Bible was not the only correct one. She cast her desire for religion as a future goal, although she was uncertain if she could adopt a perspective different from what others taught her. Cognitively, she experienced dissonance as she learned about multiple perspectives, but she was not yet prepared to adopt her own. KT's interpersonal development also interacted with her understanding of the relationship between her sexual orientation and religion. Despite her lesbian friends' negative attitudes toward religion, KT tentatively believed she could be religious and a lesbian. Still, she primarily defined herself through her relationships with her friends and hid her religious beliefs. During the second study phase, KT more confidently believed there were multiple ways to be a lesbian and religious, and started creating her own perspectives on this relationship, deciding that she could practice Catholicism even if not in church. A new, supportive relationship mediated her intrapersonal and interpersonal development because her girlfriend respected her religious beliefs. This support allowed KT to reflect on prior relationships and see how she had allowed others to define her identity. KT demonstrated development in all three domains. She was coming to understand multiple perspectives on the relationship between religion and sexual orientation (cognitive development); gaining a stronger sense of how she wanted to reconcile these two aspects of her identity (intrapersonal development); and hoping to maintain her religious beliefs in a relationship (interpersonal development). In the third phase, KT discussed these same perspectives with increased confidence. She knew that God loved her and that she could practice religion as she chose, aware that at some point she would find a church that welcomed her and in which she could openly be true to her identity.

Sexual Orientation and Social Class

KT also sought out concrete examples to help her learn that a stereotype with which she was familiar, specifically that lesbians typically inhabit a lower social class, was not necessarily true. Again, she was exposing herself to and seeing validity in multiple perspectives. Based on comments from her mother and exposure only to lesbians who were college students, KT believed for many years that identifying as a lesbian and identifying as an upper-class professional were mutually exclusive. Through a relationship at the time of the first study phase with a "professional" woman, KT attended parties at nice homes owned by lesbians. Seeing these professional women allowed KT to tentatively consider the possibility that identifying as a lesbian might not preclude her from achieving her professional goals. During the second phase, KT was more confident that her sexual orientation need not dictate her social class. KT attributed her new perspective to her growing confidence that resulted from graduating from college and becoming a successful teacher. By accomplishing her educational goals, which her mother told her she could not do as a lesbian, KT gained the confidence to accept perspectives different from what her mother taught her and to believe in her own thinking. KT's confidence in her thinking grew in the third phase. A successful teacher, she had financial stability and knew she would be able to securely raise her family. Based on her experience, she did not see her sexual orientation limiting her social class, a significant shift from her earlier thinking. KT's evolution in how she perceived the relationship between her sexual orientation and social class demonstrated development in all three domains, as she was integrating into her sense of self (intrapersonal) her own perspectives on the relationship between her sexual orientation and social class (cognitive), rather than defining these possibilities through her mother (interpersonal).

Sexual Orientation and Gender

One of KT's obstacles in her journey toward reconciling her social class ambitions with her sexual orientation was her assumption that other people perceived lesbians to be masculine women. It was important to KT to always be professional in all aspects of her life, and she associated being professional with being feminine. From her perspective, "masculine women" were not perceived as professional women. KT assumed many people would think that because she was a lesbian she was also masculine and therefore unprofessional, which would hurt her career. This perception, again based on what others told her, was especially troubling as a physical education teacher because of a stereotype that lesbians are typically associated with this profession. However, by meeting other lesbians whom she considered to be professional and feminine, she was coming to realize, again tentatively, the possibility of being perceived by others as feminine.

KT did not give as much thought to her gender at the time of the second phase of the study. Still, she conflated gender and social class. When asked to describe her gender, KT, who was confident wearing short hair and stylish, athletic clothes, responded by saying "professional." Although she continued to equate "professional" with "feminine," she was starting to define her own meaning of feminine rather than defining it through stereotypes. Despite her worry about being fired from teaching if others knew she was gay, she grew more comfortable portraying her gender in a way that made her comfortable and that allowed her to feel professional, rather than according to other people's standards. Again, KT's confidence grew at the time of the third study phase. She dressed in ways that pleased her rather than seeking to please others by fulfilling certain gender expectations. Not only did she understand that her sexuality was not tied to how she portrayed her gender but also she defined for herself the meaning of professional, which was not tied to a particular gender expectation. As with religion and social class, KT was entertaining the possibility of multiple perspectives as well as starting to develop her own perspectives (cognitive development) and defining her own identity (intrapersonal development), rather than losing herself in others' perceptions of her (interpersonal development).

Moving closer to self-authorship, KT reflected at the end of the second study phase that by gaining the ability to define her identities for herself and in less conflict with one another, she was "allowing [her] true self to evolve." In the third phase, KT was very reflective on the nature of her identities and especially how she perceived her relationship with her mother and her mother's influence on her identity. In doing so, she explained that she did not necessarily perceive her identities as influencing one another, but that she was able to influence the nature of her identities, indeed allowing her to be her true self.

Figures 5.4 and 5.5 depict differences in how the RMMDI might look for KT, depending on whether she is making meaning externally or at a

FIGURE 5.4 KT AND EXTERNAL MEANING MAKING

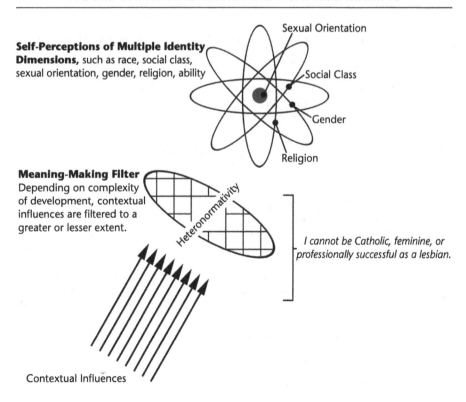

Self-Perceptions of Multiple Identity Dimensions, such as race, social class, sexual orientation, gender, religion, ability

Sexual Orientation

Social Class

Gender

Religion

Meaning-Making Filter Depending on complexity of development, contextual influences are filtered to a greater or lesser extent.

Heteronormativity

I cannot be Catholic, feminine, or professionally successful as a lesbian.

Contextual Influences

crossroads, respectively. In both figures, the context in which KT is making sense of her identity is steeped in heterosexism. In Figure 5.4, which portrays external meaning making, heterosexism passes through a permeable filter, and she defines her identities through a heterosexist lens that results in her sexual orientation's being part of her core, and in her social class, gender, and religion's being distinct from her core and distinct from one another. By putting sexual orientation, a social identity, in her core, she is interpreting the nature of the core somewhat differently from how Jones and McEwen (2000) originally described it.

In Figure 5.5, which represents meaning making at a crossroads, KT filters that same heterosexism through an increasingly less permeable filter that represents her growing awareness of her ability to make her own meaning of context. With context having less influence on her identity than it previously did, KT's social class, gender, and religion are able to move closer to her core and to each other as she desired that they do.

FIGURE 5.5 KT AND EARLY CROSSROADS MEANING MAKING

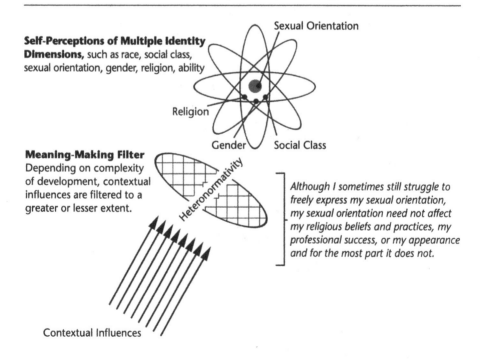

Carmen's Story: The Reconceptualized Model and Systems of Inequality—Considering a More Flexible Model

Although the manner in which the RMMDI is drawn depicts an orderly relationship between context, meaning making, and identity salience, the relationships among these elements are not always that neat and predictable.[2] Instead, there is flexibility in how the elements interact with each other. Contributing to this flexibility in the RMMDI is that the context in which identities are situated is laden with inequitable power structures, resulting in privilege and oppression. As we discussed in Chapter Two, these structures have an impact on the nature of identity, and more specifically as it relates to the RMMDI, how the meaning-making filter operates. Although we did not explicitly integrate power differences into the model, a limitation of the way it is currently portrayed, the interactions among the elements invite such a critique, opening the door for more complex ways of depicting identity. We illustrate some of this necessary flexibility through the narrative of Carmen, another one of the participants in our study (Abes & Jones, 2004). Carmen, a nineteen-year-old biracial (Puerto Rican and White) sophomore, typically defined her identity using external meaning making, even as she started to realize the limitations of doing so. Such tentativeness and conflicting perspectives are consistent with meaning making at a crossroads between internal and external meaning making (Baxter Magolda, 2003). Although it was increasingly frustrating to her, she still allowed relatively unfiltered influences from her family, stereotypes, and social norms to determine relationships among her sexual orientation, gender, religion, and culture. Although Carmen participated in only the first phase of our research, the richness of her story warrants its inclusion as an example of the importance of a more flexible MMDI and RMMDI.

Carmen, for whom identifying with Christianity was important, explained that she did not allow her family's insistence that she would go to hell for being gay influence her attitude about her sexual orientation. Carmen found it hypocritical to use religion, which teaches the importance of loving everybody, as a basis for disapproving of gay people. Still, she was not certain she would ever practice her religion because of the

---

[2]Much of Carmen's story is drawn from Abes & Jones, 2004.

opinions of other Christian people who did not believe her lifestyle was normal. Although she did not believe that dating a woman would necessarily preclude being religious, she explained that she was more likely to go to church if the woman portrayed herself in a feminine manner, both in and out of church. Carmen expressed frustration with these external expectations that did not coincide with her evolving internal beliefs, yet she still relied on them, allowing them to contribute to her perceptions of the relationships among her gender, sexual orientation, and religion. Likewise, Carmen's perceptions of the relationship between her ethnicity and sexual orientation wavered, revealing inner conflict between wanting to be her own person and resigning herself to the expectations of others. Some of Carmen's closest relatives disapproved of her sexual orientation, based in part, she believed, on traditional Puerto Rican values about the roles of men and women. Although Carmen questioned their opinions' merit, she nevertheless resigned herself to believing that her sexual orientation and culture, both of which were important to her, were unlikely to be integrated; further, she attempted to convince herself she was satisfied with that relationship.

As part of her participation in our research (Abes & Jones, 2004), Carmen depicted her identity using the original MMDI. She explained that sexual orientation touched her core sense of self, as it was the aspect of her identity to which she gave the most thought and that most influenced her behavior. Using meaning making at an early crossroads between external and internal meaning making, she explained that it touched her core because she was "abnormal" in society's eyes. Similarly, Carmen explained that her gender was close to her core, but only because of social norms with which she did not agree but from which she did not believe she could escape. She further explained that gender would be one of the least important aspects of her identity if it were not for the influence of social norms that frowned on her preferred way of dressing. Also a result of meaning making at a crossroads, she depicted religion in two different ways. She drew religion as a separate identity ring apart from the others, given the complications involved in understanding how religion fit into her life. She also drew religion in her core because she believed that once she had religion in her life, it would be central to her identity. She believed religion would change in salience more than any other aspect of her identity. This dual role of religion was a product of her new and tentative questioning of external influences and her nascent internal belief that she could define her own relationship with God despite her family's opinion.

FIGURE 5.6 CARMEN AND EARLY CROSSROADS MEANING MAKING

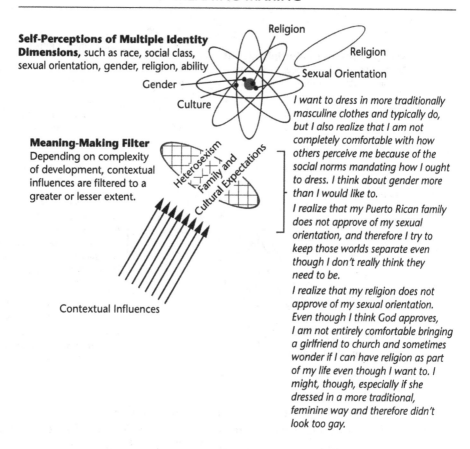

Self-Perceptions of Multiple Identity Dimensions, such as race, social class, sexual orientation, gender, religion, ability

Religion

Religion

Sexual Orientation

Gender

Culture

Meaning-Making Filter Depending on complexity of development, contextual influences are filtered to a greater or lesser extent.

Heterosexism

Family and Cultural Expectations

Contextual Influences

I want to dress in more traditionally masculine clothes and typically do, but I also realize that I am not completely comfortable with how others perceive me because of the social norms mandating how I ought to dress. I think about gender more than I would like to.

I realize that my Puerto Rican family does not approve of my sexual orientation, and therefore I try to keep those worlds separate even though I don't really think they need to be.

I realize that my religion does not approve of my sexual orientation. Even though I think God approves, I am not entirely comfortable bringing a girlfriend to church and sometimes wonder if I can have religion as part of my life even though I want to. I might, though, especially if she dressed in a more traditional, feminine way and therefore didn't look too gay.

Depicted on the RMMDI, Carmen's meaning-making filter would be likely to have varying permeability, allowing some contextual influences to pass through reinterpreted and reshaped by Carmen and others to be defined externally and left relatively unchanged. We portray in Figure 5.6 one possibility for how the RMMDI might represent her identity. We used the model she drew as part of the research and added the meaning-making filter to it. To further illustrate how the RMMDI operates, we also include Figure 5.7 as a point of comparison to portray how Carmen's model might look if her meaning making were further along in the crossroads, closer to internal meaning making.

FIGURE 5.7 CARMEN AND LATER CROSSROADS MEANING MAKING

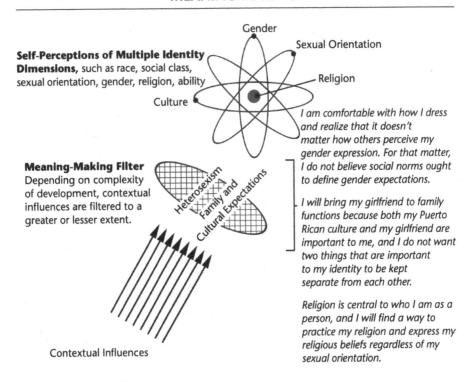

Gender

Sexual Orientation

Self-Perceptions of Multiple Identity Dimensions, such as race, social class, sexual orientation, gender, religion, ability

Religion

Culture

I am comfortable with how I dress and realize that it doesn't matter how others perceive my gender expression. For that matter, I do not believe social norms ought to define gender expectations.

Meaning-Making Filter
Depending on complexity of development, contextual influences are filtered to a greater or lesser extent.

Heterosexism

Family and Cultural Expectations

I will bring my girlfriend to family functions because both my Puerto Rican culture and my girlfriend are important to me, and I do not want two things that are important to my identity to be kept separate from each other.

Religion is central to who I am as a person, and I will find a way to practice my religion and express my religious beliefs regardless of my sexual orientation.

Contextual Influences

Figures 5.6 and 5.7 depict heteronormativity, as well as family and cultural expectations, as the contextual influences that move through Carmen's meaning-making filter. In Figure 5.6, she is making meaning at an early crossroads, and she filters context accordingly through a relatively permeable filter. The result of the way she reshapes context is that her gender and sexual orientation are close to her core; her culture is further removed; and her religion is both in the core and an identity dimension distinct from all of the others, portrayed as separate from the rest of the model.

In Figure 5.7, she is making meaning at a later place in the crossroads. The same contextual influences move through a less permeable filter, and therefore fewer oppressive conditions and challenging expectations directly influence how she perceives her identity. Instead, she understands her identity in a manner that is more consistent with her growing internal voice. Religion is now only at her core, as she desires it to be, and sexual orientation, gender, and culture move further out, not aspects of her identity that she chooses to be central to her sense of self.

A comparison of KT's models and Carmen's models illustrates that there is no one way that context influences the meaning and salience of social identities. Rather, as individuals move closer to self-authorship, they can determine for themselves the meaning and salience of their identities. For KT, more complex meaning making meant that the identities most personally important to her were close to her core and intersecting with each other. For Carmen, complex meaning making meant she did not have to think about certain aspects of her identity that were not as personally important to her, making them further from her core.

The varying ways in which Carmen depicted her religion, the aspect of identity most central to how she saw herself or would have liked to see herself, facilitate a discussion about how the RMMDI addresses a critique of the MMDI's core. As discussed in Chapter Four, the MMDI has been said to portray what appears to be an essentialized core identity that is distinct from a person's social identities (Jones, Kim, & Skendall, 2012). This critique has been launched especially in regard to social identities that lack privilege in dominant-subordinate hierarchies. Although a distinction between social identities and the core emerged in the data from which the MMDI was conceptualized (Jones, 1997), several of the participants in our later study (Abes & Jones, 2004) included social identities, most often sexual orientation, as part of their core. Their reasons for doing so differed, in part dependent on meaning-making capacity. Some participants with complex meaning-making capacity considered sexual orientation to be part of their core because they perceived this identity to be internally defined and fully incorporated into their sense of self rather than as the one identity that defined who they were. In contrast, other participants considered sexual orientation as part of their core because they perceived their core identity to be directly influenced by external factors; these participants resisted the notion that the core could be wholly defined internally. Typically undertaking meaning making at a crossroads between external and internal meaning making, these participants recognized that social norms were catalysts for sexual orientation's being in their core, regardless of whether sexual orientation was something they wanted to be central to their identity. For example, Carmen reluctantly perceived her sexual orientation and gender as being in the core because she realized that external influences (grounded in oppression, although she did not have the language to articulate that concept) caused these aspects of her identity to be central to who she was as a person despite her preference that they not be. Carmen's example demonstrates that placing a social identity within one's core does not always imply positive self-perceptions of that identity. A social identity could be in the core, but still be externally defined, often for reasons associated with inequitable power structures.

Carmen's story also demonstrates that a person's meaning-making capacity might differ as it relates to different social identities. For instance, a person might have a more internalized understanding of his or her gender than of religion, suggesting that perhaps the screen openings in the meaning-making filter are not uniform or that there might be multiple filters within the model. Although the original drawing of the RMMDI did not necessarily allow for these options, these are possibilities to be considered.

In regard to the various reasons why some social identities are more salient than others, with some touching the core, the RMMDI demonstrates how certain contextual influences are more challenging to filter than others, regardless of a person's meaning-making capacity. Specifically, identities shaped by systemic forms of oppression, such as racism and heterosexism, might prove to be more challenging to filter in a complex manner as a result of the deeply rooted and pervasive ways in which privilege and power define the meanings of these identities. No matter how complex a person's meaning-making capacity might be, systemic forms of oppression might still contribute to an identity's being salient to one's core, despite the personal preference for it not to be. This realization speaks to how meaning making alone does not shape identity perceptions; it must be coupled with the specific nature of the context.

Moreover, this flexibility addresses how the nature of meaning making is dependent on identity differences and context. For instance, the external-to-internal meaning-making trajectory represented by the filter might not apply to all students in the same manner, depending on their particular social identities and the contexts in which they are situated. Researchers have explored and continue to investigate variations in development toward self-authorship that depend on a person's identity, for example in studies concerning high-risk college students (Pizzolato, 2005); Latino/a college students (Torres & Hernandez, 2007); lesbian college students (Abes & Kasch, 2007); and students with intersecting marginalized identities (Jones, 2009; Jones et al., 2012). Studies are also exploring non-Western cultures to determine if the external-to-internal meaning-making trajectory and the notion of self-authorship are grounded in Western beliefs (Hofer, 2010). For example, in regard to lesbian identity, KT struggled to internally define her relationship with her mother, whose beliefs were rooted in a system in which heterosexuality was the privileged norm. KT had to overcome not only her role as a deferential daughter but also a system of power deeply engrained in society. As we will examine in depth in Chapter Eight when we discuss queer theory, this demanding burden placed on KT redefined the nature of her development toward self-authorship and thus her meaning-making filter. Because development toward self-authorship is dependent on identity differences, the meaning-making filter as portrayed in the RMMDI needs to be applied with flexibility and caution.

Related to this cautious application of the meaning-making filter, it is important to consider the influence of identity on context. Although the RMMDI portrays context as shaping identity, it does not take into consideration how identity also shapes context. Another possibility for rethinking how the RMMDI might be drawn therefore involves portraying the filter as two-directional rather than one-directional. As currently depicted, context moves through the meaning-making filter prior to interacting with social identities. If the filter were to be portrayed as two-directional, the RMMDI would demonstrate that just as context shapes identity, so, too, does identity shape the nature of the context. For example, with whom a person interacts and the experiences a person encounters depend in some measure on a person's identity. These interactions and experiences contribute to the nature of the context in which the person is situated. Thus, context influences identity, and identity influences context. We believe that a further reconceptualization of the model ought to represent this symbiotic relationship.

Summary

In this chapter we presented the Reconceptualized Model of Multiple Dimensions of Identity. We began with an explanation of the meaning-making filter that we incorporated into the MMDI by reviewing the scholarship of Kegan and Baxter Magolda. We then introduced Elisa's longitudinal study and the RMMDI that emerged from this study's results using the narratives of two study participants. These two narratives illustrate the relationship between meaning making and perceived relationships among social identities, as well

(Continued)

as the flexibility with which the RMMDI ought to be applied, especially in light of systems of inequality.

Although the RMMDI offers an important step forward in understanding identity in that it simultaneously considers multiple social identities and multiple domains of development, examining systems of inequality within contextual influences reveals some of the limitations of how the RMMDI is portrayed. Although the absence of an exploration of systems of inequality is a limitation of the current model, the model invites important questions about identity by prompting an examination of how systemic oppression contributes to the nature of relationships among social identities. For instance, what is the nature of identity? Is it how that person perceives his or her identity in spite of systemic oppression, or through systemic oppression? Is it how others perceive his or her identity? Is it how the individual perceives his or her own identity despite the salience of particular social identities? In what ways does identity shape context, which in turn reshapes identity? We take up these questions, and others, in the remainder of the book through a discussion of the application of critical theoretical perspectives to the RMMDI.

Discussion Questions and Activities

1. Using the model of your identity you drew based on the MMDI in Chapter Four, add a meaning-making filter that portrays how you think you currently make meaning. What are some of the challenges of doing so? In what ways have changes in your meaning making affected your perception of your identity over time?

2. Are there some social identities for which your meaning-making filter is more complex than others? Are there some contextual influences that are more difficult for you to filter than others? If so, why might that be, and how do these differences play out in your life? How might you portray this variability in meaning making in your model?

3. To what extent does the RMMDI help you understand the college students with whom you work in ways you hadn't previously considered? Provide two examples of college students with whom you

work, being sure to protect the anonymity and confidentiality of the students as much as possible, and indicate how the RRMDI helps you understand them in new ways.

4. What do you see as some of the other strengths and limitations of the RMMDI, in addition to the ones discussed in this chapter?

5. Considering possibilities for further understanding the RMMDI, design a research project in which you explore the multiple ways in which the meaning-making filter might operate. For instance, how might you explore the symbiotic relationship between context and meaning making, or between context and identity? Or how might you explore differences in filtering among a person's different social identities?

CRITICAL THEORETICAL FRAMEWORKS AND MULTIPLE IDENTITIES

Interludes

Susan

The origins of my interest in critical theoretical approaches to student development and identity grew out of my doctoral course work. In addition to my course work in student development and women's studies, I also took a course on phenomenology that required a significant amount of writing every week as well as a research project. My project explored the phenomenon of difference. This particular class and writing project took me into the realm of philosophy as I explored the work of Derrida, Levinas, and Heidegger in relation to the concepts of difference, otherness, and authenticity, and the question of "What is it like to be different?" As a child and young adult, I always knew I was different, even before I could put words to this feeling. This project enabled me to explore my own identity negotiations, which really serve as the foundation for all my scholarship, to this day. This project was also a creative one in that I could integrate into my work so many writers who had influenced my thinking and provided me with a "home" in my othered world. Such writers as June Jordan, Audre Lorde, Patricia Hill Collins, and Toni Morrison were introduced to me in my class with Bonnie Thornton Dill, and I quickly connected their work to the constructs of identity, difference, and otherness. Quotations from these writers made their way into my dissertation, including the lines from an opening soliloquy from the play Angels in America *(which had just come out as I wrote my dissertation) about change and the nature of theory. A character described as "unimaginably old and totally blind" (Kushner, 1994, p. 12) exhorted, "Change? Yes, we must change, only show me the Theory . . . Show me the words that will reorder the world, or else keep silent" (p. 14). I loved this quote because it elevated the role of theory in social change, which, by illuminating unheard voices in student development scholarship and focusing on multiple identities rather than putting forth a singular view, is what I hoped to accomplish.*

All of these influences served as a precursor to my interest in intersectionality and other critical theoretical frameworks as a way to add depth to an understanding of identity. I found that if I were going to explore such topics as race, sexual orientation, and multiple identities, particularly through a nonlinear, purely developmental lens, I needed to wade into the world of epistemology and different epistemological frameworks for studying and examining the topic of identity. This led me to critical theory and postmodern perspectives advanced by such scholars as William Tierney and Robert Rhoads, Patti Lather, Michel Foucault, and Susan Talburt. What these scholars and others provided were ways of thinking about issues of difference, identity, privilege, and oppression that were not present in the student development scholarship at the time. They also emphasized, as did the phenomenological approach I learned in my class, the importance of lived experience, both as a starting point to ground research and as a means to elevate the experiences of those often left out of scholarly discourse.

It is probably not entirely coincidental that my work in the area of intersectionality coincided with my return to the University of Maryland as a faculty member and my renewed connection with Dr. Thornton Dill, who was writing extensively in this area. At this time I was giving great consideration to what the next step in my multiple identities research should be. As I've noted earlier, I was humbled by the number of individuals contacting me from all over the world for permission to reproduce the Model of Multiple Dimensions of Identity (MMDI) and knew that there was more to be said on this topic. During an advanced student development theory class, it dawned on me that my students were asking great questions about the model and were extending my thinking in exciting ways. I began to consider ways to engage them in research or a project, beyond a discussion or reading group. I recalled reading an article on an autoethnographic project focused on Latinos/as in doctoral programs (see González & Marin, with Figueroa, Moreno, & Navia, 2002) and went back to reread this article to see if the methodology might be appropriate for a project focused on multiple identities and intersectionality. This was the idea that transformed into what was fondly referred to as "ARG," or the autoethnographic research group, eight individuals (including me) engaged in the study of multiple social identities for over a year, using intersectionality as a framework (this study is discussed in detail in Chapter Six). Reading primary sources in critical race theory, queer theory, and intersectionality, and applying intersectionality in my research, have enabled me to understand identity differently and to ask new kinds of questions. Likewise, studying identity using these frameworks brings out different results and tells a different story—just like my identity story took on a new voice when told using the constructs of difference and otherness rather than sameness and commonality.

Elisa

As discussed in Section Two, my work with the Reconceptualized Model of Multiple Dimensions of Identity (RMMDI) was a result of my gravitation as a graduate student toward ideas associated with the MMDI, self-authorship, and privilege and oppression. When developing the RMMDI, Susan, Marylu McEwen, and I were concerned about its orderly presentation of the relationships among context, meaning making, and identity perceptions. Related to that concern, I also sensed we were missing part of the story by not explicitly considering the role of power structures. Although my own experiences, especially with religion and social class, have drawn me to ideas related to difference, at that time I was considering ideas about the relationship between power structures and meaning making primarily from an intellectual standpoint. Since then I have done more reflection, also from a personal standpoint. For instance, now in my forties, I believe I have fairly complex meaning making. Still, my lesbian identity occasionally is more salient to my sense of self than I would prefer. (I am someone who would prefer that it not be something central to who I am.) To elaborate further, our daughter is now a precocious three-year-old who soon will be asking about our family structure, and I need to be prepared for the ways that it will potentially influence her self-understanding. I gave birth to our second child during the time I was writing this book. I needed to invest in the time and expense of working with an attorney to procure documents that created legal protections in regard to the relationship between my partner and our children. (Our state, Ohio, does not permit second-parent adoptions.) I also know that despite my pure joy in being a mother, I cannot always expect a positive reaction from others, some of whom do not condone my family structure. Thus, despite my relatively complex meaning making, systemic oppression makes it challenging for me to determine for myself the salience of social identities and thus the nature of my identity.

I was initially drawn to queer theory because of how it interrogated the meaning of normal. I am certain that part of my resistance to the notion of a power-defined normal is a result of believing that I am about as "normal" a person as there is as a Jewish woman with a same-sex partner and two children. I typically forget that my beliefs and how my family looks are different from the beliefs and family structures of most others. Perhaps the most significant impetus toward my use of critical theoretical perspectives in general, and specifically queer theory, was my dissatisfaction with the story that a constructivist perspective was telling about the participants in my longitudinal study. This notion of asking who gets to define normal was one I heard from nearly all of the participants in the study, and there was something intuitively compelling to me about the idea of people having the agency to define their own norm. When the meaning-making development of the study participants appeared to be stalled, despite their efforts to work through challenging heteronormative dynamics within their respective families and peers, I questioned the normative assumptions behind student development theory. I reflected on the RMMDI's meaning-making filter, and I questioned what it means to say someone is more developed than another person. More or less developed according to whose norm?

I was very fortunate to then collaborate with Dave Kasch, who at the time was working toward a master's degree at Miami University, undertaking a student development theory project using queer theory. Dave, who was less socialized than I in constructivist scholarship as the primary approach for researching student development, and who also is one of the brightest thinkers about queer ideas I know, was instrumental in pushing me past some of my initial apprehensions. Although our work was challenging, the end product felt right to us in terms of the way we conceptualized the meaning of development, absent some of the normative assumptions against which college students are compared.

Although my work with critical theoretical perspectives began with an interest in queer theory, I don't consider myself a queer theorist. My approach has been to take some of its complex ideas and apply them in an accessible manner. Indeed, there have been times over the past year when I haven't been sure how much more I had to say in this arena. But then, very recently, the importance of continuing with queer ideas, especially how queer tenets can be extended beyond sexuality and gender, has touched me in a deeper way than it ever has. While finishing up the process of writing this book, my nephew was born with Down syndrome. Despite prenatal screenings, the disorder went undetected prior to his birth. The shock of this reality has caused me to grapple again with the meaning of normal. Sometimes I look at his beautiful face and I am saddened by the limitations he will most likely have in his life, how some of our dreams for him, like the dreams I have for my own children, will not be realized—how his life will be different. Then I catch myself. I question—different from whose life? Different from a norm? Whose norm? I remind myself that my nephew will lead a life that is his *normal, not one that is defined by those with different abilities than he has. As with the lesbian students I have studied, the problem does not lie with my nephew, it lies with the ways in which society creates disabling conditions. It is difficult, though, to shift ingrained perceptions of reality, one's own and those of others. It is my nephew's story that is my impetus to continue this work about critical theoretical perspectives on identity and the meaning of normal with renewed vigor.*

◆ ◆ ◆

We were fortunate to have two of our colleagues join us in writing two chapters in this section. Stephen John Quaye brings expertise in critical race theory, and David Kasch, whom we previously mentioned, in queer theory. Here they share their stories of how they came to these theories.

Stephen

I started thinking about my racial identity for the first time as a master's student. I always knew I was Black, but I never contemplated what that meant for me or those around me until studying college student development theories at the graduate level. As I reflected on my emerging sense of what it meant to be a Black man who was situated within a predominantly White context, I thought about what being Black meant to me personally and individually, as well as what it meant to be a member of a larger group of Black people both within my institutional context and in the larger U.S. context. I became increasingly frustrated that student development theories that were grounded in psychology tended to focus mostly on the individual, with some attention to the individual as a member of a group. But I realized that these theories usually did not enable me or my peers to consider the larger systems that had an impact on our individual identity constructions.

As I struggled with making sense of my identity as a Black man, I turned to a Black faculty member in my department to ask questions about Blackness. I completed an independent study with him in which we identified readings to help me grapple with the systemic influence of race on my life. We started with Cornel West's Race Matters, *and then shifted to bell hooks's* Teaching to Transgress, *and Herbert Marcuse's* One-Dimensional Man, *which enabled me to explore critical theory for the first time. As I learned more about critical theory, I became fascinated with how this theory enabled me to critique social structures and provided me with a new language to understand issues of power and privilege. Yet the ideas by Marcuse seemed divorced from racial influences. Although West and hooks discussed race, I never saw language of critical theory in their work; similarly, I noticed that race was largely left out of critical theory analyses.*

During this time, I came upon a reading on critical race theory that combined the critique of systems from critical theory with the racial awareness of West and hooks. I started immersing myself further in critical race theory, which enabled me to reflect on my Black racial identity but also consider the influence of systemic racism on my life. Thus, with critical race theory, I was able to focus on the individual situated within larger systems that are racist and make sense of what that meant for me as well as others. I continue to be interested in how to overlay critical race theory with student development theory to explore the challenges and outcomes of doing so.

David

My work with queer theory and student development began as an unexpected opportunity. During my first semester of graduate school, I approached Elisa about working together on a summer research practicum. I was a student in one of her classes and thought her research on lesbian students covered an important area of higher education that closely aligned with my personal and professional experiences. At that time, I had virtually no academic background in queer theory or lesbian, gay, and bisexual studies—just a wealth of experiences with gay and lesbian students who struggled within normative higher education. Fortunately, Elisa took me on as a research supervisee. To help me prepare for our work together, she suggested a doctoral course on queer theory in the English department. The class would provide me with some academic grounding for our work and would help her engage in some of the newer literature in the field via literature reviews I would write.

My experience that spring was overwhelming on all levels. Even with a liberal arts background and a particular interest in a wide range of philosophy, I had never encountered anything like the complexity and instability of queer theory. I came to class every week having spent countless hours reading with the feeling that I only marginally understood what I had read, at best. My peers, in contrast, seemed to be well versed in the readings and had spirited discussions in which they pulled apart some of the rich nuances of the readings. Complicating my academic experience was my positionality. As a straight White male in a class space that was a safe haven for queer and gay identities, I felt like an interloper. Not only did I not want to interrupt the class with my limited understanding of the material but also I didn't want to threaten the safety of the classroom space with my normative sensibilities. Although I would have described myself as an ally before the class, my time in this class fundamentally changed how I perceive, conceive of, and understand intersections of power and identity. It literally changed how I think about knowledge and the entire world around me.

The nuance and complexity of poststructuralism caught fire in my mind, and I found myself unable to think of student development without also thinking about forms of intersectionality present in that development. Queer theory had begun to answer some of my questions about how to make sense of the messiness of holistic development implied by intersectionality. As the classroom experience gave way to my collaboration with Elisa, she and I worked through what it meant and looked like to apply queer theory to constructivist-developmental data from lesbian college students. Finding a way to place constructivism and queer theory into conversation proved to be a challenging and rewarding task. For me, it was a constant process of digging into the data with the ideas of power, identity, and intersectionality to explore the missing space of existing theory. Our collaboration resulted in a dual analysis of one student from both the constructivist-developmental perspective as well as a queer perspective. That same conversation returns in our current effort to put queer theory into conversation with the RMMDI. In particular, I appreciate the opportunity and potential within the RMMDI to do more to address the developmental contexts in which students find themselves, and against which students generate forms of resistance. Much like other forms of constructivist-developmental theory, the RMMDI provides a rich background from which to explore what we collectively understand as identity and development.

◆ ◆ ◆

Chapters Six, Seven, and Eight introduce the use of critical and poststructural theoretical perspectives in conjunction with the MMDI and RMMDI. A theoretical perspective offers a point of view from a particular framework, including assumptions about different aspects of a phenomenon. The perspective's assumptions lead to particular types of questions about the phenomenon (Jones & Abes, 2011). As previously discussed, the MMDI and RMMDI both grew out of research using a constructivist perspective, which holds that there are multiple realities and knowledge is socially constructed. Although a possible constructivist reality might be one in which power structures, such as racism, heterosexism, and classism, are relevant, the constructivist perspective does not explicitly hold assumptions and raise questions about power dynamics. Indeed, although the RMMDI built on the MMDI by adding in the constructivist meaning-making filter, it did not expand on the nature of the contexts, and the power structures that shape those contexts, in which one's identity is situated. Assumptions and questions about power structures, and the resulting systems of privilege and oppression, are explicitly the focus of critical and poststructural theoretical perspectives, including the three that we include in this section: intersectionality, critical race theory, and queer theory.

As is clear from our interludes, we each bring an interest in how student development theory—and, especially for Susan and Elisa, the

MMDI and RMMDI—can be more representative of the ways in which privilege and oppression mediate the nature of identity development and developmental theory. We have selected these three particular theoretical perspectives for inclusion because we value the contributions they make to an understanding of multiple social identities, recognizing that this is not a comprehensive review of such perspectives and knowing that others might want to consider additional or different perspectives that also interrogate power. To assist in understanding some of the key ideas of intersectionality, critical race theory, and queer theory while reading Chapters Six, Seven, and Eight, we include a chart that describes and compares some of the ideas espoused by each of the theoretical perspectives (see Table 6.0). It offers a brief summary of the manner in which each perspective depicts relationships among social identities and between social identities and context. It also briefly describes some of the strengths and limitations of each perspective.

We begin this exploration in Chapter Six with a discussion of intersectionality as a framework for understanding college student identity. First, we introduce the historical origins of intersectionality, and then discuss in some detail its core tenets, including centering the experiences of people of color, complicating identity, unveiling power in interconnected structures of inequality, and promoting social justice and social change (Dill & Zambrana, 2009a). Next, we present examples of the application of intersectionality as a theoretical foundation for higher education research through the work of scholars who have used intersectionality as a theoretical framework to guide all or parts of their research. Few of these examples from higher education research focus on the application of intersectionality to student development theory. We also explore some of the critiques of an intersectional approach as well as the challenges of application. Finally, we revisit the MMDI through the lens of intersectionality. Although the MMDI's focus on relationships among multiple identities reflects some aspects of intersectionality, it was not designed with an intersectional framework in mind. We first discuss several considerations and possibilities for how the theoretical interventions might be applied to the model. We then conclude the chapter with a redrawn version of the MMDI, the Intersectional Model of Multiple Dimensions of Identity (I-MMDI), grounded in the core tenets of intersectionality. Among the key features of this model are intersecting identities surrounding a core of authenticity, both of which are nestled within intersecting systems of power as context.

We want to point out that in this chapter and subsequent chapters in which we provide different iterations of redrawn models, the starting point

TABLE 6.0 OVERVIEW OF RELATIONSHIPS AMONG THREE THEORETICAL PERSPECTIVES

Theoretical Perspective	Paradigm	Approach to Understanding Relationships Among Social Identities	Nature of the Relationships Between Social Identities and Context	Strengths	Limitations
Intersectionality	Critical	Critically examines how intersecting systems of inequality shape individuals' lived experiences, resulting in intersectional rather than additive social identities	Focus on context (intersecting systems of inequality) as central to identity	Situates identity in lived experience as integral to social change; highlights identity as comprising both privilege and oppression	Without a focus on one particular identity, allows the individual to overlook nonsalient identities (often those associated with privilege) as influencing the nature of lived experience
Critical Race Theory	Critical	Focuses on race and racism as central to identity and intersecting with other social identities	Focus on context (racism) as central to identity	Foregrounds racism through counterstories; facilitates social change	Focuses primarily on race, which overshadows other identities
Queer Theory	Poststructural	Recognizes social identities as fused performatives, constantly changing (fluid) as contexts change, resulting in an identity that is always becoming	Focus on context (heteronormativity) as central to identity; symbiotic relationships between social identities and context	Offers resistance to oppressive social conditions (heteronormativity) through the deconstruction of identity categories	Has difficulty reconciling the deconstruction of identity categories and the fluid nature of identity with lived experience and social change; focuses primarily on gender and sexuality, which overshadow other identities

for each extension is the MMDI. The elements of the RMMDI, including the meaning-making filter, are present in these new versions of the MMDI because the RMMDI was the first extension of the MMDI. We therefore refer to the redrawn models as newer versions of the MMDI rather than of the RMMDI.

In Chapter Seven, we, along with Stephen John Quaye, use critical race theory (CRT) as a framework to examine college student identity when race and racism are placed at the center of analysis. Regarded by some as an intersectional perspective, CRT does consider relationships among social identities, but has as its central focus the realities of race and racism. We begin with a brief overview of CRT and offer examples of how it has been used in the context of higher education, noting again that it has been infrequently applied in the student development theory literature. We then discuss in more detail five tenets of CRT and connect them to college student identity development: the ordinariness of racism, interest convergence, social construction and differential racialization, intersectionality and anti-essentialism, and counterstorytelling (Delgado & Stefancic, 2001). We apply these tenets to the MMDI to explore how CRT reinterprets each of the elements of the model. As in Chapter Six, we first discuss several considerations and possibilities for applying CRT to the model. The chapter then culminates with a redrawn MMDI grounded in a CRT perspective, the Critical Race Theory Model of Multiple Dimensions of Identity (CRT-MMDI). Among the key features of the CRT-MMDI are the depictions of racism as context and race as simultaneously in the core and an identity dimension that varies in salience.

We are aware that our application of intersectionality and CRT to the study of identity is not typical. Rather than addressing identity per se, intersectionality typically refers to "sites of intersections," such as education, policymaking, or politics (Dill & Zambrana, 2009a). Likewise, many critical race theorists perceive the study of identity as not sufficiently activist in nature to bring about meaningful change, unlike its application in such contexts as law and education (Delgado & Stefancic, 2001). Still, we have taken the liberty of applying both of these theoretical perspectives to identity, believing that doing so offers an important new understanding of how one's own identity and the identities of others are shaped by inequitable systems of power.

Unlike scholars of intersectionality and CRT, who are reticent to apply those theories to the study of identity, queer theorists use the tenets of that theory to deconstruct identity, which is what we, along with David Kasch, explore in Chapter Eight. As with intersectionality and CRT, queer theory is critical in nature given its focus on power structures associated with privilege and oppression. Unlike intersectionality and CRT, however, queer theory is a poststructural theory—that is, a theory that challenges the construction and reality of power structures, resulting in a more fluid perspective on identity. Despite the differences between critical and poststructural theories, we often refer to intersectionality, CRT, and queer theory in the collective as critical theories given their emphasis on power structures. We realize that some people might take exception to the critical label for queer theory.

We begin Chapter Eight with a comparison between the poststructural assumptions of queer theory and the assumptions grounding the student development theories that have typically characterized research on lesbian, gay, and bisexual identity development. We then explore how queer theory has been applied in the higher education literature, again noting the scarcity of its application in student development theory. The chapter then provides a more detailed review of some of the tenets of queer theory. We focus on four concepts central to the theory: heteronormativity, performativity, desire, and becoming. Our intention is not to offer a comprehensive review of queer theory, which is complex and nuanced, but instead to review the concepts most relevant to our purpose of reenvisioning the MMDI—and to do so in an accessible manner. With its inclusion of these four tenets, queer theory, like CRT, shares some ideas with intersectionality, but considers relationships among social identities in a much more fluid manner. We conclude the chapter by applying the four tenets to the MMDI, again first considering various possibilities and then culminating in a Queered Model of Multiple Dimensions of Identity (Q-MMDI). The queered MMDI incorporates all of the elements of both the MMDI and RMMDI, but reinterprets them in a queer manner, resulting in a new depiction of the elements and the ways in which they relate to one another. Among the key features of the queered model are the depictions of an ever-changing (becoming) core, nestled within a filter of desire, each of which has intrasecting social identity performatives coiling through it, all within heteronormativity as the larger context.

In preparing all three chapters, we did not lightly embark on the task of creating the redrawn models. In fact, we went back and forth about whether or not it was appropriate to attempt this task. Our hesitation related to two issues. The first is that it is easier to gravitate toward a model, rather than all that goes into the creation of a model. We did not want to create a visual representation that contributed to the oversimplification of complex and dynamic processes. The second, related issue is that it is daunting to try and capture graphically what we know to be a very complex process, and to do that process justice. For example, we know that despite an assumption that students of color progress more quickly in certain domains of development, this is often at some emotional cost to the individual, an identity consideration difficult to portray graphically. However, we leaned toward the other side of this argument and redrew the models because we think the benefits of doing so outweigh our concerns. We are always being asked to redraw the models based on our current research and understandings, so we thought we should make the attempt. Further, the exercise of drawing models provides an excellent means of ensuring the clarity of the concepts and ideas that go into them. We want readers to know that we view these redrawn models as evolving and representing possibilities and new ways to think about identity, rather than as the last word on how to apply critical theoretical frameworks to identity.

It is also important to be clear that whereas the constructivist MMDI and RMMDI are intended to depict the ways in which people perceive their identities, the critical models are intended to be theoretical interpretations of identity, not necessarily showing how people understand their own identities. Individuals are not always explicitly aware of the ways in which power structures affect their identities. The critical models offer a way of conceptualizing identity when these systems of inequality are brought to the forefront. The redrawn models therefore attach meaning to some of the elements of the MMDI in ways that diverge from the original intentions for the MMDI. We understand that it might feel somewhat unsettling to have identity described in a way that does not necessarily describe one's own perception of identity, but we invite the reader to consider the possibilities associated with identity descriptions that make visible these often invisible systems of inequality.

CHAPTER SIX

INTERSECTIONALITY

Noted sociologist and leading scholar on intersectionality Bonnie Thornton Dill wrote that "to a large extent, intersectional work is about identity" (Dill, McLaughlin, & Nieves, 2007, p. 630), and many identity scholars are increasingly drawn toward this theoretical perspective. Intersectionality has become popular in educational contexts and among student development scholars because, on the face of it, intersectionality appears to capture more fully the complexity of who we are as individuals, acknowledges that each of us possesses multiple identities, and addresses the argument that "there *are* multiple dimensions of social life operating in every micromoment" (Luft, 2009, p. 104). However, with its growing presence in the scholarship of higher education and student affairs, and specifically in its application to identity, there has been "some slippage of the term among educational researchers" (Renn, 2010b, p. 7), resulting in distancing from the historical origins and contemporary intentions of intersectionality. As will be discussed further in this chapter, intersectionality is not just about the individual; instead, it "helps us understand the multidimensional ways people experience life—how people see themselves and how they are treated by others" (Dill et al., 2007, p. 630). With an explicit focus on locating individuals within larger structures of privilege and oppression, intersectionality as an analytic framework for understanding identity insists on both a more holistic approach to identity and an examination of "how both formal and informal systems of power are deployed, maintained, and reinforced through axes of race, class, and gender" (Berger & Guidroz, 2009b, p. 1) and other systems of oppression.

In student development theory and research, we have seen growing attention to models of identity that draw on the holistic conceptualizations of some foundational models *and* incorporate underrepresented social identities. However, to connect these models with the structural analysis required by intersectionality is a difficult task. Patricia Hill Collins (2009) aptly characterized the movement toward narratives and away from critical analysis in identity research:

> In recent years, intersectional analyses have far too often turned inward, to the level of personal identity narratives, in part, because intersectionality can be grasped far more easily when constructing one's own autobiography. This stress on identity narratives, especially individual identity narratives, does provide an important contribution to fleshing out our understandings of how people experience and construct identities within intersecting systems of power. Yet this turning inward also reflects the shift within American society away from social structural analyses of social problems. (p. ix)

The goals of using an intersectional approach are the dismantling of structural inequalities and promoting social justice, which may prove daunting when trying to apply this approach to the realities of everyday life. Nonetheless, Dill and Ruth Zambrana (2009a) described intersectionality as "an innovative and emerging field of study that provides a critical analytic lens to interrogate racial, ethnic, class, physical ability, age, sexuality, and gender disparities and to contest existing ways of looking at these structures of inequality" (p. 1).

In this chapter we explore intersectionality as an analytic framework for understanding identity. We introduce the historical origins of intersectionality and the scholarship that serves as the foundation for this approach, and provide a discussion of the core tenets of intersectionality through the presentation of four theoretical interventions (Dill & Zambrana, 2009a). Next, we present examples of the application of intersectionality in higher education by referencing the work of several scholars who have used intersectionality as a theoretical framework for research, in the design of research, or to analyze data. Despite intersectionality's currency in higher education and student affairs, we also explore some of the critiques of an intersectional approach as well as the challenges of application. Finally, we examine the Model of Multiple Dimensions of Identity (MMDI) and the Reconceptualized Model of Multiple Dimensions of Identity (RMMDI) through the lens of intersectionality. Although these two original models reflect certain aspects of intersectionality, they were not designed with an intersectional framework in mind, so in this final section of the chapter we explore how the MMDI might look different if designed as one that reflects the core tenets of intersectionality.

An "Intersectional Approach"

Michele Tracy Berger and Kathleen Guidroz (2009a) introduced their book *The Intersectional Approach: Transforming the Academy Through Race, Class, and Gender* by stating, "Intersectionality of experience in society has been a driving theoretical focus, beginning specifically with women-of-color-theorists trying to create relevant theory about the concept of multiple oppressions" (p. 4). Despite an emphasis in their title on *the* intersectional approach, intersectionality emerged out of a rich and interdisciplinary scholar-activist tradition. However, like other intellectual traditions that capture the attention of scholars, intersectionality should not be understood or applied "as a single analytical category" (McCall, 2005, p. 1771), and thus, although defining intersectionality brings some clarity to its core characteristics, tensions emerge as researchers and practitioners apply the concept.

Historical Origins

Legal scholar Kimberlé Crenshaw is credited with first naming the term *intersectionality*, yet in doing so "she basically named a heterogeneous set of practices that had gone on for some time" (Collins, 2009, p. viii), primarily emanating from women of color scholars who sought to illuminate the complexities of their own lived experiences. In her landmark article "Mapping the Margins: Intersectionality, Identity Politics, and Violence Against Women of Color," Crenshaw (1991) used intersectionality to frame an analysis of violence against women by arguing that the more typical gender-only analysis did little to explain violence against women of color. Instead, the phenomenon of violence against women is more clearly and completely understood when analyzed through a framework of "intersecting patterns of racism and sexism" (p. 1243) that then illuminates how the experiences of women of color are the result of these intersecting patterns. Crenshaw, and those who followed her, emphasized the lived experiences of groups historically marginalized and oppressed, and thus insisted on a structural analysis of social issues rather than a sole focus on individual identities and narratives. As Stephanie Shields (2008) captured, "The theoretical foundation for intersectionality grew from study of the production and reproduction of inequalities, dominance, and oppression" (p. 303).

Much of the groundwork for intersectionality emerged from the fields of ethnic studies and women's studies, particularly from the scholarship of women of color, and is grounded in the lived experiences of women of color (Dill et al., 2007). Dill and Zambrana (2009a) were quick to point out that intersectionality not only grew out of academic boundaries but also is situated in the realm of lived experience and social action so as to broaden the "intellectual appeal and practical applicability of intersectional approaches to questions of identity and social life" (p. 3). The intent of intersectional analysis is therefore not simply theory building or knowledge creation but also undertaking real, on-the-ground practices that result in social change and social justice. An emphasis on intersecting structures of inequality, dominance, and oppression is reflected in the work of other intersectional scholars, even though they did not always adopt the label of intersectionality. In her groundbreaking book *Black Feminist Thought,* sociologist Collins (1991) discussed race, class, and gender as interlocking systems of oppression framed by a "matrix of domination" (p. 225). Her emphasis on interlocking systems reconceptualized additive approaches to understanding race, class, and gender as discrete systems, which emphasized the adding up of one privilege or oppression after another without paying attention to the connections among these. A focus on interlocking systems offers a new framework in which "race, class, and gender constitute axes of oppression that characterize Black women's experiences within a more generalized matrix of domination" (p. 226). Extending Collins's earlier conceptualization of the matrix of domination, Margaret Andersen and Collins (2007b) more recently wrote:

> A matrix of domination sees social structure as having multiple, interlocking levels of domination that stem from the societal configurations of race, class, and gender relations. This structural pattern affects individual consciousness, group interaction, and group access to institutional power and privileges. Within this structural framework, we focus less on comparing race, class, and gender as

separate systems of power than on investigating the structural patterns that join them. (p. 6)

What we see in this framework of intersectionality is the conceptualization of race, class, and gender as systems that reflect privilege and oppression rather than individual identities. This is not to suggest that individual narratives and identities are not important, but that individual identities are products of these larger systems and are situated within them.

Intersectionality and Multiple Identities

Although Dill and colleagues (2007) claim that intersectionality is *about* identity and that a presumption of multiple identities is a starting point, clearly defining the differences between additive approaches and intersectional approaches to identity is more difficult to accomplish, both in theory and in practice. Although the following example is not grounded in the notions of intersecting systems of power, we offer it to illustrate the differences between the additive and intersectional approaches to understanding multiple social identities. This example is drawn from a paper written by Jenny Williams, a master's degree student in one of Elisa's student development theory classes, in response to an assignment asking her to react to several different theories describing social identities. Although Jenny did not intend to write about intersectionality, a theoretical framework with which she was not familiar at the time, her perceptions and illustrations of relationships among social identities creatively represent conceptualizations of additive and intersectional identities.

Her response included a critique of the way in which many theories of identity development do not consider the role of multiple identities. She used three different portrayals of a color palette, with each color representing a particular social identity, to illustrate the different ways of conceptualizing relationships among social identities. Using a traditional painter's color palette, she described an approach whereby multiple identities are perceived as "distinct, separate, and capable of being explored in isolation," requiring an "intricate surgical separation of individuals from themselves" (Williams, 2008, pp. 4, 5).

Jenny critiqued that individualized approach, explaining that "categories of identity aren't discrete pieces that can be popped out, examined, and plugged back in. They're interwoven through the person. Inseparable. In the DNA" (p. 4). To portray relationships among social identities taking what we describe as an additive approach, whereby multiple identities are considered in relation to each other but not as inseparable, Jenny drew a more blended model, explaining,

> There are still some distinct areas of color but they've become gradient. The borders are a little messy, perhaps indicating society's influence on identity categories. In this model, where does blue really begin and end? What do we call the area where blue and green overlap? (Williams, 2008, p. 5)

In her third illustration, a swirl of mixed colors, she illustrated an intersectional approach in which identities are "interrelated and interdependent" (Williams, 2008, p. 5). Referring to the blending of colors, she noted the impossibility of theorizing distinct social identities: "Try theorizing on green. You can't. It's wrapped up in all the other colors" (p. 5).

Although Jenny did not address intersecting systems of power through her illustrations, several other scholars have done so. Lynn Weber, professor of women's and gender studies and psychology, developed a conceptual framework for understanding race, class, gender, and sexuality as interrelated systems of oppression. Weber's framework for analysis (2001, 2010) highlights five themes that characterize these systems as "(1) historically and geographically contextual (2) socially constructed (3) power relationships that operate at (4) macro social-structural and micro social-psychological levels and are (5) simultaneously expressed" (Weber, 2010, p. 90). These themes highlight the importance of analyzing race, class, gender, and sexuality (and other systems of oppression) as situated within and influenced by particular times and places; as gaining meaning through the perceptions, experiences, and realities of specific groups and individuals; as based in a matrix of domination (and subordination) that defines power relationships and can be located in both macro social institutions and micro individual interactions; and as operating simultaneously all the time. As Weber (2010) commented,

> At the societal level, these systems of social hierarchies are connected to each other and are embedded in all social institutions. At the individual level, we each experience our lives based on our location along *all* dimensions, and so we may occupy positions of dominance and subordination at the same time. (p. 92)

This comment gets to the heart of intersectionality, and in these themes we see the core tenets of intersectionality as advanced by scholars Dill and Zambrana (2009a), which will be discussed in the next section.

Before moving to a discussion of the core tenets of intersectionality, it is important to note a central tension in the application of intersectionality to the study and understanding of identity. Shields (2008) made the following point:

> Intersectionality first and foremost reflects the reality of lives. The facts of our lives reveal that there is no single identity category that satisfactorily describes how we respond to our social environment or are responded to by others. It is important to begin with this observation because concern about intersectionality from a theoretical or research perspective has grown directly out of the way in which multiple identities are experienced. (p. 304)

As Shields's comment implies, this attention to multiple identities and lived experience is the starting point for an intersectional analysis. However, despite Dill and others' (2007) claim, noted earlier, that intersectional work is about identity and that intersectional scholars intend intersectionality to more accurately and completely describe the lived experiences of marginalized groups, intersectionality is not *only* about identity. The tension therefore revolves around placing an analytic focus on the individual or on larger structures of inequality. If the analysis remains focused solely on the individual, then it is not truly an intersectional analysis.

Those in higher education and student affairs are drawn to intersectionality because of the clarity it brings to identity narratives when the starting point is "We all have multiple identities." However, this claim becomes reductionist if the analysis does not include connecting individuals to groups; groups to society; and individuals, groups, and society—all in connection to structures of power (B. T. Dill, personal communication, September 11, 2008). We see the focus on both the micro and macro levels of analysis that an intersectional approach requires in the content of Crenshaw's seminal work on domestic violence (1991) (and in her more recent work on the "emergency discourses" that characterize disaster relief efforts [K. Crenshaw, personal communication, April 21, 2011]), as well as in chapters from two major texts addressing intersectionality in higher education, Berger and Guidroz's *The Intersectional Approach: Transforming the Academy Through Race, Class, and Gender* (2009a), and Dill and Zambrana's *Emerging Intersections: Race, Class, and Gender in Theory, Policy, and Practice* (2009b). Rather than simply addressing specific populations or groups, these chapter authors have foregrounded social issues that have a disproportionate impact on particular groups. For example, the Berger and Guidroz (2009a) text includes such chapters as "Black Women and the Development of Intersectional Health Policy in Brazil" (by Kia Lilly Caldwell), "The View from the Country Club: Wealthy Whites and the Matrix of Privilege" (by Jessica Holden Sherwood), and "Repairing a Broken Mirror: Intersectional Approaches to Diverse Women's Perceptions of Beauty and Bodies" (by Elizabeth Cole and Natalie Sabik). Similarly, chapters in Dill and Zambrana's (2009b) edited volume include "The Intersection of Poverty Discourses: Race, Class, Culture, and Gender" (by Debra Henderson and Ann Tickamyer); "Racial, Ethnic, and Gender Disparities in Early School Leaving" (by L. Janelle Dance); and "Racial, Ethnic, and Gender Disparities in Political Participation and Civic Engagement" (by Lorrie Ann Frasure and Linda Faye Williams). One other notable example is the work of Rachel Luft (2008) in her intersectional analysis of the relief efforts in New Orleans after Hurricane Katrina. What these examples underscore is the structural analysis necessitated by an intersectional approach. Structures of power and oppression are entangled with lived experience, so although intersectionality enables us to say something about individual narratives, the analysis must not stop with the individual. As discussed in the next section, the core tenets of intersectionality, expressed through four theoretical interventions, reflect this important cornerstone of an intersectional approach.

Theoretical Interventions of Intersectionality

Dill and Zambrana (2009a) have succinctly conceptualized the core tenets integral to intersectionality, organizing them into what they refer to as four theoretical interventions of intersectionality. The use of the term *theoretical intervention* is significant because it emphasizes the importance of and relationship between theory and practice, or praxis, which implies that theory and knowledge will be put to use in the service of a more socially just society (Torres, Jones, & Renn, 2009). The idea of praxis is derived from the writing of Paulo Freire (1997), who defined praxis as "reflection and action upon the world in order to transform it" (p. 33). This commitment to social transformation is reflected by Dill and Zambrana (2009a):

> Intersectional analysis explores and unpacks relations of domination and subordination, privilege and agency, in the structural arrangements

through which various services, resources, and other social rewards are delivered; in the interpersonal experiences of individuals and groups; in the practices that characterize and sustain bureaucratic hierarchies; and in the ideas, images, symbols and ideologies that shape social consciousness. (p. 5)

The framework of intersectionality links together individual, interpersonal, and structural domains of experience as inextricably related and for the purpose of working toward a more socially just society (Dill & Zambrana, 2009a; Shields, 2008). The framework proposed by Dill and Zambrana integrates analysis, theorizing, advocacy, and pedagogy through four theoretical interventions, which are as follows:

(1) Placing the lived experiences and struggles of people of color and other marginalized groups as a starting point for the development of theory; (2) Exploring the complexities not only of individual identities but also group identity, recognizing that variations within groups are often ignored and essentialized; (3) Unveiling the ways interconnected domains of power organize and structure inequality and oppression; and (4) Promoting social justice and social change by linking research and practice to create a holistic approach to the eradication of disparities and to changing social and higher education institutions. (p. 5)

What follows is a brief presentation of the theoretical interventions, accompanied by examples of the applicability of each intervention to higher education and student affairs contexts.

Centering the Experiences of People of Color

As evident in the historical evolution of intersectional thought, the experiences of marginalized groups are foregrounded in theory and practice, with a specific focus on how race and ethnicity intersect with other categories of identity. This centering of the lived experiences of individuals from marginalized groups produces new knowledge that highlights the voices of those previously excluded (Jones & Wijeyesinghe, 2011). This new knowledge is unique, based on the particular experiences of those not typically represented. As Dill and Zambrana (2009a) described, "It is knowledge based upon and derived from what intersectional scholars have called the 'outsider-within,' 'subaltern,' and 'borderland' voices of society, creating counterhistories and counterstories to those based primarily on the experiences of social elites" (p. 6). These voices and the positionality from which they emerged produce what Collins (1991) referred to as a "unique angle of vision on self, community, and society" (p. 22), such that individuals are seen as experts on their own lived experiences, but also on the norms, requirements, and expectations of the dominant society by virtue of their need to navigate that world, too. By centering the experiences of people of color, the ways in which race and other dimensions of difference pattern their lives, both the opportunities and constraints, become apparent (Dill & Zambrana, 2009a).

Centering the experiences of people of color in higher education and student affairs contexts requires a rethinking of programs, policies, organizational structures, rituals, and routines from the perspective of students from racially marginalized groups. We know from the research on campus climate that students of color often perceive the campus environment and climate very differently than do racial majority students (for example, Chang, 2007; Dey, Ott, Antonaros, Barnhardt, & Holsapple, 2010; Harper & Hurtado, 2007; Solórzano, Ceja, & Yosso, 2000). An intersectional analysis of the retention of African American men, for example, would locate itself in structural inequalities rather than in the deficits and deficiencies of the individual (for example, "He didn't have good preparation for college in high school and, thus, can't succeed"; "His parents didn't go to college, so he does not have any family support"). It would also insist on an examination of how race, class, gender, and other dimensions of identity influence this dynamic. Another example might be found in an analysis of the leadership in student organizations. How might an intersectional analysis explain why students of color are primarily only leaders in identity-based student organizations and are generally absent from leadership in more general organizations, such as student government; lesbian, gay, bisexual, and transgender groups; or recycling-focused communities? Similarly, how might an intersectional approach enhance an understanding of the demographics of those students participating in community service and service-learning opportunities? For example, White women appear to be overrepresented among the participants in community service activities, but when centering the experiences of African American students we see that many are engaged in giving back to their community, but do not "count" this as community service. What would the organizational structures of divisions of student affairs look like if the experiences of students of color were centered? Placing students of color at the center of higher education and student affairs necessitates attention to the implicit goals and values of student affairs as well as to the common practices and strategies used for implementing those values.

Complicating Identity

An intersectional framework complicates identity by focusing on both individual and group identity as "influenced and shaped not simply by a person's race, class, ethnicity, gender, physical ability, sexuality, religion, or nationality—but by a combination of all of those characteristics" (Dill & Zambrana, 2009a, p. 6). This theoretical intervention highlights the complexities of lived experience by emphasizing the tendency to essentialize group identities and the need to understand the considerable intragroup differences that exist, which emanate primarily from shifting historical, political, cultural, and social contexts in which identities are embedded. According to Dill and Zambrana (2009a), "Identity for Latinos, African Americans, Asian, and Native Americans, is complicated by differences in national origin or tribal group, citizenship, class (both within the sending and host countries—for recent migrants), gender as well as race and ethnicity" (p. 7).

This theoretical intervention suggests that those in higher education and students affairs roles should never presume they know all there is to know about an individual's background or group identity, and they should not assume that students who appear to come from similar groups actually do, or that they experience their group identity similarly (Jones & Wijeyesinghe, 2011). For example, a Black woman from Kenya will most likely understand herself quite differently (when considering multiple dimensions of identity) from a Black woman who grew up in the United States, despite the fact that they will both be referred to by others as "African American." Student affairs administrators and faculty members interested in creating inclusive learning environments will need to consider what each student would want them to know about her or him rather than leaving this to assumptions. Student affairs programs that emphasize intercultural engagement and dialogues across difference, such as service-learning opportunities, intergroup dialogues, problem-based projects, and other innovative methods, will help students think more complexly about the lived experiences of individuals (Dill, 2009). Students understand more fully the complicatedness of identity when they have opportunities to develop relationships with individuals unlike them, to work on tasks with a common goal, and to gain knowledge about their own and others' cultural heritage, family background, and life circumstances.

Unveiling Power in Interconnected Structures of Inequality

In addition to centering the experiences of people of color and complicating identity, an intersectional framework attends to power and how power operates in everyday life, shaping privilege and oppression, opportunities and constraints. Dill and Zambrana (2009a) detailed a sophisticated conceptualization of power that

> provides tools for examining the ways that people experience
> inequalities [that] are organized and maintained through four
> interrelated domains:
> 1. The structural domain, which consists of the institutional structures
>   of the society including government, the legal system, housing
>   patterns, economic traditions, and educational structure;
> 2. the disciplinary domain, which consists of the ideas and practices
>   that characterize and sustain bureaucratic hierarchies;
> 3. the hegemonic domain, which consists of images, symbols, ideas, and
>   ideologies that shape social consciousness; and
> 4. the interpersonal domain, which consists of patterns of interaction
>   between individuals and groups. (p. 7)

These domains are interrelated, and different groups experience them differently based on historical, cultural, social, and institutional contexts. When these domains of power are unveiled, the ways in which inequality is perpetuated are exposed. As Dill and Zambrana (2009a) summarized, "Intersectional analyses, as knowledge generated from and about oppressed groups, unveil these domains of power and reveal how oppression is constructed and maintained through multiple aspects of identity simultaneously" (p. 7).

A commitment to unveiling power in higher education and student affairs contexts draws attention to institutional policies, bureaucratic practices, institutional rituals, mascots, and symbols present, as well as to the interpersonal practices reflected in how students, faculty, and student affairs administrators treat one another. Examples from the structural domain of power are seen in the larger societal policies that affect specific groups of individuals, such as racial segregation, affirmative action, federal financial aid policies, and differential distribution of federal resources, all of which ultimately have an impact on the pipeline to higher education.

Examples from the disciplinary domain of power are evident in bureaucratic practices that sustain inequality, such as university financial aid policies, requirements to study abroad, housing policies that require all students to live on campus, and professional service expectations of faculty and staff of color. In the hegemonic domain, power is reflected in cultural representations and images that bolster the policies and practices of the structural and disciplinary domains (Dill & Zambrana, 2009a), and that on university campuses prevail in stereotypes that are both obvious (for example, offensive mascots) and implicit (for example, Asian Americans as the model minority or Latinos/as as illegal immigrants). Both disciplinary and hegemonic power help explain the dynamics of differential access and representation in higher education and educational attainment. Finally, the interpersonal domain of power is the one that gets at the realities of everyday practices, routines, and patterns of engagement, such as "everyday racism." Dill and Zambrana (2009a) suggested that

> such practices are systematic, recurrent and so familiar that they often go unnoticed . . . It is exemplified in the simple acts of referring to White men as "men" and men of color with a racial modifier in news reports; or reports by White women of experiencing feelings of threat or fear when encountering a Black man on the street in the evening. (p. 11)

We see the interpersonal domain of power in action when we scrutinize campus patterns of interaction and intercultural or interracial contact, police reports, and student perceptions of the campus climate.

Promoting Social Justice and Social Change

The transformative potential of an intersectional approach lies in the explicit commitment to eliminating inequality and promoting social justice and social change. As the experiences of people of color are foregrounded, identity complicated, and power unveiled, social justice is promoted. Dill and Zambrana (2009a) argued, "Because intersectional work validates the lives and stories of previously ignored groups of people, it is seen as a tool that can be used to help empower communities and the people in them" (p. 12). They were also explicit that such social change includes changes within higher education and in the relationship of higher education to society. Undertaking this kind of transformation is a daunting task, but it is central to the core of intersectionality; that is, all knowledge generation and action should be inextricably tied and dedicated to the end goal of the creation of more socially just societies.

The implications of this fundamental commitment for higher education and student affairs are significant. *Social justice* is a term that easily rolls off the lips of most in higher education, and particularly those working in student affairs. As Dill (2009) succinctly stated, "Intersectionality is the intellectual core of diversity work" (p. 229), and "diversity" is an espoused goal of most institutions of higher education. However, many gaps between this espoused goal and the realities of everyday life on campuses point to the significant kind of change required to eliminate inequalities and promote social justice. Every domain of power and nearly every organizational entity within higher education may be scrutinized for examples of inequities and differential experiences among groups of individuals. Several areas for examination bolster this point, including the demographic makeup of students, faculty, and staff; the leadership provided—and by whom—for diversity initiatives; and the financial resources devoted to the kinds of activities that promote the goals of social change and equity, such as interdisciplinary research, service-learning, and intergroup dialogue programs. Student affairs educators are frequently perceived as the carriers of this mission to promote social justice; however, the kind of transformation called for in intersectional work requires a full institutional commitment and multiple collaborations. The importance and complexity of this work demands meaningful partnerships between faculty and student affairs educators as well as interdisciplinary collaborations. Faculty can facilitate classroom learning by intentionally integrating discussions of power and privilege, and by using teaching methods that help students make connections between theory and practice and assignments that enable students to think more complexly about the lived experiences of individuals from underrepresented groups (Jones & Wijeyesinghe, 2011).

Transformation that results in social justice also requires the commitment of individuals to work toward this kind of social change. And, of course, individuals make up institutions, communities, families, places of worship, and schools. "What can we do?" is the important question taken up by Allan Johnson (2006), who argued that the silence and inaction among those who know that inequities exist perpetuate structures of privilege and oppression. Johnson went on to offer several suggestions for making a difference in the effort toward social justice: acknowledge that privilege and oppression exist, pay attention to how privilege and oppression operate in *your* life and educate yourself, learn to listen attentively, take risks, and *do something*. Johnson suggested that, in the effort to start somewhere (which will be where you are), making a list of all actions you could actually imagine doing, ranking them from most to least risky, and then getting started with the least risky activity constitute a good strategy.

Applications of Intersectionality in Higher Education Scholarship

As noted earlier in this chapter, the application of intersectionality in higher education and student development scholarship is growing, yet still represents a relatively new and varied approach. A few examples exist of researchers who have used intersectionality as a theoretical framework for research, in the design of a study, or as a framework for analyzing data. Drawing on the core tenets and theoretical interventions advanced by intersectional scholars (for example, Collins, 2007; Dill, 2002), Jones (2009) suggested that central characteristics of intersectional research include

> (a) a primary emphasis and centering on the lived experiences of individuals; (b) an exploration of identity salience as influenced by systems of power and privilege and the interacting nature of such systems; and (c) a larger purpose and goal of contributing to a more socially just society. (p. 289)

Renn (2010b) described intersectionality as an "attractive approach to understanding college student development" (p. 8) because of the potential for a more holistic portrayal of the complexities of identity.

In this section of the chapter, we discuss three examples of the use of intersectionality. The examples presented are not intended to necessarily represent exemplars, but were selected because each draws on the MMDI, the RMMDI, or both, as well as the work leading up to these models.

Constructivist and Intersectional Interpretations of a Lesbian College Student's Multiple Identities (Elisa S. Abes)

Elisa's analysis of a lesbian college student's multiple social identities (Abes, 2012) was groundbreaking for two reasons. First, she provided a compelling example of how different analytic frameworks create different narratives and produce different interpretations and results. Second, she was one of the first to systematically apply an intersectional framework in data analysis. As suggested before, it is not enough to state as a researcher that you are investigating multiple social identities and therefore conducting intersectional work. Rather, the core tenets of intersectionality must be explicitly and responsibly applied; thus, interrogating the structures of inequality and unveiling power constitute a primary purpose of intersectional research, and how this purpose is engaged must be clear to the reader.

In this specific article, Elisa drew on data from her longitudinal study of lesbian college students and focused specifically on one participant, Gia (Abes, 2012). She applied both constructivism and intersectionality to the narrative data generated from interviews with Gia during a three-phase longitudinal study of relationships among lesbian college students' multiple identities. Elisa was particularly interested in the construct of power and how both constructivism and intersectionality address the influence of power structures on the construction of identity. Although, as noted earlier, intersectionality is designed to take into account the experiences of those from marginalized groups, it also explicates the relationship between privileged and oppressed identities in the context of power structures. Gia was a White, working-class, first-generation college student who identified as a lesbian. The constructivist analysis of Gia's narrative pointed to her perceptions of the relationships among multiple social identities based on her evolving meaning-making capacity (the filter in the RMMDI), whereas the intersectional analysis illuminated the relationships among shifts in context; the power structures of heterosexism, classism, and racism; and how identity is experienced (Abes, 2012).

Constructivism is often used in studies of holistic development; however, Elisa's analysis demonstrates how embedded an additive approach to identity is within the constructivist tradition. Although in the constructivist analysis Gia's social class is understood in relation to race and sexuality, the nature of that relationship is still more distinct rather than intertwined, such that new claims about identity can be made, as an intersectional analysis makes possible. Elisa identified three themes that illuminate lesbian identity when this identity is analyzed through the lens of intersectionality: lesbian identity as a product of social class, lesbian identity as a product of relationships among privileged (race) and nonprivileged identities, and lesbian identity as a product of dominant and subordinate norms (Abes, 2012). What an intersectional analysis enabled was an explicit focus on power structures as significant context as well as the relationships among power structures, meaning making, and identity.

As Elisa's analysis using both constructivism and intersectionality suggests, this kind of identity research is complicated. Getting at the depth and complexity of individual narratives, intersecting social identities that may represent privileged and oppressed identities, the influence of meaning-making capacity, and the role of power structures—all while honoring individuals' telling of their stories—is challenging to say the least. As she commented, "Ironic, complex development is necessary to make one's own meaning of interlocking inequitable social structures, while interlocking inequitable social structures make complex development challenging to achieve" (Abes, 2012, p. 204). The autoethnographic study described next represents one attempt to get at these challenges inherent in intersectional approaches to the study of identity.

Considering Multiple Social Identities Using Autoethnographic and Intersectional Approaches (Susan R. Jones, Yoolee Choe Kim, and Kristan Cilente Skendall)

Much as Elisa explored how different theoretical frameworks would shift what we know about identity, Susan and her colleagues investigated how an intersectional approach might shape an understanding of multiple social identities in new ways (Jones, Kim, & Skendall, 2012). Drawing on the core elements of the MMDI and using autoethnography as a methodological approach, Susan and her research team investigated three questions: (1) What is the lived experience of identity construction when multiple identities are considered?, (2) How is identity experienced at the intersections?, and (3) What are the sociocultural contexts and structures of power and privilege that influence and shape identity? Autoethnography "refers to a particular form of writing that seeks to unite ethnographic (looking outward at a world beyond one's own) and autobiographical (gazing inward for a story of one's self)" (Schwandt, 2001, p. 13). To that end, each member of the eight-person research team began the research process by responding to the following prompt: "Thinking about your multiple dimensions of identity (for example, race, ethnicity, sexual orientation, religion/faith, social class), describe who you are as a person" (Jones, 2009, p. 291). The next phase of the study was for each person to read his or her narrative aloud, followed by the third phase, which included over ten focus groups that served the purposes of both data gathering and analysis. Every step in the design of this study—the research questions, theoretical framework, study procedures, and data analysis—included the application of intersectionality.

In the first published article from this study, Susan explored the relationship between self-authorship and intersectionality (Jones, 2009). In particular, Susan was interested in "bringing together intersectionality, which necessarily situates identity within larger structures of power and privilege, with self-authorship and its emphasis on holistic development" (p. 289) in an effort to explore the relative contributions of each to an understanding of multiple identities. The major themes from this analysis highlighted the experience of difference: heightened visibility and seeing invisibility; tensions between privileged and oppressed identities; and the (in)visible influence of social class. An intersectional analysis enabled the research team to tease apart what at first appeared to be an over-arching theme of *negotiating identities* and illuminated what was really a dual process of internal negotiations of identity and a more externally driven process of managing the perceptions of others. The research team found that, even if internally generated, or self-authored, external forces were always present and needed to be managed, thus making it clear that the "powerful influence of changing contexts determined what it meant 'to be true to [our]selves'" (Jones, 2009, p. 301).

In the second published article (Jones et al., 2012), the research team tried to wade more deeply into an intersectional analysis, which resulted in the need to rethink the question of what it meant to be true to ourselves as well as authenticity when multiple and intersecting social identities were considered. The research team had to work hard to explicitly address *intersecting* identities and the sites of the intersections, rather than falling back on the easier analysis of examining identities that intersect, which foregrounds the identities rather than the intersections. This led us to a major theme of "troubling authenticity" and the significant influence of context. As we wrote,

> We wondered: Is authenticity also contextual? If one is constantly
> negotiating identities and managing the perceptions of others, is this
> an authentic way to live? . . . If context shapes identity and identity
> shapes context, what does this mean for authenticity of self? (p. 708)

The research team explored the question of troubling authenticity further by illuminating two central themes: wrestling with self-definition and living out authenticity. We found that authenticity was not a constant, static phenomenon, but rather one that was more fluid and dynamic given shifting contexts, all patterned by larger structures of power. An intersectional analysis elevates the importance of context to identity construction and also redraws the boundaries of social identities that intersect and produce new forms that are mutually constituted and synergistic. In this case, an intersectional analysis required the research team to explore not only the intersections of social identities but also the sites of these intersections (the contexts and settings in which intersecting identities are experienced), particularly where collisions of social identities occurred, and the influence of structures of power on both the intersections and the meaning we made of them (Jones et al., 2012).

Intersectional Model of Multiracial Identity (Charmaine L. Wijeyesinghe)

Charmaine Wijeyesinghe (2012) has developed a new model of multiracial identity using intersectionality as a guiding framework and drawing on the characteristics and assumptions shared between intersectionality and multiracial theory. Although her first model, the Factor Model of Multiracial Identity Development (Wijeyesinghe, 1992, 2001), incorporated multiple factors that influence the choices multiracial people make about their racial identity, her new conceptualization extends the assumptions behind these choices to integrate tenets of intersectionality, portraying multiracial identity in a more fluid and intersecting way. Informed by the MMDI and the RMMDI, Wijeyesinghe's Intersectional Model of Multiracial Identity (IMMI) is drawn as a galaxy "because aspects of galaxies capture many features inherent in the IMMI" (Wijeyesinghe, 2012, p. 100), including their ever-changing nature, the continuing interaction among elements of galaxies and multiple galaxies within a larger galaxy, and the presence of a center or core (see Figure 6.1).

In the IMMI, the center of the galaxy "represents choice and experience of racial identity" (Wijeyesinghe, 2012, p. 100). Similar to the content of the MMDI and the RMMDI, salience of a factor or factors to an individual's choice of multiracial identity is accounted for in the IMMI by proximity to the center of the galaxy. How an individual arranges any combination of these factors (for example, racial ancestry, early experiences and socialization, cultural attachment, physical appearance, social and historical context, political awareness and orientation, other social identities, and spirituality) constitutes his or her "personal galaxy," which is constantly changing and expanding based on new experiences, which then influence choices and decisions about multiracial identity. Wijeyesinghe (2012) also noted that the IMMI "uses the clouded nature of galaxies to represent interaction across factors, their mutual influence on each other, and the 'process in action' of identity" (p. 101).

FIGURE 6.1 THE INTERSECTIONAL MODEL OF MULTIRACIAL IDENTITY

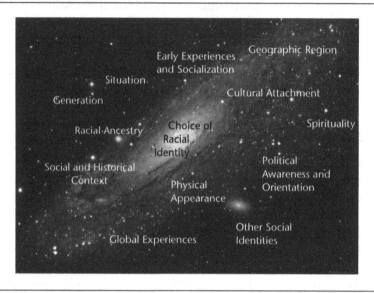

Source: Copyright Charmaine L. Wijeyesinghe, 2011 (published in Wijeyesinghe, 2012, p. 99); background galaxy photo copyright Robert Gendler, 2002. Used with permission.

In commenting about the future of theory development and analysis related to multiracial identity, racial identity, and intersectionality, Wijeye-singhe (2012) noted that "the contribution of the IMMI is less about the inclusion of additional factors that affect choice of identity in Multiracial people, and more about how to advance the discussion of how to represent and interpret Intersectional identity models" (p. 102). Presumably, and ideally as demonstrated thus far, this is because identity models informed by intersectionality offer better ways of capturing the complexity of identity and portraying a full range of factors, contextual influences, social identities, lived experiences, and structures of power that contribute to a holistic interpretation of identity. However, such models are difficult to draw given these complexities.

As noted earlier in the chapter, these three examples are not meant to be exhaustive, but were selected given their connection to the MMDI and RMMDI. We are aware of other examples that shed light on the use of intersectionality in identity-related work. For example, an entire issue of the journal *Sex Roles* from 2008 is devoted to intersectional research and includes such articles as Lisa Bowleg's "When Black + Lesbian + Woman ≠ Black Lesbian Woman: The Methodological Challenges of Qualitative and Quantitative Intersectionality Research," Stephanie Shields's "Gender: An Intersectionality Perspective," and Leah Warner's "A Best Practices Guide to Intersectional Approaches in Psychological Research." Terrell Strayhorn is editing a book titled *Living at the Intersections: Social Identities and Black Collegians* (in press); and Susan Marine (2011) addressed intersectionality and identity development in her book titled *Stonewall's Legacy: Bisexual, Gay, Lesbian, and Transgender Students in Higher Education.* We expect that additional research and scholarship applying intersectionality to the study of identity will continue to emerge.

Critiques and Challenges of Intersectionality

Before we turn to the application of intersectionality to the MMDI, and because of intersectionality's currency in the higher education and student affairs literature, we want to offer a few comments that get at critiques of intersectionality and the challenges of application. Intersectionality holds much promise for coming to an understanding of identity, but a more sophisticated adopter of intersectionality will also want to be aware of some of the potential limitations. We highlight here theoretical, methodological, and practical challenges. A theoretical and practical concern is that intersectionality runs the risk of what Luft (2009) referred to as "flattening difference." She argued, "There can be unintended consequences to the blanket applications of intersectionality. Uniform deployment may inadvertently contribute to flattening the very differences intersectional approaches intend to recognize" (p. 100). Using the example of trying to teach about race and racism to White students and the trouble they often have acknowledging the existence of race and racism, she went on to argue that there may be occasions for a race-only focus. Luft and Ward (2009) offered a compelling critique of intersectionality as a practice, suggesting "the prevalence of superficial engagements with intersectionality" and calling for "keeping intersectionality on our growing edge, a politics of 'not yet,' or just out of reach" (p. 33) to convey that most who claim to be engaged in intersectional work are far from accomplishing its objectives.

From a methodological perspective, intersectional research is very difficult to conduct. Although some research focuses more closely on the micro analysis of individual narratives, this is not true to intersectional tenets, as macro considerations—variables and constructs in research terminology—must also be integrated. Several scholars have written about intersectionality from a methodological perspective, pointing to the challenges (Bowleg, 2008; Jones, 2010; McCall, 2005; L. Warner, 2008). Making a point of particular relevance to identity research, Bowleg (2008) described the importance of considering data within a "macro sociohistorical context of structural inequality that may not be explicitly or directly observable in the data" (p. 320) and the need as a researcher to "make explicit the often implicit experiences of intersectionality, even when participants do not express the connections" (p. 322). This results in what Abes (2012) described as "overlaying a sociohistorical analysis onto the individual's story" (p. 193). Finally, Warner (2008) cautioned researchers to focus on methods and the kinds of questions asked in an intersectional approach. She wrote:

> I want to encourage researchers dedicated to an intersectional approach to pay attention to and be critical not only of the questions they ask and the phenomena they test, but also the questions they do not ask and the phenomena they don't test. Truly, one of the central issues in the study of intersectionality is that of visibility—who is granted attention, who is not, and the consequences of these actions for the study of social issues. (p. 462)

These challenges hardly scratch the surface of those that exist but provide a springboard for thinking through the contributions and limitations of adopting an intersectional framework. More important, they encourage students of intersectionality to be knowledgeable about this framework and practice so that they do not fall into the band of those adopters referred to as superficially engaged, and as using intersectionality because it is "catchy and convenient" (Davis, 2008, p. 75).

Applying Intersectionality to the Model of Multiple Dimensions of Identity

Applying the four theoretical interventions of intersectionality as described by Dill and Zambrana (2009a)—centering the experiences of people of color, complicating identity, unveiling power, and promoting social justice and social change—to the MMDI raises new questions about the model and provides for new insights into the construction of identity. In some ways, in part because both the MMDI and the RMMDI were first drawn with intersecting identities as the underlying premise, points of congruence exist between intersectionality and the MMDI, such as the emphasis on context, the attention to identity salience, and the assumption of multiple social identities. However, the ways in which these components are understood shift with the application of intersectionality to the MMDI, giving rise to the question of how the MMDI would look different if the core tenets of intersectionality were applied. In this section we raise questions about the application of intersectionality to the MMDI and highlight some of the shifts, ending with a redrawn model that more closely represents an intersectional approach (see Figure 6.2 later in this chapter).

Context

Because intersectionality provides for a macro level of analysis, context is a crucial and central element and thus would be elevated in importance in a redrawn model. An intersectional definition of context insists on a structural one, without which the unveiling of power is not possible. The tenets of intersectionality are specific about the nature of context in that it is represented as interlocking systems of inequality or a matrix of domination, as defined by Dill and Zambrana (2009a) and Collins (1991), respectively. An intersectional perspective on context in relation to the MMDI also suggests that context is so omnipresent that there is not a need to make the influence of context explicit; context is always an influence on individual life circumstances, including the construction of identity. This raises the question of how context is related to the core and what role it plays in determining how an individual defines him- or herself, as well as how the individual is perceived by others. An intersectional view would hold that it is impossible to disentangle the individual from the larger context. Bronfenbrenner's ecological model (1979) may be helpful here in its depiction of the individual nested within various systems, ranging from the micro and proximal level of the individual to the more distal contexts of society. This model also suggests that identity development involves an interactive process between the individual and these contexts (Torres et al., 2009).

Identity Salience

The salience of particular social identities is also tied to context. As Dill and Zambrana (2009a) noted, "Individual identity exists within and draws from a web of socially defined statuses some of which may be more salient than others in specific situations or at specific historical moments" (p. 4). An intersectional perspective on salience suggests that salience is also determined by the larger sociohistorical context, and not just by the importance an individual attaches to specific identities. Taking such a perspective results in a focus on the sites of intersections. When structures of privilege and oppression are taken into account, as is called for in an intersectional approach, particular social identities may become salient whether or not the individual was intentional about this. For example, social class may become a particularly salient identity for a first-generation college student from a working-class family who encounters students from upper-class families for the first time when entering college, and thus higher education becomes a site of intersection. In the MMDI, salience is represented by the proximity of a particular social identity to the core. An intersectional analysis raises the question of whether or not salience should also (or only) be drawn in relation to context or the intersecting systems of power, because these influence identity salience. The addition of the filter in the RMMDI begins to make this connection between context and core, but it is more implicit than explicit. The idea that salience is related to context is expressed in the findings of Susan's autoethnographic study discussed earlier, which understood intersectionality as a framework whereby what constituted the core was responsive to sociocultural influences and had an impact on the experience of living authentically (Jones et al., 2012). This suggests that from an intersectional perspective, salience, context, and core are all inextricably linked.

Core

The core may be interpreted using an intersectional framework in at least two ways. First, intersectionality places the experiences of people of color at the center, as the core of any analysis. This perspective places at the core the lived experiences of people of color and their personal narratives or counterstories and raises the level of analysis of the core to a structural one rather than one only focused on individual identities. This application also reinforces a central theme of intersectionality, that a micro analysis of individual narratives is never complete; the redrawn MMDI would therefore be used for purposes of either situating the individual in a larger structural context of relationships to groups and groups to society or analyzing sites of intersections and the ways in which these disproportionately affect certain groups.

The second way in which an intersectional analysis might frame the core is in relation to the interactions among context, social identities, and the core. Susan and her colleagues referred to these interactions as "wrestling with self-definition" (Jones et al., 2012) and discussed the shifting nature of the core as it pertained to living authentically. In particular, results demonstrated a blurring of the boundaries between personal identity (in the core) and social identities that complicated the process of self-definition. Further, because of the central role of context, the interactions among context, social identities, and the core added challenges to the effort of finding an authentic sense of self, ultimately raising questions about the nature of authenticity. However, living authentically was at the core of one's identity, even when living authentically meant managing others' perceptions, negotiating one's internal sense of self, and masking certain elements of one's identity to succeed in certain contexts.

Multiple Identities

An intersectional framework presumes not only the existence of multiple identities but also that they are intersecting in mutually reinforcing ways. In fact, Warner (2008) wrote, "Intersectionality theory leads us to question the very usefulness of considering social identities separately from each other" (pp. 454–455). In addition, Shields (2008) summarized:

> A consistent thread across definitions [of intersectionality] is that social identities which serve as organizing features of social relations mutually constitute, reinforce, and naturalize one another. By *mutually constitute* I mean that one category of identity, such as gender, takes its meaning as a category in relation to another category. By *reinforce* I mean that the formation and maintenance of identity categories is a dynamic process in which the individual herself or himself is actively engaged . . . By *naturalize* I mean that identities in one category come to be seen as self-evident or "basic" through the lens of another category. (p. 302)

This definitional clarity emphasizes the importance of both intersecting social identities and the sites of the intersections, neither of which are represented well in the MMDI or the RMMDI. Both models portray the existence of intersecting social identities but are silent on the nature of these intersections. An intersectional portrayal of multiple intersecting social identities may show certain social identities on top of one another (for example, race and gender), combining into some new identity form. Further, as discussed earlier in this chapter, Weber (2010) identified five themes that characterize social identities operating as "systems of oppression." Again we see the importance of conceptualizing all dimensions of the MMDI, including multiple social identities, from a structural perspective.

Filter

What role does the filter play in an intersectional MMDI? The question of meaning making is not explicitly addressed in intersectionality, although an intersectional perspective may hold potential for explaining why some individuals make meaning of structural systems of inequality more readily than others. As discussed in Chapter Five, the filter was added to the MMDI to incorporate the connection between meaning-making capacity and self-perceived relationships among multiple social identities and to introduce the idea that context is filtered differently based on an individual's meaning-making capacity. This addition reinforces the central theme represented in both the MMDI and the RMMDI that identity is always constructed within contexts.

An intersectional view of the filter illuminates the relationships among context, social identities and their salience, and meaning-making capacity. Rather than (or in addition to) the meaning-making filter's allowing context to pass through it, the larger sociostructural context is shaping the filter based on structures of privilege and oppression. For example, in the earlier section of this chapter on the challenges of intersectionality, we drew on the example provided by Luft (2009) to illustrate the problems that may occur when intersectionality is unquestionably and universally applied. In regard to this example of a White student arguing that racism no longer exists, Luft would suggest that educators must start with teaching about race, racism, and White privilege before moving to an intersectional framework that may be more difficult to grasp without a prior understanding of racism. Although Luft does not use the language of meaning-making capacity, we could extend Luft's argument to this realm by suggesting that structures of privilege and oppression influence meaning-making capacity, making it more difficult for a White student to make sense of race and racism, or leading such a student to conclude that racism is no longer an issue. Similarly, these structures would make the reality of race and racism more apparent for a student of color. More broadly, what we are suggesting is that intersectionality emphasizes how structures of privilege and oppression contribute to differences in the nature of students' meaning-making capacity (the filter) depending on where they are positioned within these structures. It is not simply that privilege or oppression might make someone more or less developed than another, but rather that the nature of the developmental process is itself qualitatively different depending on one's intersecting identities. The nature of these differences depends on the individual. For instance, a context laden with daily assaults on a person's race and sexual orientation in which a gay African American student lives results in a meaning-making process for that student that is qualitatively different from those typically associated with the experiences of heterosexual White students.

Intersectional Model of Multiple Dimensions of Identity

The Intersectional Model of Multiple Dimensions of Identity (I-MMDI) incorporates these ideas about how the elements of the models might shift when an intersectional framework is applied (see Figure 6.2). The I-MMDI

FIGURE 6.2 INTERSECTIONAL MODEL OF MULTIPLE DIMENSIONS OF IDENTITY

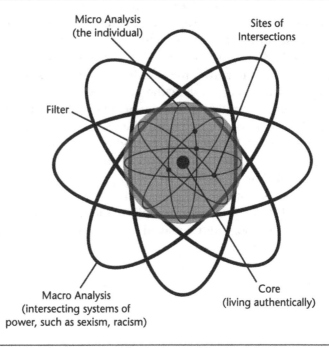

Source: Developed by Susan R. Jones, Elisa S. Abes, and Stephen John Quaye.

illustrates the presence of both micro (individual) and macro (structural) levels of analysis. The micro level of the I-MMDI comprises the original MMDI, with multiple intersecting identities, a core, and varying salience among social identities, and the filter that is part of the RMMDI is also included. The individual is nested within the macro level, which is represented by rings illustrating intersecting systems of power. The salience of various social identities is still represented by dots and their proximity to the core. In the I-MMDI, however, at the micro level, these dots illustrate the salience of intersecting social identities, and at the macro level, dots would represent intersecting structures of power at the sites of the intersections of social identities (for example, school, work, church). The core is defined less as made up of personal characteristics and more as an active process of living authentically as the individual interacts with varying and shifting contexts.

This micro MMDI, which represents the individual, is situated within the macro context of intersecting systems of power, such as racism, sexism, and heterosexism. Situating the individual within power structures illustrates how the micro and macro are inextricably connected. An intersectional lens insists on the central role of this macro context, which is structural in nature. Because intersectionality suggests that these larger structures of power are always present, we have drawn them as intersecting systems without the more defining line of an outside circle that is part of the MMDI. Both systems, the micro and the macro, are dynamic in nature. The filter from the RMMDI is drawn as a layer between the micro and macro systems to show the ways in which meaning making influences experience at both the micro and macro levels of analysis, at the same time that experience influences the nature of the meaning-making process. These three elements, the individual, power structures, and meaning making, are nested within one another. This representation of an intersectional view of the MMDI, by foregrounding a structural analysis that emphasizes systems of oppression, permits the centering of the experiences of students of color, complicates identity, and makes power dynamics explicit, components that taken together hold the potential for promoting a more socially just society.

Summary

In this chapter we introduced intersectionality as a framework for understanding identity that insists on situating individuals within larger structures of inequality. We provided a brief discussion of the historical origins of intersectionality in an effort to keep central the original intent and goals of an intersectional approach. We then presented the four theoretical interventions that characterize intersectional analyses as defined by Dill and Zambrana (2009a), and related these to higher education and student affairs contexts and issues. We also offered several examples of the application of intersectionality in higher education and student affairs scholarship. Finally, we discussed the primary elements of the MMDI (context, salience, the core, multiple identities, and the filter) using an intersectional analysis and offered a newly conceptualized model, the I-MMDI, for which we incorporated the central tenets of intersectionality into the MMDI. Our analysis pointed to the inextricability of these elements as well as the central role of context, defined by intersecting systems of power, in influencing the core, multiple identities, and the meaning-making filter.

Discussion Questions and Activities

1. Write your own autoethnographic narrative (as did the participants in Susan's study), responding to the following prompt: "Thinking about your multiple dimensions of identity, describe who you are as a person" (Jones, 2009, p. 291).
2. Thinking about your own identity, how would you describe it from an additive perspective and from an intersectional perspective? What challenges do you face in trying to apply either an additive or intersectional perspective in describing your identity? In what ways do these approaches describe different ways of understanding yourself and your experiences?
3. In what ways do you understand your privileges and lack of privileges differently depending on whether you are thinking about

(*Continued*)

your social identities individually or from an intersectional perspective?

4. In what ways does an intersectional perspective influence how you think about what it means to live an authentic life or have an authentic identity?

5. What are the "sites of intersections" that are most significant to you? What are the contexts or settings in which intersecting identities are most salient to you?

6. Thinking about your work as a student affairs educator, faculty member, or researcher, how might you use an intersectional perspective to create social change?

7. Consider this case study in light of the core tenets and theoretical interventions of intersectionality:

> Dr. Smith recently accepted a position as the first director of a newly configured multicultural center at a large public university that prides itself on its forward thinking in regard to diversity, equity, and inclusion. For many years, student organizations dedicated to underrepresented student populations (for example, an African American student organization, Caribbean American student organization, Pride [LGBT] Alliance, Latino/a student organization, Asian American student organization, Muslim women student organization, and Black engineers student organization) have provided a vibrant cocurricular experience for their student members as well as safe places on campus. However, these groups operate autonomously and rarely come together for joint programs or coalition building around areas of common interest or concern.
>
> The multicultural center must at a minimum house these organizations under the same roof and in the same space. However, Dr. Smith's vision is for much more than simply an organizational structure, and he begins talking about the idea that each student inhabits multiple identities and therefore might seek affiliation in multiple groups. He wonders aloud if the old structure, in which organizations operate fairly autonomously, still works, and muses about taking down the borders that separate each student organization from one another and creating a structure that allows for greater collaboration and acknowledgment of the complexities of identities. On first learning of Dr. Smith's vision, the staff in each of these areas

grows very nervous that this will be perceived as a step backward and argues against his ideas.

Dr. Smith knows that you have an understanding of the framework of intersectionality, and he asks you for your advice.*

*Susan's work in the area of intersectionality has benefited enormously from her scholarly collaborations with Charmaine Wijeyesinghe, consultant in organizational development, multiracial identity, and social justice education. Both recognized complementarity in their scholarship, Charmaine's in the area of multiracial identity and Susan's in multiple identities, and together they have written and presented in the areas of intersectionality and representations of social identities. This case study was first developed for use at a National Conference on Race & Ethnicity in American Higher Education (NCORE) program that they facilitated together in June 2010.

CHAPTER SEVEN

CRITICAL RACE THEORY

with Stephen John Quaye

The appearance and application of critical race theory (CRT) in the student development literature is growing and provides a useful framework through which to examine college student identity. Critical race theorists, defined by Richard Delgado and Jean Stefancic (2001) as a "collection of activists and scholars interested in studying and transforming the relationship among race, racism, and power" (p. 2), place race at the center of analysis and experience. CRT is most often used in studies exploring the experiences of underrepresented students, such as African American or Latino/a students, and very little is written that connects CRT with identity more broadly defined. An emerging area of critical Whiteness studies (for example, Frankenberg, 1993; Owen, 2007) interrogates the structures of race and racism and their impact on White individuals, but again, this framework is only applied to White students and is rarely used in studies about college students' identity development. Such theories as CRT and critical Whiteness emphasize the omnipresence of race in U.S. society, and thus highlight the impact of race and racism on institutions, environments, and identities. Our focus in this chapter is on the centrality of race and critical race theory. We do want to point out that additional scholarship addresses other frameworks developed to illuminate the differential experiences of race and racism among non-Black people of color, such as LatCrit, TribCrit, and AsianCrit.

As pointed out in Chapter Two, the evolution of theories in student development, and identity development in particular, portrays the movement from more general theories in which race is absent from inclusion (for example, Chickering & Reisser, 1993; Josselson, 1987), to those more focused on specific underrepresented groups in which race, ethnicity, culture, or other marginalized identities are situated as important to be developed (for example, Cross, 1971, 1995; Helms, 1993). Postmodern and poststructural theories (for example, Gergen, 1991; Lather, 2007; Sullivan, 2003) trouble the taken-for-granted nature of identity as well as the presumed developmental nature of identity. Critical race theory draws from these postmodern and poststructural frameworks but centers race as the core category of analysis. This evolution was influenced by societal movements, demographic changes that brought greater diversity to college campuses, and a call for social justice. These more recent theories provided a significant contribution to the literature, addressing identity development processes and experiences of students of color. However, they left unscrutinized students from more privileged social identities and failed to take a holistic view of the multiple identities all students possess. In commenting on this evolution, Vasti Torres, Susan R. Jones, and Kristen Renn (2009) noted:

> The tensions between understanding the whole without erasing its
> distinctive parts and between working with postmodern and
> critical theories in tandem with some of the useful and informative
> structural theories will become central to the study of college student
> identities in the next decade. (p. 590)

Because CRT places race at the center of analysis and assumes that racism is omnipresent, whether recognized by individuals as such or not, understanding the constructs of race and racism is important. A full discussion of these constructs is beyond the scope of this chapter, but we offer here some important definitions and ways of thinking about race and racism as they relate to the understanding of identity. Three concepts are important to our discussion in this chapter: race, racial identity, and racism. *Race* is both biological and socially constructed. However, as Andersen and Collins (2010a) pointed out, the consequence of race results "from its social significance. That is, the meaning and significance of *race* stems from specific social, historical, and political contexts. It is these contexts that make race meaningful, not just whatever physical differences may exist among groups" (p. 69). *Racial identity* refers to perceptions of a shared racial heritage with members of a particular group and the "belief systems that evolve in reaction to perceived differential racial-group membership" (Helms, 1993, p. 4); and according to racial identity theorists, such as Janet Helms, this evolution is developmental in nature. *Racism* is defined as a "system of advantage based upon race" or "racial prejudice when combined with social power—access to social, cultural, and economic resources and decision-making" (Tatum, 1997, p. 7). What is important to this definition of racism, and to an understanding of CRT, is that racism is both psychological and attitudinal (as in racial prejudice), as well as institutional and structural (as in access to power and resources). Given racism as a system of advantage, individuals from dominant racial categories stand to benefit more than do those from nondominant groups and often do not see racism at work. In fact, as Johnson (2006) pointed out, "That's all that's required of most White people for racism to continue—that they not notice, that they do nothing, that they remain silent" (p. 106). As we present CRT in this chapter, it is important to emphasize that CRT explicitly addresses race and racism but does not address racial identity.

By suggesting the usefulness of CRT—a framework that emphasizes the centrality of race—to an understanding of college student identity, we are not advocating for an essentialist view of race. A critique against the use of CRT is that in highlighting the significance of race and pervasiveness of racism, it inadvertently "treats all people of color the same" (Delgado Bernal, 2002, p. 118). However, as Dolores Delgado Bernal pointed out, critical race theorists emphasize multiple sites of oppression, meaning that "one's identity is not based on the social construction of race, but rather is multidimensional and intersects with various experiences" (p. 118). Further theoretical tensions exist within postmodern and poststructural conceptualizations of identity, such as CRT, which are characterized by Patti Lather (2008) as being "between modernist authenticity and poststructural conceptions of identity and subjectivity" (p. 222); that is, between "strategic essentialism" (p. 222) that necessarily foregrounds race and the more fluid, dynamic, ever-changing ambiguity in identity.

In this discussion of CRT we examine college student identity when race is placed at the center of analysis. This chapter will complement other chapters in its attention to the importance of social identities and the role of power and privilege when seeking an understanding of college student identity. In this chapter we focus on the centrality of race by introducing CRT in relation to the literature in higher education and student affairs, and in relation to research on identity. We present and discuss the historical origins and core tenets of CRT as they connect to identity development and the experiences of college students. We will then turn to a discussion of applying CRT to the Model of Multiple Dimensions of Identity (MMDI) to explore how CRT might explain and extend various elements of the model, such as the core, multiple identities, identity salience, contextual influences, and the filter. Finally, we offer ideas about future research, theory, and practice related to CRT and identity, including a conceptual illustration of the MMDI that reflects the tenets of CRT—the Critical Race Theory Model of Multiple Dimensions of Identity (CRT-MMDI).

Critical Race Theory and Higher Education

Much of the current application of CRT in the higher education and student affairs literature is focused on the larger landscape of higher education. Although our focus is on a more micro analysis of college student identity, students are critically affected by and influence the larger contexts in which they live. Put simply, it is impossible to fully understand college student identity without also addressing more macro elements, such as the campus environment, campus climate, campus programs and policies, and student success. The scope and purpose of this chapter on CRT and identity do not enable a full explication of the literature in these areas. However, because of the significant influence of the environment on identity development (Torres et al., 2009), we highlight here several exemplary uses of CRT in the higher education scholarship—specifically, in the areas of campus climate, service-learning, and cultural centers.

Arguably the most prolific and consistent in their application of CRT in educational research, scholars Daniel Solórzano, Miguel Ceja, Gloria Ladson-Billings, Tara Yosso, and Octavio Villalpando tackled such issues as campus racial climate, racial microaggressions, cultural capital, community and a sense of belonging, and educational inequities experienced by Chicano/a, Latino/a, and African American college students. What these scholars highlighted through the framework of CRT were perspectives on campus climate, as told through the narratives and voices of those students experiencing the climate. CRT enables this telling through counterstories that locate the problem of microaggressions, the everyday occurrences of racism and assaults on an individual's sense of self, not within the students themselves but in the climates they encounter. For example, Susan Iverson (2007) provided a critical race analysis of university diversity policies that demonstrated how well-intentioned policies designed to improve campus climate can actually reinscribe exclusionary practices. In an example from the service-learning research, Jennifer Gilbride-Brown (2008) conducted "three reads" of her data, including a critical race theory read. This analysis produced results that suggested that the African American participants in her study perceived service-learning as a "White, do-gooder" phenomenon (p. 118) and that the service-learning site (typically the site of discomfort for White college students) was a safe space in which they were more relaxed and comfortable than on their college campus, where they were racially underrepresented. Finally, Yosso and Corina Benavides Lopez (2010) examined campus cultural centers through a CRT analysis and positioned these centers as sites of resistance that "disrupt the White privilege and entitlement pervasive on historically White university campuses" (p. 84). As discussed later in this chapter, this kind of analysis reflects the core tenets of CRT.

Critical Race Theory and Identity

To introduce the connection between critical race theory and identity, we turn to the question made poignant by psychologist and college president Beverly Daniel Tatum (1997) in the title of her book *"Why Are All the Black Kids Sitting Together in the Cafeteria?" and Other Conversations About Race.* This question highlights CRT as a framework for understanding both identity dynamics as well as campus environments that embrace certain identities more than they do others. The question itself opens up the possibility for a counterstory related to perceived campus segregation and balkanization. For example, who notices that all the Black students are sitting together? Most typically, White students do, because they may notice groups of Black students sitting together in ways that would not be suspect to Black students. Rarely is the corresponding question posed, "Why are all the White students sitting together?" In addition, White students may question the motivation of these groups, or may begin to perceive them as "suspect" as they ponder, "Why *are* all the Black students sitting together?" Oddly enough, as individuals or in pairs, these same Black students are often overlooked. Even when race is seen, it may not be acknowledged, as when a White student tells a Black student that she did not "notice" that the other student was Black because she does not see color. Structures of privilege and oppression, and their integral relationship to one another, are evident in the question raised in the title of Tatum's book. Although Black students' convening is seen by the dominant group as self-segregation and exclusion of individuals from other groups, what is not acknowledged is that Black students, or other students from underrepresented groups, sit together because this offers an opportunity to overcome the isolation and invisibility that characterize much of their college experience. This critical analysis of a specific college context foregrounds race as the most salient identity, which in many settings is how Black college students are treated and perceived by others.

This example also reflects a central paradox in the student development literature. Although the question of "Why are all the Black students sitting together?" (or Latino/a students or Asian students or Indian students) implies the presence of others, these others go unnamed. Similarly, in much of the scholarship on identity development—which either focuses on race specifically and discretely or ignores race altogether—these others again go unnamed. In a chapter titled "Critical Race Perspectives on Theory in Student Affairs," authors Lori Patton, Marylu McEwen, Laura Rendón, and Mary Howard-Hamilton (2007) described the "racelessness" in student development theory. They summarized:

> Unfortunately, except for racial identity development theories and race as one social identity in Jones and McEwen's (2000) and Abes, Jones, and McEwen's (2007) models of multiple identities, little attention has been devoted to incorporating race into the theories most widely used in the profession. (p. 41)

They pointed specifically to three well-used and highly regarded theories in student development that ignore race and racism: those of Arthur Chickering and Linda Reisser (1993); Marcia Baxter Magolda (1992, 2001); and Lawrence Kohlberg (1975). Examples do exist in the student development literature of studies that use these theories as an anchor but with more diverse samples, such as McEwen, Larry Roper, Deborah Bryant, and Miriam Langa's pioneering article (1990) analyzing Chickering and Reisser's vectors with African American students at the center; the research of Torres and Hernandez (2007), Pizzolato (2005), and Abes and Jones (2004) extending the concept of self-authorship for use with Latino/a, high-risk, and lesbian students, respectively, as sample populations; the work of Corinne Maekawa Kodama, McEwen, Christopher Liang, and Sunny Lee (2001, 2002) addressing Asian American students in relation to psychosocial theory; and Vanessa Siddle Walker and John Snarey's examination (2004) of African American perspectives on care and justice. Although these studies extended the theories on which they were based, they were epistemologically grounded in a manner similar to the work of the original theorists. None was approached with a critical lens, which, as we will discuss later in this chapter, shifts an understanding of identity and raises important issues that are otherwise shadowed. Patton and others (2007) have suggested that critical race theory fills this void and offers an important contribution to theories focused on student development and identity.

Critical Race Theory: Historical Origins and Core Tenets

Critical race theory began as a movement in the mid-1970s, primarily in the field of law and legal studies. The goal of this movement was to place race at the center in thinking more broadly about legal cases and to question the very foundation on which the law was based. A central question that guided this movement was: Whose interests are served? By placing the interests of silenced voices at the center (that is, the voices of people of color), observers could examine the law and legal cases differently. In more recent years, scholars in other fields, such as education, have used CRT to critically examine the influence of race and racism within educational systems. For example, in the late 1990s Ladson-Billings (1998) posed the following question in the title of her article: "Just what is critical race theory and what's it doing in a nice field like education?" She illustrated how a critical race analysis would critique some important movements in education, such as multiculturalism, to understand their limitations when race is placed at the center of analysis. She also told a story about sitting in the VIP lounge of a hotel reading a newspaper in her "best (and conservative) 'dress for success' outfit" (p. 8) and being asked by a White man when she would be serving drinks and food at happy hour. These two components, conducting a critical analysis of how race is seen within various settings and using storytelling from people of color, are hallmarks of the CRT movement that endure today. Scholars use CRT to explore how race, racism, and power intersect to create different circumstances for people of color within society broadly and in postsecondary institutions in particular (Delgado & Stefancic, 2001).

In more recent years, CRT has developed several subgroups that endeavor to devote focused attention to particular groups under the larger CRT umbrella. Included in these subgroups are AsianCrit (Asian American CRT), critical race feminism, queer crit, and LatCrit (that is, Latino/a CRT). Although not seen as a subgroup of CRT, critical Whiteness emerged as a lens through which to examine issues of Whiteness, privilege, and power. Scholars using this theory still center race, as do critical race theorists more broadly, but they do so by placing an examination of Whiteness and White people at the center (Frankenberg, 1993). The goal is to focus on how White became constructed as the privileged race and to suggest actions White people can take to problematize Whiteness and challenge the power associated with it. A specific discussion of the emphasis areas of each of these subgroups is beyond the scope of this chapter; instead, we concentrate on the larger CRT to highlight its contributions to a discussion of identity. Given its burgeoning use in education, CRT has emerged as a theory with specific tenets that enable users to examine the centrality of race and racism in the context of education. Although scholars cite different major elements of CRT, in this chapter we rely heavily on those tenets offered by Delgado and Stefancic (2001). In particular, these authors contend that five core tenets form the basis of CRT: the ordinariness of racism, interest convergence, social construction and differential racialization, intersectionality and anti-essentialism, and counterstorytelling. We discuss each of these tenets in isolation for ease of understanding, but where possible we highlight the ways in which they are interconnected.

Ordinariness of Racism

Although members of U.S. society no longer live in an era in which legalized racism is the norm, critical race theorists assert that racism is still an everyday occurrence. The challenge with noticing racism in today's society is that it is not as overt as it once was. Even though one might not usually hear the use of racial epithets, for example, racist practices are still embedded systemically in institutions and organizations. An example of this is seen in many university "diversity plans." Using discourse analysis and a CRT lens to examine diversity plans from twenty land-grant institutions, Iverson (2007) reported how racist norms are embedded within these seemingly positive plans to create more racially equitable campuses. For instance, Iverson pointed out language from the University of Wisconsin in 1999 that indicated closing the "gap in educational achievement, by bringing retention and graduation rates for students of color in line with those of the student body as a whole" (p. 594). One reads this line as a well-intentioned goal—surely it is important for students of color to be retained and ultimately graduate. However, the use of "in line with those of the student body as a whole" places Whiteness at the center by regarding the "student body as a whole" as White, suggesting that people of color need to be "in line" with this White student body. Iverson contended that a CRT analysis challenges this language to reveal how racist practices are ingrained within postsecondary institutions, even within diversity plans that appear to be steps in the right direction. CRT scholars (for example, Delgado & Stefancic, 2001; Delgado Bernal, 2002; Solórzano, Ceja, & Yosso, 2000) have asserted that the ordinariness of racism means color-blind policies are accepted as the norm, whereby the mantra is to treat everybody the same and not focus on differences based on race. This practice, seemingly positive and neutral, actually works to maintain racial hierarchies because people's inability to achieve is seen as a fault that lies within the individual, not within racist practices and norms. CRT encourages people to challenge these color-blind practices and to name the ordinariness of racism in society.

A notable example of this common, everyday notion of racism occurred in November 2008 when Barack Obama was elected president of the United States. He is the son of a White mother from Kansas and a Black father from Kenya; he identifies as African American and is often labeled as the first Black president of the United States. Immediately following his election, media pundits and journalists often talked and wrote articles about living in a postracial society given the election of a person of color to the highest office in the country. Their rationale was a Black man's being president means Americans have crossed the racial divide—and that now all Americans have the same ability to become president, irrespective of their racial background. This belief reinforces the achievement ideology, whereby achievements or the inability to succeed are solely tied to the individual's work ethic and not racist norms and practices engrained in institutional structures. Jay MacLeod (2009) described this achievement ideology within a higher education context:

> The familiar refrain of "behave yourself, study hard, earn good grades, graduate with your class, go on to college, get a good job, and make a lot of money" reinforces the feelings of personal failure and inadequacy that working-class students are likely to bear as a matter of course. By this logic, those who have not made it only have themselves to blame . . . Because it shrouds class, race, and gender barriers to success, the achievement ideology promulgates a lie. (p. 264)

Critical race theorists challenge this achievement ideology to show how race still affects the lives of people of color differently than it does the lives of White people, even in an era in which overt forms of racism are not as prevalent. Because racism is more difficult to detect in today's society, using CRT would enable educators to examine the more subtle forms of racism that exist, often referred to as microaggressions, in an effort to demonstrate how racism is still prevalent. To undertake this examination would require collaboration from both people of color and White people, as the next tenet suggests.

Interest Convergence

Interest convergence is tied to the previously mentioned question, Whose interests are served? Racism is a system that puts White people at an advantage while simultaneously putting people of color at a disadvantage. Even if White people do not see direct advantages based on their membership in the White race, given racism's privileging of some and marginalizing of others according to skin color, the beneficiaries of this system of racism are those who identify or present as White. Critical race theorists assert that it is challenging to eradicate racism because of the benefits it confers on White people. For White people to challenge this system that benefits them, they must see how they are also harmed by it. In other words, their interests must converge with the interests of people of color, who are often more willing to see, name, and challenge racism. Interest convergence, as will be explained further in this subsection, is seen in studies of campus climate in which students of color usually perceive the campus climate as more chilly, unwelcoming, and racist than do their White counterparts (Ancis, Sedlacek, & Mohr, 2000; Cabrera & Nora, 1994). To create more favorable campus climates that benefit all students, White students must see the potential benefits of doing their part to maintain a campus climate that is welcoming to students of color.

One way to make a predominantly White campus feel more welcoming for students of color is by increasing these students' representation. Yet, as Patricia Gurin, Eric Dey, Sylvia Hurtado, and Gerald Gurin (2002) found, the mere presence of more students of color does not automatically make the campus climate more welcoming. The authors argued that there must be structured opportunities for students of color to engage with their White peers across racial differences. Alongside this demonstrated need for structured dialogue opportunities between White students and their peers of color is research that suggests that many businesses want their new employees to be able to work with others who differ from them (Association to Advance Collegiate Schools of Business, 2010). This desire stems, in part, from the presence of U.S.-based businesses in other countries; being able to work across differences will enable college graduates to be successful in the business arena in an increasingly global context.

Given these corresponding demands placed on college students in regard to interacting across racial differences and collaborating with those who differ from them in the workplace, the interests of White people converge with the interests of people of color. White people can succeed in the workplace and benefit financially from knowing how to engage with people of color, and people of color experience a work environment that is more welcoming due to their White colleagues' interest in engaging with them. As H. Richard Milner IV (2008) argued, the "binary perspectives of 'I lose—you win' prevent the convergence of interests" (p. 335). In the preceding example, both people of color and White people gain now and in the future from improving the campus climate through structured dialogues about race. For students of color, they experience a campus climate that is more welcoming, thereby enabling them to pursue their college degree in a healthier environment, and for White people, they gain necessary skills in interacting across racial differences that will be helpful in their future career.

Social Construction and Differential Racialization

Andersen and Collins (2010b) have argued that race only has meaning based on the ways in which members of society construct it. The social construction tenet of CRT asserts that even though there are physical differences between members of different races, race maintains its significance only because members of society socially construct racial categories and meanings. Thus, White is seen as the privileged and better race because people have constructed it as such over time. Whiteness is not inherently imbued with power and privilege; members of the White race have constructed Whiteness in this way. Despite the socially constructed nature of race, critical race theorists also maintain that race still has real implications for people of color. For example, there is a historical legacy of people of color in the United States being treated differently and being discriminated against because of the color of their skin. The film *Race: The Power of an Illusion* (Adelman, 2003) also depicts how people of color were denied opportunities to buy homes; this decision by White people affected the ability of people of color to earn capital over time and created a large wealth gap between White people and people of color. This discrimination due to a socially constructed view of race led to real implications for people of color. Critical race theorists wrestle with the tension between socially constructed races and the real ramifications of constructing race through privileging White people and marginalizing people of color.

An extension of social construction is the concept of differential racialization, meaning that the "dominant society racializes different minority groups at different times, in response to shifting needs such as the labor market" (Delgado & Stefancic, 2001, p. 8). An example of differential racialization lies in that the definition of "White" has changed over time based on when it has been convenient or politically expedient to label some people as "White" and others as "non-White" (Delgado & Stefancic, 2001). According to John Tehranian (2000), who set a historical context by commenting on the 1790s:

> Many individuals of European descent were not readily integrated into mainstream American society. If anything, they found themselves caught on the dark side of the White/Black binary. The Irish, for example, endured heavy prejudice in the United States, and, for years, they were considered the Blacks of Europe. Similarly, Italians, Greeks, and Slavs suffered from low social status, and their racial status was a matter of great controversy that remained unresolved for years.
> (pp. 825–826)

Further on in his article, however, Tehranian (2000) noted that Italians, Spaniards, and Slavs were later granted "White status and naturalization rights" (p. 827) by the U.S. government through a skin color test—a socially constructed and imprecise measure of one's skin tone. The fact that Irish people, for instance, were seen as Black and later as White corroborates the differential racialization tenet of CRT. Even as race is placed at the center of analysis, CRT invites people to challenge the stability of race and to instead see race as having many different interpretations and layers that shift depending on the context and a person's own construction of her or his race.

Intersectionality and Anti-Essentialism

In Chapter Six, in which we discussed intersectionality, we presented the notion that no person has a stable and fixed, unitary identity, but rather that various social identities intersect to form the basis of one's identity. Thus, even though critical race theorists place race at the center of their analysis, they also maintain that it is important to examine how other social identities intersect with race, thereby making identities complex. Intersectionality helps explain why people of color might see strong evidence of racism that occurs every day in society (that is, the ordinariness of racism), whereas some White people might question the significance of race. For example, a White woman who is from a working-class background might have difficulty understanding the ways in which she is privileged because she is White. Her class identity might be so salient that she sees her life through only that lens. Similarly, a Latino man who is from an upper-class background might also believe that he has never experienced racism because of what he has achieved in life based on his class background. Both of these examples portray the complicated nature of race and how other social identities, such as gender and class, intersect to create a multifaceted experience of race among people.

Given the intersecting nature of social identities even when race is placed at the center of analysis, critical race theorists promote an anti-essentialist stance, whereby they advocate against seeing one social identity, such as race, as the only category that defines one's life. As Delgado and Stefancic (2001) noted: "Everyone has potentially conflicting, overlapping identities, loyalties, and allegiances" (p. 9). Maintaining an anti-essentialist stance is tricky because critical race theorists also acknowledge the power when people of color organize and unify based on a shared experience of marginalization due to their race. Yet, even under the "people of color" umbrella, there are various subgroups with unique experiences that are overlooked when they are lumped together. One cannot presume that all people of color share the same experiences and that all White people, because of their shared race, have the same experiences. The various ways in which a person's social identities overlap create a complex interplay of meanings for that person. Critical race theorists encourage people to think about the multifaceted ways in which people experience how race intersects with their other social identities.

Counterstorytelling

The final tenet of CRT, counterstorytelling, relates to the unique experiences of people of color. A counterstory is a challenge to the dominant narrative about racism and people of color. When people of color tell their stories, they counter conventional notions about race and enable White people (and other people of color) to understand race in more nuanced ways. Given the racism experienced by people of color and the ways they are continuously viewed and judged because of their race, they have unique stories to tell about their experiences dealing with racism and living their lives as people of color. Related to the tenet of anti-essentialism, one person's experience of being Black, for example, does not automatically make him or her an expert on racism. Rather, awareness of being a Black person and the daily experiences of being Black are what make this person capable of telling her or his story in a unique way that challenges preconceived notions about Black people.

The story Ladson-Billings (1998) told about being mistaken for a server at a hotel by a White man is an example of a counterstory and reflects the storytelling dimension of CRT. In higher education settings, it is rare to see African American women as faculty members, especially those at the rank of full professor, such as Ladson-Billings. Within hotels, it is more common to see Latina and African American women as servers and cleaners. Thus, seeing an African American woman in her "'dress for success' outfit" (Ladson-Billings, 1998, p. 8) must have been confusing and unconventional for this White man, and his belief that she was a server reflects the reality of how African American women have historically been positioned in society—and his responsibility to know different. Ladson-Billings's counterstory challenges the dominant view of African American women, which often positions them as subordinate to White people. As another example, Shaun Harper's counterstory (2009) of Black men in college challenges conventional thinking about Black men as incarcerated felons and mostly underachievers in the college setting. Finally, Delgado Bernal (2002) shared stories from Chicano/a students to demonstrate the knowledge that these students possess is often not given space within college settings. These three examples represent efforts to challenge the dominant narrative about people of color, and to illustrate how their stories contribute to a newfound understanding of race in society.

Using CRT with Student Identity Development

Having provided a brief overview of the major tenets of CRT, we shift now to an explicit discussion of the benefits of using CRT to think about identity development among college students. Because student development theory has roots in psychology (Torres et al., 2009), it tends to focus on the individual as the unit of analysis. Critical race theory shifts attention away from solely the individual to an examination of how structures and systems influence the individual. Urie Bronfenbrenner's ecological model (1993, 2005) offers a good example here of the benefits of paying attention to the impact on the individual of larger structures. The microsystem is the individual's most proximal system, including, for example, family, friends, and peers. The exosystem is the next-closest system, including parents' work environment, the student's school environment, and the neighborhood or community in which the student is situated. The macrosystem, the most distant system, reflects such areas as culture, social conditions, and historical realities. The macrosystem is the most relevant for CRT as it relates to identity. Critical race theorists assert that the individual is always situated in a larger system in which race and racism are central. If race is always at the center, as critical race theorists argue, then how this macrosystem, of which one element might be racism, influences the individual in turn affects how the individual constructs an understanding of her or his race. People of color cannot construct their identities separate from the realization of how they are treated by White people because of their race. In addition, White people also construct their race in this same racist macrosystem, but because of their racial privilege, they may not recognize how racism influences the construction of their Whiteness. CRT encourages researchers and educators to pay attention to how these larger structures, systems, and environments affect students.

We noted in the previous section the postracial social conditions that some have claimed to exist following the election of Barack Obama as president of the United States. This perception of a postracial society influences how students develop an understanding of their identities. If people of color are engaging in conversations with their White peers about living in a postracial society, this experience will affect how they construct their identities and perceive the importance of race. CRT draws attention to how these larger structures or social conditions affect how one views identity. CRT enables researchers to examine how race is always present in an individual's life, even if the person does not see race. Whether or not the White man in the Ladson-Billings example recognized it, race was present in his assumption that Ladson-Billings was a server. The challenge becomes how to think about identity through a CRT lens while simultaneously allowing room for people to construct their racial identity in a way that might not place race at the center. We explore this point further in the next section.

Critical Race Theory and the Model of Multiple Dimensions of Identity

We turn now to an exploration of the MMDI in relation to the core tenets of CRT. In other words, how might we understand differently the central elements of these models (for example, the core, multiple social identities, identity salience, and contextual influences and filtering) when they are viewed through a CRT lens? What is gained in an understanding of identity when a CRT analysis is applied? How does an application of the core tenets of CRT shift the elements of the MMDI, either incrementally or transformatively, thus resulting in another reconceptualization of the MMDI or a dramatically redrawn model?

Perhaps the first point to be made before examining each of the elements of the model is that CRT scholars may argue against the utility of any model of identity. It may be telling that there are very few studies that focus on identity using CRT as a framework. In fact, Delgado and Stefancic (2001) described a tension related to identity and CRT:

> A great divide separates two broad types of current critical race scholarship. One group (the "real world" school) writes about issues such as globalization, human rights, race and poverty, immigration, and the criminal justice system . . . and they set out either to understand, analyze, criticize, or change conditions that afflict communities of color. Another group of scholars ("discourse analysts") focus on the system of ideas and categories by which our society constructs and understands race and racism. Writers in this camp are apt to emphasize issues, such as identity and intersectionality, that have to do with words and categories. (p. 120)

Although Delgado and Stefancic's (2001) point implies impatience on the part of one group toward the other, the central issue, regardless of approach, is the ability to advance the central tenets of CRT—that is, the ability to expose the pervasiveness of race and racism in U.S. society and to work toward a new social order. In the context of identity, this means that identity may never be considered only at the micro level, but must always be situated within a much larger context that includes history, culture, economics, institutions, legislation, and policy. Although not using the label of CRT, Andersen and Collins (2010b) captured some of the complexity of considering identity at both the micro and macro levels, an underlying theme of CRT:

> Fundamentally, race, class and gender are *intersecting* categories of experience that affect all aspects of human life; thus, they *simultaneously* structure the experiences of all people in this society. At any moment, race, class, or gender may feel more salient or meaningful in a given

person's life, but they are overlapping and cumulative in their effects. (pp. 5–6)

Another more general point when applying CRT to the MMDI is that CRT illuminates the inextricable relationships among all elements of the model. Although the original MMDI was described as a dynamic and fluid model, CRT makes more evident the precise ways in which various elements are so linked that it becomes difficult to understand one element, such as the core, without also understanding another, such as context. We also see in the application of CRT to the MMDI how particular social identities, race in the case of CRT, can constitute multiple elements. That is, race may be simultaneously the core identity, a social identity, and a contextual influence. We now turn to a discussion of each of these elements individually to explore how an application of CRT might shift an understanding of the elements and of identity. A visual representation of this application is found in the redrawn model following our discussion.

Core

The application of CRT to the core would seem to suggest that race should constitute most of the core because of CRT's premise of the centrality of race. However, CRT complicates the MMDI's conception of the core as an individual's personal identity, or "inner self" that is less susceptible to outside influences, because race may be part of one's personal, core identity as well as a social identity. As core to one's identity, race is seen as something that is central to a person's sense of self. When a person is asked to describe him- or herself, therefore, this person might respond, "I am a Black person," highlighting the centrality of race. Implied in this answer are historical notions about being Black in the United States and a sense of attachment to other people who identify similarly. As an individual's personal identity, race would be considered as central to how that person sees him- or herself. To think of most of the core as a social identity would mean considering all of the sociohistorical notions of what it means to be a member of a racial group. Thus, race is not just something that each person makes meaning of differently depending on particular experiences. Race is also tied to sociocultural and systemic influences that have been socially constructed by many people and have group meanings as well. Consequently, the addition of CRT to the understanding of the MMDI means a person constructs her or his own unique understanding of what it means to be a racial being while simultaneously considering the larger implications of being a member of a racial group that has a history.

Although the original research (Jones & McEwen, 2000) and resulting conceptualization of the core (Abes et al., 2007) described the core as comprising personal characteristics, internally claimed and protected from external view and scrutiny, CRT positions the core as more dynamic and as also composed of those dimensions of the self that are externally defined. The intent in the original MMDI was not to portray the core as fixed but more to suggest that what constituted the core was important and central to the individual's self-definition, as claimed by the individual. The application of CRT to the core raises questions about the centrality of race, whether or not the individual claims race as core. It also makes way for additional social identities to occupy the core, such as religion or culture, implying intersecting elements at the core. As we move to our discussion of multiple social identities, it bears mention that CRT also suggests the possibility of race as both a social identity and part of the core. In addition, this conceptualization shows race as a social identity intersecting with the core, but not necessarily in close proximity to the core. If race is at the core, then social identities would always be understood in relation to race, emphasizing the CRT tenet of the omnipresence of race. What an application of CRT does to the conception of a core sense of self is elevate race as an absolute cornerstone of identity. Race is represented in the redrawn MMDI as a social identity passing through the core; it is at the core whether or not this is how an individual sees him- or herself and how others might perceive the individual. As posited as a central tenet of CRT, race and racism are so "ordinary" that an individual may not experience or recognize them.

Multiple Social Identities

CRT also presumes the importance of multiple identities. With the MMDI, the person chooses the aspect or aspects of her or his identity that are at the core. However, as noted previously, CRT places race at the center. Balance is therefore needed in placing race at the center while also considering how other social identities intersect with race. In other words, an application of CRT to the MMDI would suggest that multiple social identities may intersect with race at the core and with one another. As Ruthellen Josselson (1987), Helms (1993), and other identity scholars have asserted, how people identify is always a reflection of how others see them. Therefore, CRT asks individuals to negotiate the centrality of their race and the intersection of their other social identities and to manage perceptions from others. For example, even if race is placed at the core, how other multiple social identities intersect with race will complicate the person's experience of her or his race.

The MMDI and RMMDI highlight the reality that all individuals possess multiple social identities, whether they are cognizant of these or not, and draw attention to the intersecting and relational nature of social identities, again, whether these are experienced in this way or not. Social identities may be experienced simultaneously (for example, race and gender) and as more or less salient in relation to others. As with the core, a CRT analysis complicates the dynamic interplay of social identities because, according to CRT, race would always be salient and racism would always exist as a contextual influence affecting these intersecting social identities and identity salience. How a person experiences race and racism, however, would be dependent on how race intersects with the person's other social identities. Thus, even though CRT asserts that race is always at the center, the person's experience and understanding of race will shift depending on the other social identities she or he recognizes. A discussion of identity salience helps explain this point further.

Identity Salience

Because of the primacy of race, a CRT analysis would suggest that race is always salient and thus should be represented on the redrawn model as closest to the core. However, a tension exists when people do not see race as salient to their lives. How does one reconcile these differing views? For instance, there is a tension between oppressed and privileged identities in that it is more difficult for people to see identities that are privileged. Also, when a person has other social identities that are marginalized, she or he might not see how race is central given the dominance of these other identities. Identity salience thus complicates CRT. As previously discussed, race, understood as socially constructed, has been experienced and constructed differently at various points in history. As noted earlier, Delgado and Stefancic (2001) referred to this phenomenon as differential racialization. If a person does not see race as salient but critical race theorists assert that race is always central, who is right in this case? The answer to this question is that both parties are right, hence the messiness of a CRT analysis in conjunction with the MMDI. CRT allows both positions to exist in the same space. How people experience the salience of their multiple identities and the presumed centrality of race are both important considerations in this case.

We wrote earlier about the experience of a Latino man who comes from an upper-class background. Even if this person might not see the salience of race or might believe he has not been discriminated against because of his race, race is still salient for him, in part because of how others see him. For people of color, race tends to be what others notice first about them. Thus, this noticing of race places race as the most salient aspect of this person's identity, even if the person does not experience it as such. Adding CRT to a discussion of the MMDI does not mean that how a person experiences her or his identity is meaningless; rather, it means race is always present given the historical significance of race in society, and therefore always influences how individuals are perceived by others. However, the redrawn MMDI provides for the possibility that an individual may identify race as a social identity as less salient and consequently further from the core, even though race, according to CRT, is much of the core. An exploration of the role of contextual influences and the filtering process, elements of the MMDI, help explore this potential ambiguity.

Contextual Influences and Filtering

Context is important in the MMDI and the RMMDI because it influences how people experience their multiple identities. A central contextual influence when applying CRT to the MMDI would be the presence of racism. Related to Delgado and Stefancic's point (2001) about differential racialization is that the contextual influence of racism is experienced differently in different historical times. In a "postracial" contemporary context of racism, for example, a person might experience racism differently than he or she would have in an era in which overt racism was more common. In either case, racism is still present, omnipresent according to CRT, and must be negotiated in relation to how one experiences her or his identities.

We situate our discussion of contextual influences and filtering together in relation to CRT because the two seem integrally related, just as context and the filter are integrally related in the Intersectional Model of Multiple Dimensions of Identity (I-MMDI). More so than with intersectionality, the centrality of race deepens the relationship between contextual influences and filtering. This symbiotic relationship between context and the meaning-making filter is reflected in the redrawn model. That is, the

omnipresence of racism requires the individual to make meaning of this
significant contextual influence at the same time that racism mediates
the ways in which the person makes meaning. As with our discussion in
Chapter Six of how a student of color might be more developmentally
prepared than a White student to recognize the nature of racism, CRT
suggests the necessity of a student of color's continuously making meaning
of racist contexts. The ability of a person to do so depends in part on
developmental capacity. For example, Torres (2009) used the framework
of self-authorship to analyze how Latino/a students made meaning of
racist thoughts, concluding:

> The cognitive dimension seemed to serve as the entry experience for
> both the privileged and the oppressed to recognize how racism
> influenced their lives and other dimensions in their own development.
> In essence, the cognitive dimension allowed them to have a different
> interpretation of the racist ideas, which then created a critical
> developmental tool for challenging these negative beliefs (racism).
> (p. 518)

As one of the first scholars in higher education and student affairs to
address dealing with racism as an explicit developmental task, Torres has
provided evidence of the importance of the developmental nature of
identity construction, a process not included in CRT.

At the same time, an application of CRT to the MMDI raises questions about a developmental trajectory from following external formulas
to establishing internal foundations in a meaning-making process.
Again, similar to our discussion of intersectionality, the omnipresence of
racism results in a developmental process that is qualitatively different
for a student of color than for a White student. For instance, to say a
person of color wrestling with racism has a sense of identity that is less
developed than that of a White student confident in her or his sense of
self overlooks the realities of racism and inappropriately assumes sameness in the nature of development across races. Likewise, the process a
student of color is likely to undergo in achieving a complex sense of self
in the face of racism requires a different developmental process from
that experienced by White students. And those differences also depend
on the specific nature of the context, with certain contexts being more
prone to microaggressions than others. Not only is coping with racism
an additional developmental task as suggested by Torres (2009) but also
it is a task so different from those required of others not steeped in

oppression that it results in a departure from an external-to-internal process of development.

Critical Race Theory Model of Multiple Dimensions of Identity

Figure 7.1 presents a redrawn MMDI that reflects an application of the core tenets of critical race theory—the Critical Race Theory Model of Multiple Dimensions of Identity. As noted throughout this chapter and more specifically highlighted in the preceding discussion of the elements of the MMDI when CRT is considered, the CRT-MMDI highlights the centrality of race. Incorporating the omnipresence of race and racism shifts the meaning of particular elements of the MMDI and their relationship to one another. As with the I-MMDI, the original elements of the

FIGURE 7.1 CRITICAL RACE THEORY MODEL OF MULTIPLE DIMENSIONS OF IDENTITY

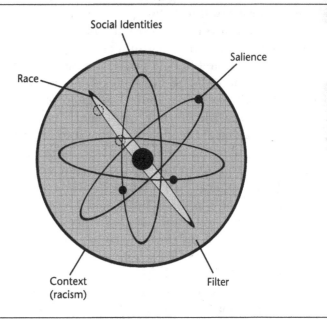

Source: Developed by Susan R. Jones, Elisa S. Abes, and Stephen John Quaye.

MMDI and RMMDI are still recognizable in the CRT-MMDI, but their configurations are reshaped because each must be understood in relation to the centrality of race. Thus, in the CRT-MMDI we see race as core, central to one's sense of self, yet interacting with the other elements of the model, including race as a social identity, other social identities, context, and the filter. The application of CRT to the MMDI does not preclude the core's incorporating personal characteristics and qualities as consistent with the original MMDI, but it does suggest that at the same time, the core will necessarily include race. One of the more important contributions of CRT, and one of the consequences of incorporating it into the MMDI, is that race is always present and central, yet the individual may not always perceive it as such, and this, too, may shift depending on the context in which the individual is situated. In the CRT-MMDI, this is represented by race as a social identity orbit passing through the core, and by the presence of two salience dots on the race orbit. The dots are drawn with broken lines to suggest the dynamic nature of salience, and two dots are shown to reflect that race, as a socially constructed and historically constituted social identity, may be more or less salient to the individual at any given time. Despite the changing salience of race as a social identity, given the tenets of CRT, it will always pass through the core.

Context and filtering in the CRT-MMDI are drawn to both reflect the symbiotic relationship between the two and to position the individual as nested within context. Given the ordinariness of racism as posited by CRT, racism as a contextual influence is always present. This rendering of context and the filter eliminates the directionality implied in both the MMDI and the RMMDI, in which context influences the individual and context is filtered by the individual based on meaning-making capacity. In the CRT-MMDI, the filter represents the developmental process of meaning making at the same time that it troubles the external-to-internal pathways by allowing openness and flexibility in regard to the nature of meaning making when race and racism are central.

What an application of CRT to the MMDI most notably and poignantly illustrates is the intersectionality and blurred boundaries of the core, social identities, and contextual influences, as well as the role of the filter in making sense of the everyday nature of racism. When something is so pervasive as racism, as CRT scholars argue, the meaning of the core, social identities, and filtering shifts, resulting in a counterstory about identity. Racism as a contextual influence is also elevated in importance, even if race as a personal identity or social identity is not perceived as significant by the individual. CRT also emphasizes the influence of the sociohistorical context and the socially constructed nature of race, and draws attention to how the meaning of race shifts across different moments in time. Critical race theory insists on the scrutiny of race and racism and thus disrupts normative assumptions about identity.

Summary

In this chapter we used critical race theory as a framework to examine college student identity when race and racism are placed at the center of analysis. We began with a brief overview of CRT and offered examples of how it has been used in the context of higher education. We then discussed in more detail five tenets of CRT and connected them to college student identity development. We applied these five tenets to the MMDI to explore how CRT reinterprets each of the elements of the model. In doing so, we first discussed several considerations and possibilities for applying CRT. We then redrew the MMDI to create a model grounded in a CRT perspective, the CRT-MMDI. Among the key features of the CRT-MMDI are the depictions of racism as a contextual influence and race as simultaneously core and a social identity that varies in personal salience.

Discussion Questions and Activities

1. How central is race in your life? Reflect on and discuss how race operates in your life as core, as a social identity, as a contextual influence, or a combination of these.
2. In what ways does your current understanding of your racial identity reflect the influence of context in your answer to the first question?
3. What is your response to "Why are all the Black kids sitting together in the cafeteria?" How do you explain this phenomenon? What tenets of CRT help explain it?

(Continued)

4. Do you believe we are living in a postracial society? If so, how do you merge your belief with CRT's assertion of the ordinariness of racism? What does this postracial thinking mean for how you construct your identity?

5. Are there counterstories about how you experience your racial identity that you believe need to be heard?

6. Interest convergence suggests that White people will work toward racial justice only if it is in their own best interest. How does this idea relate to White people's thinking about their own racial identity and Whiteness? In what ways is CRT relevant to an understanding of the identities of White people?

7. In considering the question "Who am I?" how does CRT help you think about who you are? What's missing from CRT when you are using it to think about who you are?

8. Design a study addressing some aspect of the college student experience using CRT as a framework. How would CRT influence each element of your research design?

CHAPTER EIGHT

QUEER THEORY

with David Kasch

Just as intersectionality (described in Chapter Six) and critical race theory (described in Chapter Seven) offer ways to reenvision the Model of Multiple Dimensions of Identity (MMDI) by situating the model more explicitly within societal power structures, so, too, does queer theory. Queer theory specifically addresses societal power structures associated with sexuality and gender and their relationships with other forms of identity. Contrary to common misunderstandings, queer theory does not refer to a particular identity, that is, a *queer* identity; instead, queer theory "critically analyzes the meaning of identity, focusing on intersections of identities and resisting oppressive social constructions of sexual orientation and gender" (Abes & Kasch, 2007, p. 620). Similar to intersectionality and critical race theory, queer theory considers identity to be a social construction and critiques the power structures in the social environment that construct identity. But more so than intersectionality and critical race theory, queer theory challenges the meaning of identity itself, considering identity to be an unstable, fluid notion that is a product of continuous resistance to oppressive social constructions (Butler, 1990).

Introducing queer theory's perspective on identity to the realm of college student development has the potential to significantly alter how college student identity, in particular gender and sexuality, is conceptualized. Rather than incorporating a queer perspective, most college student identity development theories that focus on lesbian, gay, bisexual, and transgender identity typically draw from a developmental stage perspective and, to a lesser extent, a social constructionist life span perspective (Renn, 2010a). This is consistent with the description in Chapter Two of the disciplines on which student development theory has typically been grounded, namely developmental psychology and sociology.

From a developmental perspective, sexual orientation identity, often categorized as gay, lesbian, or bisexual identity in the student development literature, is typically described as evolving along a somewhat linear trajectory through a series of stages. The trajectory describes a process of early recognition of one's sexual orientation and moves toward the integration of sexual orientation into one's sense of self (Renn & Bilodeau, 2005). Assumptions grounding this developmental path include that the self is central to development and that a stable social environment and a stable understanding of what it means to be gay or to be a lesbian exist. These assumptions describe an essentialist perspective on identity—that is, one in which there is a fixed set of characteristics ascribed to the identity, offering limited possibilities for the nature of sexual orientation identity development (M. Warner, 1991). Among the frequently applied examples of developmental theories include that of Cass (1979, 1996), which describes gay and lesbian identity, and that of McCarn and Fassinger (1996), which describes lesbian identity. Although some of these stage theories acknowledge that identity development is influenced in some measure by the context in which the person is situated, context takes a backseat to the focus on the individual and the development of an integrated sense of self.

In contrast to the developmental perspective, social constructionist theories of gay and lesbian identity development place at the forefront the role of context in shaping identity. Anthony D'Augelli's life span theory of gay, lesbian, and bisexual identity development (1994) is a frequently used example of a social constructionist theory applied in the context of college students. D'Augelli examined three aspects of context that shape identity development, including personal subjectivities and actions (individuals' perceptions of their sexual identity and behaviors); interactive intimacies (constituting the influence of family, peers, and intimate relationships); and sociohistorical conditions (social norms, values, policies, and laws that are part of individuals' geographical, cultural, and historical location). Because of their attention to the role of the social environment in constructing identity, social constructionist theories do not assume that identity is a fixed entity, but instead that identity changes over one's life as context changes. This assumption is referred to as identity fluidity (D'Augelli). As part of the social constructionist recognition of the role of context in shaping identity, this perspective often acknowledges the inequitable power structures that shape identity, such as racism and heterosexism. It does not, however, necessarily critique these structures.

Queer theory moves beyond only the foregrounding of context and "enables a more contextual, less categorical examination of development that considers the mutual influences of multiple, fluid identity domains (for example, race, social class, ability, religion, nationality)" (Renn, 2010a, p. 135). With its primary emphasis on the power structures that interact with identity, queer theory deconstructs identity categories. It urges, for example, the study of sexuality rather than of gay or lesbian or bisexual or heterosexual identity, and of gender rather than of masculine or feminine identity. It does so on the premise that those categories are grounded in inequitable power structures, especially heterosexism, that privilege some and marginalize others (Britzman, 1997). Rather than categorizing and labeling identity and focusing on identity as sameness, queer theory offers a perspective on identity as difference, highlighting the interaction between changing contexts and changing multiple intersecting identities that renders an individual's identity ever changing (Fuss, 1989). This focus on identity as difference contributes to queer theory's emphasis on identity fluidity. Queer theory has infrequently been applied in the context of student development theory.

The purpose of this chapter is to introduce queer theory to the MMDI, exploring new possibilities for understanding context, meaning making, social identities, and the core, as well as the relationships among these four concepts. To do so, we first provide a brief overview of queer theory, and explore how queer theory has been applied in the higher education and student development literature. We then introduce some of the key tenets of queer theory that we find most relevant to reenvisioning the MMDI, and we apply these tenets to the model. As in the chapters on intersectionality and critical race theory, our analysis culminates with a new portrayal of the MMDI, the Queered Model of Multiple Dimensions of Identity (Q-MMDI).

Philosophical Roots of Queer Theory

Queer theory began to form as an emerging school of thought in the early 1990s to question and challenge the assumption that heterosexuality is normal, natural, and preferred. From the start, queer theory had both political and scholarly purposes (Sullivan, 2003). As an area of scholarly research, it falls under the category that William Tierney and Robert Rhoads (1993) described as critical social science, which provides critiques of knowledge and power as social constructions that serve to create oppressive social conditions.

Drawing from the philosophical roots of poststructuralism, feminism, and Marxism, queer theory has historically offered a broad interdisciplinary base from which to study gender, sexuality, and society. Note that some scholars use the term *sexual orientation* rather than sexuality; however, we favor the term *sexuality* because it encapsulates a wider range of sexual expression and because it does not as readily reinforce the binary of heterosexual and nonheterosexual. The texts of such French poststructural theorists as Michel Foucault (1978, 1980), Jacque Derrida (1967/1978), and Jean-François Lyotard (1984) provide the major foundation for queer theory. Central to their work are the guiding poststructural notions that knowledge and truth are social constructions that reflect the prevailing interests of those who hold the most social power; that knowledge and truth are neither objective nor universal; and that all knowledge and truth reflect the specific cultural and historical contexts in which they were developed (Sullivan, 2003).

Applying these ideas to gender and sexuality, feminist scholars Judith Butler (1990) and Eve Sedgwick (1990) argued that identities are social constructions that reflect the time, place, and culture in which they exist for the individuals who enact them. This viewpoint differs from the essentialist notion of reality in that identities are not able to have a constant and fixed meaning because they are under continuous construction and change with each new and individual expression of them. Furthermore, Butler and Sedgwick maintained that only forms of identity expression that conform to norms of heterosexuality are seen as socially acceptable. The major purpose of their work was to challenge this socially constrained understanding of gender and sexuality and argue that identities have the capacity to be flexible and change with each new and individual expression of them. This loosening of definitions of identity laid important conceptual groundwork for queer theory. It offers an interpretation of identity as fluid and dependent on the individual, provides a way of challenging rigid social norms, and creates broader social inclusion of people who do not identify with heterosexuality.

Queer Theory, Higher Education, and Student Identity

Kristen Renn (2010a) pointed out that queer theory has been quite slow to emerge in higher education research, and especially so in research on college student identity. In the context of higher education, there are few published pieces that employ queer theory. Of those that are published, several focus on faculty, curriculum, and pedagogy. Tierney and Susan Talburt, both of whom used queer theory to study identity, have written some of the most influential work. In one of the earliest examples of published scholarship in the discipline of higher education that incorporates queer theory, Tierney (1997) called for cultural change in the academy through the infusion of queer theory, focusing especially on faculty identity. Talburt (2000) employed queer theory in an ethnographic study of lesbian faculty members. In doing so, she wrestled with the contradictions inherent in studying faculty identity when identity is deconstructed and presumed to be fluid. Focusing on curricular issues, Sean O'Connell (2004) suggested the use of queer theory to examine the heterosexist narratives in the context of general education requirements that perpetuate beliefs about what is legitimate knowledge. Within the realm of the classroom, Deborah Carlin (2011) discussed the use of queer theory to inform an intersectional teaching approach in an English literature class; Mel Lewis (2011) considered how queer theory allows the body to be a site of knowledge in a women's studies classroom; and Dennis Frank and Edward Cannon (2010) suggested that queer theory be used for diversity education in training counselors to challenge the status quo and mainstream discourse that masks how current curricula are gendered, political, historical, racial, classed, and aesthetic. Although there is limited scholarship that employs queer theory in a higher education setting, the previous review is not intended to be exhaustive, but instead to provide a few examples.

Drawing from this range of contexts, we will focus this chapter on queer theory and college students, and more specifically on the relationship between queer theory and identity. This relationship emphasizes the intersections of social identities and the resistance to oppressive social constructions of sexuality and gender. Scholars who have used queer theory in the study of college student identity include Brent Bilodeau (2005, 2009); Jeffrey McKinney (2005); and Rob Pusch (2005), each of whom has used queer approaches to study transgender college students. Patrick Dilley (2002) used queer theory to explore the history of nonheterosexual men on college campuses, focusing in part on the evolving meaning of queer identity. Mitsu Narui (2011) studied Asian American gay, lesbian, and bisexual student identity using a Foucauldian poststructural theoretical perspective with a particular focus on the coming-out process.

Renn (2010a) noted that Elisa Abes and David Kasch (2007) have done some of the most compelling research using queer theory in conjunction with college student identity. Applying queer theory to data from the longitudinal research on lesbian identity and meaning-making capacity described in Abes and Jones (2004), which we discussed in Chapter Five, Abes and Kasch (2007) argued that the theory describing development toward self-authorship is steeped in power relationships that privilege heterosexual students and is therefore not an entirely appropriate description of development for all students. Using three key tenets of queer theory to analyze the story of one of the participants from Abes and Jones, Abes and Kasch proposed a notion they deemed "queer authorship" (p. 630). Queer authorship challenges the normative assumptions on which Baxter Magolda's theory (2001) describing development from external to internal meaning making (self-authorship) are grounded, and offers a more fluid perspective on development that focuses on individual resistance to inequitable power structures and incorporates a symbiotic relationship between self and context. Queer authorship suggests that through an individual's resistance both to inequitable power structures and to the socially constructed nature of identity, identity formation results in social transformation and social transformation results in identity formation. Through its emphasis on identity formation as fluid and its critique of the power structures inherent in the concept of self-authorship, queer authorship challenges the external-to-internal meaning-making filter in the Reconceptualized Model of Multiple Dimensions of Identity (RMMDI). We will revisit some of Abes and Kasch's ideas in more detail throughout this chapter as we explore the application of queer theory to the MMDI.

Queer Theory and Its Key Tenets

Defining queer theory is a difficult task. Building on the poststructural critiques of knowledge and truth as culturally and historically specific, queer theorists have resisted establishing a single concrete definition of what queer theory is because such a definition would restrict the meaning of the term to a narrow set of cultural and historical interests, thereby ignoring one of the major intellectual tenets of poststructuralism (Jagose, 1997; Sullivan, 2003). As a result, queer theory is just as often defined by what it is not. This approach to the definition of queer theory allows for wider application and interpretation of its ideas, but it also makes those ideas more difficult to understand at an early stage of study. Scholars and practitioners new to queer theory often find it difficult to understand and interpret at first pass (and sometimes second and third pass).

For the sake of the present discussion we offer our working definition of queer theory, and then expand on that definition by exploring key tenets of queer theory that we found relevant to reenvisioning the MMDI. Our hope in this chapter is to offer an interpretation of queer theory as it applies to the MMDI for scholars and practitioners ranging from those who have little previous knowledge of queer theory to those with extensive knowledge of queer theory. We understand that offering concrete definitions of terms and ideas does violate some of the philosophical and political intentions of queer theory, but we see this accommodation as necessary to make the material more accessible for readers who are new to queer theory.

Queer Theory

Queer theory is a theoretical perspective within critical theory that examines, challenges, and deconstructs social norms attached to gender and sexuality. The central argument of queer theory is that social norms and meanings linked to gender and sexuality are only and always culturally and historically constructed, therefore lacking objective or value-neutral truth and knowledge, and serve to marginalize one group for the benefit of another (Sullivan, 2003). These social norms must therefore be questioned, challenged, and deconstructed to correct the social power inequalities they create. Defining characteristics of queer theory include an emphasis on the intersectionality of social identities (Wiegman, 1995); an explicit focus on an activist and liberatory social agenda (Eng, with Halberstam & Muñoz, 2005); and an ongoing purpose of destabilizing and delegitimizing social norms related to gender and sexuality (Halperin, 1995).

Heteronormativity

Heteronormativity is perhaps the most important and central concept of queer theory. It describes the use of heterosexuality as the social norm against which all expressions of identity (not just those of sexuality) are measured (M. Warner, 1991). As such, it serves as the primary context for understanding social power and the social inequalities that queer theorists seek to challenge and transform. The core of the queer theorists' objection to heteronormativity is that it is a social construction that serves to promote the power of a dominant group over multiple nondominant groups (M. Warner, 1991).

Heteronormativity creates and reinforces this power inequality by emphasizing a binary between heterosexuality as normal (or superior) and any expression of identity that is not explicitly heterosexual as abnormal (or inferior). At a basic level, heteronormativity defines normal as men being masculine and sexually attracted to women, and women being feminine and sexually attracted to men. Any variations of these social roles are deemed abnormal. Queer theorists argue that this binary of normal and abnormal creates a context in which members of the nondominant groups are always necessarily considered to be less capable, valuable, or important than members of the dominant group. That is, the label of *abnormal* limits the social power of nondominant group members, encourages members of nondominant groups to conform to the definition of "normal," and reinforces the social hierarchy created by heteronormativity (M. Warner, 1991).

Common examples of heteronormativity include the assumption that gay and lesbian couples involve a pairing of a masculine person with a feminine person; the belief that heterosexual men are emotionally aloof or should not be emotionally sensitive and that gay men are or should be emotionally sensitive; the belief that marriage is the culminating event of serious dating relationships; and the expectation that men will wear clothes that reflect their masculinity and women will wear clothes that reflect their femininity.

What makes heteronormativity such a rich concept for queer theory is the intersections of gender and sexuality with other social identities (for example, race, religion, socioeconomic status, nationality, and ability) and the application of the normal-abnormal binary to these other social identities. In their early examination of heteronormativity, queer theorists focused primarily on expressions of gender and sexuality (Butler, 1990; Sedgwick, 1990; Turner, 2000; M. Warner, 1991); however, over time this focus expanded to include the intersections of gender and sexuality with other identities, such as race, religion, nationality, and ability. In exploring the intersection with race, Siobahn Somerville (2000) examined how race was used in the post–Civil War South to help construct the notion of homosexuality and exert control over newly freed Black men and women. Her argument is complex, but the central idea is that maleness was defined as being a White male and femaleness was defined as being a White female, so anyone who was not a White male was less than masculine and anyone who was not a White female was less than feminine; Black men were portrayed as effeminate and less than masculine (that is, less than male), or as hypermasculine and a sexual threat to White women; Black women were fetishized as hyperfeminine and submissive sexual objects (that is, less than female) or portrayed as masculine and not to be treated as "real" women. Making a similar argument concerning the intersection with religion, Daniel Boyarin, Daniel Itzkovitz, and Ann Pellegrini (2003) discussed the social interpretation of being Jewish as a form of homosexuality, or nonheterosexuality, and the implication that Jewish men are too feminine and Jewish women are too masculine. In regard to the intersection with nationality, several authors have explored the interpretation of sexuality outside of the United States as nonconforming to heterosexuality or as forms of homosexuality (for example, Cruz-Malavé & Manalansan, 2002; C. Patton & Sánchez-Eppler, 2000). And in regard to the intersection with ability, several authors (for example, McRuer, 2003; Sandahl, 2003; White, 2003) have pointed to the notion of physical ability as comprising markers of normative and abnormal sexuality, namely that individuals with physical disabilities require training or assistance to have normal sexualities or simply are unable to have normal sexualities, thereby being less than fully heterosexual.

Performativity

Performativity describes the process in which individuals create their social identities through the behaviors of their day-to-day lives (Butler, 1990). Queer theorists use the concept of performativity to argue that identity occurs as an ongoing process of expression and enactment, rather than as an end product of development (Butler, 2004; Morris, 1995; Muñoz, 1999). Of particular importance to this concept is the idea that identity is fluid, meaning that it is in a constant state of creation and change. Fluid in nature, such social identities as gender, race, sexuality, and religion are something individuals *do* rather than something individuals *are.* For example, the meaning of one's gender identity is a product of one's actions, rather than one's actions being the product of a particular gender identity. How a person dresses and behaves, and that person's interests and preferences, create a gender identity; gender identity does not create these behaviors and characteristics. The combination of these behaviors and characteristics results in an identity performative. Because behaviors and characteristics change, identity performatives are fluid. Forms of identity therefore do not exist until individuals enact them, and identities do not have inherent meaning outside of individuals' performatives of them.

Performativity, therefore, has a close relationship with heteronormativity. Under heteronormativity, social identities have stable, socially constructed meanings. For example, the heteronormative relationship between gender and sexuality (that is, men are masculine and sexually attracted to women; women are feminine and sexually attracted to men) is stable and socially constructed. Queer theory challenges such fixed interpretations of identity to emphasize how intersections of identities result in unique expressions of identity that challenge and resist constraining social norms of identity and create social space in which identities take on complex, heterogeneous meanings. For example, in the intersection of gender and race, both gender and race inform what it means to be a Black woman, and this meaning varies for each Black woman as she continuously interprets and expresses what it means to be Black as a woman and what it means to be a woman who is Black.

There are three ideas that guide the concept of performativity. First, performativity emphasizes that identities have symbolic and material content that individuals express through their behaviors (Butler, 1990). The symbolic and material content of identity is often ubiquitous and mundane, such as clothes, music, films, and style of speech. Each of these elements reflects culturally and historically symbolic content embedded in material objects (Butler, 1990). For example, wearing expensive clothes of the latest fashion suggests affluence, interest in current fashion, or a desire to fit in with peers who are affluent or fashionable. The clothes alone are just objects, but their meaning comes from their symbolic value in how the individual and others interpret them. Second, performatives reflect social identities as *both* individual threads of identity *and* intersections of identity. This "both/and" quality of performativity is important to queer theory and creates a layered and complex expression of identity (Butler, 1997). Third, the performatives of complex intersecting identities influence the meaning of any one identity, thereby challenging the stability of meaning attached to social norms (Wiegman, 1995). For example, and as we discussed in Chapter Six on intersectionality, Bowleg (2008) offered provocative discourse on the nonadditive qualities of intersectionality and how Black plus lesbian plus woman does not equal Black lesbian woman. Instead, race, sexuality, and gender each modify the meaning of individual social identities.

The combination of these three guiding ideas is what gives performativity such force within the queer theory literature. José Esteban Muñoz (1999) discussed the use of drag and drag performances to challenge the stability of meanings attached to gender, sexuality, race, and nationality. As Muñoz argued, the act of dressing in drag creates high levels of ambiguity and uncertainty around who is a man and who is a woman, around what it means to be masculine or feminine, around the influence of race in the expression of sexuality and gender, and around how these performatives take on new meanings depending on the national context. One purpose of this type of drag performance is to make it unclear whether a person is a man or a woman, whether that person is attracted to men or women, whether a style of clothes belongs to men or women, or whether the act only carries meaning for an event (for example, dressing for a drag ball) (Markson, 2008). The instantaneous ambiguity of drag complicates the firm binary of heteronormativity (that is, men are masculine, wear men's clothing, and are attracted to women) and creates the need for alternative interpretations (Muñoz). This is what Butler (1990) meant in her description of performatives as bringing an identity into being.

Desire

The concept of desire plays a complex role within the queer theory literature. Researchers and scholars have taken the idea of erotic desire and complicated it with a wide range of applications to emphasize its deeply personal and individual nature and the centrality of desire to identity: sexual object desire (Sedgwick, 1990); interpretations of the identities of others through understanding their desires (Butler, 2004); desire for a meaning of gender that does not reinforce a superior-inferior binary (Wiegman, 2006); and desire as biological constitution, social role, and individual choice (Wilkerson, 2007). Common to these multiple uses of the concept of desire is the idea that desire is the compelling force behind the actions that individuals take.

Desire figures prominently into the social and legal debates about socially acceptable identity performatives that do not conform to heterosexuality. Major critiques of heteronormative desire (that is, desire in which men desire feminine women and women desire masculine men) by queer theorists include that heteronormativity promotes the objectification of people as possessions (M. Warner, 1991); things to be consumed (Butler, 1993); or objects to control (Elliott, 2010). Related to these critiques is the idea that heteronormative desire reinforces social binaries, providing some groups with power at the expense of others (Foucault, 1978). Queer theorists argue that by contrast, queer desire, or desire that does not conform to heteronormativity, emphasizes the agency and subjectivity of individuals and provides a necessary force behind taking actions to challenge heteronormativity, frequently in the form of performatives.

The concept of desire as applied here is not a mere wanting. Instead, desire describes a compulsion and an incompleteness that needs fulfillment. The queer theory literature uses this sense of desire to implicate desire as one of the forces behind identity development (Wilkerson, 2007). Discussions of identity development within the queer theory literature emphasize the political and personal qualities of longing—a quest for a socially intelligible, or "accepted," identity that is also personally authentic (Butler, 2004). The concept of desire offers a way of describing where performatives come from and what purposes they serve. Performatives are the actualization of desires in the form of behaviors intended to help satisfy deep personal longings. In a later section of this chapter we will take this framing of desire further to suggest that desire serves a filtering function, influencing how individuals make meaning of their lives and create their identity performatives.

Becoming

Becoming refers to a fluid and changing process of development in which an individual's identity unfolds over an extended period of time without a fixed developmental end point (Halberstam, 2005), and it plays a complicated role within the idea of performativity. Whereas performativity emphasizes the process of action rather than the product or outcome of action, becoming is both the process and the product of action—the outcome of a queer performative is an ongoing state of becoming. Well captured in the work of Elizabeth Grosz (2004) as the "continuity of duration" (p. 155), becoming reflects the way in which performativity parallels features of traditional models of human development (for example, increases in complexity, related to previous expressions of identity, and the connected nature of person and environment) because performatives over time constitute a more stable or interpretable identity than only fluid and ever-changing performatives do.

This interpretation of becoming allows the individual to have a fluid and changing identity as well as a coherent identity that is able to resist well-established social norms. As Abes and Kasch (2007) stated, "[Becoming] facilitates flexible genders and sexualities and reflects how an individual may perform a seemingly contradictory performative in ever-changing ways" (pp. 621–622). Within the queer theory literature, becoming is the product and the process of resisting heteronormativity (Butler, 1990). Individuals adopt an ongoing state of change as their way of being, a form of resisting cultural and social norms, which helps them resist the restrictiveness of embedded social norms. In the language of student development theory, this constitutes a process of developing rather than arrival at a state of development. As the term *becoming* suggests, there is no location of arrival. Individuals' identities are endlessly transforming into some new form, meaning, or interpretation of identity.

The idea of becoming takes multiple names within the queer theory literature. Wilkerson (2007) called this idea "emerging fusion" (p. 4), emphasizing the not-yet-settled quality of identity and the development of identity as a synthesis of sexual orientation and sexual identity in a continuous process. Abes and Kasch (2007) framed this idea as liminality on the conceptual level, to emphasize the in-between quality of becoming as an unstable and undetermined state of being. They later used the term *becoming* to describe the functional or applied version of this idea in their discussion of the outcome of liminality for lesbian college students. Finally, Halberstam (2008), in discussing a work by Butler (2000), drew attention to "liminal subjects" (p. 28) as individuals for whom exclusion and outsider status are fundamental identity elements that create an identity in a steady state of flux due to always being outside of accepted norms.

Applying Queer Theory Concepts to the MMDI: Queering the Model

We now apply the four queer theory concepts we reviewed, heteronormativity, desire, performativity, and becoming, to the MMDI to queer the model. A distinction needs to be made here: rather than offering a "queer MMDI," a version of the MMDI that would apply only to students who identify as queer, we are suggesting a queering of the MMDI, a version of the MMDI that emphasizes the intersectionality of identities and challenges power relationships promoted by heteronormativity. In queering the MMDI, we are foregrounding gender and sexuality in the construction of intersectionality among threads of identity. In other words, the queered MMDI uses gender and sexuality to complicate the meaning and interpretation of intersections of identity. Such foregrounding does not occur in the intersectional framework as described in Chapter Six. To achieve this queering, we have applied each concept to one element of the model—heteronormativity to context; desire to the meaning-making filter; performativity to the social identities; and becoming to the core. Although we use the four elements of the model as our points of comparison, we have replaced each with a queer concept, resulting in a model that portrays a very different conceptualization of identity than that offered by the MMDI.

We find the process of queering the MMDI a creative, liberating one that challenges us to consider possibilities that defy identity categories that privilege some and marginalize others, to create relationships among social identities that otherwise are at odds with one another, and to embrace a fluidity that challenges the stability that is often an assumed aspect of identity. Still, we realize that developing a queered model defies queer theory's resistance to being defined and to presenting identity as an orderly construct. Although depicting a model is perhaps not entirely consistent with the nature of queer theory, we believe the manner in which we incorporate the tenets of queer theory is true to these tenets' meaning. Creating a model is also consistent with our goal of portraying queer theory in an accessible manner that enables its tenets to be applied in multiple contexts. To readers who are queer theory purists, we simply ask that you approach our model in this spirit of utility.

Heteronormativity

In the MMDI the *context* in which an individual's identity is situated is varied and changes with time. This context includes such notions as relationships with family and peers, the college culture, policies and laws, and the often unspoken norms of one's environment. Queer theory makes apparent how each of these aspects of context is shaped by the pervasiveness of heteronormativity. Context is therefore heteronormativity. Queer theory deconstructs this context, simultaneously making visible how heteronormativity shapes reality and also resisting this power structure in favor of a reality not grounded in an oppressive heterosexual-nonheterosexual binary. If context is heteronormativity, an individual therefore transforms context through resistance. It is this resistance to heteronormativity that results in the identity formation and social transformation that Abes and Kasch (2007) described as queer authorship.

Desire

In the RMMDI the meaning-making *filter* regulates the influence of internal and external sources of authority on the individual. The addition of the meaning-making filter was a significant change to the original MMDI because it provided a mechanism through which the other three elements of the model (the core, social identities, and context) could interact. In the queered model, desire also links the other elements of the model and provides a mechanism for enacting resistance to heteronormativity, regulating the influence of heteronormativity on students' identity performatives and construction of fluid self-concepts.

Desire as a queering force directly challenges the notions of truth and authority behind the constructivist foundation of the RMMDI and helps explain how social transformation occurs as part of Abes and Kasch's concept (2007) of queer authorship. In the RMMDI the meaning-making filter determines the degree to which students rely on external or internal sources of authority when evaluating knowledge, relationships with others, or their understanding of themselves. In the queered MMDI, desire transforms the meaning-making filter by influencing how the individual makes meaning and how others around her or him are able to make meaning. Like the other elements of the model, the desire filter is interactive and unstable. As desire influences social identity performatives, it changes external definitions of what identity is and means. Individuals are therefore able to change the social meaning of identity based on their expression of desires through their identity performatives. Drawing on the literature of queer theory, this ability of desire to help define performatives suggests that desire also helps define how individuals understand and interpret themselves and their expressions of self. In one sense, the desire filter challenges individuals to redefine and reinterpret how and whom they understand themselves to be through desires that motivate the actions they take (and self-expressions they make).

For the students represented in the work of Abes and Jones (2004); Abes, Jones, and McEwen (2007); and Abes and Kasch (2007), meaning making occurred around the idea of how "normal" or "natural" their gender or sexualities were. All of the women highlighted, to varying degrees, the challenges they faced in gaining acceptance from others for their performatives of gender and sexuality. Undergirding these performatives was a desire for their external experiences of identity to correspond to their internal experiences of identity. That is, they wanted to express, experience, and have others understand their identity in a manner consistent with how they internally understood their identity. The notion of queer authorship, as described by Abes and Kasch, suggests that as the women adopted more complex expressions of their desire, they were increasingly capable of transforming their social context through resistance to heteronormativity. Although this resistance to heteronormativity was important to transforming their social context, this queered context started with their desires and the power those desires conferred in regard to imagining and creating resistance to heteronormativity. The desires these women felt, both for and of gender and sexuality, violated the social norms of heteronormativity, and these violations created a need both to filter external sources of authority in favor of an internal one as well as to transform the external authority by contesting definitions of acceptable identities. In this way, desire is critical to the creation and expression of queer authorship.

Performativity

As heteronormativity moves through the desire filter, it is enacted through performatives. These performatives are the queered version of the *social identities* portrayed in the MMDI. The key distinctions to be made between these performatives and the social identities of the MMDI are that these performatives reflect the intersectionality of gender and sexuality with other social identities and that they are fluid and continuously changing. Rather than portraying distinct and separate social identities, a queered model features fused unisons of social identities in which the particular social identities are mutually influencing and possibly inseparable from gender and sexuality. In this way, social identities are performed more holistically. Intersectionality with threads of identity other than gender and sexuality occurs, as discussed in Chapters Six and Seven; however, one of the elements that constitutes a queered MMDI is the centrality of gender and sexuality to examining identity performatives and the meanings those performatives enact. Queer performatives also emphasize gender and sexuality as a process of constantly constructing new meanings for the concepts of gender and sexuality and their relationships with other threads of identity.

Becoming

Rather than there being a *core* identity as portrayed in the MMDI, the fluid nature of performatives results in an identity that is always evolving, or becoming. Rather than asserting that there is an essential nature to identity, as the core of the MMDI suggests, the queered model has as a central notion that identity is a process rather than a product. Because all identity is performed, the performatives are central to the process of becoming. Performatives and becoming are therefore interconnected. Using the terms of the MMDI, no distinction exists between the core and social identities. Varying salience of social identities in relation to the core therefore no longer exists. Instead, all performatives are interconnected, or fused, as part of a process of becoming. A result of that fusion is that if one aspect of identity changes, all others change. Because context is always shifting, and thus how one resists heteronormativity through desire is always changing, all aspects of identity are continuously changing. This continuous process of becoming, therefore, is also a continuous process of resisting heteronormativity. Again using MMDI terms, the context and core are therefore interconnected in the queered model. In the language of queer theory, resistance to heteronormativity, performativity, and becoming are all interconnected. This interconnectedness speaks to the symbiotic relationship described by queer theory: identity formation results in social transformation, while social transformation creates identity formation. In essence, this portrayal of identity is consistent with the nature of queer authorship: individuals create and re-create their fluid, intersecting identities through desires that resist heteronormativity, resulting in an identity that is always in a state of becoming.

By replacing the core identity with the notion of identity as becoming, the queered model addresses one of the primary critiques of the MMDI. As we discussed in Chapters Four and Five, the MMDI has been critiqued for its representation of the core as a fairly fixed aspect of identity that is distinct from social identities. The relationships among resistance to heteronormativity, context, performatives, and identity as becoming result in the incorporation of all aspects of a person's identity as fluid intersections rather than distinct components.

A Queered MMDI

In Figure 8.1 we offer the Queered Model of Multiple Dimensions of Identity as an example of how the four concepts from queer theory relate to the MMDI. Two guiding ideas inform this model. First, all of the elements in the model are interactive with and influence each other. Second, each element of the model exhibits the fluid quality of queer theory through motion and movement. We encourage the reader to think of the model as a series of vibrating elements that move in irregular patterns, which serve to undermine the stability of each individual element. To more thoroughly explain this model, we will discuss each of its elements in relation to the others.

FIGURE 8.1 QUEERED MODEL OF MULTIPLE DIMENSIONS OF IDENTITY

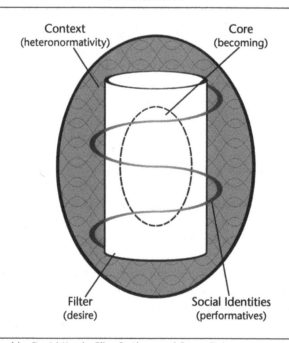

Source: Developed by David Kasch, Elisa S. Abes, and Susan R. Jones.

Heteronormativity (Context)

As noted earlier, heteronormativity is the context in which identity is situated within a queered MMDI. In the Q-MMDI, we represent heteronormativity as a viscous fluid that encircles the other three elements. Within heteronormativity, the social identity performatives, the desire filter, and the becoming core exist as a unified entity made up of interconnected elements. Singly and as a group, those three elements serve to disrupt and agitate heteronormativity, thereby undermining its stability.

Performatives (Social Identities)

Social identities in the Q-MMDI take the form of identity performatives. Performatives are the primary means through which students challenge the context of heteronormativity and change the social meanings ascribed to individual and intersecting identities. In this model, performatives form a spiraling thread, or "performative coil," that encircles and bisects the desire filter, such that the performative coil links the filter of desire to the larger context of heteronormativity. The social identities are drawn as an inseparable coil, rather than distinct rings, to highlight the impossibility of separating them. The social identities are intrasecting rather than intersecting (Abes & Kasch, 2007). As opposed to intersecting rings, which represent the joining together of separate identities (intersectionality), the performative coil represents how identities share a common thread that cannot be separated (intrasectionality). As students perform their intrasecting identities, their performative coil plays a complex role in linking elements of the model together. First, it bisects the desire filter and exerts influence inward onto the meaning of desire in the students' lives. Second, it allows the desire filter to exert influence outward to shape the performatives that students enact. Third, it enables both the desire filter and a given individual's performatives to agitate the surrounding context of heteronormativity and disrupt social norms.

Desire (Filter)

Within the performative coil, the desire filter envelops the becoming core, similar to how heteronormativity envelops the rest of the model. The desire filter is a closed cylinder surrounding the becoming core and bisected by the performative coil. Similar to the performative coil linking the desire filter and heteronormativity, the desire filter serves as an intermediary between both the becoming core and the social identity performatives. Desire is a driving force that exerts influence outward and inward. Outwardly, it generates social identity performatives from the ever-evolving sense of self within the becoming core. Inwardly, it influences the form taken by the becoming core. In this way, the desire filter shapes the meaning and expression of social identity performatives and the individual's internal sense of a core self based on an understanding of his or her motivations for performatives and definitions of his or her core self.

Becoming (Core)

The heart of this model is the core self as a state of becoming. In the Q-MMDI there is no fixed personal sense of self. Instead, individuals experience their sense of self as an act of unending creation. Within this model, this constant transition and flux occur through a motion of an expanding and contracting core. As the becoming core expands, it exerts more influence and control over the desire filter and the performative coil. As the becoming core contracts, it exerts less influence and control. This process of expansion and contraction reflects changes in personal agency over the other elements of the model. This shifting or flux in agency is not to be confused with the idea of development. Agency reflects the individual's ability to act on elements within the model, whereas development involves the ability to influence that action across the sum total of the model toward a directed or intentional purpose. The question of what constitutes development within a queered model is a complex one. To answer this question, we draw on the concept of queer authorship (Abes & Kasch, 2007) to suggest that queer development in this model revolves around the degree to which individual students are able to manage the individual elements represented within the model and thereby direct their influence on the larger heteronormative context. In other words, the more developed the individual student is, the more that student will be able to manage the motion and movement of individual elements in the model—directing how and the degree to which each element influences other elements.

Summary

In this chapter we introduced queer theory as a theoretical perspective that offers a poststructural view of the fluid nature of identity, resulting in identity as a form of resistance against heteronormativity. We provided an overview of the differences between constructivist and queer perspectives on identity, explaining how student development theory has typically been grounded in a constructivist perspective that does not have as its focus a critique of the power structures that shape both development and developmental theory. We then briefly looked at some of the ways in which queer theory has been used in research in higher education, noting the relative absence of its application to student development theory. We then presented in some detail four key tenets of queer theory: heteronormativity, performativity, desire, and becoming. We concluded by redefining each of the elements of the MMDI using those four tenets of queer theory and presenting a queered model. The queered model, or Q-MMDI, includes the elements of the MMDI (the core, social identities, the filter, and context), but redefines them and portrays them in a fashion quite different from before. This analysis and new model show the inseparability of the elements of the model and how the ways in which identity and the contexts in which identity is situated influence each other, resulting in a fluid identity and resistance to the inequitable systems of power that create context.

Discussion Questions and Activities

1. Describe examples of heteronormativity that exist in your life or your surroundings. What might resistance to this heteronormativity look like?
2. In what ways are your sexual and gender identities performatives? For example, in what ways do you interact with others or present your appearance that give meaning to your identity?
3. Using the Q-MMDI, how do you portray and understand your own identity? In what ways does the Q-MMDI help you to portray your identity, and in what ways does it fall short?

(Continued)

4. In what ways could the Q-MMDI be applied in higher education and student affairs practice? What are the benefits and challenges of doing so?

5. How might the Q-MMDI be used in research? For instance, how might the queered model be employed in a study of college students that is grounded in queer theory? How might the model be incorporated as part of the study's conceptual framework in an effort to more richly understand how the key tenets of queer theory interact with college student identity?

EDUCATIONAL APPLICATIONS AND FUTURE DIRECTIONS

Interludes

Susan

For a number of years before becoming a full-time faculty member in a higher educa-tion and student affairs program, I was a practitioner. When I began my doctoral program as a full-time student, I had spent about ten years working in student affairs, the last three years as a dean of students at a small liberal arts college in Vermont. Always comfortable in the world of ideas, I went back to pursue my doctor-ate in part because I knew the scholarship in the field of higher education and student affairs had advanced considerably since my master's degree experience. To locate myself in the evolution of theory, I should mention that Carol Gilligan pub-lished her groundbreaking text In a Different Voice *the year after I completed my master's degree! Our primary text in student development theory was the one we referenced heavily in Chapter Two,* Applying New Developmental Findings, *which was published in 1978. I learned about the theories of Chickering, Perry, Kohlberg, Loevinger, and the Heaths, some names that are probably unfamiliar to today's graduate students. Ten years later, I knew that as a busy senior administra-tor I had not kept fully abreast of the new scholarship emerging in the student development area, and that a doctoral program would fully immerse me. I was also motivated to pursue a doctorate because as a practitioner, I was perplexed by what I perceived as our inability as a profession to solve, or at least make progress on, some of the vexing problems facing educators. Indeed, many of the issues I dealt with as a dean of students are still prevalent today, such as alcohol and substance abuse; incivility; strained town-gown relationships; hazing; sexual assault; and the predominance of siloed existence along multiple identifiers, such as race, religion, and culture, and along functional lines, such as academic affairs and student affairs, to name but a few. Surely, I thought, learning new theories and immersing myself in the current scholarship of the field would help me think more deeply about these issues.*

Well, I did think more deeply and theoretically, and in some ways this took me away from the realm of practice. The best way for me to describe my scholarly path is as a rock rolling down a mountain, gathering moss (greater substance) as it goes (I guess this is counter to the old proverb "A rolling stone gathers no moss"!). What I mean by this is that I started with an original idea (the stone) about self-perceived identities when such dimensions as race, gender, sexual orientation, culture are considered. Yet with every study (and what I learned from participants)—and as I engaged in the reading of contemporary scholarship—new questions emerged for me, leading me into new areas of scholarship, including varying methodological approaches. As emphasized in Chapter Ten, identity is complex both as a theoretical construct and as a lived experience, such that no one theoretical framework can capture the complexity and present a complete picture (if one even exists). My initial dissertation study was prompted by my reaction to the theories available to me at the time I began my work—I just didn't see my own most pressing identity questions reflected in these theories. I now know that I was probably too quick to critique at the time, but nonetheless, my own identity preoccupations led me in this direction. My introduction to the scholarship in women's studies through my doctoral program gave me a new theoretical lens and concepts through which to view identity. This scholarship necessarily required much more explicit attention to issues of power, privilege, and oppression, which more foundational student development theories ignored. My coming to terms with my own sexual orientation had everything to do with how I came to understand my identity and involved complicated intersections of race, gender, social class, and sexual orientation.

I am incredibly fortunate to work in a profession in which I can teach what I learn through my scholarship and research. Similarly, my students teach me, as they are often on the cutting edge in terms of both generating scholarly questions and lived experience. They also push me to translate the abstract and theoretical, worlds in which I am comfortable, to the realities of practice. In fact, in class I sometimes get asked, "When will we get to the practical applications?" and all the while I was *thinking I had been talking about applications! These questions also force me to constantly ask myself how I am **really** contributing to the goals of equity and inclusion, values of mine and our profession, on a daily basis—in the classroom, through my research, and in my daily interactions with others. Critical theoretical frameworks help me think through these questions, but they don't always provide specific guidance for changing practice. As challenging as these final chapters were for us to write (because they forced us to dwell on practical applications and to think creatively about future directions), I think they point us down a path that holds great potential for bringing theory and practice closer together in the important areas of privilege, power, oppression, equity, and inclusion. Time, and our continued collective efforts, will tell.*

Elisa

One of the positive outcomes of my legal training is my capacity to analyze complex ideas. This training has facilitated my ability to consider new ways of thinking about relationships among the constructivist, critical, and poststructural perspectives. I so appreciate having the opportunity to analyze ideas and consider theoretical possibilities that I believe are necessary for creating more inclusive and critically conscious campuses and enabling students to understand themselves and others in more authentic ways. I also know, however, that I have a tendency to get lost in theoretical possibilities and sometimes struggle with the practical application. Happily, I surround myself with bright students who gravitate toward the application piece.

Still, I often think about my own practice, critical consciousness, and places where I hope to grow as a faculty member in the application of these theoretical perspectives. Although much of my writing and teaching has a critical bent to it, I know I have many ways in which I need to continue learning about difference, especially as a well-educated, White, able-bodied, and able-minded person. I also know I need to continuously reexamine my commitment to critical work, making sure I don't take the "path of least resistance," as described by Allan Johnson (2006, p. 80), despite the emotional cost associated with this work.

Over the past few years, I developed and taught three intergroup dialogue classes for the Student Affairs in Higher Education program at Miami University. We focused on a number of different identities, including race, sexual orientation, religion, ability, social class, and gender. Although it was some of the most rewarding teaching I have done, and although I continue to be in touch with several of the students about their learning, it also took a personal toll on me, as I know it did for some of the students. The toll was greatest when a student might have been hurt as a result of my privileged lack of recognition concerning the emotional weight of an assignment, my failure to ask an appropriate follow-up question as a facilitator that contributed to a student's pain, or my underestimation of the courage it took for a student to come to class. Moving forward, I know I need to continue developing the breadth of my critical awareness to heighten my facilitation abilities and resist the temptation to leave the facilitation to others while taking refuge in courses that are less personally challenging.

I also know that I will continue teaching student development theory using critical theoretical perspectives, despite the challenges that this, too, brings. I have had a lesbian student silently stare at me with her arms crossed for multiple class sessions because I allowed space for another student to discuss how her religious beliefs made her not want to study queer theory due to its challenge to the idea of a "normal" sexual orientation. I agree with my decision to allow this conversation, despite its toll on at least one of the queer students in the class. Still, I want to continue learning different pedagogical approaches for engaging in this material that more effectively take into consideration relationships among students' multiple identities. I'm now giving more thought to how the new models introduced in earlier chapters of this book as well as the theoretical perspectives on which they are based would bring more equity to these classes. What would an intersectional, critical race theory (CRT), or queer theory intergroup dialogue or course in student development theory look like?

Moving forward, I intend to continue thinking with increased vigor about how to make complex theoretical ideas accessible and have practical value in students' lives. Despite my tendency to get lost in theoretical ideas, I have occasionally questioned the utility of such thinking and wondered what difference I am making. I am certain that my questioning is a result of my working-class/lower-middle-class upbringing and the values I maintain from my childhood about practicality, making one's way through daily concerns, and the importance of taking care of one another. I continue to understand how the theories we are discussing and the ways in which we are discussing them, although complex in nature, are indeed addressing the everyday concerns of many people, and are at their essence all about caring for one another and thus very practical.

◆ ◆ ◆

Section Three of this book, in which we presented intersectional, CRT, and queered models of multiple identities, represents a new direction in higher education and student affairs scholarship. In Section Four, we now build on those ideas and continue looking to the future by presenting considerations for applying these concepts, in conjunction with other theoretical perspectives, in research and practice. The integration of multiple theoretical perspectives is relatively uncharted territory in theorizing about multiple identities. Exploring new ways of thinking, we present more questions than answers.

Chapter Nine describes various approaches to and considerations for applying the Model of Multiple Dimensions of Identity (MMDI), the Reconceptualized Model of Multiple Dimensions of Identity (RMMDI), and the critical models presented in Chapters Six through Eight. We first provide some examples of how the MMDI and RMMDI have been used as frameworks in empirical research, in scholarly articles as contributions to new theoretical developments, and in student affairs practice. We then consider the application of the intersectional, CRT, and queer theory approaches. Rather than offering numerous specific strategies for applying the critical models, we discuss the paradigmatic shift in practical approaches needed to do so. We discuss two considerations pertaining to this paradigmatic shift and application of the critical models: the continuous education required for practitioners to understand their own and others' identities and the importance of gaining the ability to tap into students' narratives. These two considerations can probably be translated into any educational context, and we offer examples of the application of these models in three specific contexts. Using the critical models, and consistent with the paradigmatic shift in practice that we encourage, we examine those contexts from the perspectives of both privileged and marginalized identities.

In Chapter Ten we offer some of our thinking about future directions for conceptualizing relationships among multiple social identities. We begin by considering ways of making more inclusive some of the theoretical perspectives we discussed in this book, in particular CRT and queer theory, by incorporating within the theories a focus on other identities and by extending the application of the theories to other identities. The ideas we next present in this chapter revisit the theme we introduced in Chapter One about the danger of the single story. Rather than using only one theoretical perspective, or story, to reexamine the MMDI as we did in Chapters Six, Seven, and Eight, we introduce the concept of theoretical borderlands, or the idea of simultaneously using multiple theoretical perspectives to make sense of the MMDI. Basing our assertions on the notion that all theories offer an incomplete perspective on identity, or one partial story, we make the case for using multiple theoretical perspectives to more richly describe relationships among identities. Rather than depicting one borderland version of the MMDI, which is inconsistent with the borderland approach of opening up numerous theoretical possibilities, we conclude the chapter with five examples of borderland models that incorporate ideas from more than one of the critical models. Current graduate students drew these models in an effort to depict their own identities, and later reported the challenging yet freeing nature of this exercise as a way of making sense of one's identity. It is our hope that others will also be simultaneously challenged and freed by moving in this new direction in understanding identity. We also invite thinking about how this new direction in theorizing might be applied in practice. We then conclude the book with final interludes that bring us full circle as we summarize the contents of *Identity Development of College Students: Advancing Frameworks for Multiple Dimensions of Identity* as well as offer a final reflection on the evolution of our thinking as we wrote this book.

CHAPTER NINE

APPLICATION OF THE MODELS IN EDUCATIONAL CONTEXTS

Having discussed the origins and details of the Model of Multiple Dimensions of Identity (MMDI) and the Reconceptualized Model of Multiple Dimensions of Identity (RMMDI), as well as having offered intersectional, critical race theory (CRT), and queer theory iterations of these models, we now consider these models' applications. Certainly there are no formulaic ways of applying the models, and in fact the critical models suggest a paradigmatic shift in the nature of much of student affairs practice more than they indicate specific modes of application. We begin this chapter by presenting ways in which the MMDI and RMMDI have been applied in research and practice. These applications build primarily on our discussion of those models in Chapters Four and Five. We then explore ways of thinking about applying the critical models and suggest the necessity of educators' continuously working to make sense of themselves and others in relation to these critical theories and models. Further, we provide some examples of how the models might be applied in various educational contexts that have a focus on student identity, as well as contexts not typically associated with identity.

Application of the Model of Multiple Dimensions of Identity

In an effort to identify both the strengths and the limitations of the MMDI and RMMDI, we provide in this section a discussion of some of the specific ways in which these models are being used by theory creators, researchers, and practitioners. As a reminder, we refer here to the application of the MMDI because it serves as the foundation for the RMMDI. However, in the examples we provide, both the MMDI and the RMMDI are presented because this is how these models are being used by others. To that end, we divide this discussion into three areas: (1) scholarly and empirical research that uses the models as the frameworks for studies; (2) scholarly articles and book chapters that discuss the models as theoretical contributions; and (3) application of the models in practice. Our goal is to provide a diverse array of examples in these areas, rather than an exhaustive review of all the uses of the models in the literature.

MMDI as a Framework for Scholarly and Empirical Research

An increasing number of studies focused on identity are using the MMDI and the RMMDI as theoretical frameworks. The starting point for these studies is typically some combination of multiple identities, such as race and sexual orientation in Lori Patton and Symone Simmons's research on Black lesbians; veteran status for those who reenroll after deployment in war zones by Corey Rumann and Florence Hamrick; and race, ethnicity, and gender among Asian Americans in Grace Chen's work. What follows is a brief summary of each of these studies, how the MMDI and RMMDI were used as theoretical frameworks, and the strengths and limitations of the models given the results of these studies.

Black Lesbians in a Black College Environment. Patton and Simmons (2008) investigated the developmental experiences of first-year women who self-identified as Black and as lesbians in the context of a historically Black university in an article titled "Exploring Complexities of Multiple Identities of Lesbians in a Black College Environment." Using a phenomenological approach, Patton and Simmons had five Black lesbians participate in in-depth interviews in an effort to address four research questions:

> What are the developmental experiences of women who identify as lesbians at HBCUs [Historically Black Colleges and Universities]? What role does the environment at HBCUs play in facilitating this development? How do the women perceive their own identity? How do they negotiate multiple aspects of their oppressed identities? (p. 201)

Patton and Simmons (2008) were explicit in their article, and detailed in their discussion, that both the MMDI and RMMDI served as theoretical frameworks for their study. Although less attention is given to this model, they indicated that Reynolds and Pope's Multidimensional Identity Model (MIM) (1991) also served as a framework in this study, and came back to this model in the discussion of their results. Patton and Simmons wrote:

> Given the nature of this study, these models are particularly relevant. The multiple identities of our participants . . . include race, gender, and sexual orientation within the context of a historically Black college setting. Not only were we interested in how participants perceived themselves, we also sought to understand how they understood their oppressed identities. (p. 201)

Patton and Simmons (2008) returned to the models when discussing their results, which illuminated the complex dynamics between an internal sense of self and external expectations and among three oppressed identities. Drawing on the RMMDI, Patton and Simmons found that their participants relied on transitional meaning making to navigate the tensions they experienced among their identities and the challenges associated with finding acceptance as a result of multiple oppressed identities. When exploring how participants experienced identity salience, they noted that "participants in this study had awareness of three oppressed identities but at different times these identities moved further away from or closer to their core identity" (p. 210). Their results raised important questions about what constitutes salience and how salience comes about, as well as highlighting the dynamic nature of salience. Oppressed identities may be more or less salient (like privileged identities as posited in the MMDI) as a result of contextual influences, such as attending a historically Black institution, or a number of other identity factors and experiences. That is, even if an oppressed identity is personally important, it might not be salient given an individual's lack of comfort with that identity in relation to another identity or in a particular context.

Student Veterans in Transition. Rumann and Hamrick (2010), in an article titled "Student Veterans in Transition: Re-Enrolling After War Zone Deployments," investigated the transition experiences of six college student veterans who were reenrolling in college after returning from active duty in the armed services (in Iraq, Afghanistan, and Kuwait). Rumann and Hamrick approached their constructivist study using semi-structured interviews according to a phenomenological design. Drawing primarily on Schlossberg's transition theory (Goodman, Schlossberg, &

Anderson, 2006), Rumann and Hamrick also incorporated the RMMDI into their theoretical framework because the RMMDI "emphasizes individuals' meaning-making and identity self-perceptions in light of multiple, concurrent social identities such as, in this case, 'student' and 'veteran'" (p. 435). Because of the significant contextual influence of war zone deployment, Rumann and Hamrick were interested in the identity constructions and reconstructions that occurred as a consequence of "new social identities of 'servicemember' and 'veteran'" (p. 436).

In analyzing their results, Rumann and Hamrick pointed to the RMMDI to help explain how powerful contextual influences shaped a newly emerging sense of self given newer identities as servicemember and veteran. They wrote:

> The reconceptualized model of multiple dimensions of identity (Abes et al., 2007) provides insight into these identity constructions through its attention not only to individuals' experiences within different contexts that can influence constructions of identity, but also to individuals' active meaning-making about these various and potentially competing influences such as peer group interactions and encounters with stereotypes and biases. (p. 453)

What is unique about Rumann and Hamrick's (2010) use of the RMMDI is their employment of servicemember and veteran as social identities. This is consistent with how social psychologist Deaux (1993) defined social identities—that is, as including roles and group memberships. More typically in higher education and student affairs, social identities have been used to describe socially constructed categories of race, class, and gender, for example, rather than social roles that could include such categories as mother, student, and sister. Their use suggests the versatility of the RMMDI, as well as the MMDI, in their application to both socially constructed identities and social roles.

Asian American Identity. Chen's dissertation research (2005), *The Complexity of "Asian American Identity": The Intersection of Multiple Social Identities,* is notable because it is one of the few identity studies, particularly focused on multiple identities, to employ a quantitative design. Using a variety of measures (for example, the Rosenberg Self-Esteem Scale, the Satisfaction with Life Scale, and the Social Group Identification Scale), she investigated the management of multiple identities and identity salience among 287 Asian Americans, representing sixteen different Asian ethnicities and ranging in age from eighteen to sixty-three (Chen, 2005). Chen used

Reynolds and Pope's MIM (1991) as her theoretical framework because of her interest in validating components of the MIM, such as identification with single or multiple dimensions of identity in either active or passive ways, using an Asian American sample. However, she was also interested in the interactions among privileged and oppressed identities, exploration that the MIM does not allow given its exclusive focus on oppressed identities. Chen therefore turned to the MMDI to explore a more dynamic process of identity management and salience. In particular, in discussing her results, Chen noted, "The study results reflected that marginalized identities were often more salient, which supports the Multidimensional Identity Model and other models of multiple identities (Jones & McEwen, 2000)" (p. 89).

In extending the results of her initial research in this area, Chen (2009) drew more heavily on the MMDI and the RMMDI to explore the complexities of multiple social identities among Asian Americans. She highlighted that "increasingly, identity development scholars are recognizing factors in identity development, namely (a) identity salience, (b) internal definition versus external definitions of identity, and (c) the role of context" (p. 175), all of which are illuminated in the MMDI and the RMMDI. Using illustrative quotations from the participants in several of her studies, Chen highlighted the three factors just identified as well as the possible strategies for managing multiple identities: focusing on a single social identity, compartmentalizing multiple social identities, and integrating multiple social identities. In the first two strategies, the components of the MIM are recognizable, and in the third, integrating multiple social identities, the MMDI and RMMDI come to bear. Chen discussed these models using examples from the experiences of Asian Americans, such as when she addressed the relationship of social identities to the core in the MMDI: "For instance, in a family where the daughter attended Chinese language school on the weekends and the parents insisted on speaking Chinese at home, the daughter's ethnic identity (being Chinese) may be more salient and closer to her core identity" (p. 184). One of Chen's contributions to and extensions of the MMDI and RMMDI is the idea of identity management given shifting contexts and her emphasis on personal identity as core to one's sense of self.

Theoretical Contributions of the MMDI

Whereas the previous examples highlighted the use of the MMDI and the RMMDI in empirical research as theoretical frameworks that guided the design and analysis of particular studies, a number of scholars have incorporated these models into their theoretical contributions to understanding a variety of topics, including marriage and family therapy and multiracial identity. Here we provide a brief overview of both to offer a glimpse into how the MMDI and the RMMDI have been theoretically applied to other content areas beyond student affairs.

Marriage and Family Therapy. In the fifth edition of *Ethical, Legal, and Professional Issues in the Practice of Marriage and Family Therapy*, authors Allen Wilcoxon, Theodore Remley Jr., and Samuel Gladding (2012) introduced both the MMDI and the RMMDI in the introductory chapter, "Values as Context for Therapy." Wilcoxon and colleagues engaged the models to explore such foundational concepts as acculturation, worldview, values, and identity, a discussion that served as a reference point in subsequent chapters. The audience for this text is marriage and family therapists, and the orienting idea for the entire book is that of "value-sensitive care." The authors argued that value-sensitive care is filtered through one's particular worldview and identity and the meaning made of these. In specifically addressing the models and their contribution to these ideas and to the context of marriage and family therapy, Wilcoxon and colleagues noted:

> Jones and McEwen (2000) illustrated how the dimensions of acculturation can converge into psychosocial identity and worldview. [The MMDI] reveals how one's identity and worldview is influenced by a variety of factors throughout the span of one's life. The unique combination of these factors yields a unique value structure for both therapists and clients. These acculturated value distinctions are significant contributions for therapists when they consider mandatory or discretionary elements of dilemmas in their duty to clients and their role as professionals. (p. 9)

The authors then went on to discuss the reconceptualized model and the addition of meaning making to the MMDI. In applying the RMMDI to their audience, the authors wrote:

> For example, one's acculturation and worldview in a context of affluence is quite different than one's acculturation and worldview in the context of poverty. For one living in wealth, socioeconomic status may be a given, while for one living in impoverishment, socioeconomic status dominates their value structure. Similarly, one's acculturation and worldview in a context of strong religious tradition is quite different

than one's acculturation and worldview in a context of religious and spiritual indifference . . . From [the RMMDI], we see that our worldview and psychosocial identity can form a value structure that filters our interactions with others as well as our decision-making. Thus, the dominant value structures of therapists can be particularly significant in their decisions about client care. (Wilcoxon et al., 2012, p. 10)

Wilcoxon and colleagues' use of the MMDI and the RMMDI is intriguing in regard to both the models' application to a professional group of practitioners (marriage and family therapists) and, perhaps more significant, these authors' translation of identities, meaning making, and context into what they referred to as acculturation and value structure. They were also addressing therapists rather than their clients in endorsing the use of the models to support the self-knowledge required to be effective as clinicians providing value-sensitive care.

Multiracial Identity. Charmaine Wijeyesinghe, who became a pioneering scholar on multiracial identity with the creation of her factor model of multiracial identity (Wijeyesinghe, 1992), has revisited her earlier model, in part as a result of her familiarity with the MMDI and the RMMDI. In a new chapter in the second edition of *New Perspectives on Racial Identity Development,* edited with Bailey Jackson III, Wijeyesinghe (2012) presented a new multiracial identity development model, the Intersectional Model of Multiracial Identity (IMMI), which she noted was "informed and inspired by" (p. 99) the MMDI. The IMMI includes such factors as the geographic environment, situational differences, global influences, and generation. (See Chapter Six for more specifics about the model itself, which differs from the new Intersectional Model of Multiple Dimensions of Identity [I-MMDI] in its focus specifically on multiracial identity.) A strength of the MMDI as perceived by Wijeyesinghe as she applied it to multiracial identity is the explicit attention to contextual influences (some of which are reflected as factors in her model) and the representation of the dynamic, fluid, and complex nature of identity construction and a developing sense of self.

Practical Applications of the MMDI

Practical applications of the MMDI and the RMMDI are harder to access because they typically do not appear in published forms. We have plenty of anecdotal evidence of their use in practice settings through e-mails we receive, conferences we attend at which the MMDI and RMMDI are referenced, and program designs we see in which students are asked to plot their own MMDI elements on a worksheet. Here we highlight some of the uses for which we have evidence through documents, personal forms of communication, and online materials. What follows represents how the models have been applied by others, and our hope is that these descriptions may inspire reflections on how the models might be applied to readers' own settings.

Student Learning. A variety of institutions have integrated the MMDI and RMMDI into student workshops and classes focused on leadership development, working with diverse peers, identity development, and self-reflection.

- The Academic Success Center at Iowa State University incorporates the MMDI into the workshop topics for its Peer Educator program (http://new.dso.iastate.edu/asc/peered/workshops/). The description of the specific workshop reads, "Learn about this research-based theory, and use it to help you understand how identity affects your leadership as a Peer Educator, and how identity may affect other students' ability to be academically successful."
- Vivian Garay Santiago at the University of Vermont integrated the model into a training program for students of color called Racial Akido. The goal of the program was to assist students of color in addressing the stressors of being at a predominantly White institution.
- Patience Whitworth incorporated the MMDI into an academic skills strategy course she teaches at the University of Vermont to at-risk, first-year admitted students. She used the model to demonstrate how the salience of ethnic and social class identities might differ for students depending on context, specifically the differences between college and home environments. Her use of the model created accessible ways to discuss dominant and subordinate identities, privilege, race, and class.

Staff Development. The MMDI and RMMDI are also important tools in helping staff and educators think more critically about the students with whom they work and the value of integrating theories and practice.

- Mark Torrez presented the program Beyond the Single Story: Negotiating Multiple Marginalized Identities in Institutions of Higher

Education at the ACPA-College Student Educators International. The program explored person–environment interactions by integrating the MMDI with Urie Bronfenbrenner's ecological systems theory (2005) and Ethier and Deaux's (1994) scholarship on social identity and changing contexts. Participants discussed how the environment influences meaning making in regard to identity as well as the need for environmental assessment of programs and services to ensure institutions are meeting student needs related to intersections of identities.

- Jeff Grim incorporated the MMDI and RMMDI into a presentation to student affairs staff at Washington University as part of a workshop on student development theories. He focused on the evolution of the models and the role of context in contributing to identity salience. He also presented practical applications of the MMDI and RMMDI to assistant directors and residential community directors in residence life at Southern Methodist University, discussing campus climate by comparing the salience of identities at home and at work.
- Greg Roberts, Michele Glik, Amy Sandler, and Debbie Yunker incorporated the MMDI into a presentation at the 2004 Hillel Professional Staff Conference in Princeton, New Jersey, on the topic of Jewish students' multiple identities and the importance of Hillel staff's being multiculturally competent.

Additional Innovative Applications. The MMDI and RMMDI are being used for purposes that are innovative and unanticipated beyond educational sessions. For instance, they have been used to guide an organization, make a statement about an organization's values, and provide the context through which to determine a student's fit with an organization.

- The Asian & Pacific Islander American Scholarship Fund (APIASF) integrated the RMMDI into their "Guiding Principles of APIASF" (www.apiasf.org/programs_guiding_principles.html). The Web site provides the ideas and the research supporting these principles. The specific principle that draws on the RMMDI is the following: "Racial identity is only one of myriad social identities that our scholarship recipients possess; social class identity may be equally or more salient, as may be gender identity, sexual orientation, religious/spiritual identity, or ability, to name a few."
- At the University of Vermont, Vivian Garay Santiago incorporated the MMDI into the interview process for residence life positions.

Applicants were introduced to the model and asked to apply it using their own life experiences.

Whether it be in research, new theoretical contributions, student learning, or staff development, the MMDI and RMMDI have proven useful in their accessibility and flexibility. What is more, the infusion of critical theoretical perspectives offers additional possibilities for applying permutations of both, as discussed in the next section.

Considerations for Applying the Intersectional, CRT, and Queered Models

We now consider possibilities for applying the intersectional, CRT, and queer theory models of multiple identities in practice. As stated at the beginning of this chapter, applying critical perspectives is more about a philosophical shift in the nature of typical student affairs practice than about the specifics of how these theories and models can each be precisely used. That is, applying critical theories and models means shifting practice so that the inequities that result from power structures are at the forefront of how practice is shaped, with an aim at undoing these power structures' influence on students' identities and experiences. This paradigmatic approach shares some similarities with changes in student affairs practice that others have demanded for more than two decades (Manning, 1994; Rhoads & Black, 1995), many of which have gone unrealized, but which bring additional theoretical possibilities and a heightened focus on multiple social identities.

It is also difficult to outline precise application specifics because how a practitioner applies the theories and models depends on the nature of his or her own identity, as well as the context in which they are applied. For instance, the way a practitioner might interact with and apply the Critical Race Theory Model of Multiple Dimensions of Identity (CRT-MMDI) is likely to differ depending on the person's race and the context in which he or she is applying the model, whether the context is, for example, the institution as a whole, a campus program, or a classroom. A professional's place in a career trajectory might also influence how that person applies critical models, depending on what is personally at stake. Still, we suggest some possibilities for consideration, recognizing that they merely skim the surface of how the models might be applied. The two considerations we offer in this section can probably be translated into any context. In the next section we offer examples of specific contexts documented to promote learning. As we discuss these applications, we refer to applying both the critical theories and the critical models. Although we believe that applying these models is as much about applying the critical theoretical perspectives as it is about the models themselves, we also believe that the models provide a tangible way of putting the theories into practice by serving as a means for educators and students to apply the theories to their own identities and contexts.

Educating the Educator

Regardless of the specific application of the critical models, it is important that student affairs educators learn about the critical theories on which the models are based and reflect on the meanings of the models and the ways in which they inform how a person understands his or her own identity. This is the first consideration. Students cannot be expected to do the difficult work of understanding the influence of systems of privilege and oppression if educators have not engaged in their own meaningful exploration. Indeed, despite spending significant time with these critical theoretical perspectives and models, we still are making sense of our own identity in relation to them and of how these ideas shift our thinking about teaching and research, as our final interludes suggest. We therefore encourage educators to use the models as part of professional development opportunities, in much the same way that the MMDI and RMMDI have been applied, as reviewed earlier in this chapter. It is beneficial for educators to consider their own identity in relation to the various elements in each of the models, exploring while they do so how power structures shape the various contexts in which they work.

One of the goals of professional development of this nature is to foster a critical understanding of one's own identity; the identities of the students with whom one works; as well as the contexts in which the work is done, ranging from the campus as a whole to the more narrow circles in which students interact with one another, such as student organizations and courses. Possessing a critical understanding of identity means having the ability and inclination to recognize how identities are shaped by inequitable power structures and the desire to change them at least within one's own "sphere of influence" (Tatum, 1997, p. 204). Developing this perspective is a process that takes continuous work, including, for instance, learning about differences, reflecting on one's own intersecting identities, challenging oneself to recognize one's own privileges and oppressions, and sharpening one's ability to be aware of inequities both subtle and not so subtle in the ways that systems of inequality shape reality. Some individuals may have a heightened awareness of these inequities but still need to refine their understanding of particular forms of oppression that they do not personally encounter as frequently. Regardless of where one's development toward a critical understanding resides, the continued development necessary is something to which one must commit despite some of its emotional cost and the lure of taking the "path of least resistance" (Johnson, 2006, p. 80). Educating students without also educating oneself is not a viable option when truly engaging in critical practice.

Developing and acting on one's critical understanding can be accomplished in subtle yet important ways. For instance, a student in one of Elisa's student development theory classes reflected on how her increasing knowledge of critical race theory and the CRT-MMDI informed her practice as a supervisor within residence life. She stated:

> As an entry-level residence life professional, one of the most important components of my position is student staff supervision . . . I propose that my racial identity as White and my understanding of various theories related to race have a direct impact on the way I approach and understand my supervisory style. In my first year of graduate school, my supervisory style had three parts: 1) setting clear and high expectations of my student staff early; 2) consistent accountability to those expectations; and 3) role modeling strong professional and ethical practice. I found these expectations to be reasonable, my staff (of predominantly White individuals) found this style to be direct and effective, and by stating my supervisory style early on, I could effectively implement this style. However, a closer analysis of this style has revealed several significant realizations in the way I have approached supervision in my second year.
>
> My understanding of critical race theory . . . as well as my Whiteness and its associated privilege . . . has allowed me to evolve my supervisory style in my second year. I have taken a more inclusive approach to the underlying "non-negotiables" of my supervisory style. Instead of setting the same clear . . . expectations for all student staff members, I have taken a more developmental approach to supervision that focuses on getting to know students and their experiences, and creating expectations that are developmentally appropriate to students' growth. While some expectations are set by the department, I am able to tweak expectations that allow me to situate learning in students'

experiences . . . My understanding of critical race theory, which focuses on storytelling and the experiences of people of color, also allows me a stronger ability to get to know students and their experiences related to their identity before creating expectations that I expect them to follow and "fit." (Newman, 2012, p. 11)

Here this student is recognizing the centrality of race in the notion of meeting students where they are, commenting on race as central to students' experiences and development. Further, she recognizes the centrality of race for herself as a White supervisor. In doing so, her reflection raises interesting questions about the application of CRT to White individuals. She is reflecting on the extent to which she is comfortable applying CRT to her own identity, recognizing that race is not central to her in the same way that it is to a person of color, despite race overtly and subtly shaping her experiences. She is also considering how her application of CRT in her practice is likely to be different from the way a person of color might apply the theory. This student's thinking represents the type of ongoing professional development that is crucial for meaningful application of the critical theories.

Tapping into Students' Stories Through the Critical Models

The critical models can be applied in any educational context, regardless of whether or not the context is one specifically focused on student identity. We believe that one of the most effective ways of applying the models in various contexts, and the second consideration for applying the critical models in practice, is by using them to tap into students' narratives. Considering the extent to which critical perspectives and the ideas portrayed in the critical models are challenging for professionals to make sense of, these concepts can be extremely difficult for many traditional-age college students and adult learners, especially those with multiple privileged identities. We believe, however, that challenging students to learn about elements from the critical models can be an effective way to help them understand critical perspectives. The models combine to provide a framework that enhances students' ability to see their own stories within the critical theories.

Returning to Chimamanda Adichie's (2009) perspective on the "danger of a single story" to which we referred in Chapter One, we encourage educators to elicit students' multiple narratives. These multiple narratives bring to the surface the apparent and less apparent ways in which all students are part of inequitable systems of power and possess identities that can be portrayed within the critical models. (We present examples of student narratives and their various relationships with the critical models in Chapter Ten.) To illustrate the importance of students' narratives, we share with you a note we received from two students in Elisa's student development theory class. These students facilitated a presentation with traditional-age college students about queer theory and identity. Specifically, they presented about the relationships among heteronormativity, performativity, and gender roles in same-sex relationships. With much enthusiasm, the presenters commented afterward:

> As we presented the material, you could see the lights go off in their heads that they had experienced what we were discussing, but now had language to describe it. They were applying heteronormativity and performativity to their own lives and telling stories of their own experiences. One ally said he had never heard of heteronormativity and was blown away that it existed. One woman came out as lesbian and talked of her experience in the military. A masculine performing man also talked about the difficulties of gender roles/expectations in his relationship, because he doesn't meet many of the stereotypes of masculinity and "just likes to cuddle" with his male partner. Just a few of the awesome stories we heard! We also talked about how they could bring these conversations back to their campuses and peers. They were WONDERFUL!! AND provided such great insight into how some of these theories can really be applied. (K. Altenau & E. Gudmundson, personal communication, February 15, 2012)

Similar ideas drawn from queer theory and the queered model can be extended to multiple contexts within student affairs. For instance, conversations about heteronormativity and gender performance could be had within fraternities and sororities to explore the social constructions of masculinity and femininity and the impact these social constructions have on rituals, behaviors, and relationships. Likewise, conversations about heteronormativity and gender performance might be relevant within offices of student conduct, given potential relationships between conduct issues and student perceptions of behaviors associated with masculinity. Similar conversations are important within offices of residence life in regard to body image and disordered eating. Within race-based student organizations, such conversations could explore intersections of racial, gender, and sexual identity performatives. Using a queered approach, students' narratives ought to be heard in the context of continuous shifts in the meanings of their identity, and in space provided for students to explore that fluidity. Regardless of the context, tapping into student narratives and perceptions of compulsory ways of performing one's identity and the influence of context on these performances might expose students to new understandings about the meaning of their identity and associated behaviors.

Likewise, using elements from the intersectional and CRT models as starting points for discussion can be productive in helping students both discover new identity narratives about themselves and develop an understanding of identity narratives of students different from them. For instance, educators in orientation and first-year student programming might use elements of the I-MMDI to elicit the narratives of first-generation college students and students from low socioeconomic backgrounds as a way for those students to make sense of and be supported in their college experience. Academic advisers, residence life staff, or those working in multicultural offices, among others, might use elements of the CRT-MMDI to elicit narratives of students of color at predominantly White institutions as a way of partnering with them to make meaning of their experiences. Students with multiple privileged identities could benefit from exploring their narratives through the lens of the I-MMDI as a way of learning about ways they have benefited from intersecting systems of power. Such conversations are relevant in numerous contexts, such as offices of campus activities and student government, as students consider the meaning of inclusive campus programming, or offices of residence life, as students learn how to negotiate roommate conflicts grounded in different worldviews. Educators will bring their own skills to drawing out these narratives, in some instances through planned programs and in others through organic conversation. Regardless of the approach, the importance of bringing forth narratives highlights the need for educators to continuously develop their own understandings of critical practice, and also to be open to learning together with students as new perspectives emerge from their narratives.

Educational Contexts That Foster Students' Critical Understanding of Identity

The two considerations described earlier, educating the educator and tapping into students' narratives, are relevant to numerous contexts. In this section we present examples of four specific contexts in which these considerations could be applied. For educational contexts to promote students' critical understanding of identity, a combination of certain key characteristics is necessary. Each of these characteristics is an important component of any context that would promote students' critical understanding of identity, although not all characteristics will be present in every context. We developed this list of characteristics based on themes we found in the literature on identity-focused educational contexts (for example, Butin, 2010; Chang, Denson, Saenz, & Misa, 2006; Dessel, Rogge, & Garlington, 2006; Milem, Chang, & antonio, 2005; Nagda & Gurin, 2007; Quaye, Tambascia, & Talesh, 2009; Rhoads, 1997; Rosenberger, 2000), as well as on the ideas we reviewed throughout Section Three of this book. These characteristics are presented in Table 9.1.

We now describe some examples of contexts that include several of these key characteristics for fostering students' critical understanding about their identity and the identities of others. Each of these contexts is specifically focused on students' identities. These contexts range from broad issues related to campus climate to individual interactions with students in the curriculum and cocurriculum. What follows are only a few of the numerous possible examples of contexts found to be effective. We note that much of the literature concerning these contexts focuses on raising the consciousness of dominant students as a result of their interactions with the "other," the "other" being students with marginalized identities. Consistent with our application of the intersectional, CRT, and queered approaches, we include contexts from the perspectives of both dominant and marginalized groups.

Campus Climate and Critical Perspectives: Counterspaces and Supports for Marginalized Students

One way to think about using the critical models is to consider how educators might apply them in practice to shape campus climate. It is well documented that interactions across difference within a diverse campus environment produce positive outcomes associated with developing openness to diversity, a necessary condition for developing a critical understanding about identity. Much of this research is in the context of cross-racial interactions. In their oft-cited report on campus climate, Sylvia Hurtado, Jeffrey Milem, Alma Clayton-Pedersen, and Walter Allen (1999) described how the presence of and interactions among racially and ethnically diverse peers in the learning context produce positive

TABLE 9.1 CHARACTERISTICS OF CONTEXTS THAT FOSTER STUDENTS' CRITICAL UNDERSTANDING OF IDENTITY

Characteristic	Description
Critical analysis of systems of power and oppression	Offers experiences and opportunities that focus on recognition and analysis of systems of inequality
Critical self-reflection	Offers opportunities for reflection concerning the ways in which systems of inequality contribute to one's own identity and actions
Interaction with the "other"; cross-cultural interaction	Provides meaningful opportunities for interactions with people with identities and worldviews different from one's own
Sustained engagement	Offers opportunities for time-intensive engagement with critical analysis or critical reflection, and for deep reflection and learning fostered by sustained engagement in a subject area
Immersion	Provides opportunities to be part of a culture different from one's own for sustained periods of time with little access to one's own culture
Border crossing	Facilitates an internal process of reflection concerning changing conceptualizations of one's identity and creation of new frameworks for understanding how the world works as a result of interactions with the "other" and different contexts
Challenging stereotypes	Provides opportunities for exposure to realities different from those typically assumed about people different from oneself
Dialogue across difference	Provides opportunities to engage in conversations with people with identities different from one's own in which the purpose is to understand, rather than to analyze or debate, differing perspectives
Dissonance, decentering, disequilibrium	Provides learning opportunities that introduce new ways of thinking and worldviews that are inconsistent with one's current understanding, resulting in a need for reflection concerning how to resolve these inconsistencies
Resistance	Makes apparent one's opposition to new worldviews, ideas, or change; although not a paralyzing state, requires educators to support students through this process and challenge them to deconstruct their resistance

outcomes, such as "improvements in students' ability to engage in more complex thinking about problems and to consider multiple perspectives, and improvements in intergroup relations and understanding" (p. 7). Building on that work, Milem, Mitchell Chang, and anthony antonio (2005) explained that when students experience cross-racial interaction, they encounter dissonance, which enhances their cognitive and identity development. Opportunities for cross-racial interaction were found to increase according to growth in compositional diversity on campuses. Similarly, Chang and colleagues (2006) studied the implications of cross-racial interaction for producing increased openness to diversity, cognitive development, and self-confidence. They found peer cross-racial interaction to be significant for achieving openness to diversity. Most recently, Chang, Milem, and antonio (2011) offered further evidence that cross-cultural interaction is a key factor in realizing the educational benefits of campus diversity. They put forth the following recommendations for professionals: recognize policies that limit student interaction across difference; implement diversity as a policy across all areas of campus, ensuring retention and success for underrepresented students; and conduct assessments that investigate the impact that diversity on campus is having on students and the institution.

Although diverse campus climates that allow for interactions across difference might contribute to developing more openness to diversity, these same campus climates often perpetuate systems of oppression through microaggressions. Therefore, the critical theories and models become relevant to the conversation surrounding campus climate. As discussed in Chapter Seven, Solórzano, Ceja, and Yosso (2000) used critical race theory to examine racial microaggressions and their impact on the college racial climate. They explored the connections between racial stereotypes, racial microaggressions, the campus racial climate, and academic performance. Findings illuminated how African American students experienced racial microaggressions in academic and social contexts on campus, which had a negative impact on their academic performance and campus involvement. For instance, discussions of African Americans in the curriculum were stereotypical or nonexistent, and many African American students felt invisible in the classroom, which led to feelings of self-doubt. Class study groups were often racially segregated, which students thought reflected their peers' belief that Black people were not intelligent. Outside the classroom, students conveyed a similarly negative racial climate that caused them to feel discomfort, and that discouraged them from participating in programs or services. Solórzano and others advocated for the role of counterspaces, such as African American student organizations, Black fraternities and sororities, and Black student-organized study halls, to respond to microaggressions. These researchers found that counterspaces allowed African American students to learn in a supportive and validating environment. Yosso, Smith, Ceja, and Solórzano (2009) expanded on that study by using critical race theory to understand how Latino/a students experienced racial microaggressions. They found that Latino/a students claimed empowerment from the margins through building community and developing critical navigation skills.

Using critical race theory, Lori Patton (2006) explored an example of counterspaces used to claim empowerment, Black cultural centers, to understand how Black students made meaning of their experiences in these centers. Patton used a CRT framework to understand the ongoing realities and struggles with discrimination that Black students experience. She also used CRT to make sense of the Black students' use of counter-storytelling and counterspaces, which reflected their need for safe spaces to resist the chilly campus climate. Patton also viewed Black cultural centers as stories (through their programs, buildings, and services) of Black culture. Finally, Patton's CRT approach highlighted the possibility that Black cultural centers outwardly may be viewed by White people as a representation of the university's commitment to diversity, yet inwardly may be viewed by White people as a method to avoid controversy and protest. Among other findings, Patton explained that Black cultural centers were linked to the personal and historical identities of Black students and were considered a home for many of them. The findings support the belief that these centers play a significant role for Black students in recognizing Black culture and history, offering students a chance to learn about themselves and providing a safe and supportive space.

Using the CRT-MMDI to understand student identity adds another layer to this CRT-based campus climate literature. The model's depiction of race as central to the identity of students of color, regardless of whether or not they perceive it as salient, contributes to the ways in which educators might create contexts that foster resistance against racism. Recognizing differences in the salience of race for different students enables educators to understand students' varied perceptions of the role of racism, allowing for multiple approaches to resistance. For example, African American students for whom race is not salient might not be interested in engaging with a Black cultural center. The same is true for participation in Black student organizations, despite the positive outcomes associated with participation for some students (Harper & Quaye, 2007). Still, these students are likely to encounter microaggressions, and appropriate support ought to be available across the campus from faculty and staff in multiple arenas in the students' lives. One of the most visible forms of support is the vibrant presence of faculty and staff of color who are engaged with the students' experience.

Likewise, the model's portrayal of racism as intersecting with other forms of inequality, such as heterosexism and classism, and thereby affecting how race interacts with other social identities, also contributes to the ways in which practitioners might create and work within contexts that foster resistance. Whether in a race-based cultural center or elsewhere on campus, racism will look different for individual students depending on how it intersects with other forms of oppression relevant to their identity. The relevance of these intersections will differ depending on context and the changing salience of social identities. Putting students' experiences with intersecting forms of oppression at the center of practice shifts the nature of student affairs practice from working within systems of inequality to resisting these systems, and doing so in partnership with the students whenever possible. For example, in the context of academic advising, an African American woman in a STEM (science, technology, engineering, mathematics) major might voice perceptions of invisibility in how her professors and peers treat her in the classroom. The CRT-MMDI informs the advisor's understanding of racism as central to the student's identity, and as inseparable from sexism. Inviting the student's counterstory about her otherwise silenced presence in the classroom and interrogating the role of gendered racism in the student's experience might empower her to exert herself as knowledgeable in the classroom, a means for this student to resist classroom power dynamics and more richly understand her own identity.

Although much of the literature on campus climate focuses on race and ethnicity, the Queered Model of Multiple Dimensions of Identity (Q-MMDI) and I-MMDI also contribute to an understanding of how students with other marginalized identities might experience the campus climate. For instance, just as racial microaggressions are detrimental to the campus climate for students of color, microaggressions related to sexuality are harmful to students who do not identify as heterosexual. Examples of sexual orientation microaggressions include the use of heterosexist terminology; the endorsement of heteronormative culture and behaviors; assumptions of a universal lesbian, gay, and bisexual (LGB) experience; and the exoticization of LGB identities (Nadal et al., 2011). Renn (2010a) noted that there is very little research that examines higher education and queer identities using a queer theory analysis. Applying the Q-MMDI to this heteronormative context enhances educators' ability to address these microaggressions. For instance, applying the Q-MMDI to students' experiences, educators can make sense of students' identities each as a series of performatives that challenge these microaggressions, rather than perceiving their identities and experiences as essentialized reflections of these microaggressions. This agentic perspective on identity lends itself to practitioners' accommodating students' desires in regard to how they perform their identities and letting the "power" reside within the student, unlike a perspective that only "helps" support students within a heteronormative context. For example, an office of campus activities might partner with a student who identifies as gender nonconforming or genderqueer in hir desire to be on the homecoming court despite not identifying as either male or female. Rather than boxing the student into the heteronormative structure, the nature of a homecoming court might be rethought and not gender-bound. At the same time, the office might consider the presence of other gendered spaces on campus, beyond the most obvious ones, such as residence halls and restrooms. These spaces can be identified by inviting and listening to the stories of gender nonconforming students, a process that might also facilitate their own understanding of their identity.

Regardless of student affairs practitioners' best efforts, heteronormative microaggressions do contribute to the lived experience of queer students, and these students experience the campus climate differently depending on how their sexuality intersects with other social identities. The I-MMDI helps make sense of their identities in these contexts. By way of example, cultural centers and student organizations focused on sexuality are places where the theory of intersectionality can be put into practice. These contexts prove fruitful for some students (for example, Renn, 2007; Renn & Bilodeau, 2005). However, the intersection of racism and heterosexism, and the different meanings of being a queer person of color versus a queer White person, might prevent some students of color from feeling comfortable being involved in such centers and organizations on a predominantly White campus. The intersections of their sexual orientation and race might be salient as a result of the intersections of heteronormativity and racism, but not because the person authentically chooses these social identities to be salient. This student might not choose to be involved in the queer community through a center or student organization, but might seek out other forms of support from peers who share some similar intersections. Creating supportive contexts that recognize these intersections is an important aspect of student affairs practice.

Although much of the research on campus climate focuses on predominantly White institutions, the salience of the intersection of racism and heterosexism suggests the need for forms of support other than student organizations for queer students of color at an HBCU, a Hispanic-Serving Institution, or an Asian American and Pacific Islander–Serving Institution. Lori Patton (2011) examined the experience of six African American men at an HBCU, exploring how they viewed and disclosed their sexual identity and how they navigated the campus environment. She found that all the participants referred to themselves as Black and male, with their sexual identity taking less prominence in how they identified themselves. Within the campus environment, students believed that the climate on their campus was more open and welcoming than at other HBCUs, but that to be involved in campus life meant to put the "gay thing on the backburner" (p. 91). Not many students were members of lesbian, gay, bisexual, and transgender student organizations because it would increase the visibility of their sexual identity and had political implications for those who wanted to be leaders in other areas of campus. These findings suggest that the African American gay and bisexual men had to choose between identities as a result of external pressure, which resulted in race and gender's taking precedence over their sexual identity. Although hers was not an intersectional study, Patton's results highlight the importance of forms of support that are less prominent than student organizations and cultural centers based on sexual orientation. Rather, it is important that topics related to sexual orientation be infused throughout campus, such as in residence hall education, campus programs, and course work, as well as through supportive university policies, and this effort must be undertaken in a manner that does not falsely separate sexual orientation from other forms of identity, including race and gender.

Diversity-Focused Courses, Intergroup Dialogue, and Critical Perspectives

Courses specifically focused on diversity have the potential to develop students' critical understanding of identity. Diversity courses focused on racial, ethnic, and gender identities have been shown to promote cognitive changes as well as attitude and value shifts; decrease forms of sexism and racism; increase students' ability to notice racism and privilege; support student gains in cultural awareness; and improve interactions with racially and ethnically diverse peers (Bowman, 2010). For instance, focusing on the experiences of White students, Chang (2002) investigated whether diversity courses meet the goals associated with reducing racial prejudice, particularly toward African Americans. He found that these courses can result in reduced racial prejudice when students critically examine the systemic marginalization of others and challenge their stereotypes and assumptions. However, developing such an understanding is complex and not easily accomplished. Nicholas Bowman noted that students expressed resistance to integrating new perspectives from these diversity courses with their preexisting worldviews, a process that created a sense of disequilibrium for them. Bowman identified student resistance and disequilibrium as aspects of course experiences that can have a positive impact on student learning, provided that these reactions are addressed and students' disequilibrium is worked through.

A particular type of diversity-focused class that has demonstrated significant potential for developing students' critical understanding of identity is one that allows for intergroup dialogue (IGD). In addition to being part of a course, IGD can also be included as part of the cocurriculum. Biren Nagda and Patricia Gurin (2007) defined IGD as

> an educational endeavor that brings together students from two or more social identity groups to build relationships across cultural and power differences to raise consciousness of inequalities, to explore the similarities and differences in experiences across identity groups, and to strengthen individual and collective capacities to promote social justice. (p. 35)

The crucial components of IGD are critical analysis of understandings of difference and dominance, discursive engagement across difference, and sustained community building and conflict engagement (Nagda & Gurin, 2007). IGD strives for students to understand inequalities in the "context of sociostructural and power relations, such as institutional racism or patriarchy" (Nagda & Gurin, p. 36). Adrienne Dessel, Michael Woodford, and Naomi Warren (2011) reported such positive outcomes associated with an intergroup dialogue course on sexual orientation, stating:

> Similar to what occurs in intergroup dialogue groups on other topics (Nagda, Gurin, Sorensen, & Zúñiga, 2009), our participants generally reported a more complex awareness of institutional and structural oppression . . . Students became aware of the explicit and often subtle

nature of heterosexism and the complex ways in which it is maintained. Contributing to this is the recognition and claiming of privileged identities. Parallel to students in other dialogue groups (Nagda et al., 2009; Rozas, 2007), our participants reported a commitment to engage in social change actions, and some had undertaken notable change activities while members of the sexual orientation dialogue group. We believe that both the commitment and the action taken are indicators of the empowerment that was realized. (pp. 1145–1146)

Emotionally and intellectually challenging work, intergroup dialogue provides provocative opportunities for developing new perspectives on identity. Still, if employed in a noncritical manner, dialogue could be harmful to some of the student participants.

Indeed, much of the research on diversity-related courses has focused on the learning of White students about students of color, or the learning of those with other dominant identities in relation to that of those who are marginalized. It has been noted that students of color often experience diversity-related courses, especially the first courses they take, as places where their role is to educate others rather than to learn from others (Bowman, 2010). Intersectionality, critical race theory, and queer theory provide approaches to analyzing the experiences and identities of those students on the margins in the classroom. For instance, understanding the identities of students of color through the CRT-MMDI would assist faculty in making sense of the ways in which racism is central to students' identity (their core) despite varying salience of race for individual students. Using critical race theory, as well as stereotype theory and student development theory, Quaye and colleagues (2009) explored how to respond to the needs of racial and ethnic minority students in the classroom, where "far too often, the onus is put on racial/ethnic minority students to assimilate to predominantly White classroom norms and divorce their cultures and identities from the learning process" (p. 158). Asserting that this problem is not limited to diversity-related courses, Quaye and others identified five obstacles faced by racial and ethnic minority students in predominantly White classrooms and illustrated why it is important to focus on engagement among these students. The obstacles they identified are inattentiveness by faculty to differences in racial identity development; being one of few racial and ethnic minority students; a lack of same-race or same-ethnicity faculty; noninclusive curricular content; and a lack of culturally responsive pedagogy. The process of racial identity development was highlighted as essential to assisting students in understanding their own and others' views of knowledge. Racial and ethnic minority students often encounter questions of their academic capabilities because of deficit-minded approaches and stereotypes related to affirmative action. Faculty of the same race or ethnicity are crucial for racial and ethnic minority students to have as mentors. They help create more inclusive environments, and encourage students to experience diverse perspectives on learning. Curricular content that infuses the voices of racial and ethnic minority cultures has the powerful effect of validating the knowledge and experiences of racial and ethnic minority students.

The critical models could be applied in the context of intergroup dialogue, not only to prompt educators to rethink modes of facilitation but also to shape learning outcomes associated with this form of instruction. As suggested by the I-MMDI, listening for and encouraging students' authenticity at their core, nestled within intersecting systems of power and intersections of social identities, accomplishes this objective. Offering opportunities for students to explore and reflect on their identities, the meaning of authenticity, and the challenges associated with authenticity is useful given the push and pull on identity from external expectations. As the Q-MMDI encourages educators to recognize, it is important to assume that students' identities are constantly evolving rather than stable. This assumption that social identities are always in motion and fused rather than moving toward an end destination means that little can actually be predicted about students based on their "list" of social identities. Rather than "doing for" students by calling out systems of power, it is important to partner with students who are engaged in dialogue, as they are their own best agents in resisting systems of inequality that try to confine them. One way to partner with students is by encouraging authenticity in identity performatives that result in such resistance. For example, as a facilitator, it is important to probe for and support student stories of identity performatives that are not in line with dominant expectations, either as part of the larger dialogue or in smaller affinity groups in which students might feel more support. At the same time, a facilitator ought to be aware that students' lived experiences are shaped by the systems of inequality that they are resisting. Again, this is one of the challenges of the push and pull on identity and is a place where intergroup dialogue facilitators ought to provide significant support. Considering the CRT-MMDI, a facilitator would center the perspectives of students of color, pay heightened attention to the role of microaggressions in the dialogue, and offer examples of racism that counter some of the dominant ideas emerging from discussions. Recognizing that race is at the core for all students of color despite the differences in the salience of race, the facilitator must help make racism apparent to all and offer varying challenges and supports to different students. Intergroup dialogue is a challenging approach to teaching and learning, but it has significant transformative potential that can be realized in new ways when framed through these critical models.

As with Quaye and others' research (2009), the examples in the rest of this subsection of critical perspectives in course work do not apply only to diversity-related courses, but instead show how critical models are relevant in general in the classroom. Approaching identity from an intersectional perspective can also address the experiences of marginalized students in the classroom by leading to an understanding of how their identities are situated within intersecting systems of inequality that affect the nature of intersections among their social identities. In the following example, Jones and Wijeyesinghe (2011) applied four core tenets of intersectionality to classroom dynamics, course development, and teaching in diverse classrooms. *Centering the experiences of people of color* implies a commitment to teaching about power and privilege and examining the discipline through a lens of inequality that is integrated throughout the course. *Complicating identity* requires educators to refrain from assuming they understand an individual's or group's identity fully and encourage students to do the same. *Unveiling power in interconnected structures of inequality* reflects the notion that policies, teaching practices, interpersonal practices, and resources help shape the interactions between students and faculty. Power dynamics can influence which students dominate discussions and whether students are engaged in cocreating knowledge. Finally, *promoting social justice and social change* is fostered through incorporating discussions about power and privilege. Again, there are challenges inherent in bringing intersectionality into teaching practices, including the difficulty of attending to multiple identities while citing the oppression of one larger identity group, creating space to acknowledge marginalization while also recognizing the identities of individuals who benefit from power, working collaboratively across disciplines, and addressing the need for faculty to demonstrate personal commitment to social justice.

Queer theory also is relevant in the classroom. For instance, Brenda Brueggemann and Debra Moddelmog (2002) explained how they teach about identities, specifically sexual orientation and disability (an example of queer theory applied to disability), as performatives through the way they present their identities to the students. They represent their identities as fluid and challenge students to explore their heterosexist and ableist assumptions. Mel Lewis (2011) described how she incorporated queer theory and intersectionality into her women's studies classroom. She stated:

> I examine the ways in which women's studies can address the predicament of black lesbian erasure and silence; black queer studies; black feminist studies. I teach what I am, I am what I teach . . . I live and perform my multiple social identities, both visible and invisible, and teach both through institutional knowledge and my own "embodied text" (Henderson, 1994, p. 436) . . . I identify as a black woman, a lesbian, queer, a feminist, a scholar, and a teacher—thus living and teaching at their intersections. The ways in which my students understand my identities becomes part of the project as they sort out the complicated ideas of race, gender, sexuality, and class through the interpretation of course texts, including my own embodied text. (p. 50)

Just as professors speak to the ways in which they bring their own multiple, intersecting identities to the classroom and present them to students as fluid performatives, professors and student affairs educators ought to assume that their students have multiple, intersecting identities that act as fluid performatives. As depicted by the I-MMDI and Q-MMDI, it is important to recognize difference among students despite similarity of social identities. The inseparability of social identities and the prominence of context result in students' each experiencing their identity differently. Likewise, the differences in how students experience their identity result in differences in how they experience the campus environment (Museus, 2009).

Service-Learning and Critical Perspectives

Service-learning is a form of pedagogy that has proven to be especially effective in creating the conditions that foster students' critical understanding of identity. Service-learning is "a form of experiential education in which students engage in activities that address human and community needs together with structured opportunities intentionally designed to promote student learning and development" (Jacoby, 1996, p. 5). It can be implemented both as part of a course or as part of the cocurriculum. In a thoughtful and interdisciplinary book on service-learning,

Robert Rhoads (1997) suggested that service-learning increases students' understanding of self and community, placing particular emphasis on the development of a caring self. Important aspects contributing to this outcome are fostering mutual relationships based on equity and collaboration, community building, and integrating reflection and action. Rhoads developed a critical service-learning approach focused on creating opportunities that challenge students to think more deeply about service, how service shapes them and others, and the potential to build caring communities. Jones and Abes (2004) explored the lasting impact of a critical service-learning course on identity development. They found that service-learning had an enduring influence on students' developing greater complexity and empathy in thinking about themselves and others, becoming open to new ideas and experiences, and establishing new commitments to community and social responsibility, resulting in a more "integrated identity" (p. 149).

Cynthia Rosenberger (2000) highlighted that service-learning educators need to create experiences in which students develop a critical consciousness, not just empathy. Without developing among students an awareness of their place in society and their capacity to create change, there is potential for service-learning to reproduce power and privilege dynamics. Critical theoretical approaches to service-learning foreground power and privilege and engage students in critical examinations of the structural inequalities that create the social issues service-learning seeks to address (Jones, LePeau, & Robbins, in press). Dialogue, which occurs "between subjects who are open to seeing the world through the eyes of others and who grant others the right of naming the world" (Jones et al., in press), is a crucial aspect of developing such a critical understanding. Dialogue can occur between students and service recipients, as well as among students. These conversations are an opportunity to name and explore the systems of power, and the intersections among these systems, that structure the contexts in which the service recipients are situated, such as racism, classism, and heteronormativity. Michelle Dunlap, Jennifer Scoggin, Patrick Green, and Angelique Davi (2007) offered strategies for supporting students though a critical service-learning experience, including encouraging frequent and consistent critical reflection; allowing freedom and appropriate boundaries for exploring socioeconomic status, gender, sexual orientation, and race in reflections; highlighting the diversity within and among the students; offering curricular resources; providing prompting questions for critical reflection; and emphasizing the support systems available to the students.

Despite evidence that service-learning fosters new understandings of self and others, Jones and colleagues (in press) raised the difficulty of developing a critical understanding of identity through service-learning, specifically understanding the systems of inequality that ground the social problems addressed through service. They presented the results of a narrative study that explored the possibilities and limitations of service-learning through an alternative spring break trip focused on HIV/AIDS. They used an antifoundational and critical theoretical framework for the study. An antifoundational approach to service-learning "is about disrupting unacknowledged binaries that guide much of our day-to-day thinking and acting to open up the possibility that how we originally viewed the world and ourselves may be too simplistic and stereotypical" (Butin, 2010, p. 13). The results of this antifoundational and critical study suggested that "perspective transformation and analysis of root causes will not occur for most students" (Jones et al., in press). Jones and others examined through a critical lens the stereotypes, discrimination, privilege, and assumptions often unrecognized by participants. The study's findings raised questions about the reality of reciprocity in service-learning, the feasibility of addressing or examining root causes of social problems, the potential for sustaining students' commitment to social change, and the need for more critical examination of service-learning practice. Although service-learning is a meaningful context for examining systems of inequality, the work is difficult to do in a manner that truly gets at the critical understanding of how power shapes identity.

Further highlighting the difficult yet beneficial nature of service-learning work, Jones, Claire Robbins, and Lucy LePeau (2011) used a critical and antifoundational framework to explore the development and challenges associated with service-learning for students with privileged identities and those with marginalized identities. Participants crossed developmental, interpersonal, and cultural borders through their work with an HIV/AIDS service organization, which created powerful learning experiences through their internal grappling with the new identities and worldviews to which they were being exposed. Incorporating service-learning and immersion literature and applying critical and multicultural theories, the researchers investigated the developmental border crossing and decentering students encountered. Participants confronted their own privilege, which destabilized their understanding of identity and prompted them to think more critically about their beliefs, values, and behaviors. Although border crossing was a significant aspect of participants' experiences, "not all borders were crossed by all students and not all border crossings were sustained" (p. 35). In particular, students with marginalized social identities experienced less conflict in border crossing than did their peers with dominant social identities. These results suggest the importance of considering the nature of service-learning when students with marginalized identities are participating, a subject to which we now turn.

For instance, Gilbride-Brown's work (2008) provides an example of research that considers the service-learning experiences of students with marginalized identities and offers a crucial call for infusing critical perspectives into service-learning work. Using critical race theory, among other critical perspectives, Gilbride-Brown addressed the lack of understanding about the experiences of students of color in service-learning through her case study. Participants described service-learning as working "within" community. Findings also indicated that students of color were less inclined to participate in service-learning because it was perceived as a "White, do-gooder activity" (p. 118). Gilbride-Brown interrogated the ways in which students of color faced the complex issues they encountered, which caused others to characterize them as disengaged. Yet these issues were not addressed or attended to as part of the service-learning experience. These results suggest that critical service-learning may fall short of the transformational ideals it espouses.

Dialogue and other forms of reflection are fertile opportunities for considering identities, both marginalized and dominant, from the perspectives of the critical models. Whether an intersectional, CRT, or queered lens is used influences the primary focus of the service-learning experience. Students can reflect on how systems of power within the contexts of their service sites, viewed according to a particular theoretical perspective, shape the identities of the people with whom they are serving and their own identities. For example, using the I-MMDI as a guiding framework might help students with marginalized identities who did not believe they experienced border crossing reflect on intersections of identities and systems of power that render their identity different from the identities of those they are serving. Reflections might focus on similarities and differences in identity salience between the students and those they serve, including explorations of how differences in the ways they experience power structures might influence these comparisons. Students can also reflect on the impact of their intersecting identities on their service experience, which depends in large measure on the context and nature of the service work. For example, a Black gay student serving at an HIV/AIDS organization might think about the nature of his identity differently than when he is serving at a homeless shelter. The queered model could be used to facilitate reflections about the performed nature of students' identities, focusing on the different meanings of race, sexuality, and gender depending on an individual's actions. This focus on the instability of identity could enable students to rethink the meaning of border crossing by encouraging them to resist the notion of fixed identities and sameness. Using critical models to guide reflections allows for an exploration of these important differences. We encourage continued creative thinking about the potential of these models to guide reflection, recognizing that the precise ways in which these models can be incorporated will depend on differences in students' identities and the nature of the service work.

Challenges and Opportunities: "A Call to Action"

The nature of practice that we are calling for in this chapter brings with it some challenges, none of which are insurmountable, but which require a commitment from educators to embrace and educate themselves about the realities of critical student affairs practice. We conclude by considering one of these challenges, not to discourage readers, but rather to inspire the continued learning opportunities and determination necessary to create change.

One of the challenges in effectively practicing from a critical theoretical approach is that students' development in other domains also makes a difference in how they respond to this framework, and not all students will necessarily have the developmental capacity for understanding or acting on the critical perspectives. As described in Chapter Five, student development can be organized in three domains: cognitive (complexity in making meaning of the nature of knowledge), interpersonal (complexity in making meaning of relationships), and intrapersonal (complexity in making meaning of one's own identity). Movement from external toward internal meaning making in each of these domains is necessary for development toward self-authorship (Baxter Magolda, 2001). The capacity to recognize multiple possibilities for the meaning of identity, the capacity to construct one's own identity and understand the authenticity of the identities of others, and the capacity for recognizing and making one's own sense of how power structures shape reality require movement toward self-authorship that is beyond the development of most traditional-age college students (Baxter Magolda, 2001). Therefore, effectively applying these critical models in practice requires knowledge of how to work with students in a developmentally appropriate manner. Given the complex relationship between identity and student development and students' emotional investment associated with identity and difference, this is an obstacle that some practitioners find difficult to surmount.

Despite this challenge, we believe that these critical theories and the models based on them offer important opportunities—opportunities to learn how they are relevant to our own identities and contexts and opportunities to challenge ourselves to learn how to implement them in practice. As one of Elisa's students noted: "If you don't think these theories apply to a particular student affairs functional area or competency, think again, because they do. Exposure to these theories and models is a call to action" (E. Gudmundson, personal communication, May 7, 2012). Just as we are continuing to understand our own roles in this call to action, we urge others to do the same.

Summary

In this chapter we presented some of the ways in which the MMDI and RMMDI have been applied in research, theory development, and practice. We then considered possibilities for implementing the critical models in practice, an undertaking that requires continuous personal and professional learning and a philosophical shift in the nature of typical student affairs practice. We presented considerations relevant to multiple educational contexts, and also offered application possibilities for specific contexts. Applying the critical models opens up opportunities for considering the influence of systems of inequality on how students with marginalized identities experience educational contexts and the empowering ways in which these contexts can be reshaped. We recognize that there are challenges to effectively applying critical theoretical approaches in practice, and what we have presented is intended as the start of further conversation.

Discussion Questions and Activities

1. In addition to the examples provided of ways in which the MMDI and RMMDI have been applied in practice, what other applications of these models do you envision across multiple student affairs functional areas or other contexts?

2. Reflect on the development of your own critical understanding of identity. Is having such an understanding something that is important to you? In what areas do you see room for further development of your critical understanding? What educational contexts have been most beneficial to you in developing such an understanding? What contexts or practices could help you further develop your critical understanding?

3. In addition to some of the suggestions we included in this chapter, in what ways do you envision applying the intersectional, CRT, and queer theory models in practice? What are some of the opportunities and challenges of doing so? In what ways might these challenges be addressed?

4. Talk to a current student affairs practitioner about possibilities for applying the intersectional, CRT, and queered models in practice. You might want to choose a practitioner who works in a functional area with a focus on learning across difference. Before doing so, carefully consider how you will explain these models to this person, recognizing that they are founded on complex ideas with which many are not familiar. Consider what questions this practitioner might ask and how you would respond. What would you like the outcome of these conversations to be? How might you be able to continue such conversations, and with what intended outcomes?

5. Have a conversation with one or more undergraduate students about at least one of the critical models. In doing so, try to elicit the students' multiple identity narratives as a means of discussing how they understand their identities in relation to the models. Use this opportunity to practice talking to undergraduate students about critical theories in ways that they understand as relevant to their lives.

CHAPTER TEN

FUTURE DIRECTIONS

Considering Theoretical Perspectives in Conjunction with One Another

The various versions of the Model of Multiple Dimensions of Identity (MMDI) we presented in this book are grounded in different theoretical perspectives: constructivism, intersectionality, critical race theory, and queer theory. Each of those perspectives offers a way of understanding identity through the lens of one particular theory, focusing primarily on understanding students' perceptions of identity (constructivism), intersecting systems of inequality (intersectionality), the centrality of racism (critical race theory), or resistance to heteronormativity that results in fluid identities (queer theory). Considering the MMDI in light of these theoretical perspectives offers some of the newest thinking in the student affairs literature on the relationships among multiple identities, and there is still more work to be done in learning how to apply the critical perspectives in practice. Still, each of these theoretical perspectives is incomplete, as are all theoretical perspectives, meaning that each lens provides a partial understanding of reality grounded in one particular perspective, or, said another way, represents one reality among multiple possibilities (Abes, 2009). There might, therefore, be times when researchers or practitioners want to draw from one perspective or another, depending on such considerations as their own values and interests, the nature of the students with whom they are working, or the environment in which the institution is situated. There also might be times when they want to draw from multiple perspectives simultaneously.

As a way of continuing to think about future directions in the exploration of multiple identities, we consider in this chapter interactions among the four theoretical perspectives we have presented. We discuss relationships among their tenets and ways in which they inform one another when considered in conjunction with one another. For instance, we address the possibility of new theoretical perspectives that draw on ideas from multiple theories, such as concepts from queer theory and critical race theory considered together. We focus extra attention throughout the chapter on relationships between and among intersectionality, critical race theory, and queer theory because each foregrounds and critiques systems of inequality in ways that readily speak to one another. We also explore the application of these theories' tenets to social identities other than those they were originally intended to address, such as the application of ideas from queer theory to disability studies. We then discuss an approach we call "theoretical borderlands" (Abes, 2009, p. 143), which involves the simultaneous embrace and application of multiple theoretical perspectives, even when these contradict one another. To illustrate the borderland analysis, we conclude this chapter by presenting examples of five borderland models and corresponding narratives drawn and described by graduate students, and we urge readers to consider how other borderland analyses and models might represent relationships among multiple identities.

Exploring Relationships Among Constructivism, Intersectionality, Critical Race Theory, and Queer Theory

The four theoretical perspectives we have discussed, constructivism, intersectionality, critical race theory, and queer theory, each bring a unique perspective to the nature of relationships among social identities, as well as the relationships between these social identities and the context in which they are situated. To help guide the analysis of the ways in which these perspectives might be thought of in relation to one another, including relationships among social identities and relationships between social identities and context, we reintroduce Table 6.0 from the introduction to Section Three. Appearing in this chapter as Table 10.1, this chart now also includes constructivism, as well as additional information about the critical nature of each of the paradigms.

TABLE 10.1 RELATIONSHIPS AMONG THEORETICAL PERSPECTIVES

Theoretical Perspective	Paradigm	Critical Nature of the Theory	Approach to Understanding Relationships Among Social Identities	Nature of Relationships Between Social Identities and Context	Strengths	Limitations
Constructivism	Interpretivist	Understand: possibility of recognition of power structures, but not a theoretical assumption	Seeks to understand how individuals perceive relationships among social identities	Focus on the individual in relation to the context; defining oneself either through the context (external meaning making) or in relation to the context (internal meaning making)	Offers an understanding of individuals' self-perceptions, minimizing the tendency to make assumptions about others	Does not intentionally interrogate systems of inequality
Intersectionality	Critical	Praxis: putting theory into practice to create change in the nature of power structures	Critically examines how intersecting systems of inequality shape individuals' lived experiences, resulting in intersectional rather than additive social identities	Focus on context (intersecting systems of inequality) as central to identity	Situates identity in lived experience as integral to social change; highlights identity as comprising both privilege and oppression	Without a focus on one particular identity, allows the individual to overlook nonsalient identities (often those associated with privilege) as influencing the nature of lived experience
Critical Race Theory	Critical	Resistance: resisting racist power structures through counterstories	Focuses on race and racism as central to identity and intersecting with other social identities	Focus on context (racism) as central to identity	Foregrounds racism through counterstories; facilitates social change	Focuses primarily on race, which overshadows other identities
Queer Theory	Poststructural	Resistance: resisting heteronormative power structures through performatives that result in fluid identities	Recognizes social identities as fused performatives, constantly changing (fluid) as contexts change, resulting in an identity that is always becoming	Focus on context (heteronormativity) as central to identity; symbiotic relationships between social identities and context	Offers resistance to oppressive social conditions (heteronormativity) through the deconstruction of identity categories	Has difficulty reconciling the deconstruction of identity categories and the fluid nature of identity with lived experience and social change; focuses primarily on gender and sexuality, which overshadow other identities

Distinctions Among Intersectionality, Critical Race Theory, and Queer Theory

With their emphasis on inseparable social identities, queer theory and critical race theory have been characterized as types of intersectional scholarship (Dill, McLaughlin, & Nieves, 2007; Renn, 2010b). This is a reasonable characterization, as the emphasis on inseparable social identities that inform one another is a fundamental tenet that the three perspectives share. However, important distinctions exist among them as well. Specifically, as we discussed in Chapters Six, Seven, and Eight, intersectionality and critical race theory, both critical theories, encourage social change, focusing on how inequitable social systems shape one's identity and lived experience, whereas queer theory, a poststructural theory, emphasizes the deconstruction of identity and therefore the process rather than the product of identity creation. Queer theory's focus on performativity makes it difficult to describe how one experiences identity, because identity is always in a process of becoming. Performativity and fluidity can also make social change more elusive because it is challenging to undo power structures associated with an identity when that identity is considered unstable, without a firm category to ground it (Sullivan, 2003). For instance, how does one challenge heteronormativity without the leverage of the experiences of lesbian, gay, bisexual, or transgender people to hold on to?

At the same time, as described in Chapter Eight, queer theory suggests that inequitable social structures are eroded through performativity. Performativity, a constant process that re-creates identity through everyday behavior, is a form of resistance that is different from critical race theory's espousal of intentional counterstories as a means of overcoming structural determinism. Indeed, tenets of critical race theory challenge queer theory's focus on resistance through performativity. Critical race theorists argue that the study of identity in and of itself is insufficient to address the realities of racism. Resistance that is more direct and radical than the study of identity allows is necessary to accomplish social change (Delgado & Stefancic, 2001). Queer theory, intersectionality, and critical race theory, therefore, each portray the inseparability of identities in a distinct manner and with a different purpose, as either a phenomenon that affects one's lived experience (intersectionality and critical race theory) or a phenomenon that is a form of resistance to oppressive social conditions reified through identity categories (queer theory).

Unlike these critical and poststructural perspectives, constructivism, which reveals how individuals perceive their identities, allows for social identities to be considered as distinct from one another. An individual's perception of distinctions among social identities might or might not be related to meaning-making complexity. People who undertake complex meaning making might construct their identity as comprising distinct social identities, if that is how they experience, or would like to experience, identity. Such a perception might not take into consideration the role of power structures. Although a person might make meaning of power structures as part of assessing the surrounding context, and although that person might choose to resist such structures, doing so is not a necessary aspect of constructivism. The possibility of being unaware of the influence of power structures begs the question of whether a person who does not consider power structures in the construction of identity is unknowingly defined by these external influences and therefore not internally defining the relationships among social identities. For instance, if a White person is not aware of White privilege, is it possible for that person to internally define relationships among identities? Without an awareness of White privilege, it seems that the relationships between race and other social identities are products of external influences. This challenging question speaks to the difficulty of understanding social identities through only one theoretical perspective, a nod to the importance of considering multiple theoretical perspectives together.

Merging Aspects of Queer Theory, Critical Race Theory, and Intersectionality into New Theoretical Perspectives

Despite some of the fundamental differences among the three critical theoretical perspectives, there is good reason to consider ideas from these theories in relation to one another. Indeed, when taken together, these three perspectives create possibilities for conceptualizing identity that none can accomplish alone. Recognizing this potential, scholars have considered new takes on queer theory and critical race theory that bring together some of the ideas from each in an intersectional manner. For instance, queer theory has been frequently critiqued for giving insufficient attention to race (for example, Anzaldúa, 1991; Barnard, 1999), and critical race theory has been critiqued for overlooking sexual orientation (Carbado, 2002). Nikki Sullivan (2003) noted the problem with separate queer and race analyses, explaining:

> One of the many problems with disassociating race, gender, and sexuality and focusing primarily on one of the terms is that such an

approach can lead to the production of accounts of race that are (at least implicitly) sexist and/or homophobic, theories of gender that are (at least implicitly) racist and/or homophobic, and analyses of sexuality that are (at least implicitly) racist and/or sexist. (p. 66)

Bringing together ideas from queer theory and critical race theory results in an analysis in which gender, sexuality, and race, as well as heterosexism and racism, are each central to identity and interconnected. Including intersectionality, and the multiple systems of inequality with which it is concerned, broadens possibilities for considering more inclusive conceptualizations of identity.

The critique of queer theory for giving insufficient attention to race is a frequent and longstanding one. Gloria Anzaldúa (1991) stated, "It is White middle class gays and lesbians who have produced queer theory and for the most part their theories make abstractions of us colored queers . . . their theories limit the way we think about being queer" (p. 251). A decade later, Michael Hames-García (2001) encouraged a new critical queer theory that considers race and also social class as central aspects of queer theory. He noted that even when some of the dominant texts in queer theory have included the experiences of people of color, these people have typically been portrayed as an "other." Specifically, he stated that race tends to be addressed as

either a silence that projects Whiteness as universal or an inscription of race onto the bodies of people of color, leaving the normative claims of Whiteness intact and inscribing the existence of people of color into a reified category of otherness. (p. 215)

Rather than portraying race as a marginalized concept, as was the case in the foundational works on queer theory, he called for a radical shift in which race is central to queer theory—a proposed change that has still not become a reality. Hames-García (2011) drew on the notion of mutually constitutive identities, with social identities depending on each other for their meanings, to urge the centrality of race within queer theory. He acknowledged that the concept of mutually constitutive identities grounds an intersectional perspective. However, he argued that beyond some of the foundational intersectional work, intersectionality is sometimes misappropriated, used to describe multiple but not necessarily intersecting identities. We include in Chapter Six the concept of mutually constitutive identities and the misappropriation of intersectionality.

Despite Hames-García's critique of some intersectional scholarship, he is in essence arguing for an intersectional perspective on queer theory that spotlights sexuality and race, as well as social class. From that perspective, then, he is bringing together some of the central notions of intersectionality, queer theory, and critical race theory to more fully represent lived experience. He applied his theorizing to analyze the U.S. prison system, arguing that the mutually constitutive nature of masculinity, race, and sexuality—specifically, the dominant discourses around these ideas— determines the nature of prison dynamics (Hames-García, 2011). Similar analyses more closely related to student development theory might consider how intersections among gender, race, and sexuality structure such concepts as perceptions of identity, educational contexts, and student learning.

Just as Hames-García urged the inclusion of race and social class in queer theory, others have urged the inclusion of sexuality in critical race theory, known as a queer crit perspective (Delgado & Stefancic, 2001). Mitsunori Misawa (2010) explained that queer crit theorists emphasize the intersection of race and sexuality, noting that the experiences associated with race are significantly influenced by sexuality. This dynamic is in part a result of the underlying assumption that people of color are heterosexual. Considering ideas from queer theory and critical race theory together more pointedly challenges what race looks like when sexuality is also centrally located. Misawa explained that queer crit literature has made several contributions to critical race theory, including (1) recognizing the centrality of the intersection of racism and heterosexism; (2) challenging mainstream ideologies by empowering queer people of color to critique racial and sexual stereotypes; (3) introducing a contextual and historical analysis of queer people of color and putting the lived experiences of queer people of color at the forefront of critical race theory, challenging ideas surrounding the intersection of racism and heterosexism; and (4) introducing a multidisciplinary perspective on racism and heterosexism that can contribute to social change for queer people of color. In essence, queer crit is an intersectional perspective on critical race theory that highlights the intersection of race and sexuality. Given the roots of both queer theory and critical race theory in an intersectional perspective, critical queer theory and queer crit theory could also consider race and sexuality in conjunction with inequitable social structures associated with an individual's other social identities. Doing so is not to take the spotlight off of race and sexuality, but to consider them as informed by other social identities.

Extending Theoretical Perspectives Beyond the Identities at Their Forefront

In addition to considering new conceptualizations of the theoretical perspectives, intersectionality, critical race theory, and queer theory also inform each other when their tenets are extended to identities not typically at their forefront. For instance, extending tenets to other identities works well with some of the ideas associated with queer theory. Queer theory stretches one's thinking about how identity could be conceptualized if power structures were truly dismantled; extending some of queer theory's ideas to intersectionality and critical race theory allows that dismantling of power structures to be situated in the realities of people's lived experiences. Considering queer theory in conjunction with intersectionality and critical race theory raises the possibility of applying concepts from queer theory to identities other than gender and sexuality. Given intersectionality's focus on interlocking systems of oppression, it makes sense to think about such queer notions as performativity, resistance, and fluidity in relation to such social identities as race, social class, and ability.

For instance, just as sexuality and gender are performances that resist power structures, so, too, can other identities be performed. Consider race, by way of example. In her study of race and identity among Black alumni of a historically Black university and of a predominantly White university, Sarah Susannah Willie (2003) used ideas from queer theorists, especially Judith Butler's explanation (1991) of performativity, to explain race as a performed, evanescent identity. Willie stated, "Butler provides us with a model for understanding that racial identity . . . [is] continuously reinstituted and reinvented" (p. 127). Although Willie does not specifically discuss performance of race as a form of resistance against racism, this appears to be the phenomenon in play. Rather than dominant norms' defining the meaning of one's race, race is instead shaped through one's actions. These racial performatives result in race as a fluid construct that defies the imposition of racist norms. Such an analysis of race does not eliminate the reality of racism, the critique launched by critical race theorists toward the study of identity, but it does allow for a possible erosion of racist norms through performatives that resist dominant understandings of race, as well as perhaps a freeing of internalized racial oppression.

Scholars have also noted the potential of applying queer theory to identities other than sexuality and gender. For instance, Mark Sherry (2004) analyzed some of the similarities between queer theory and disability studies, such as their "opposition to hegemonic normalcy, their strategic use of universalist and minority discourses, their deconstruction of essentialist identity categories and their use of concepts such as performativity" (pp. 781–782). Given some of these similarities, he encouraged more discussion of how the two ideas can be cross-fertilized. Indeed, more recently, the similarities in some of the tenets of queer theory and disability studies, in particular the notion of normalcy, have formed the basis for crip theory, a theoretical perspective that weaves together disability and sexuality (McRuer, 2006). Explaining the basis of crip theory, Robert McRuer (2006) explained:

> I put forward here a theory of what I call "compulsory able-bodiedness" and argue that the system of compulsory able-bodiedness, which in a sense produces disability, is thoroughly interwoven with the system of compulsory heterosexuality that produces queerness: that, in fact, compulsory heterosexuality is contingent on compulsory able-bodiedness, and vice versa. (p. 2)

Through crip theory, McRuer has not merely extended queer theory to disability studies but instead is working within a new theoretical perspective that draws on intersecting ideas. Although we have discussed here only the application of queer theory's tenets to other social identities, similar analyses could be performed using critical race theory and intersectionality. Such analyses extend the possibilities of how the theoretical perspectives might be applied in conjunction with one another.

Theoretical Borderlands

Still another way of thinking about the relationships among these theoretical perspectives is through the concept of theoretical borderlands (Abes, 2009). Basing her assertion on the premise that all theoretical perspectives are incomplete, Abes (2012) suggested, "To realize the complexity of student development it is important to use multiple theoretical perspectives in conjunction with one another, even when they contradict" (p. 190). To use multiple theoretical perspectives—that is, to work in theoretical borderlands—means to simultaneously embrace multiple perspectives about college students, even if these perspectives espouse differing ideas about reality. Although simultaneously embraced as multiple realities, these multiple theories are not necessarily merged into one new theory. For instance, a person might believe identity is performed (queer theory), while at the same time viewing racism as central and resisted through counterstories (critical race theory). Or a person might perceive identity to be a product of intersecting systems of power (intersectionality), while at the same time respecting students' evolving perceptions of their identities, even if these are perceived as distinct social identities (constructivism). Although Abes (2009) described her use of theoretical borderlands in the context of conducting research, a borderland analysis is relevant also to the application and development of theories. Regardless of whether it is used in research, theory development, or theory application, undertaking a borderland analysis is not something that is easily done, but instead requires operating out of a somewhat ambiguous space that respects multiple realities.

Abes (2009) borrowed the term *borderlands* from Anzaldúa (1999) but used it somewhat differently when applying it to theoretical perspectives. Speaking to the relationships among her identities, Anzaldúa described a borderland identity as a third space where individuals move between two worlds, participating in both and wholly belonging to neither, "none of them 'home,' yet none of them 'not home'" (p. 528). Abes adopted the idea of borderlands to explain how researchers apply multiple theories, using notions from each to portray a more complete picture of identity. "Given the theories' different assumptions, none are complete on their own, and none can be used together in their entirety. A new theoretical space is created that requires thinking beyond distinct theoretical categories" (Abes, 2012, p. 190). She asserted that "rather than being paralyzed by theoretical limitations or confined by rigid ideological allegiances, interdisciplinary experimentation of this nature can lead to rich new research results and possibilities" (Abes, 2009, p. 141). Likewise, such theoretical experimentation can also lead to new ways of thinking about the nature of identity.

Noted researcher and teacher Patti Lather informed Abes's thinking about theoretical borderlands. Lather (2006) argued that the use of multiple research paradigms is necessary given the multiplicity of reality. She explained that "rather than searching for the common elements underlying difference," there should be a "freeing of difference" that is about "divergence, dispersed multiplicities, the possibilities of that which is in excess of our categories of containment" (p. 47). Multiple paradigms allow difference to be embraced. Other scholars have urged researchers to put aside their theoretical silos to uncover the potential of using multiple theoretical perspectives. For instance, Joe Kincheloe and Peter McLaren (2005) have advocated for a bricolage approach, which is typically understood "to involve the process of employing . . . [multiple] methodological strategies as they are needed in the unfolding context of the research situation" (p. 316). Referring to a bricoleur, someone who takes a bricolage approach, they explained:

The bricoleur exists out of respect for the complexity of the lived world and complications of power. The task of the bricoleur is to attack this complexity, uncovering the invisible artifacts of power and culture, and documenting the nature of their influence on not only their own works but on scholarship in general. (p. 317)

Bringing together multiple theoretical perspectives to explore the power structures underlying the MMDI and the RMMDI exemplifies this notion of bricolage.

Borderland Analysis Examples in the Literature

Several examples exist of bricoleurs who have incorporated multiple theoretical perspectives in their research. Although bricolage is an underused idea, it is not a new one. William Tierney (1993) brought together critical theory and postmodernism in his research on communities of difference in higher education. The impetus behind his use of critical postmodernism was that neither perspective sufficiently addressed his participants' realities. For instance, in his research with gay faculty, a postmodern analysis focused on differences among the participants' social identities, whereas a critical perspective facilitated the participants' ability to challenge their marginalized status. The combined analysis of difference and change more thoroughly addressed the experiences of gay faculty. Tierney and Rhoads (1993) thoughtfully discussed the merging of postmodernism and critical theory. They explained that the two frameworks share several key assumptions, such as the existence of multiple social realities and the role of power in structuring subjectivity. Critical theory, with its emphasis on praxis, offers an approach to applying postmodernism in practice (Tierney & Rhoads, 1993).

More recently, Abes and Kasch (2007), in their research described in Chapter Eight, applied a borderland analysis to their study of lesbian college students' multiple social identities, using both constructivism and queer theory. Focusing on the stories of one study participant, they analyzed data from a constructivist perspective to understand how development toward internal meaning making contributes to an ability to negotiate the ways in which context, which includes inequitable power structures, shapes relationships among social identities. They then reanalyzed the same data using queer theory. Rather than focusing on how the participant understood her identity within an inequitable society, the queer analysis deconstructed her identity, revealing how she resisted inequitable power structures through the performance of her identity. Together, these two perspectives embrace multiple ways in which power structures mediate identity, as well as multiple realities about this phenomenon. Queer theory uncovers some of the power-laden assumptions in characterizations of lesbian identity development. However, because students are not always aware of the influence of power structures on their identity, the application of this queer theory analysis is enhanced by juxtaposing these findings with students' self-perceptions uncovered through constructivism. A constructivist perspective explores how participants make meaning of their identities, whereas a queer perspective challenges the very notion of identity. Seeing value and limitations in both queer theory and constructivism, Abes and Kasch applied both of these theoretical perspectives to analyze the same data, despite their fundamental differences, and merged the results to shape a new perspective on student development theory.

Although partnering constructivism with queer theory is a rich way of conceptualizing identity, it is challenging to connect some of the tenets of queer theory with the realities of students' experiences. Intersectionality, which also offers a framework for exploring how social inequalities shape the meaning of identity, creates a bridge between queer theory and constructivism by focusing on the relationship between lived experience and power structures (Dill & Zambrana, 2009b; Valentine, 2007). Abes (2012) applied a borderland analysis of constructivism and intersectionality to explore relationships among one lesbian college student's multiple identities. We described this research in some detail in Chapter Six. The constructivist analysis of the participant's narrative pointed to her perceptions of the relationships among multiple social identities based on her evolving meaning-making capacity. This analysis demonstrated how a constructivist perspective often uses an additive approach to relationships among multiple social identities. The intersectional analysis illuminated the relationships among shifts in context; the interlocking power structures of heterosexism, classism, and racism; and how identity is experienced (Abes, 2012). Gia, the participant featured in that story, read through the borderland analysis three years after the completion of data collection. She explained that she saw herself in the intersectional analysis, which captured her lived experience, but also that she could reflect on how her increased meaning-making capacity contributed to understanding her identity differently at different points in her life. As with Abes and Kasch's borderland analysis (2007) using queer theory, the simultaneous application of constructivism and intersectionality provided a nuanced portrayal of student identity.

Borderland Analysis of Intersectionality, Queer Theory, and Critical Race Theory

In the previous examples from Elisa's research, constructivism was partnered with queer theory and intersectionality, respectively. We now consider relationships among intersectionality, critical race theory, and queer theory. Bringing those perspectives together highlights some of the similar and differing ideas about identity that emerge when applying critical and poststructural perspectives, both of which deconstruct systems of inequality, to the MMDI. We then analyze those ideas in relation to constructivism in the following subsection. This analysis of the four theoretical perspectives in relation to one another results in new understandings about identity in general and relationships among social identities in particular. Table 10.1 is intended to help guide this analysis, especially through the description of each theoretical perspective's portrayal of relationships among social identities as well as the nature of relationships between social identities and context.

Intersectionality, critical race theory, and queer theory all have in common the intersecting nature of social identities and the centrality of context to identity. More specifically, they share the notion that context comprises systems of inequality, and that these systems of inequality are central to the manner in which social identities intersect. The three perspectives differ to some extent, however, in how they perceive the individual's relationship to that context. As a poststructural theory, queer theory suggests that the individual resists the oppressive social systems through everyday identity performatives. Resistance is therefore a central aspect of identity. Critical race theory describes intentional counterstories as forms of resistance, at the same time that it brings racism to the forefront. Intersectionality, although a praxis-based theory that seeks social change, most notably portrays the realities of living within systems of inequality, particularly for marginalized populations.

A borderland analysis among these three perspectives, therefore, portrays identity as made up of systems of inequality that are simultaneously shaping the nature of relationships among social identities and being reshaped by these relationships. The reshaping of relationships occurs both through everyday behaviors (queer theory) and through intentional acts of social change (intersectionality and critical race theory). Yet power structures seemingly refuse change, engrained in individuals' realities. For all inseparable social identities, therefore, identity is composed of resistance to or efforts to change both context and the limiting systems of inequality within context that at times seem to defy resistance and change.

That is, an individual's identity is intertwined with inequitable contexts, and identity emerges from ongoing and evolving performances and counterstories that shape who we are and the contexts in which we live. Yet identity is also constrained by context. Inequitable power structures have a grip on people that will not let go and that shapes our identities in both subtle and not-so-subtle ways. A borderland analysis challenges individuals to live within this seemingly inconsistent conceptualization.

For example, a Latina lesbian at a predominantly White university in the Midwest might resist the racist and heteronormative, and intersecting racist-heteronormative, campus climate through her everyday behaviors, such as her mode of dress, the people with whom she interacts, the forms of campus involvement in which she engages, and the ways in which she makes herself visible on a campus where she might otherwise be invisible. Her performatives change the meaning of Latina lesbian by contributing to the fluidity of her identity, and her behaviors resist systems of power through the counterstories they tell. Simultaneously, this racist-heteronormative climate shapes her identity. For instance, an unwelcoming climate contributes to the salience of her social identities in ways over which she might not have agency; it unnaturally contributes to a false separation of her Latina and lesbian identities; and it compels her to perform her identities in particular ways to create change. No matter how much she resists power and creates change, she cannot escape the reality of power structures. This student resides at the center of resistance to power and the implications of power for identity.

Regardless of whether individuals are resisting or being shaped by systems of inequality as an aspect of identity, the poststructural and critical perspectives vividly illuminate the taxing and sometimes emotional struggle often associated with defining one's own identity. Indeed, they illustrate, perhaps more than does the constructivist perspective, Josselson's observation (1996) that "identity is what we make of ourselves within a society that is making something of us" (p. 28). The push and pull between systems of inequality and an individual's sense of self is challenging, given how engrained these systems are in the fabric of society and in one's own identity.

Borderland Analysis of Constructivism, Intersectionality, Queer Theory, and Critical Race Theory

The constructivist perspective also illuminates how individuals must define their own identity while others try to define it for them. In some respects, it seems that constructivism offers ideas similar to those of the poststructural and critical perspectives, but two significant differences exist: the absence of an intentional focus on power and the possibility of separating social identities. The constructivist meaning-making filter reveals that a person who externally makes meaning defines identity through context. In comparison, a person who internally makes meaning defines identity in relation to context. Although context is an important component of constructivism, this theoretical perspective does not intentionally address systems of inequality within context. An externally defined person is unknowingly defined by systems of power. An internally defined person is making meaning of her or his identity within systems of power. A person might choose to resist systems of power, but that choice is an individual decision and not a theoretical assumption. Constructivism therefore focuses on context in relation to the self rather than context as part of the self. Furthermore, as discussed earlier in this chapter, because the constructivist perspective reveals how individuals perceive their multiple identities, social identities might be portrayed as distinct from one another, different from the intersectional notion of interconnected identities that mutually define and reinforce one another.

A borderland analysis brings together the ideas that (1) identity and context are joined in a relationship with each other, and the nature of the relationship is dependent on an individual's meaning-making capacity (constructivist perspective), and (2) identity comprises systems of inequality that are simultaneously shaping the nature of relationships among social identities and being reshaped by these relationships (critical and poststructural perspectives). There is not a simple way to bring together these two ideas, nor should there necessarily be one. One might suggest that a person's meaning-making capacity contributes to his or her ability to make meaning of the possible relationships between systems of inequality and intersecting social identities. Using the example of the Latina lesbian student introduced earlier, if she has a complex meaning-making filter, she might have greater ability to resist, through her performatives and counterstories, the ways in which the campus climate tries to separate her racial and sexual identities as distinct. That is, she could resist the campus's treating her sexual orientation no differently from that of a White lesbian, and her race no differently from that of a heterosexual Latina. At the same time, however, and as discussed in previous chapters, systems of inequality, including racism and heterosexism, mediate how a person makes meaning, resulting in a different conceptualization of development than what constructivism suggests (Abes & Kasch, 2007; Jones, 2009). Rather than trying to neatly merge these perspectives, the borderland analysis suggests that these multiple realities, although inconsistent in some respects, are occurring simultaneously. Meaning making serves as a filter, but systems of oppression complicate the nature of meaning making, as described in our earlier discussions about intersectionality, critical race theory, and queer theory.

In essence, then, a significant benefit of a borderland analysis is that it brings to light the multiple realities about relationships among social identities, and therefore offers a more complex portrayal of the possibilities concerning the nature of identity. A significant limitation, however, is that bringing together multiple perspectives results in the omission of some of the important aspects of each perspective that make them unique views on reality. For instance, the queer theory desire filter and the notion of identity as becoming get lost, as do ideas from critical race theory, such as the centrality of race as an aspect of one's core, one's social identities, and the context. These are not mere theoretical nuances, but rather are central to the theories' contributions to understanding identity. A place exists for more than one approach to understanding identity. The complexity of understanding relationships among social identities warrants both a borderland approach that highlights the necessity of juggling multiple perspectives and a more traditional application of one theoretical perspective in all of its richness.

Applying a Borderland Analysis to the MMDI

Having considered some of the ways in which the four theoretical perspectives relate to and at times interact with one another, we now consider how these relationships might be applied to the MMDI through a borderland analysis. We did not believe it was appropriate for us to draw one model to represent the borderland analysis as we did with the intersectional, critical race theory, and queer theory models. A borderland analysis allows for many possibilities for how a model might look, depending on how the theoretical perspectives are used in conjunction with one another. Therefore, rather than drawing one prototype model, we asked five graduate students from diverse backgrounds to draw how they would represent their identities through a borderland model—that is, a model that pulls from multiple theoretical perspectives. All of these individuals have been students in our classes and have some knowledge of the four theoretical perspectives we used throughout this book. To prepare them to draw their own borderland model, we reviewed with them the new intersectional, critical race theory, and queer theory models. We then asked them to reflect on the ways they understand their identities as depicted through these three critical models and to consider whether or not each model tells a complete story of their identity. Based on that reflection, we asked them to draw a borderland model that would best represent their identity. We asked that they not stray too far from the original elements of the MMDI in drawing their model, but indicated that they could represent those elements in ways that fit with their own self-perceived identities. After we gave them these directions, the students worked on this project on their own time. We did not interact with them as they reflected on their identities, the theories, and possibilities for a borderland model. We offer here the borderland models each student drew, followed by an explanation written by the student.

Derrick

FIGURE 10.1 DERRICK'S BORDERLAND MODEL OF MULTIPLE DIMENSIONS OF IDENTITY

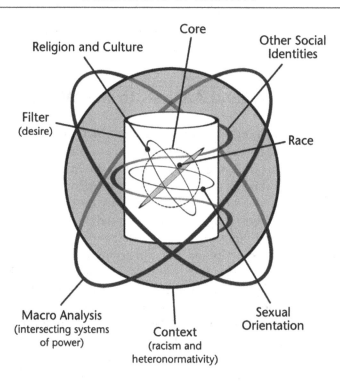

Core

Religion and Culture

Other Social Identities

Filter (desire)

Race

Macro Analysis (intersecting systems of power)

Context (racism and heteronormativity)

Sexual Orientation

I am Black . . . I am Christian . . . I am gay . . . I am male . . . From very early on, I came to understand that I was a Black boy. Whether the messages were about "our" (Black) people being disadvantaged or "those" (White) people thinking they were better than everyone else, my family articulated a significance in being Black and having a family raised in the South, particularly Louisiana and Arkansas. These messages were often tied to my being a Black boy—suggesting some additional potential hardship from authority figures generally, law enforcement and teachers specifically. Perhaps after recognizing that I was a Black person in a White society, I came to choose to be Christian. My parents made sure that we (my siblings and I) went to church for the major holidays, but they never attended with us. Over time, I came to want to attend church, to want to be among other people who relied on a "higher being" to provide guidance, wisdom, and protection. But as I grew in my understanding of Christianity, I also grew in my dislike of my parents' not making such a commitment. Church, the Black church particularly, became my safe place from my feelings of not belonging. Even before deciding to practice the Christian faith, I knew I liked boys; however, it was not until after I recognized myself as a Black Christian that I came to understand "gay." Although it is an imperfect word, primarily because of society's denigration of the term, I struggled with the idea of being (or identifying as) gay; I struggled with the articulated expectation of an outward acknowledgment of my sexual interest in the same sex, of being flamboyant. So here's this Black gay Christian what? I recalled being told that I was a handsome, smart, thin Black boy, but does that equate to Black male? As much as my family wanted to shield me from the hardship of society for being Black and male, I think their focus on "Black boy" actually perpetuated racist perceptions that Blacks are lesser than Whites—rather than calling me a young Black man, there was a constant use of "boy," reverting to a childlike assumption of ability, worth, and so on. As I grew I began to take ownership of my maleness, ownership of being a worthy participant in society. Now, I have come to understand myself to be a Black, gay, Christian male. The positioning of those words highlights their importance to my understanding of self. I am at all times Black and Christian; however, I tend to disclose my gay identity in more selective spaces. The male identity plays an interesting role for me, as I often think of myself as a Black male; a Black Christian male; or a Black gay male, but rarely as simply male.

My borderland model represents this reality in several ways (see Figure 10.1). At its core are three social identities: race, sexual orientation, and religion and culture. As I believe that race is at the core of my identity and influences how I understand all other identities, it has been placed prominently through the core in my model. Sexual orientation and religion and culture are also prominent in my understanding of self, so they are also featured in the core; however, as these social identities have been fundamentally shaped by my understanding of my race, they are both shown as intersecting my racial identity. Specifically, my race, as a meaning-making filter, has dictated how and with whom I discuss being gay as well as how I participate and include my "secular" life within the church and what church means for me. In addition, although there are other identities (for example, gender or socioeconomic class) that are important in my understanding of self, they tend to play a less significant role and therefore are combined into one larger strand surrounding the core. Furthermore, outside of my core self, I recognize that my life experiences, my understanding of being a Black gay Christian male, are significantly influenced by a societal context steeped in racism and heteronormative expectations. Specifically, I constantly see my understanding of self conflict with societal norms and the Black church's explicit and implicit assumptions of what a Black man should be. I find that as the Black church attempts to combat racism, it perpetuates this sense of division among its members by demeaning sexual difference (particularly homosexuality) and aligning it with nonmaleness and at times non-Blackness.

Ian

FIGURE 10.2 IAN'S BORDERLAND MODEL OF MULTIPLE DIMENSIONS OF IDENTITY

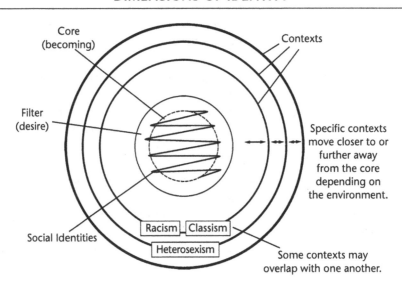

Moving us to the United States from the Philippines when I was very young, my parents wanted me to have a better life, a life that they wished they had had growing up. Being the first child of immigrants was a difficult responsibility. The expectations and demands of my parents were never questioned because of the sacrifices they made and hardships they experienced for me. Instilling the strict values of the Catholic faith in their everyday lives, my parents raised me to believe that having a strong work ethic and a belief in God will get you anywhere. They have taught me that the "Land of the Free" will give me that "American Dream" if I just work hard and follow directions. Growing up, that is what my parents did to make a living in the United States; they worked every day. With my dad working three different jobs and my mom working two, their working-class income went to supporting me and my two siblings.

As a Filipino American growing up in a predominantly Latino neighborhood in a suburb of Los Angeles, I struggled to find my place in the community in which I lived. As one of the only few Filipinos living in this working-class neighborhood, I feared losing my identity and losing my Filipino-ness. Throughout high school, I always adopted this belief that I was Mexican American, or at least I wanted to be Latino because all my friends were Mexican. I was Filipino at home with my parents and family, but I was Latino at school with my friends. Although I was aware that I was not Mexican American, the community in which I grew up played an intricate part in how I understood my Asian and Pacific Islander identity, as well as how I culturally embraced my Mexican American upbringing.

It was in college that my race and ethnic identity, as well as my socioeconomic class, were challenged quite often. As I attended school at the University of Vermont, I struggled defining what it means to be Filipino American. Attending this predominantly wealthy and White institution in the Northeast, I found it difficult to balance who I know I am with what I needed to be. Being from a working-class Filipino American household, I constantly had to think critically about how I was portrayed to my peers. The organizations and clubs that I joined in college were the same groups that challenged my various identities.

As I was trying to seek support from the cultural clubs on campus, it was difficult to find a club that would take me for who I am. Having been a member of the Asian American Student Union and Alianza Latina, I struggled to find a place that had my interests in mind. In the Asian American Student Union, being Filipino wasn't an identity that resonated with many of the members; therefore, my voice was left out because I wasn't Asian enough to be heard. Joining Alianza Latina was my opportunity to seek out a community like the one I have established back in Pico Rivera; however, again I struggled fitting in because I wasn't Latino enough to understand the issues and problems of the club members. Participating in both cultural clubs, but not necessarily fitting into either mold, has forced me to identify as a person of color, rather than identifying with a particular race or ethnicity.

In addition to having difficulty owning and understanding my racial and ethnic identities in these cultural organizations, I also struggled with my class and sexual orientation identities when I made the decision to join a fraternity. Being a member of a historically White fraternity, which had members who were predominantly heterosexual males of higher socioeconomic class, as I was questioning my sexual orientation, I knew I had to restructure and redefine my identity to fit in comfortably.

In applying my borderland identity model to my personal experiences, context is the most important element (see Figure 10.2). The contextual influences are the many ideas and environments that contribute to shaping, changing, or conforming to who I am as an individual. The contextual influences also shape the way individuals and the society gain an understanding of who I am within the given context. Depending on the environment or situation, the contexts expand or contract (move closer or further away) from the core. Because my social identities intrasect and are constantly in motion within the core, the performatives shake up the various contexts (that is, racism, classism, heterosexism) that I may or may not be experiencing.

For example, at this moment in my life, my sexual orientation is a social identity that I have started to reflect on and redefine. Since college, I have always questioned my sexual orientation and never really explored it until now. Looking at the various theoretical models on lesbian, gay, bisexual, and transgender identity, I found it difficult to understand my sexual orientation identity development alone without factoring in how my other identities (that is, race, religion, class) affect my sexual orientation. As I begin to grapple with the idea that I might not be straight, the environment that I am in has helped me come to that realization. In my graduate program, Student Affairs in Higher Education, I am often encouraged and forced to reflect on my identity and challenge who I really am as an individual. The program itself is designed to be an accepting and inclusive environment for all graduate students, and recognizes the importance of growth and personal development within these two years. In the process of deconstructing power structures in society and thoroughly recognizing privileges and oppressions of various identities in the classroom, certain contexts (the -isms) were made more apparent to me than before. Looking at the other contexts in my lifetime, I understand that my sexual orientation was not as salient to my identity as were race and class because the environments were not set up for me to acknowledge my questioning sexuality.

Growing up in East Los Angeles with very Catholic parents, the sexual orientation (heterosexism) context was close to my core; however, it was not close enough for me to be more aware of it because of the environment. When I joined a fraternity in college, my sexual identity was again foremost in my core; however, the environment was not set up for me to overtly express my sexual orientation. Reflecting on my time in college, there were definitely moments when I had enough support and guidance from mentors and classmates to come "out"; however, a lot of my struggles centered on my racial identity. My racial identity and the racism context were closer to my core than my questioning sexuality. The contexts of which I have been most aware in these past couple of years have influenced and determined how I perform my identities and what I find most authentic and important to me, as well as what identities have no salience with me. Part of the reason why these contexts have influenced so many aspects of my identity would have to do with my meaning-making filter.

The meaning-making filter sorts and determines what contextual factors lead me to be aware of how to perform in the environment. The ability to sift through these contexts (for example, racism, classism, sexism) depends on my development and how I am able to organize and arrange the information I receive from society. My identity will always be influenced and shaped by contexts; however, some contexts are more influential than others. In an environment such as Miami University, my race and class will always be two identities that intrasect constantly. Given such an environment, which is very White and upper-middle class, I acknowledge that racism and classism will play a huge part in how I perform or do not perform my identities. It may be that race and class for me are very visible—thus explaining why I am aware of these contexts. Factoring in my sexual orientation, that identity has begun to intrasect and fuse with race and class because of the context and how I am making meaning of my identity and life through the other environments in which I am involved (that is, my graduate program). However, I am aware that who I am and who I am not at Miami University are always changing, whether I leave or come back to the environment.

As I continue to explore my sexual orientation, I know that my meaning-making filter had stopped me from pursuing my sexual identity in college. Joining a fraternity and growing up in a Catholic household, those environments allowed me to recognize the contexts at play and showed me how to maneuver and perform my identity. Recognizing that building and maintaining relationships with people plays a role that is so important to who I am, I knew that coming "out" to my parents and to my fraternity brothers during college would destroy those relationships and friendships. However, in the student affairs graduate program environment, relationships are built on being able to open up with each other and learn through the experiences and stories of others. Therefore, my sexual orientation has intrasected with other identities in my core because my meaning-making filter has allowed me to recognize the heterosexist context.

When I started to create my borderland identity model, I felt that context was a prevalent part of the model that I needed to revisit. Because the heteronormative context and the racist context are lenses used in queer theory (QT) and critical race theory (CRT), respectively, I saw the value of the intersectional model as a way of seeing the other intersecting systems of power. In my model, context is and will always be nestled in my lived experience; however, I may or may not be aware of the various systems of power in place. Depending on my environment, the contexts in my model move closer or further away, expand or contract from the core. In the Miami University environment, as a working-class Filipino questioning my sexual orientation, those three contexts (heterosexism, racism, and classism) are much closer to my core than, for example, gender (sexism). Although all of these systems of power are in place in society (whether I am aware of it or not), I see how racism and classism affect the salience of my identity, more than heterosexism and more than sexism.

Very similar to the QT model, in my model all social identities enter and exit from the core and the filter and are absolutely inseparable and must be interconnected with one another. In queer theory, the performatives in the social identities shake up the context. Just like the QT model, mine shakes up the contexts that are closer to and more prevalent in my core. As a Filipino American, categorizing myself and identifying as having particular racial and ethnic identities is complicated. Depending on my awareness of the racism context, I may identify my Filipino-ness as Asian American, Pacific Islander, person of color, Filipino/ Japanese/Spanish, or another label. The filter in my model wants to resist the systems of power contributing to racism, sexism, classism, heterosexism, and so on, and tries to define and desires what is truly authentic and whole. Like in the CRT model, the filter is identifying the relationships between the contexts (macro) and the core (micro).

The core is ever changing and ever moving. In QT, the concept of becoming was created. Because identity is constantly in motion, I recognize that the values and beliefs that I hold may change and modify depending on the contexts and environments. This idea can be reflected in my borderland identity model. In understanding my sexual orientation and class identities, I recognize that these are and will continue to be ever changing and always moving. The individual that I am and the beliefs and values that I hold right now in this moment may or may not be the same in an undefined amount of time. The core might not be salient to me; however, I recognize my own authenticity as always changing and in motion.

Kira

**FIGURE 10.3 KIRA'S BORDERLAND MODEL OF MULTIPLE
DIMENSIONS OF IDENTITY**

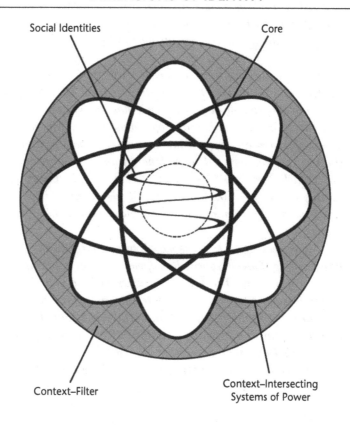

Social Identities   Core

Context–Filter

Context–Intersecting
Systems of Power

The ways I make use and meaning of the perspectives presented in this book are a direct result of my identity and personal story. I identify as a White, Jewish, upper-middle-class, more masculine-identified woman, with a strong affinity and personal passion for understanding and increasing awareness of systems of racial oppression, and the effects of racism on our interactions with the world around us. I attended a liberal arts undergraduate institution in the San Francisco area, and have since moved to rural Ohio in my pursuit of a master's degree in student affairs. My passion for all things race began as a sophomore in college, when I took the required "diversity" course and felt an internal fire that I have never felt before. I continually immerse myself in literature that places race at the forefront of my own identity and the ways in which I interact, as a White woman, as a part of systems of oppression that award me opportunities that are not inherently awarded to people of color. I consider myself more than a White ally in this sense, and am constantly seeking out ways to raise awareness of these systems within higher education. I have been an out and proud lesbian woman for two years, and I had the fortune of coming out in a liberal, self-pronounced "gay mecca" of San Francisco, with an extremely supportive community of family, friends, mentors, and colleagues. The transition to rural Ohio has not been an easy one and, through more overt homophobia, has brought my sexual orientation to the forefront of my personal and professional image. My gender presentation and identity performance as a lesbian woman have been significant in my work with students and colleagues. I have done my best to remain authentic in this transition, which I go into in my presentation and discussion of my own model of identity (see Figure 10.3). I don't just like to stir things up, I like to think I create sparks of dissonance in those around me that have the potential to lead to change.

My model borrows from the models presented earlier in the text, highlighting the true meaning of using student development theories in conjunction with one another as a sort of bricolage. The model emphasizes the fluid nature of identity and personal meaning making, my changing contextual influences, my racial identification as a White woman with a personal and academic affinity for deconstructing racism, and the nature and meaning of authenticity in a world that is making meaning of me while I am making meaning of myself.

The most significant part of the model I present is the core. I understand the core as authenticity, which is in a constant state of evolution and change, and thus is displayed on the model with a dashed line (permeability). The permeability of my core (the changing nature of my authenticity) is based on contextual and environmental factors, and thus my authentic identity performance is relative to the context in which I am situated. My authentic identity performance of my sexual orientation, for example, changed drastically in my contextual move from a politically liberal undergraduate institution to a rural, Midwestern, politically conservative graduate institution. In San Francisco, I felt comfortable and authentic in publicly showing affection to my partner; however, I do not feel as comfortable doing so in rural Ohio, and thus I feel less authentic. I do not think this makes me any less "developed," because I am aware of the contextual factors that affect my authenticity, and I make *conscious, informed decisions based on situational context. So, although my enactment of authenticity may change, authenticity remains nonetheless at the core of my identity.*

Running through my core is an "axis" of intrasectionality, similar to the one presented in the queer theory model. I use this in the same way it is used in the queer theory model, to show the fluidity and connected nature of my social identities. I chose to show them this way because I struggle with pulling my social identities apart on individual orbitals because they never have and never will be independent of each other. I cannot focus on one more than another, or see one as more salient than any other. My gender and sexual orientation are so tightly connected and intersected that it takes away from this connectedness to show them as independent. Similarly, my race and socioeconomic status are so connected that I lose something by trying to pull them apart. One has such a direct impact on the other, and my race has played such a large part in helping me reach where I am today that I cannot ignore its implications and ties to my socioeconomic status. Although I have the capacity to understand them individually, they do not play out that way in the real world. The axis of intrasectionality runs through my core because based on context (and the systems that exist within context), certain identities directly affect the nature of my changing authenticity, whereas at other times they may not. For example, in the context of Jewish religious services, my religious social identity (which may be in my core) may be a more significant factor in that context of authenticity than, say, my race (which may move out of my core for that context). Because context is always changing, the salience of these identities to my core, and thus my authenticity, are always changing.

The orbitals around my core represent systems of privilege and oppression that always affect the salience of my social identities. These systems include racism, homophobia, sexism, and so on; they may have different implications in different contexts, but they are the very reason why my core and authenticity are always changing. They affect how I understand and thus perform my social identities, thereby having a direct impact on my authenticity. These systems are situated within context, shown on the model with a filter to represent the way I personally filter context to understand the implications of the intersecting systems of power and privilege, and how they are going to affect the salience of my social identities in relation to my core.

Overall, the model I present is one that works from the outside in. It begins with context, which passes through my filter of meaning making and has a direct effect on the implications of systems of power and oppression, which then affect my social identities and my performance of an authentic identity, existing in my core.

Alex

FIGURE 10.4 ALEX'S BORDERLAND MODEL OF MULTIPLE DIMENSIONS OF IDENTITY

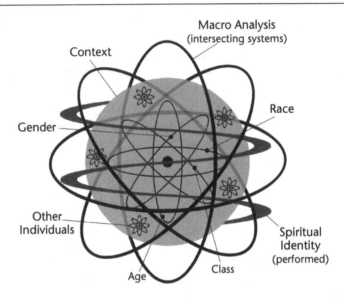

My identity is a fluid construct, shaped by past experiences and influenced by environmental factors. After evaluating systems of power that exist in our society and reflecting on my privileges that extend from the systems, I found that the Intersectional Model of Multiple Dimensions of Identity (I-MMDI) and the Queered Model of Multiple Dimensions of Identity (Q-MMDI) illuminate how I view my identity. However, these models do not fully capture my values or showcase my nuanced social identities. Through combining parts of both of these models, as well as infusing additional components and contextual forces, I begin to paint a more detailed picture of myself (see Figure 10. 4).

Micro Analysis. *The original MMDI largely reflects how I conceptualize my identity. I believe I carry several core qualities that remain constant across contexts, and my various social identities shift in salience as I encounter different situations. However, the MMDI does not display two areas that have a critical impact on my identity: spirituality and interpersonal relationships. To more fully explain how I view my identity within the construct of a model, I will elucidate the individual components.*

My Core. I vividly remember sitting in my student development theory seminar and hearing classmates vehemently oppose the composition of a "core." Several of my peers refused to acknowledge that any part of our identity remains static, and they believed that individuals embody different qualities across contexts. I sat on the opposite end of that debate, and I have always felt that certain values define who I am and hold true in any situation.

True to its name, my core sits at the heart of my identity model. The values I associate with my core were fostered during my childhood and galvanized during my undergraduate years at a Jesuit institution. The reflective milieu of my college's campus encouraged students to understand themselves on a deeper level, and various retreats and exercises allowed me to articulate a sense of self. Ultimately, I feel that my core can be captured in three words: loyalty, empathy, and intellect. These qualities represent my compassion for friends and family members, my relational nature, and my appreciation for thinking and learning.

My Social Identities. *Over the past two years of graduate school, my understanding of my social identities has become far more complicated. I can better articulate who I am as a White man, and I have identified innumerous privileges that accompany these identities. Race and gender, specifically, represent visible parts of myself, and there have been few cases in which these identities were not reflective of the greater context around me. I represent my social identities as rings that gravitate around my core. As demonstrated in the original MMDI, these rings carry salience nodes. The nodes revolve around my core as they shift in salience, and different settings and people dictate how powerfully I feel my social identities.*

Earlier this year, I investigated Black male identity as part of a class project and observed several meetings of a Black male student group. I remember initially stepping into the students' meeting, and I quickly realized I was the only White man in the room. My Whiteness became far more apparent, and I felt hypervigilant of how my words and actions might essentialize my racial identity. This is not to say I was unaware of my Whiteness prior to entering that meeting; I simply did not have to think as deeply about my race when I was surrounded by so many other White people. This experience highlighted the distinction between identity development and identity salience. Though I have internalized what it means to be a White man and reflected on various external factors that construct the larger narrative of Whiteness in our society, I never truly feel my White identity until it becomes marginalized.

Spirituality. *In addition to my core and social identities, I believe my spirituality largely shapes who I am. My spirituality is not to be confused with a religious identity, and it exists outside of any specific faith system. I chose to represent my spirituality as a coil that passes through my core and intersects with my social identities. I view my spirituality as a performative, much like the social identities in the Q-MMDI, and it is a part of my identity that ebbs and flows with my actions and interactions. My spirituality is grounded in interconnectedness and humanist beliefs, and I enact my spiritual identity through meaningful conversations with friends, deep reflections, and service work. My spirituality represents a foundation of purpose and meaning, and I attempt to infuse it into my personal and professional life through authentic discussions, genuine listening, and suspended judgment. My spirituality transcends my social identities and reflects my core, and I am most spiritually fulfilled when I enact my values and feel connected to those around me.*

Context. Context dictates the salience of my social identities, and various geographic regions and environments showcase different parts of my identity. The sphere around my core, my social identities, and the spirituality coil represent the various contextual influences in my life. I also borrow the meaning-making filter from the RMMDI, and this filter coats my sphere of influence. My meaning-making filter controls the various factors that influence my identity, and it allows me to analyze how power systems and people shape my self-image.

During my two years as a graduate student, social class became a more salient part of my identity. I constantly budgeted my assistantship stipend and negotiated how to live independently from my parents. Similarly, whenever I left my graduate school campus and visited friends and family members in other cities, I encountered individuals who were not twenty-five years old. In these instances, age became more salient to my identity.

It is impossible for me to remove interpersonal relationships from my sphere of context. Other people influence the salience of my social identities and draw out different parts of my personality. Given my interconnected spiritual identity, people also play an instrumental role in allowing me to enact my spirituality. I highlight the presence of other individuals in my identity model because I feel they are often overlooked as a driving contextual force.

Macro Analysis. *As I described in my anecdote about working with Black male students, the environment shapes the salience of my social identities. My race, gender, class, and age all shift in their salience depending on the context. The constant movement of these identities showcases the various privileges I possess and underscores larger systems of power that exist in our society. Racism, sexism, genderism, classism, and ageism all provide me with unearned advantages and feelings of comfort, simply because I am almost always surrounded by individuals who look like me and hold similar social identities. Pulling from the I-MMDI, I illustrate these power systems through larger rings that surround my sphere of context. My* *various privileges stem from these systemic rings, and my meaning-making filter allows me to process and internalize the greater impact of these privileges.*

Mei-Yen

FIGURE 10.5 MEI-YEN'S BORDERLAND MODEL OF MULTIPLE DIMENSIONS OF IDENTITY

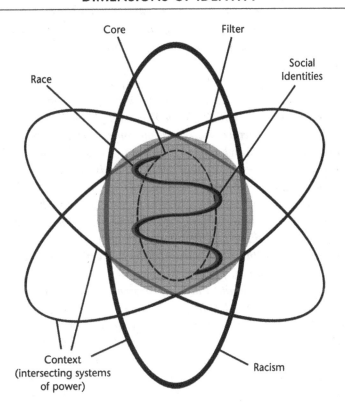

Growing up biracial (White and Asian) in a predominantly White environment, I struggled to understand my racial identity and often felt out of place. I came to embrace my identity as "different" but struggled to fully embrace being "biracial" because it seemed too rigid. I never felt that I was just one identity, such as biracial, or even that I had two identities (White and Asian), but rather felt that I represented some kind of mixed state. I learned that I have the privilege of "passing" as White or "passing" as a person of color and can do so when it benefits me. Sometimes, though, I am not in control of what identity I "pass" as because people often decide

for me based on their own understanding of difference or their need to categorize me. The idea of passing and choice in relation to identity reflects my belief that there are many complex factors that influence how I define my identity. Determining what is most salient to me in a given situation is an intensely personal experience that is influenced by a variety of external and internal factors, contexts, social identities, lived experiences, and structures of power that are fluid and interacting. I believe that various identities continually intersect to form my identity, and I view my core as a process that is fluid and ever changing. In my model the core is a fluid representation of this process of self-definition (see Figure 10.5).

I highlight the idea of performativity and choice in my model by drawing from QT's concept of social identities that are fluid, combined together, and mutually influencing. Depending on the context, my social identities will look different and interact with each other differently. This feature comes from QT, but I believe that it also reflects my connection to intersectionality's recognition of multiple, overlapping identities and CRT's notion that multiple social identities interact with race and with each other. Depending on the context, my identity as a woman of color or my identity as a straight mixed person may resonate. No matter the context, though, race always is present, in part because this is the identity that I have internally struggled and evolved with for so long. In my model race is the one identity that is separate while still fluid and constantly interacting with, influencing, and being influenced by other social identities. However, it has been pulled out from the single strand of identities to highlight that it is always present. Race forms its own strand that interacts with and is influenced by the combined social identities strand and other factors (context, filter, and so on).

"Passing" as White and being straight are two identities from which I derive significant privilege. I recognize the socially constructed way in which the world operates that privileges Whiteness and heteronormativity. Through my work in community service and service-learning as a student and later as a professional, I am attentive to social justice and understanding the role of systems of power in creating social issues, such as poverty, HIV/AIDS, and educational inequality. I view race and racism as underlying factors in perpetuating these social issues. Given the internal salience of race to me and my recognition of the external role of racism, race is the lens through which I see the world, interact with it, am influenced by it, and try to change it. Context is represented using the macro analysis of intersecting systems of power from intersectionality. I believe that social identities are culturally and sociohistorically constructed, which results in structures of power. I highlight the interlocking depiction of racism to reflect the centrality of race to my lived experience and my view that racism is a dominant aspect of how the world is organized. Because I hold race as a primary lens through which I see and interpret the world, race is also an important aspect of my meaning-making filter. I believe in working

toward social justice and resistance against oppression as an important part of identity. I therefore see my core as being influenced by and also influencing the context through my filter, which is depicted through the ways in which the filter overlaps and intersects with context in the model. The centrality of race and a commitment to create change place the meaning-making filter as both a way in which context influences my core and a way in which I influence and seek to change the context.

◆ ◆ ◆

These five students also provided us with reflections on the process of considering their identity from a borderland perspective. Most all of them commented on the freedom they felt in having the ability to describe their identity as they truly perceive it rather than being confined by a particular theory's description of their identity. They also commented on the challenge of articulating and making sense of their identity given such freedom, recognizing that student development theory has typically not afforded them such leeway. For example, Mei-Yen commented:

> Describing my identity using a borderland approach was an exciting and scary process. I was energized by the freedom of creating a model that truly reflected how I experience my identity. Yet this freedom was somewhat overwhelming. Rarely do we allow for the creativity and blending of models and theories to fit our individual experience and identity. Often it is easier to plot oneself in a rigid model and then critique the ways in which it does not fit. The process of actually describing and exploring what precisely we want to convey about ourselves is a much more challenging experience. Additionally, while I tried to capture the fluidity with which I think about my identity in the model, it was scary to put something definitive down in the form of a model. I believe this model is just a snapshot of how I was thinking about my identity at a moment in time but the process pushed me to consider more deeply where I have come from, who I am, and what my authentic self might look like. (M-Y. Ireland, personal communication, January 5, 2012)

Likewise, Kira noted:

> I thought it was really powerful to be able to find parts of different approaches that really fit me. It made me think critically about student

development theory in general, and it was really challenging to find the right language for describing my identity. So many other theories feel partially complete, or it's so easy to see the limitations. With this process, I felt like I could pull different strengths of each perspective and bring them together in a personally meaningful way. This was different than just mapping myself on other theories, and I felt empowered to create my own model and approach specific to my identity, context, and experiences. (K. Newman, personal communication, January 4, 2012)

Reflecting on similar ideas, Ian also explained that the borderland approach enabled him to better appreciate the relevance of student development theory and its application in higher education, stating:

When I first took a student development course in my graduate program, I was hesitant and doubtful that I would be able to take my own personal experiences and place them in a simple and linear development model. Either forcing myself to fit in a particular model or simply just disregarding the theory, I found it difficult to truly find my voice, my story. Using the borderland approach enabled me to really incorporate the identities I find salient to my development and understand how various contexts affect who I am at that moment. There are a lot of models that resonate with me; however, they all seem to capture chunks of who I am. Creating my own borderlands identity model has helped me fully encapsulate the full me, the real Ian. Describing my identity in this way has allowed me to see the value of student development theory and recognize its importance in higher education. (I. Prieto, personal communication, January 10, 2012)

Derrick commented on similar ideas, and also observed how the borderland analysis required him to think about his identity with more precision than he otherwise might have done. Specifically, he observed:

Considering the difficulty in fully articulating one's identity, I found that with the borderland approach I was better able to create a comprehensive representation of my multiple identities. On first attempt, writing the description to accompany the visual representation proved difficult, mostly because of my initial reluctance toward becoming too personal; however, with some probing questions and further consideration of my identities, I found the writing component a beneficial chance to articulate the salience and intersection of my various social identities. Furthermore, the borderland exercise required me to become more intentional in choosing words (and social memberships) to voice as descriptions of who I am as a Black gay Christian male. (D. Tillman-Kelly, personal communication, January 6, 2012)

Alex appreciated the ability to consider multiple models, but still struggled to fit his identity into one model—and one with which he wasn't already familiar. His observation underscores the value of a borderland approach and how infrequently we encourage people to draw from multiple perspectives and think about themselves in new, unfamiliar ways, especially when they possess predominantly privileged identities. He commented:

Representing my whole self in a single model proved to be an incredibly daunting task. Though this may highlight the essence of identity research, any singular model feels reductive, incomplete, and flawed. I struggled in thinking beyond existing models and theories in crafting something new without being influenced by my studies in student development during graduate school. Though I ultimately adopted much of Jones and Abes's current work, I felt that the additional components I infused into my model, especially relationships with other individuals and my spirituality, underscore who I am. (A. Hirs, personal communication, May 11, 2012)

We found the students' models and narratives to be quite rich, demonstrating how a borderland approach enhanced the students' ability to think about their identity in relation to power structures in new, unconfined ways. We also were struck by the differences among the portrayals of the models, illustrating for us how people will connect with and interpret differently ideas from the theoretical perspectives. Still, a limitation of the borderland models is that they omit important details unique to each of the theories that distinguish them from one another and highlight the implications of particular power structures while ignoring others. Although we acknowledge and have some concerns about this limitation, we encourage future research and practice that draw on the strengths of the borderland analysis, including the opportunity for new possibilities in understanding one's own identity in relation to power structures, the illustration of the incomplete nature of each theoretical perspective individually, and the reminder of the necessity of managing multiple perspectives concerning the nature of reality.

Summary

In this chapter we presented what we believe to be stimulating but challenging material about possibilities for new directions in thinking about relationships among multiple identities. Whether considering how theories could be used in conjunction with one another through new theoretical perspectives or through borderland analyses, we have introduced largely untested ideas. We believe there is much potential for understanding multiple identities in ways that truly challenge assumptions about the relationships among identities and between identity and context. It was intriguing for us to see how the five students included in this chapter applied a borderland analysis, and we believe the idea of using multiple theoretical perspectives together will continue to take shape as it is further considered with identities in diverse contexts. We invite you to bring your own identities, contexts, and worldviews and join this conversation about your own borderland analysis and how borderland analyses more broadly might be applied in practice.

Discussion Questions and Activities

1. Engage in a process similar to that of the five students featured in this chapter. Using the intersectional, CRT, and queer theory models that we drew in Chapters Six, Seven, and Eight, reflect on how you understand your identity as depicted through these three critical models. Consider whether or not each model tells a complete story of your identity. What is represented well? What is left out? Based on that reflection, consider how a borderland model, or a model that pulls from multiple theoretical perspectives, represents your identity, and make your best effort at drawing that model. What are the strengths and limitations of your model? What are strengths and limitations of borderland analyses and models in general?

2. What are the strengths and limitations of applying theoretical perspectives to the social identities not intended to be at their forefront, such as applying ideas from queer theory to religion? What are your perceptions of theoretical perspectives that highlight intersections among identities, such as a theoretical perspective drawn from both queer theory and critical race theory that has the intersection of heteronormativity and racism at the center?

3. In what ways might a borderland analysis or model be applied in practice? What are the strengths, challenges, and limitations of doing so?

4. In what ways might a borderland analysis be applied in a research design? What are some of the strengths and challenges associated with applying such an approach to studies in higher education and student affairs?

5. We offered borderland analyses and models as future directions in understanding relationships among multiple social identities. What other future directions do you envision?

FINAL INTERLUDES

Throughout this book we have incorporated interludes, or pauses in the presentation of more typical academic material, for us to reflect on our evolving understandings of identity, both our own identities and what we have learned about identity conceptually through our theoretical and empirical investigations. We embarked on the writing of these interludes inspired in part by the connections made between theories and stories by psychiatrist and writer Robert Coles (1989) in his book *The Call of Stories*, and also by a commitment to grounding the content we were presenting in our own stories. We hoped to model the reflexive process we think is integral to understanding identity. Early in the book we included references to a line from an e. e. cummings poem, which interestingly came from a piece titled "A Poet's Advice to Students," and to a talk by Nigerian author Chimamanda Adichie (2009) titled "The Danger of a Single Story." In these final interludes, we see ourselves not offering advice to readers of this book, but instead coming full circle in reflecting on what such an understanding of multiple dimensions of identity as presented in these pages suggests for us, for researching and teaching about identity, and for higher education and student affairs practice. In short, we reflect on the connections we see between e. e. cummings's poem and Chimamanda's talk. That is, "to be nobody-but-yourself—in a world which is doing its best day and night to make you like everybody else" (e. e. cummings, 1958, quoted in Firmage, 1965, p. 335) means to constantly work against the single story.

Susan

Although the idea of the "single story" was not familiar to me when my scholarly interests in identity took root, I now realize that what I saw in the theories presented to me in my education were theories that encouraged a single story, either about students as a whole or about particular populations of students. I also didn't see my own story represented in the theories about which I was learning. I wondered how a theory could hold up as a theory if it captured the complexities and particularities of multiple life stories. How do we as teachers, researchers, and administrators honor what is unique about individuals and their own identity constructions, as well as recognize the developmental principles and concepts that have stood the test of time? In many ways, the writing of this book—seeing it unfold as it was written—returned me to these earlier questions, causing me to revisit what I learned long ago in my master's program at the University of Vermont, and to situate that within my evolving knowledge and experience. I am reminded, yet again, of a favorite quote of mine (and Elisa's) from Rabbi Abraham Heschel, which is, "It is far easier to see what we know than to know what we see." My process of studying, writing, and teaching about identity, and the process of writing this book, have been about learning to "know what we see." In this book, we have tried to incorporate multiple frameworks for understanding identity, necessarily connecting individual stories to larger structures of inequality. Doing so changes the story of identity and ideally allows for multiple stories within a larger framework of identity.

In the writing of this book, and to help ground the newer frameworks we put forward, I returned to a number of the earlier theorists whose work many are too quick to dismiss as no longer relevant. Although the world is very different today than it was when these early theories were created, I spent time learning about the life stories of such individuals as Erik Erikson and Arthur Chickering, because just as my life story has influenced my scholarly interests and commitments, so too have theirs. Returning to these earlier works at this moment in my scholarly life also enabled me to understand them in the context of my current knowledge, and to appreciate in new ways such constructs as developmental trajectory, which I too might have been quick to dismiss a few years ago. My understanding of newer conceptualizations of identity and theoretical frameworks is deepened and enriched by reengaging with foundational theories.

Nearing the conclusion of this book brings me to an abiding concern with how to grapple with all the complexities of identity. For me, this is both a research question and a pedagogical one. How do we study both the particular domains of identity and the whole of identity? How do we incorporate the very real influences of social identities, such as race, and the intersecting relationships among social identities? How do we teach about identity in the presence of those with both privileged and oppressed identities? How do we teach those for whom race, for example, has been salient for most of their lives, especially in relation to how they are perceived by others, and for whom such emotions as anger and frustration are real? And how do we teach them alongside those for whom these conversations are just beginning and such emotions as shame and guilt are lurking beneath the surface?

An advisee of mine from the University of Maryland, Claire Robbins, just defended her beautifully written and sophisticatedly analyzed dissertation, titled Racial Consciousness, Identity, and Dissonance Among White Women in Student Affairs Graduate Programs *(Robbins, 2012). Among other findings, the results of her study provide compelling evidence of the intersections of developmental trajectories and constructs (for example, a progressive pathway marked by dissonance) with the tenets of critical theories (for example, performativity and resistance) that foreground the importance of placing individual identities in larger structures of power and privilege. The recognition of these intersections requires attention to the developmental nature of identity, a holistic view that integrates interpersonal, intrapersonal (identity), and cognitive development, and places emphasis on the important influence of social identities and larger sociohistorical contexts. This is a lot to take in! And it suggests that for both research and teaching purposes, there should be not only an emphasis on the evolution of theory but also recognition that contemporary perspectives cannot be fully understood without knowledge of past theoretical constructs on which newer theories are based (even if these older constructs are rejected). However complicated this work may be, I am as firmly committed as ever to the importance of honoring foundational theories of the past while also developing more contemporary perspectives of identity. This combination brings multiple stories to the forefront and highlights the possibility of more authentic living.*

Elisa

I am a better teacher today than I was when I began writing this book with Susan. This is in part a result of the writing process, which inspired personal and professional reflection, but more so it is a result of teaching draft chapters of this book in one of my student development theory classes. This course provided me with the opportunity to move closer to the reality of shaping a critical student development theory class. The "teaching" to which I refer was a partnership through which the students taught me a great deal about the complexities of being an inclusive educator, a label I work toward claiming, all the while realizing its seeming elusiveness.

The ways in which the students engaged with this material through personal reflections about their identities within intersecting systems of power compelled me to listen to their individual perspectives more intently than I think I had done before, despite my previous work with intergroup dialogue, and despite typically being known as a caring instructor. Their efforts at authenticity inspired me to try to genuinely connect with their stories to understand how their identity was mediating the ways in which they were making sense of themselves and student development theory. In other words, the material compelled me, in the words of Rabbi Heschel, to try to "know what I see" about students and not only "see what I know."

At the same time that I felt an increased responsibility to know what I see in students, the critical perspectives also facilitated my attempts at doing so by allowing me to tap into students' multiple stories. I knew most of the students in this class through a previous and also highly reflective course for which I was their instructor, but I now learned about them in new ways. For instance, a student typically quiet about her lower socioeconomic status was inspired by intersectionality to share narratives about her shifting identity perspectives as a result of working in a predominantly upper-class university. Likewise, a student constructed a notion of her mental health identity using intersectionality to make sense of how this identity intersected with her other social identities. Queer theory prompted a student's insights about body type among gay men and also about more comfortable coming-out processes. These critical perspectives and narratives transformed our classroom into a space that was moving toward an authentic intellectual community.

But did they also do just the opposite? As we tried to move toward this authentic community, our own limitations as a class became starker. For instance, the reality of having only one student of color in the class was palpable. Despite some of the White students' wrestling with their privileges in quite meaningful ways, a result of learning about critical race theory, the student of color still endured what we called the "duh" versus "huh?" realizations about privilege (realizations that some individuals necessarily take for granted, but that others do not yet understand). This starkness causes me to question some of my assumptions about how I teach identity. How often do I fall into the trap of teaching dominant perspectives first, followed by the "alternate" critical perspectives? How often do I focus attention on those struggling to understand their privilege at the expense of those with fewer privileged identities? How do I create and teach a course that shifts who is comfortable and who is not? How do I create and teach a course that shifts power dynamics concerning which are the dominant and subordinate perspectives on identity?

In some ways, this particular student development theory class, structured around critical theoretical perspectives, approached some of these possibilities. Students with multiple privileged identities typically had to stretch themselves to find their home in the material, whereas those with multiple marginalized identities more easily saw themselves. Still, I step away from writing this book knowing that I must keep learning about my own and others' perspectives, and continue rethinking my teaching in light of the critical perspectives on identity so that I am more fully embracing the potential of the perspectives I am teaching. As we stated in Chapter Nine, the first and continuous step is educating the educator.

◆ ◆ ◆

The second edition of *Student Development in College* (Evans, Forney, Guido, Patton, & Renn, 2010) concluded with final thoughts on the nature of student development theories and models and with a nod to the evolution of theories:

> As more is learned, some theories receive more attention than others. For instance, Abes, Jones, and McEwen's (2007) model is cited more than any other in this book. As developmental research based in constructivism, its popularity may signal a move away from stage models toward more intersection and integration of student development theory . . . A consideration of integration and intersection of all parts of student development provides a warrant for new and creative ways to examine the whole. (p. 372)

Our interest in this book, *Identity Development of College Students: Advancing Frameworks for Multiple Dimensions of Identity,* was to provide "new and creative" perspectives on college student identity. In doing so, we also wanted to acknowledge the rich foundation and disciplinary origins on which newer theories are developed. Just as recognizing only a single story about an individual is diminishing and inaccurate, so, too, is presenting a singular theoretical perspective on identity. We are more likely to "know what we see" if we bring to bear a diverse array of theories, models, and lived experiences on our understanding of such a complex phenomenon as identity. In our work with college students, if we know what we see, then every day we *see* the complexities of identity at work as students construct a sense of self that is anchored in their particular background and personal characteristics as well as influenced by specific contexts and social structures.

The five borderland models in Chapter Ten provide, in our minds, a fitting and compelling end to this book. They represent both a drawing on what has come before (the elements of the Model of Multiple Dimensions of Identity) and an extension into innovative representations of and ideas about identity. They present the complexities of individual identities, both in how individuals understand themselves and in how they are perceived by others. They allow for great individual variation, yet are organized around common elements. They also make explicit larger structures and contextual influences that pattern individual identity construction. And they represent students' *application* of our work, rather than our own renderings of what we thought their models might look like. We hope that these models and the content in this book inspire others toward "new and creative" approaches to teaching, research, and interactions with college students.

REFERENCES

Abes, E. S. (2009). Theoretical borderlands: Using multiple theoretical perspectives to challenge inequitable power structures in student development theory. *Journal of College Student Development, 50,* 141–156.

Abes, E. S. (2012). Constructivist and intersectional interpretations of a lesbian college student's multiple identities. *The Journal of Higher Education, 83,* 186–216.

Abes, E. S., & Jones, S. R. (2004). Meaning-making capacity and the dynamics of lesbian college students' multiple dimensions of identity. *Journal of College Student Development, 45,* 612–632.

Abes, E. S., Jones, S. R., & McEwen, M. K. (2007). Reconceptualizing the Model of Multiple Dimensions of Identity: The role of meaning-making capacity in the construction of multiple identities. *Journal of College Student Development, 48,* 1–22.

Abes, E. S., & Kasch, D. (2007). Using queer theory to explore lesbian college students' multiple dimensions of identity. *Journal of College Student Development, 48,* 619–636.

Adelman, L. (Producer). (2003). *Race: The power of an illusion* [DVD]. Available from www.pbs.org/race/000_General/000_00-Home.htm

Adichie, C. (2009, July). *Chimamanda Adichie: The danger of a single story* [Video file]. Retrieved from http://blog.ted.com/2009/10/07/the_danger_of_a/

American Council on Education. (1994). The student personnel point of view. In A. L. Rentz (Ed.), *Student affairs: A profession's heritage* (2nd ed., pp. 66–67). Lanham, MD: University Press of America. (Original work published 1937).

Ancis, J., Sedlacek, W., & Mohr, J. (2000). Student perceptions of campus cultural climate by race. *Journal of Counseling & Development, 78,* 180–185.

Andersen, M. L., & Collins, P. H. (2007a). Systems of power and inequality. In M. L. Anderson & P. H. Collins (Eds.), *Race, class, and gender: An anthology* (6th ed., pp. 61–90). Belmont, CA: Thomson/Wadsworth.

Andersen, M. L., & Collins, P. H. (2007b). Why race, class, and gender still matter. In M. L. Anderson & P. H. Collins (Eds.), *Race, class, and gender: An anthology* (6th ed., pp. 1–16). Belmont, CA: Thomson/Wadsworth.

Andersen, M. L., & Collins, P. H. (2010a). Systems of power and inequality. In M. L. Andersen & P. H. Collins (Eds.), *Race, class, and gender: An anthology* (7th ed., pp. 61–86). Belmont, CA: Thomson/Wadsworth.

Andersen, M. L., & Collins, P. H. (2010b). Why race, class, and gender still matter. In M. L. Andersen & P. H. Collins (Eds.), *Race, class, and gender: An anthology* (7th ed., pp. 1–16). Belmont, CA: Thomson/Wadsworth.

Anzaldúa, G. (1991). To queer the writer: Loca, escrita y chicana. In B. Warland (Ed.), *InVersion: Writings by dykes, queers, and lesbians* (pp. 249–263). Vancouver, BC, Canada: Press Gang.

Anzaldúa, G. (1999). *Borderlands: La frontera* (2nd ed.). San Francisco, CA: Aunt Lute Books.

Association to Advance Collegiate Schools of Business. (2010). *Eligibility procedures and accreditation standards for business accreditation.* Retrieved from www.aacsb.edu /accreditation/AAACSB-STANDARDS-2010.pdf

Astin, A. W. (1984). Student involvement: A developmental theory for higher education. *Journal of College Student Personnel, 25,* 297–308.

Barnard, I. (1999). Queer race. *Social Semiotics, 9*(2), 199–212.

Baxter Magolda, M. B. (1992). *Knowing and reasoning in college: Gender-related patterns in students' intellectual development.* San Francisco, CA: Jossey-Bass.

Baxter Magolda, M. B. (1999). *Creating contexts for learning and self-authorship: Constructive-developmental pedagogy.* Nashville, TN: Vanderbilt University Press.

Baxter Magolda, M. B. (2001). *Making their own way: Narratives for transforming higher education to promote self-development.* Sterling, VA: Stylus.

Baxter Magolda, M. B. (2003). Identity and learning: Student affairs' role in transforming higher education. *Journal of College Student Development, 44,* 231–247.

Baxter Magolda, M. B. (2004). Evolution of a constructivist conceptualization of epistemological reflection. *Educational Psychologist, 39,* 31–42.

Baxter Magolda, M. B. (2009). *Authoring your life.* Sterling, VA: Stylus.

Belenky, M., Clinchy, B. M., Goldberger, N., & Tarule, J. (1986). *Women's ways of knowing: The development of self, voice, and mind.* New York, NY: Basic Books.

Berger, M. T., & Guidroz, K. (Eds.). (2009a). *The intersectional approach: Transforming the academy through race, class, and gender.* Chapel Hill, NC: University of North Carolina Press.

Berger, M. T., & Guidroz, K. (2009b). Introduction. In M. T. Berger & K. Guidroz (Eds.), *The intersectional approach: Transforming the academy through race, class, and gender* (pp. 1–22). Chapel Hill, NC: University of North Carolina Press.

Bilodeau, B. L. (2005). Beyond the gender binary: A case study of transgender college student development at a Midwestern university. *Journal of Gay & Lesbian Issues in Education, 2*(4), 29–44.

Bilodeau, B. L. (2009). *Genderism: Transgender students, binary systems and higher education.* Saarbrücken, Germany: VDM Verlag.

Bolman, L. G., & Deal, T. E. (2008). *Reframing organizations: Artistry, choice, and leadership* (4th ed.). San Francisco, CA: Jossey-Bass.

Bowleg, L. (2008). When Black + lesbian + woman ≠ Black lesbian woman: The methodological challenges of qualitative and quantitative intersectionality research. *Sex Roles, 59*, 312–325.

Bowman, N. A. (2010). Disequilibrium and resolution: The nonlinear effects of diversity courses on well-being and orientations toward diversity. *The Review of Higher Education, 33*, 543–568.

Boyarin, D., Itzkovitz, D., & Pellegrini, A. (Eds.). (2003). *Queer theory and the Jewish question.* New York, NY: Columbia University Press.

Brewer, M. B. (2001). The social self: On being the same and different at the same time. In M. A. Hogg & D. Abrams (Eds.), *Intergroup relations: Essential readings* (pp. 245–253). Philadelphia, PA: Psychology Press.

Britzman, D. P. (1997). What is this thing called love? New discourses for understanding gay and lesbian youth. In S. de Castell & M. Bryson (Eds.), *Radical in(ter)ventions: Identity, politics, and difference/s on educational praxis* (pp. 183–207). Albany, NY: State University of New York Press.

Bronfenbrenner, U. (1979). *The ecology of human development: Experiments by nature and design.* Cambridge, MA: Harvard University Press.

Bronfenbrenner, U. (1993). The ecology of cognitive development: Research models and fugitive findings. In R. H. Wozniak & K. W. Fischer (Eds.), *Development in context: Acting and thinking in specific environments* (pp. 3–44). Hillsdale, NJ: Lawrence Erlbaum Associates.

Bronfenbrenner, U. (Ed.). (2005). *Making human beings human: Bioecological perspectives on human development.* Thousand Oaks, CA: Sage.

Brueggemann, B. J., & Moddelmog, D. A. (2002). Coming-out pedagogy: Risking identity in language and literature classrooms. *Pedagogy: Critical Approaches to Teaching Literature, Language, Composition, and Culture, 2*, 311–335.

Butin, D. W. (2010). *Service-learning in theory and practice.* New York, NY: Palgrave Macmillan.

Butler, J. (1990). *Gender trouble: Feminism and the subversion of identity.* New York, NY: Routledge.

Butler, J. (1991). Imitation and gender subordination. In D. Fuss (Ed.), *Inside/out: Lesbian theories, gay theories* (pp. 13–31). New York, NY: Routledge.

Butler, J. (1993). *Bodies that matter: On the discursive limits of "sex."* New York, NY: Routledge.

Butler, J. (1997). *Excitable speech.* New York, NY: Routledge.

Butler, J. (2000). Agencies of style for a liminal subject. In P. Gilroy, L. Grossberg, & A. McRobbie (Eds.), *Without guarantee: In honor of Stuart Hall* (pp. 30–37). New York, NY: Verso.

Butler, J. (2004). *Undoing gender.* New York, NY: Routledge.

Cabrera, A. F., & Nora, A. (1994). College students' perceptions of prejudice and discrimination and their feelings of alienation: A construct validation approach. *The Review of Education, Pedagogy, and Cultural Studies, 16*, 387–409.

Carbado, D. W. (2002). Straight out of the closet: Race, gender, and sexual orientation. In F. Valdes, J. McCristal Culp, & A. P. Harris (Eds.), *Crossroads, directions, and a new critical race theory* (pp. 221–242). Philadelphia, PA: Temple University Press.

Carlin, D. (2011). The intersectional potential of queer theory: An example from a general education course in English. In M. L. Ouellett (Ed.), *An integrative analysis approach to diversity in the college classroom* (New Directions for Teaching and Learning, No. 125, pp. 55–64). San Francisco, CA: Jossey-Bass.

Cass, V. (1996). Sexual orientation identity formation: A Western phenomenon. In R. P. Cabaj & T. S. Stein (Eds.), *Textbook of homosexuality and mental health* (pp. 227–251). Washington, DC: American Psychiatric Association.

Cass, V. C. (1979). Homosexual identity formation: A theoretical model. *Journal of Homosexuality, 4*, 219–235.

Chang, M. J. (2002). The impact of an undergraduate diversity course requirement on students' racial views and attitudes. *Journal of General Education, 51*, 21–42.

Chang, M. J. (2007). Beyond artificial integration: Reimagining cross-racial interactions among undergraduates. In S. R. Harper & L. D. Patton (Eds.), *Responding to the realities of race on campus* (New Directions for Student Services, No. 120, pp. 25–38). San Francisco, CA: Jossey-Bass.

Chang, M. J., Denson, N., Saenz, V., & Misa, K. (2006). The educational benefits of sustaining cross-racial interaction among undergraduates. *The Journal of Higher Education, 77*, 430–455.

Chang, M. J., Milem, J. F., & antonio, a. l. (2011). Campus climate and diversity. In J. H. Schuh, S. R. Jones, & S. R. Harper (Eds.), *Student services: A handbook for the profession* (5th ed., pp. 43–58). San Francisco, CA: Jossey-Bass.

Charmaz, K. (2006). *Constructing grounded theory: A practical guide through qualitative analysis.* Thousand Oaks, CA: Sage.

Chase, S. E. (1995). Taking narrative seriously: Consequences for method and theory in interview studies. In R. Josselson & A. Lieblich (Eds.), *Interpreting experience: The narrative study of lives* (pp. 1–26). Thousand Oaks, CA: Sage.

Chen, G. A. (2005). *The complexity of "Asian American identity": The intersection of multiple social identities.* (Unpublished doctoral dissertation). University of Texas at Austin.

Chen, G. A. (2009). Managing multiple social identities. In N. Tewari & A. N. Alvarez (Eds.), *Asian American psychology: Current perspectives* (pp. 173–192). New York, NY: Psychology Press.

Chickering, A. W. (1969). *Education and identity.* San Francisco, CA: Jossey-Bass.

Chickering, A. W., & Reisser, L. (1993). *Education and identity* (2nd ed.). San Francisco, CA: Jossey-Bass.

Clandinin, D. J., & Connelly, F. M. (2000). *Narrative inquiry: Experience and story in qualitative research.* San Francisco, CA: Jossey-Bass.

Coles, R. (1989). *The call of stories: Teaching and the moral imagination.* Boston, MA: Houghton Mifflin.

Coles, R. (2000). *The Erik Erikson reader.* New York, NY: W. W. Norton.

Collins, P. H. (1991). *Black feminist thought: Knowledge, consciousness, and the politics of empowerment.* New York, NY: Routledge.

Collins, P. H. (2007). Pushing the boundaries or business as usual? Race, class, and gender studies and sociological inquiry. In C. J. Calhoun (Ed.), *Sociology in America: A history* (pp. 572–604). Chicago, IL: University of Chicago Press.

Collins, P. H. (2009). Foreword: Emerging intersections—building knowledge and transforming institutions. In B. T. Dill & R. E. Zambrana (Eds.), *Emerging intersections: Race, class, and gender in theory, policy, and practice* (pp. vii–xiii). New Brunswick, NJ: Rutgers University Press.

Côté, J. E., & Levine, C. G. (2002). *Identity formation, agency, and culture: A social psychological synthesis.* Mahwah, NJ: Lawrence Erlbaum Associates.

Crenshaw, K. (1991). Mapping the margins: Intersectionality, identity politics, and violence against women of color. *Stanford Law Review, 43,* 1241–1299.

Cross, W. E., Jr. (1971). The Negro-to-Black conversion experience. *Black World, 20*(9), 13–27.

Cross, W. E., Jr. (1995). The psychology of Nigrescence: Revising the Cross model. In J. G. Ponterotto, J. M. Casas, L. A. Suzuki, & C. M. Alexander (Eds.), *Handbook of multicultural counseling* (pp. 181–198). Thousand Oaks, CA: Sage.

Cruz-Malavé, A., & Manalansan, M. F. (Eds.). (2002). *Queer globalizations: Citizenship and the afterlife of colonialism.* New York: New York University Press.

D'Augelli, A. R. (1994). Identity development and sexual orientation: Toward a model of lesbian, gay, and bisexual development. In E. J. Trickett, R. J. Watts, & D. Birman (Eds.), *Human diversity: Perspectives on people in context* (pp. 312–333). San Francisco, CA: Jossey-Bass.

Davis, K. (2008). Intersectionality as buzzword: A sociology of science perspective on what makes a feminist theory successful. *Feminist Theory, 9,* 67–85.

Deaux, K. (1993). Reconstructing social identity. *Personality and Social Psychology Bulletin, 19,* 4–12.

Delgado, R., & Stefancic, J. (2001). *Critical race theory: An introduction.* New York, NY: New York University Press.

Delgado Bernal, D. (2002). Critical race theory, Latino critical theory, and critical raced–gendered epistemologies: Recognizing students of color as holders and creators of knowledge. *Qualitative Inquiry, 8,* 105–126.

Denzin, N. K., & Lincoln, Y. S. (2000). The discipline and practice of qualitative research. In N. K. Denzin & Y. S. Lincoln (Eds.), *Handbook of qualitative research* (2nd ed., pp. 1–28). Thousand Oaks, CA: Sage.

Derrida, J. (1978). *Writing and difference.* (A. Bass, Trans.). Chicago, IL: University of Chicago Press. (Original work published 1967).

Dessel, A., Rogge, M. E., & Garlington, S. B. (2006). Using intergroup dialogue to promote social justice and change. *Social Work, 51,* 303–315.

Dessel, A. B., Woodford, M. R., & Warren, N. (2011). Intergroup dialogue courses on sexual orientation: Lesbian, gay and bisexual student experiences and outcomes. *Journal of Homosexuality, 58,* 1132–1150.

Dey, E. L., Ott, M. C., Antonaros, M., Barnhardt, C. L., & Holsapple, M. A. (2010). *Engaging diverse viewpoints: What is the campus climate for perspective-taking?* Washington, DC: Association of American Colleges and Universities.

Dill, B. T. (1983). Race, class and gender: Prospects for an all-inclusive sisterhood. In R. Takaki (Ed.), *From different shores: Perspectives on race and ethnicity in America* (pp. 204–213). New York, NY: Oxford University Press.

Dill, B. T. (2002, Fall). Work at the intersections of race, gender, ethnicity, and other dimensions of difference in higher education. *Connections: Newsletter of the Consortium on Race, Gender, and Ethnicity,* pp. 5–7.

Dill, B. T. (2009). Intersections, identities, and inequalities in higher education. In B. T. Dill & R. E. Zambrana (Eds.), *Emerging intersections: Race, class, and gender in theory, policy, and practice* (pp. 229–252). New Brunswick, NJ: Rutgers University Press.

Dill, B. T., McLaughlin, A. E., & Nieves, A. D. (2007). Future directions of feminist research: Intersectionality. In S. N. Hesse-Biber (Ed.), *Handbook of feminist research* (pp. 629–637). Thousand Oaks, CA: Sage.

Dill, B. T., & Zambrana, R. E. (2009a). Critical thinking about inequality: An emerging lens. In Dill, B. T., & Zambrana, R. E. (Eds.), *Emerging intersections: Race, class, and gender in theory, policy, and practice* (pp. 1–21). New Brunswick, NJ: Rutgers University Press.

Dill, B. T., & Zambrana, R. E. (2009b). *Emerging intersections: Race, class, and gender in theory, policy, and practice.* New Brunswick, NJ: Rutgers University Press.

Dilley, P. (2002). *Queer man on campus: A history of non-heterosexual men, 1945–2000.* New York, NY: Routledge.

Dunlap, M., Scoggin, J., Green, P., & Davi, A. (2007). White students' experiences of privilege and socioeconomic disparities: Toward a theoretical model. *Michigan Journal of Community Service Learning, 13*(2), 19–30.

Elliott, P. (2010). *Debates in transgender, queer, and feminist theory: Contested sites.* Burlington, VT: Ashgate.

Eng, D. L., with Halberstam, J., & Muñoz, J. E. (2005). Introduction: What's queer about queer studies now? *Social Text, 23*(3-4), 1–17.

Erikson, E. H. (1963). *Youth: Change and challenge.* New York, NY: Doubleday.

Erikson, E. H. (1964). *Insight and responsibility.* New York, NY: W. W. Norton.

Erikson, E. H. (1968). *Identity: Youth and crisis.* New York, NY: W. W. Norton.

Erikson, E. H. (1994). *Identity and the life cycle.* New York, NY: W. W. Norton. (Original work published 1959).

Ethier, K. A., & Deaux, K. (1990). Hispanics in ivy: Identity and perceived threat. *Sex Roles, 22,* 427–440.

Ethier, K. A., & Deaux, K. (1994). Negotiating social identity when contexts change: Maintaining identification and responding to threat. *Journal of Personality and Social Psychology, 67,* 243–251.

Evans, N. J., Forney, D. S., Guido, F. M., Patton, L. D., & Renn, K. A. (2010). *Student development in college: Theory, research, and practice* (2nd ed.). San Francisco, CA: Jossey-Bass.

Fassinger, R. E. (1998). Lesbian, gay, and bisexual identity and student development theory. In R. L. Sanlo (Ed.), *Working with lesbian, gay, bisexual, and transgender college students: A handbook for faculty and administrators* (pp. 13–22). Westport, CT: Greenwood Press.

Firmage, G. J. (Ed.). (1965). *e. e. cummings: A miscellany revised.* New York, NY: October House.

Foucault, M. (1978). *The history of sexuality: Vol. 1. An introduction.* (R. Hurley, Trans.). New York, NY: Vintage Books.

Foucault, M. (1980). *Power/knowledge: Selected interviews and other writings, 1972–1977.* (C. Gordon, L. Marshall, J. Mepham, & K. Soper, Trans.). New York, NY: Pantheon Books.

Frank, D., & Cannon, E. (2010). Queer theory as pedagogy in counselor education: A framework for diversity training. *Journal of LGBT Issues in Counseling, 4,* 18–31.

Frankenberg, R. (1993). *White women, race matters: The social construction of Whiteness.* Minneapolis, MN: University of Minnesota Press.

Freire, P. (1997). *Pedagogy of the oppressed.* New York, NY: Continuum. (Original work published 1970).

Frye, M. (2007). Oppression. In M. L. Andersen & P. H. Collins (Eds.), *Race, class, and gender: An anthology* (6th ed., pp. 29–31). Belmont, CA: Thomson/ Wadsworth.

Fuss, D. (1989). *Essentially speaking: Feminism, nature, and difference.* New York, NY: Routledge.

Gergen, K. J. (1991). *The saturated self: Dilemmas of identity in contemporary life.* New York, NY: Basic Books.

Gilbride-Brown, J. K. (2008). *(E)racing service-learning as critical pedagogy: Race matters.* (Unpublished doctoral dissertation). The Ohio State University, Columbus.

Glaser, B. G., & Strauss, A. L. (1967). *The discovery of grounded theory.* Chicago, IL: Aldine.

Glesne, C. (2006). *Becoming qualitative researchers: An introduction* (3rd ed.). Boston, MA: Pearson.

González, K. P., & Marin, P., with Figueroa, M. A., Moreno, J. F., & Navia, C. N. (2002). Inside doctoral education in America: Voices of Latinas/os in pursuit of the PhD. *Journal of College Student Development, 43,* 540–557.

Goodman, J., Schlossberg, N. K., & Anderson, J. L. (2006). *Counseling adults in transition: Linking practice with theory* (3rd ed.). New York, NY: Springer.

Greene, B. (2000). African American lesbian and bisexual women. *Journal of Social Issues, 56,* 239–249.

Grosz, E. A. (2004). *The nick of time: Politics, evolution, and the untimely.* Durham, NC: Duke University Press.

Guba, E. G., & Lincoln, Y. S. (2005). Paradigmatic controversies, contradictions, and emerging confluences. In N. K. Denzin & Y. S. Lincoln (Eds.), *The SAGE handbook of qualitative research* (pp. 191–215). Thousand Oaks, CA: Sage.

Gurin, P., Dey, E. L., Hurtado, S., & Gurin, G. (2002). Diversity and higher education: Theory and impact on educational outcomes. *Harvard Educational Review, 72,* 330–366.

Halberstam, J. (2005). *In a queer time and place: Transgender bodies and subcultural lives.* New York, NY: New York University Press.

Halberstam, J. (2008). What's that smell? Queer temporalities and subcultural lives. In S. Driver (Ed.), *Queer youth cultures* (pp. 27–50). Albany, NY: State University of New York Press.

Hall, S. (1992). The question of cultural identity. In S. Hall, D. Held, & T. McGrew (Eds.), *Modernity and its futures* (pp. 273–315). Cambridge, England: Policy Press.

Halperin, D. M. (1995). *Saint Foucault: Towards a gay hagiography.* New York, NY: Oxford University Press.

Hames-García, M. (2001). Can queer theory be critical theory? In W. S. Wilkerson & J. Paris (Eds.), *New critical theory: Essays on liberation* (pp. 201–222). Lanham, MD: Rowman & Littlefield.

Hames-García, M. (2011). *Identity complex: Making the case for multiplicity.* Minneapolis, MN: University of Minnesota Press.

Hardiman, R. (1982). *White identity development: A process oriented model for describing the racial consciousness of White Americans.* (Unpublished doctoral dissertation). University of Massachusetts–Amherst.

Hardiman, R., & Jackson, B. W., III (1997). Conceptual foundation for social justice courses. In M. Adams, L. A. Bell, & P. Griffin (Eds.), *Teaching for diversity and social justice: A sourcebook* (pp. 16–29). New York, NY: Routledge.

Harper, S. R. (2009). Niggers no more: A critical race counternarrative on Black male student achievement at predominantly White colleges and universities. *International Journal of Qualitative Studies in Education, 22,* 697–712.

Harper, S. R., & Hurtado, S. (2007). Nine themes in campus racial climates and implications for institutional transformation. In S. R. Harper & L. D. Patton (Eds.), *Responding to the realities of race on campus* (New Directions for Student Services, No. 120, pp. 7–24). San Francisco, CA: Jossey-Bass.

Harper, S. R., & Quaye, S. J. (2007). Student organizations as venues for Black identity expressions and development among African American male student leaders. *Journal of College Student Development, 48,* 127–144.

Helms, J. E. (1993). *Black and White racial identity theory, research, and practice.* Westport, CT: Praeger.

Helms, J. E. (1994). The conceptualization of racial identity and other "racial" constructs. In E. J. Trickett, R. J. Watts, & D. Birman (Eds.), *Human diversity perspectives on people in context* (pp. 285–311). San Francisco, CA: Jossey-Bass.

Henderson, M. G. (1994). What it means to teach the other when the other is the self. *Callaloo, 17,* 432–438.

Hofer, B. K. (2010). Personal epistemology, learning, and cultural context: Japan and the United States. In M. B. Baxter Magolda, E. G. Creamer, & P. S. Meszaros (Eds.), *Development and assessment of self-authorship: Exploring the concept across cultures* (pp. 133–150). Sterling, VA: Stylus.

Hurtado, S., Milem, J., Clayton-Pedersen, A., & Allen, W. (1999). *Enacting diverse learning environments: Improving the climate for racial/ethnic diversity in higher education.* (ASHE-ERIC Higher Education Report, Vol. 26, No. 8). Washington, DC: George Washington University Graduate School of Education and Human Development.

Iverson, S. V. (2007). Camouflaging power and privilege: A critical race analysis of university diversity policies. *Educational Administration Quarterly, 43,* 586–611.

Jackson, B. W., III. (1976). Black identity development. In L. H. Golubchick & B. Persky (Eds.), *Urban, social, and educational issues* (pp. 158–164). Dubuque, IA: Kendall-Hunt.

Jacoby, B. A. (Ed.). (1996). *Service-learning in higher education: Concepts and practices.* San Francisco, CA: Jossey-Bass.

Jagose, A. (1997). *Queer theory: An introduction.* New York, NY: New York University Press.

Johnson, A. G. (2006). *Privilege, power, and difference* (2nd ed.). New York, NY: McGraw-Hill.

Jones, S. R. (1995). *Voices of identity and difference: A qualitative exploration of the multiple dimensions of identity development in women college students.* (Unpublished doctoral dissertation). University of Maryland, College Park.

Jones, S. R. (1997). Voices of identity and difference: A qualitative exploration of the multiple dimensions of identity development in women college students. *Journal of College Student Development, 38*, 376–386.

Jones, S. R. (2002). Becoming grounded in grounded theory methodology. In S. Merriam (Ed.), *Qualitative research in practice: Examples for discussion and analysis* (pp. 175–177). San Francisco, CA: Jossey-Bass.

Jones, S. R. (2009). Constructing identities at the intersections: An autoethnographic exploration of multiple dimensions of identity. *Journal of College Student Development, 50*, 287–304.

Jones, S. R. (2010). Getting to the complexities of identity: The contributions of an autoethnographic and intersectional approach. In M. B. Baxter Magolda, E. Creamer, & P. S. Meszaros (Eds.), *Development and assessment of self-authorship: Exploring the concept across cultures* (pp. 223–244). Sterling, VA: Stylus.

Jones, S. R., & Abes, E. S. (2004). Enduring influences of service-learning on college students' identity development. *Journal of College Student Development, 45*, 149–166.

Jones, S. R., & Abes, E. S. (2011). The nature and uses of theory. In J. H. Schuh, S. R. Jones, & S. R. Harper (Eds.), *Student services: A handbook for the profession* (5th ed., pp. 149–167). San Francisco, CA: Jossey-Bass.

Jones, S. R., Abes, E. S., & Cilente, K. (2011). Theories about college students, environments, and organizations. In J. H. Schuh, S. R. Jones, & S. R. Harper (Eds.), *Student services: A handbook for the profession* (5th ed., pp. 138–148). San Francisco, CA: Jossey-Bass.

Jones, S. R., Kim, Y. C., & Skendall, K. C. (2012). (Re-) framing authenticity: Considering multiple social identities using autoethnographic and intersectional approaches. *The Journal of Higher Education, 83*, 698–724.

Jones, S. R., LePeau, L. A., & Robbins, C. K. (in press). Exploring the possibilities and limitations of service-learning: A critical analysis of college student narratives about HIV/AIDS. *The Journal of Higher Education.*

Jones, S. R., & McEwen, M. K. (2000). A conceptual model of multiple dimensions of identity. *Journal of College Student Development, 41*, 405–414.

Jones, S. R., Robbins, C. K., & LePeau, L. A. (2011). Negotiating border crossing: Influences of social identity on service-learning outcomes. *Michigan Journal of Community Service Learning, 17*(2), 27–42.

Jones, S. R., & Wijeyesinghe, C. L. (2011). The promise and challenge of teaching from an intersectional perspective: Core components and applied strategies. In M. L. Ouellett (Ed.), *An integrative analysis approach to diversity in the college classroom* (New Directions for Teaching and Learning, No. 125, pp. 11–20). San Francisco, CA: Jossey-Bass.

Josselson, R. (1987). *Finding herself: Pathways to identity development in women.* San Francisco, CA: Jossey-Bass.

Josselson, R. (1996). *Revising herself: The story of women's identity from college to midlife.* San Francisco, CA: Jossey-Bass.

Kearney, R. (1984). *Dialogues with contemporary Continental thinkers: The phenomenological heritage.* Manchester, England: Manchester University Press.

Kegan, R. (1982). *The evolving self: Problem and process in human development.* Cambridge, MA: Harvard University Press.

Kegan, R. (1994). *In over our heads: The mental demands of modern life.* Cambridge, MA: Harvard University Press.

Keniston, K. (1971). *Youth and dissent.* New York, NY: Harcourt Brace Jovanovich.

Kincheloe, J. L., & McLaren, P. (2005). Rethinking critical theory and qualitative research. In N. K. Denzin & Y. S. Lincoln (Eds.), *The SAGE handbook of qualitative research* (pp. 303–342). Thousand Oaks, CA: Sage.

King, P. M. (1994). Theories of college student development: Sequences and consequences. *Journal of College Student Development, 35,* 413–421.

King, P. M., & Baxter Magolda, M. B. (1996). A developmental perspective on learning. *Journal of College Student Development, 37,* 163–173.

King, P. M., & Baxter Magolda, M. B. (2005). A developmental model of intercultural maturity. *Journal of College Student Development, 46,* 571–592.

Knefelkamp, L. L., Widick, C., & Parker, C. A. (Eds.). (1978). *Applying new developmental findings* (New Directions for Student Services, No. 4). San Francisco, CA: Jossey-Bass.

Kodama, C. M., McEwen, M. K., Liang, C.T.H., & Lee, S. (2001). A theoretical examination of psychosocial issues for Asian Pacific American students. *NASPA Journal, 38,* 411–437.

Kodama, C. M., McEwen, M. K., Liang, C.T.H., & Lee, S. (2002). An Asian American perspective on psychosocial student development theory. In M. K. McEwen, C. M. Kodama, A. Alvarez, S. Lee, & C.T.H. Liang (Eds.), *Working with Asian American college students* (New Directions for Student Services, No. 97, pp. 45–59). San Francisco, CA: Jossey-Bass.

Kohlberg, L. (1975). Moral education for a society in moral transition. *Educational Leadership, 33*(1), 46–54.

Kuh, G. D., Kinzie, J., Schuh, J. H., Whitt, E. J., & Associates. (2005). *Student success in college: Creating conditions that matter.* San Francisco, CA: Jossey-Bass.

Kushner, T. (1994). *Angels in America, part two: Perestroika.* New York, NY: Theatre Communications Group.

Ladson-Billings, G. (1998). Just what is critical race theory and what's it doing in a nice field like education? *International Journal of Qualitative Studies in Education, 11,* 7–24.

Lather, P. (1991). Deconstructing/deconstructive inquiry: The politics of knowing and being known. *Educational Theory, 41*(2), 153–173.

Lather, P. (2006). Paradigm proliferation as a good thing to think with: Teaching research in education as wild profusion. *International Journal of Qualitative Studies in Education, 19,* 35–57.

Lather, P. (2007). *Getting lost: Feminist efforts toward a double(d) science.* Albany, NY: State University of New York Press.

Lather, P. (2008). Getting lost: Critiquing across differences as a methodological practice. In K. Gallagher (Ed.), *The methodological dilemma: Creative, critical, and collaborative approaches to qualitative research* (pp. 219–231). New York, NY: Routledge.

Lewis, M. M. (2011). Body of knowledge: Black queer feminist pedagogy, praxis, and embodied text. *Journal of Lesbian Studies, 15,* 49–57.

Lieblich, A., Tuval-Mashiach, R., & Zilber, T. (1998). *Narrative research: Readings, analysis, interpretation.* Thousand Oaks, CA: Sage.

Liu, W. M., Soleck, G., Hopps, J., Dunston, K., & Pickett, T., Jr. (2004). A new framework to understand social class in counseling: The social class worldview model and modern classism theory. *Journal of Multicultural Counseling & Development, 32,* 95–122.

Lorde, A. (1980). *The cancer journals.* San Francisco, CA: Spinsters/Aunt Lute.

Luft, R. E. (2008). Looking for common ground: Relief work in post-Katrina New Orleans as an American parable of race and gender violence. *Feminist Foundations, 20*(3), 5–31.

Luft, R. E. (2009). Intersectionality and the risk of flattening difference: Gender and race logics, and the strategic use of antiracist singularity. In M. T. Berger & K. Guidroz (Eds.), *The intersectional approach: Transforming the academy through race, class, and gender* (pp. 100–117). Chapel Hill, NC: University of North Carolina Press.

Luft, R. E., & Ward, J. (2009). Toward an intersectionality just out of reach: Confronting challenges to intersectional practice. In V. Demos & M. T. Segal (Eds.), *Advances in gender research* (Vol. 13, pp. 9–37). Bingley, England: Emerald Group.

Lyotard, J.-F. (1984). *The postmodern condition: A report on knowledge* (G. Bennington & B. Massumi, Trans., Theory and History of Literature, Vol. 10). Manchester, England: Manchester University Press.

MacLeod, J. (2009). *Ain't no makin' it: Aspirations and attainment in a low-income neighborhood* (3rd ed.). Boulder, CO: Westview Press.

Manning, K. (1994). Liberation theology and student affairs. *Journal of College Student Development, 35,* 94–97.

Marcia, J. E. (1966). Development and validation of ego-identity status. *Journal of Personality and Social Psychology, 3,* 551–558.

Marine, S. B. (2011). *Stonewall's legacy: Bisexual, gay, lesbian, and transgender students in higher education.* (ASHE Higher Education Report, Vol. 37, No. 4). Hoboken, NJ: Wiley.

Markson, Z. D. (2008). Drag it out! How queer youth are transforming citizenship in Peterborough. In S. Driver (Ed.), *Queer youth culture* (pp. 279–294). Albany, NY: State University of New York Press.

McCall, L. (2005). The complexity of intersectionality. *Signs: Journal of Women in Culture and Society, 30,* 1771–1800.

McCarn, S. R., & Fassinger, R. E. (1996). Revisioning sexual minority identity formation: A new model of lesbian identity and its implications for counseling and research. *The Counseling Psychologist, 24,* 508–534.

McEwen, M. K. (2003). The nature and uses of theory. In S. R. Komives, D. B. Woodard Jr., & Associates (Eds.), *Student services: A handbook for the profession* (4th ed., pp. 153–178). San Francisco, CA: Jossey-Bass.

McEwen, M. K., Roper, L. D., Bryant, D. R., & Langa, M. J. (1990). Incorporating the development of African-American students into psychosocial theories of student development. *Journal of College Student Development, 31,* 429–436.

McIntosh, P. (2010). White privilege: Unpacking the invisible knapsack. In M. L. Andersen & P. H. Collins (Eds.), *Race, class, and gender: An anthology* (7th ed., pp. 99–104). Belmont, CA: Wadsworth.

McKinney, J. S. (2005). On the margins: A study of the experiences of transgender college students. *Journal of Gay & Lesbian Issues in Education, 3*(1), 63–76.

McRuer, R. (2003). As good as it gets: Queer theory and critical disability. *GLQ: A Journal of Lesbian and Gay Studies, 9,* 79–106.

McRuer, R. (2006). *Crip theory: Cultural signs of queerness and disability.* New York, NY: New York University Press.

Milem, J. F., Chang, M. J., & antonio, a. l. (2005). *Making diversity work on campus: A research-based perspective.* Washington, DC: Association of American Colleges and Universities.

Milner, H. R., IV. (2008). Critical race theory and interest convergence as analytic tools in teacher education policies and practices. *Journal of Teacher Education, 59,* 332–346.

Misawa, M. (2010). Musings on controversial intersections of positionality: A queer crit perspective on adult and continuing education. In V. Sheared, J. Johnson-Bailey, S.A.J. Colin III, E. Peterson, & S. D. Brookfield (Eds.), *The handbook of race and adult education: A resource for dialogue on racism* (pp. 187–200). San Francisco, CA: Jossey-Bass.

Morris, R. C. (1995). All made up: Performance theory and the new anthropology of sex and gender. *Annual Review of Anthropology, 24,* 567–592.

Morse, J. M. (2007). Sampling in grounded theory. In A. Bryant & K. Charmaz (Eds.), *The SAGE handbook of grounded theory* (pp. 229–244). Thousand Oaks, CA: Sage.

Muñoz, J. E. (1999). *Disidentifications: Queers of color and the performance of politics.* Minneapolis, MN: University of Minnesota Press.

Museus, S. D. (2009). A critical analysis of the exclusion of Asian American from higher education research and discourse. In L. Zhan (Ed.), *Asian American voices: Engaging, empowering, enabling* (pp. 59–76). New York, NY: NLN Press.

Nadal, K. L., Issa, A., Leon, J., Meterko, V., Wideman, M., & Wong., Y. (2011). Sexual orientation microaggressions: "Death by a thousand cuts" for lesbian, gay, and bisexual youth. *Journal of LGBT Youth, 8,* 234–259.

Nagda, B. A., & Gurin, P. (2007). Intergroup dialogue: A critical-dialogic approach to learning about difference, inequality, and social justice. In A. Kaplan & A. T. Miller (Eds.), *Special issue: Scholarship of multicultural teaching* (New Directions for Teaching and Learning, No. 111, pp. 35–45). San Francisco, CA: Jossey-Bass.

Nagda, B. A., Gurin, P., Sorensen, N., & Zúñiga, X. (2009). Evaluating intergroup dialogue: Engaging diversity for personal and social responsibility. *Diversity & Democracy, 12*(1), 4–6.

Narui, M. (2011). Understanding Asian/American gay, lesbian, and bisexual experiences from a poststructural perspective. *Journal of Homosexuality, 58,* 1211–1234.

Newman, K. (2012). *Identity as a journey: An independent study of me.* (Unpublished manuscript). Miami University, Oxford, Ohio.

O'Connell, S. P. (2004). Telling tales in school: A queer response to the heterosexual narrative structure of higher education. *Journal of Homosexuality, 47,* 79–93.

Omi, M., & Winant, H. (1986). *Racial formation in the United States from the 1960s to the 1980s.* New York, NY: Routledge.

Owen, D. S. (2007). Toward a critical theory of Whiteness. *Philosophy and Social Criticism, 33,* 203–222.

Patton, C., & Sánchez-Eppler, B. (Eds.). (2000). *Queer diasporas*. Durham, NC: Duke University Press.

Patton, L. D. (2006). The voice of reason: A qualitative examination of Black student perceptions of Black cultural centers. *Journal of College Student Development, 47*, 628–646.

Patton, L. D. (2011). Perspectives on identity, disclosure, and the campus environment among African American gay and bisexual men at one historically Black college. *Journal of College Student Development, 52*, 77–100.

Patton, L. D., McEwen, M., Rendón, L., & Howard-Hamilton, M. F. (2007). Critical race perspectives on theory in student affairs. In S. R. Harper & L. D. Patton (Eds.), *Responding to the realities of race* (New Directions for Student Services, No. 120, pp. 39–54). San Francisco, CA: Jossey-Bass.

Patton, L. D., & Simmons, S. L. (2008). Exploring complexities of multiple identities of lesbians in a Black college environment. *Negro Educational Review, 59*, 197–215.

Patton, M. (1990). *Qualitative evaluation and research methods* (2nd ed.). Thousand Oaks, CA: Sage.

Patton, M. (2002). *Qualitative evaluation and research methods* (3rd ed.). Thousand Oaks, CA: Sage.

Perry, W. G., Jr. (1968). *Forms of intellectual and ethical development in the college years: A scheme*. New York, NY: Holt, Rinehart and Winston.

Phinney, J. S. (1993). A three-stage model of ethnic identity development in adolescence. In M. E. Bernal & G. P. Knight (Eds.), *Ethnic identity formation and transmission among Hispanic and other minorities* (pp. 61–79). Albany, NY: State University of New York Press.

Piaget, J. (1952). *The origins of intelligence in children*. New York, NY: International Universities Press.

Pizzolato, J. E. (2005). Creating crossroads for self-authorship: Investigating the provocative moment. *Journal of College Student Development, 46*, 624–641.

Pope, R. (2000). The relationship between psychosocial development and racial identity of Black college students. *Journal of College Student Development, 41*, 302–312.

Pusch, R. S. (2005). Objects of curiosity: Transgender college students' perceptions of the reactions of others. *Journal of Gay & Lesbian Issues in Education, 3*(1), 45–62.

Quaye, S. J., Tambascia, T. P., & Talesh, R. A. (2009). Engaging racial/ethnic minority students in predominantly White classroom environments. In S. R. Harper & S. J. Quaye (Eds.), *Student engagement in higher education: Theoretical perspectives and practical approaches for diverse populations* (pp. 157–178). New York, NY: Routledge.

Reinharz, S. (1994). Toward an ethnography of "voice" and "silence." In E. J. Trickett, R. J. Watts, & D. Birman (Eds.), *Human diversity: Perspective on people in context* (pp. 178–200). San Francisco, CA: Jossey-Bass.

Renn, K. A. (2003). Understanding the identities of mixed race college students through a developmental ecology lens. *Journal of College Student Development, 44*, 383–403.

Renn, K. A. (2007). LGBT student leaders and queer activists: Identities of lesbian, gay, bisexual, transgender, and queer identified college student leaders and activists. *Journal of College Student Development, 48,* 311–330.

Renn, K. A. (2010a). LGBT and queer research in higher education: State and status of the field. *Educational Researcher, 39,* 132–141.

Renn, K. A. (2010b, November). *Attempting intersectionality in a sectioned world: Research and practice in college student development.* Paper presented at the annual meeting of the Association for the Study of Higher Education.

Renn, K. A., & Bilodeau, B. (2005). Queer student leaders: An exploratory case study on identity development and LGBT student involvement at a Midwestern research university. *Journal of Gay & Lesbian Issues in Education, 2*(4), 49–71.

Reynolds, A. L., & Pope, R. L. (1991). The complexities of diversity: Exploring multiple oppressions. *Journal of Counseling & Development, 70,* 174–180.

Rhoads, R. A. (1997). *Community service and higher learning: Explorations of the caring self.* Albany, NY: State University of New York Press.

Rhoads, R. A., & Black, M. A. (1995). Student affairs practitioners as transformative educators: Advancing a critical cultural perspective. *Journal of College Student Development, 36,* 413–421.

Robbins, C. K. (2012). *Racial consciousness, identity, and dissonance among White women in student affairs graduate programs.* (Unpublished doctoral dissertation). University of Maryland, College Park.

Root, M.P.P. (1990). Resolving "other" status: Identity development of biracial individuals. In L. S. Brown & M.P.P. Root (Eds.), *Complexity and diversity in feminist theory and therapy* (pp. 185–205). New York, NY: Haworth.

Root, M.P.P. (1992). *Racially mixed people in America.* Thousand Oaks, CA: Sage.

Rosenberger, C. (2000). Beyond empathy: Developing critical consciousness through service learning. In C. R. O'Grady (Ed.), *Integrating service learning and multicultural education in colleges and universities* (pp. 23–43). Mahwah, NJ: Lawrence Erlbaum Associates.

Rotheram, M. J., & Phinney, J. S. (1987). Introduction: Definitions and perspectives in the study of children's ethnic socialization. In J. S. Phinney & M. J. Rotheram (Eds.), *Children's ethnic socialization: Pluralism and development* (pp. 10–28). Thousand Oaks, CA: Sage.

Rozas, L. (2007). Engaging dialogue in our diverse social work student body: A multilevel theoretical process model. *Journal of Social Work Education, 43,* 5–29.

Rumann, C. B., & Hamrick, F. A. (2010). Student veterans in transition: Re-enrolling after war zone deployments. *The Journal of Higher Education, 81,* 431–458.

Sandahl, C. (2003). Queering the crip or cripping the queer? Intersections of queer and crip identities in solo autobiographical performance. *GLQ: A Journal of Lesbian and Gay Studies, 9,* 25–56.

Sanford, N. (1962). Developmental status of the entering freshman. In N. Sanford (Ed.), *The American college student* (pp. 253–282). New York, NY: Wiley.

Sanford, N. (1966). *Self and society.* New York, NY: Atherton Press.

Sanford, N. (1967). *Where colleges fail: A study of the student as a person.* San Francisco, CA: Jossey-Bass.

Schuh, J. H., Jones, S. R., & Harper, S. R. (Eds.). (2011). *Student services: A handbook for the profession* (5th ed.). San Francisco, CA: Jossey-Bass.

Schwandt, T. A. (2001). *Dictionary of qualitative inquiry* (2nd ed.). Thousand Oaks, CA: Sage.

Sedgwick, E. K. (1990). *Epistemology of the closet*. Berkeley, CA: University of California Press.

Sherman, G. (2009, November). Martin Heidegger's concept of authenticity: A philosophical contribution to student affairs theory. *Journal of College and Character, 10*(7), 1–8.

Sherry, M. (2004). Overlaps and contradictions between queer theory and disability studies. *Disability & Society, 19,* 769–783.

Shields, S. (2008). Gender: An intersectionality perspective. *Sex Roles, 59,* 301–311.

Siddle Walker, V., & Snarey, J. (2004). *Race-ing moral formation: African American perspectives on care and justice.* New York, NY: Teachers College Press.

Solórzano, D., Ceja, M., & Yosso, T. (2000). Critical race theory, racial microaggressions, and campus racial climate: The experiences of African American college students. *The Journal of Negro Education, 69,* 60–73.

Somerville, S. B. (2000). *Queering the color line: Race and the invention of homosexuality in American culture.* Durham, NC: Duke University Press.

Strange, C., & Banning, J. (2001). *Educating by design: Creating campus learning environments that work.* San Francisco, CA: Jossey-Bass.

Straub, C., & Rodgers, R. F. (1986). An exploration of Chickering's theory and women's development. *Journal of College Student Personnel, 27,* 216–224.

Strauss, A., & Corbin, J. (1990). *Basics of qualitative research: Grounded theory procedures and techniques.* Thousand Oaks, CA: Sage.

Strayhorn, T. (Ed.) (in press). *Living at the intersections: Social identities and Black collegians.* New York, NY: Information Age.

Stryker, S., & Burke, P. J. (2000). The past, present, and future of an identity theory. *Social Psychology Quarterly, 63,* 284–297.

Sullivan, N. (2003). *A critical introduction to queer theory.* New York, NY: New York University Press.

Tajfel, H. (Ed.). (1982). *Social identity and intergroup relations.* Cambridge, England: Cambridge University Press.

Talburt, S. (2000). *Subject to identity: Knowledge, sexuality, and academic practices in higher education.* Albany, NY: State University of New York Press.

Tatum, B. D. (1997). *"Why are all the Black kids sitting together in the cafeteria?" and other conversations about race.* New York, NY: Basic Books.

Taub, D. J., & McEwen, M. K. (1991). Patterns of development of autonomy and mature interpersonal relationships in Black and White undergraduate women. *Journal of College Student Development, 32,* 502–508.

Taub, D. J., & McEwen, M. K. (1992). The relationship of racial identity attitudes to autonomy and mature interpersonal relationships in Black and White undergraduate women. *Journal of College Student Development, 33,* 439–446.

Tehranian, J. (2000). Performing Whiteness: Naturalization litigation and the construction of racial identity in America. *The Yale Law Journal, 109,* 817–848.

Thomas, R., & Chickering, A. W. (1984). Education and identity revisited. *Journal of College Student Personnel, 25,* 392–399.

Tierney, W. G. (1993). *Building communities of difference: Higher education in the twenty-first century.* Westport, CT: Bergin & Garvey.

Tierney, W. G. (1997). *Academic outlaws: Queer theory and cultural studies in the academy.* Thousand Oaks, CA: Sage.

Tierney, W. G., & Rhoads, R. A. (1993). Postmodernism and critical theory in higher education: Implications for research and practice. In J. C. Smart (Ed.), *Higher education: Handbook of theory and research* (Vol. 9, pp. 308–343). New York, NY: Agathon Press.

Tinto, V. (1993). *Leaving college: Rethinking the causes and cures of student attrition.* Chicago, IL: University of Chicago Press. (Original work published 1987).

Torres, V. (2009). The developmental dimensions of recognizing racist thoughts. *Journal of College Student Development, 50,* 504–520.

Torres, V., & Hernandez, E. (2007). The influence of ethnic identity on self-authorship: A longitudinal study of Latino/a college students. *Journal of College Student Development, 48,* 558–573.

Torres, V., Jones, S. R., & Renn, K. A. (2009). Identity development theories in student affairs: Origins, current status, and new approaches. *Journal of College Student Development, 50,* 577–596.

Turner, W. B. (2000). *A genealogy of queer theory.* Philadelphia, PA: Temple University Press.

Valentine, V. (2007). Theorizing and researching intersectionality: A challenge for feminist geography. *The Professional Geographer, 59,* 10–21

Villalpando, O. (2003). Self-segregation or self-preservation? A critical race theory and Latina/o critical theory analysis of a study of Chicana/o college students. *Qualitative Studies in Education, 16,* 619–646.

Warner, L. R. (2008). A best practices guide to intersectional approaches in psychological research. *Sex Roles, 59,* 454–463.

Warner, M. (1991). Introduction: Fear of a queer planet. *Social Text, 29,* 3–17.

Weber, L. (1998). A conceptual framework for understanding race, class, gender, and sexuality. *Psychology of Women Quarterly, 22,* 13–22.

Weber, L. (2001). *Understanding race, class, gender, and sexuality.* New York, NY: Oxford University Press.

Weber, L. (2010). *Understanding race, class, gender, and sexuality* (2nd ed.). New York, NY: Oxford University Press.

White, P. (2003). Sex education; or, how the blind became heterosexual. *GLQ: A Journal of Lesbian and Gay Studies, 9,* 133–147.

Widick, C., Parker, C. A., & Knefelkamp, L. L. (1978a). Arthur Chickering's vectors of development. In L. L. Knefelkamp, C. Widick, & C. A. Parker (Eds.), *Applying new developmental findings* (New Directions for Student Services, No. 4, pp. 19–34). San Francisco, CA: Jossey-Bass.

Widick, C., Parker, C. A., & Knefelkamp, L. L. (1978b). Erik Erikson and psychosocial development. In L. L. Knefelkamp, C. Widick, & C. A. Parker (Eds.), *Applying new developmental findings* (New Directions for Student Services, No. 4, pp. 1–17). San Francisco, CA: Jossey-Bass.

Wiegman, R. (1995). *American anatomies: Theorizing race and gender.* Durham, NC: Duke University Press.

Wiegman, R. (2006). Heteronormativity and the desire for gender. *Feminist Theory, 7,* 89–103.

Wijeyesinghe, C. L. (1992). *Towards an understanding of the racial identity of bi-racial people: The experience of racial self-identification of African-American/Euro-American adults and the factors affecting their choices of racial identity.* (Unpublished doctoral dissertation). University of Massachusetts–Amherst.

Wijeyesinghe, C. L. (2001). Racial identity in multiracial people: An alternative paradigm. In C. L. Wijeyesinghe & B. W. Jackson III (Eds.), *New perspectives on racial identity development: A theoretical and practical anthology* (pp. 129–152). New York, NY: New York University Press.

Wijeyesinghe, C. L. (2012). The intersectional model of multiracial identity: Integrating multiracial identity theories and intersectional perspectives on social identity. In C. L. Wijeyesinghe & B. W. Jackson III (Eds.), *New perspectives on racial identity development: Integrating emerging frameworks* (2nd ed., pp. 81–107). New York, NY: New York University Press.

Wilcoxon, A., Remley, T., Jr., & Gladding, S. T. (2012). *Ethical, legal, and professional issues in the practice of marriage and family therapy* (5th ed.). Upper Saddle River, NJ: Pearson Education.

Wilkerson, W. S. (2007). *Ambiguity and sexuality: A theory of sexual identity.* New York, NY: Palgrave Macmillan.

Williams, J. (2008). *Let's get intrapersonal: The final reflection.* (Unpublished manuscript). Miami University, Oxford, Ohio.

Willie, S. S. (2003). *Acting Black: College, identity, and the performance of race.* New York, NY: Routledge.

Winkle-Wagner, R. (2009). *The unchosen me: Race, gender, and identity among Black women in college.* Baltimore, MD: Johns Hopkins University Press.

Yakushko, O., Davidson, M. M., & Nutt Williams, E. (2009). Identity salience model: A paradigm for integrating multiple identities in clinical practice. *Psychotherapy: Theory, Research, Practice, Training, 46,* 180–192.

Yon, D. (2000). *Elusive culture: Schooling, race, and identity in global times.* Albany, NY: State University of New York Press.

Yosso, T., Smith, W. A., Ceja, M., & Solórzano, D. (2009). Critical race theory, racial microaggressions, and campus racial climate for Latina/o undergraduates. *Harvard Educational Review, 79,* 659–690.

Yosso, T. F., & Benavides Lopez, C. (2010). Counterspaces in a hostile place: A critical race theory analysis of campus cultural centers. In L. D. Patton (Ed.), *Cultural centers in higher education: Perspectives on identity, theory, and practice* (pp. 83–104). Sterling, VA: Stylus.

Zinn, M. B., Hondagneu-Sotelo, P., & Messner, M. (2007). Sex and gender through the prism of difference. In M. L. Andersen & P. H. Collins (Eds.), *Race, class, and gender: An anthology* (6th ed., pp. 147–156). Belmont, CA: Thomson/Wadsworth.

NAME INDEX

SUBJECT INDEX